ROUTLEDGE LIBRARY EDITIONS:
SAUDI ARABIA

Volume 2

THE COHESION OF SAUDI ARABIA

THE COHESION OF SAUDI ARABIA

Evolution of Political Identity

CHRISTINE MOSS HELMS

Routledge
Taylor & Francis Group
LONDON AND NEW YORK

First published in 1981

This edition first published in 2015
by Routledge
2 Park Square, Milton Park, Abingdon, Oxon, OX14 4RN

and by Routledge
711 Third Avenue, New York, NY 10017

Routledge is an imprint of the Taylor & Francis Group, an informa business

British Library Cataloguing in Publication Data
A catalogue record for this book is available from the British Library

ISBN: 978-1-138-82515-4 (Set)
ISBN: 978-1-138-84576-3 (Volume 2)
Pb ISBN: 978-1-138-84667-8 (Volume 2)

THE COHESION OF SAUDI ARABIA

Evolution of Political Identity

CHRISTINE MOSS HELMS

CROOM HELM LONDON

Croom Helm Ltd, 2-10 St John's Road, London SW11

ISBN 0-7099-0441-X

Reproduced from copy supplied
printed and bound in Great Britain
by Billing and Sons Limited
Guildford, London, Oxford, Worcester

CONTENTS

FIGURES

To

MOTHER
AND
ABU CHRISTINE

ACKNOWLEDGEMENTS

This book is the outcome of five years of research for my doctoral thesis. After many alternate moments of frustration and exciting discovery, it is pleasant to find that my one remaining responsibility is to express my appreciation to all those persons who and institutions which assisted me. It is appropriate that Oxford University, the academic traditions of which are hundreds of years older than the founding of my own country, should head this list. Not only was the educational experience challenging, but also I incorporated much from the environment and living experience that cannot be classified as strictly 'academic' but was, none the less, a valuable experience. I would especially like to thank Mr Albert Hourani and Professor A. F. L. Beeston, both of whom are well known for their scholarship and selfless devotion of time and encouragement to students, and Dr John Wilkinson, whose ideas stimulated the direction of my research.

There were also many people who added to my excitement for the Middle East because they played a special part in history as explorers, diplomats or soldiers. Among those who personally gave me their time and candid opinions were Lieutenant-General Sir John Bagot Glubb, Major-General James Lunt and Wilfred Thesiger. After meeting each of these men, it was not difficult to understand why their names are legendary in the countries in which they have travelled and worked. I would also like to thank Mrs Glubb and Mrs Lunt who, on behalf of their husbands, offered the hospitality of their homes and had many stories of their own to tell me about their travels in the Middle East.

Officials at the Embassy of Saudi Arabia in London and Dr

Morsey Abdullah of the Arab Documentation Centre in Abu Dhabi contributed their time and source material. Mr William Mulligan (ARAMCO), through the kind auspices of Mr Caspar Weinberger, assisted me with a number of inquiries and also provided me with a copy of Madani's manuscript.

There are many friends in Jordan and Abu Dhabi, unfortunately too numerous to mention individually, who offered me the hospitality of their countries and homes. In this regard, however, I cannot fail to mention Mrs Maysun Oweiss and her husband, the late Ambassador from Jordan to Rumania, whose generosity, friendship and home were always open to me. Shaikh Nahyan b. Mubarak Al Nahyan and Mr Alamgir Masud also contributed to my understanding of various aspects of the badu, their social organisation, politics and language.

Colonel and Mrs F. M. Johnson are also two people with whom I have shared and learned a great deal about the Middle East and who have unceasingly offered their friendship. Finally, special thanks to my parents, without whose challenges and encouragement none of this would have been possible.

Research for this study was conducted at the India Office Records in London and the Middle East Centre at Oxford University. Unpublished Crown Copyright material in the India Office Records reproduced in this book appears by permission of the Controller of Her Majesty's Stationery Office. This material consisted of Britain's collected Political and Secret Department Papers which documented its knowledge of the activities of and its involvement with Abd al-Aziz b. Abd al-Rahman Al Faisal Al Saud from 1902 to 1931. The Middle East Centre at Oxford contained a variety of additional material: the Philby Papers, collected writings of Muhammad b. Abd al-Wahhab, *The United Kingdom Memorial* and *The Saudi Memorial* concerning the arbitration over the Buraimi Oasis dispute, and a number of recent publications in Arabic. The Saudi Embassy in London kindly provided Arabic copies of its treaties with Great Britain and Attar's biography of Abd al-Aziz. I also obtained a number of unpublished diaries and dissertations, all of which are listed in the first section of the bibliography. Among them, however, are Captain W. H. Shakespear's private papers, loaned to me by Major-General Lunt, and General S. S. Butler's journal of a trip to Northern Arabia in 1908. The significance of this fascinating journal, with photographs of the area around Jabal Shammar and of the Al

Rashid, only recently came to light when Butler's family donated the memoirs of his later life in Africa to Rhodes House at Oxford University. General Butler was undoubtedly one of the first, although uncredited, explorers of Arabia. All other sources are fully identified in the footnotes and bibliography.

Although I am deeply grateful for all the assistance I have received, I acknowledge that all conclusions in this study are my own.

Christine Helms
Oxford

CONVENTIONS

It would be impossible to enumerate every convention which has been adopted, but it is hoped the following pages will list those of greatest importance.

Transliteration

It has been decided for the sake of simplicity to omit the transliteration of Arabic words in the main body of the text although they have been transliterated in the notes, bibliography and index for those who are interested.

Personal and Tribal Names

Many aspects of an individual's life in the Arabian Peninsula are coloured by his membership in a tribe or family group. Names such as Abd al-Aziz b. Abd al-Rahman Al Faisal Al Saud reflect the importance of these relationships. The word Al, not to be confused with the definite article *al*, is a common way to denote a family or tribe. The reader should learn to associate Al Saud as the Family of Saud, Al Murra as the Family or Tribe of Murra, and so forth. The term *ibn* or 'son', abbreviated as b. in this study (see example above), indicates a man's immediate familial descent. Thus, Abd al-Aziz, the first king of Saudi Arabia, was the son of Abd al-Rahman who, in his turn, was descended from the Al Faisal branch of the Al Saud family.

The use of *ibn* with a capital 'I' as in Ibn Rashid and Ibn Saud, without a personal name preceding, is a convention which designates the ruler of a particular dynasty within a specific time period. I have avoided using the name Ibn Saud to refer to Abd al-Aziz, unless quoting sources, for two reasons: first, it was a name employed by Western sources and Arabs outside Central Arabia; and second, it caused annoyance to Abd al-Aziz. Rarely, if ever, was it used in Najd. Names are given in their nominative form as, for example, the transliteration of 'father' as *abu* rather than *aba* or *abi*. A man was often called by the name of one of his sons, so that the tribesmen of Najd frequently called Abd al-Aziz by the name Abu Turki, Turki being the name of his eldest son. The term *banu* is given in its colloquial form *bani*. When prefixed to a proper name, it literally means 'sons of', so that the Bani Khalid are a tribal group all of whom recognise themselves to be 'sons of Khalid'.

Although the vowelling of personal and tribal names presented difficulties because of the number of variant spellings, I have been guided by Arabic texts or colloquial preferences of the Arabs in Central Arabia. Many Arabs on the littoral areas of the Arabian Peninsula refer, for example, to the al-Ajman and the Ataiba tribes. The Najd Arabs, however, use al-Ujman and Utaiba and these are the forms which have been adopted. When there were a number of alternative spellings available, I have chosen the one which occurred most frequently in the Arabic sources.

Geographical Names

As with personal and tribal names, I have not italicised most geographical names. The few names which have been italicised are so because they have been used only once and an English equivalent substituted. Thus, I indicated that I would refer to Saudi Arabia rather than *al-mamlaka al-arabiya al-saudiya.*

There are a few geographical names which have not been transliterated because they are names in common English usage and would have been unfamiliar in other forms. Examples of these are Mecca and Damascus. Difficulties also arose in the usage of definite articles preceding place names. Nouns consistently associated with *al* retain this prefix, as in the examples al-Riyad and al-Khurma. Although al-Kuwait and al-Iraq are more proper forms of these names, they are referred to as Kuwait and Iraq as they are commonly known in conversation.

The Persian Gulf, as it was known until the mid-twentieth century, is called the Arabian Gulf by most Arabs today and therefore I too have chosen to refer to it as the Arabian Gulf. There are a few occasions, however, when it is also referred to as the Persian Gulf, particularly in Part II where there are quotations from British Political Agents during the early 1900s when the Persian Gulf was still referred to by that name in British administrative records.

The Turkish administrative terms *Vali*, *Vilayet*, *Muteserrif* and *Sancak* are written as Wali, Wilaya, Mutasarrif and Sanjaq.

General Rules About Other Arabic Words

There are a number of Arabic words—other than personal, tribal and geographical names—which have been used in the body of the text. All are italicised, such as *shirk* and *hima*. As in Arabic, none of these words is capitalised unless it begins a sentence. Thus, I have written *al-wahhabiya* to indicate the word for this movement in Arabic and the Wahhabi movement for its English equivalent. It should be noted that I have not capitalised any proper nouns in Arabic phrases, as, for example, *al-dawa al-najdiya*.

Frequently used words which have become current in English usage are not italicised, as, for example, Imam, shaikh and amir. Note that badu has not been italicised except in a few specialised instances.

Some Arabic words are given in their English plural forms: *dira*s and *fitna*s.

Abbreviations

There are six frequently used abbreviations: lit. (literally), sing. (singular), pl. (plural), colloq. (colloquial), gram. (grammatical) and cf. (confer).

In the footnotes, particularly in Part II, IO indicates a source obtained from the India Office Records in London.

Muslim Dates

Muslim dates are generally placed in parentheses after the English date: 13 January 1928 (20 Rajab 1346). There are a few instances, however, where it was more appropriate for the Muslim date to be placed first, as in the case of a letter from Abd al-Aziz, and it is the English date which is then placed in parentheses. The Muslim dates of publication for Arabic books in the bibliography are written 1348ه.

Quotations

Quotations appear as they did in the source material. Any explanatory material enclosed in parentheses within a quotation was written by the person who is being quoted; any explanatory material enclosed in brackets are my own remarks. There are many variant spellings in English of the same Arabic word. In many cases the similarity of these words will be easily understood by the reader, and I have therefore not added the correct transliteration. Most readers, for example, already know that Riyadh is al-Riyad and Koweit is Kuwait. However, if there is any question, I have indicated a more standardised or correct spelling: for example, Dhafir [Zafir], Rwala [al-Ruwala], *huwa* [*khuwa*]. The full transliteration, as mentioned previously, is in the bibliography and index.

Footnotes and Bibliography

If there are inconsistencies it has been primarily to assist the reader. I have listed by each book the city in which the publisher can be found, but in the case of a few unfamiliar cities I have also listed a state or country. There are also inconsistencies in many of the references for the India Office Records. This is partly because of the lack of standardisation in the material itself and partly because I listed all the available information for each reference to help those who wished to use them.

Finally, personal names of the authors appear exactly as the individual chose to write it in his own published work. There are some authors who have Arabic names, but who are or were American or European citizens, and these names are written without the Arabic transliteration: Rihani and Rashid.

INTRODUCTION

The Kingdom of Saudi Arabia as it is internationally recognised today is, historically speaking, of relatively recent origin. Within the first three decades of the twentieth century, the Al Saud recaptured al-Riyad, the city which had served as their political centre during the nineteenth century, and successfully expanded their authority over rival amirates and shaikhdoms in Central Arabia. During the same period both Arab leaders along the littoral regions of the Arabian Peninsula and European powers began to limit the expansion of Saudi authority with the result that its boundaries as an emerging nation-state began to crystallise and were formally established through a series of treaties. In 1932 Abd al-Aziz b. Abd al-Rahman Al Faisal Al Saud was proclaimed 'king' of the new nation-state, at which time both the Saudi kingship and the nation-state of Saudi Arabia were formally recognised by the international community.

The above account is, of course, superficial. Due largely to the work of the Arabian American Oil Company (ARAMCO) and its historian, George Rentz, as well as to various diplomatic histories, the history of Saudi Arabia is generally presented as synonymous with Al Saud history. These histories are biased for two major reasons. First, they follow a tradition that sees history as a product of powerful individuals and of international machinations. Although this view of history is certainly important in any research, by itself it presents a foreshortened perspective, neglecting ecological factors and the activities and attitudes of the inhabitants of the areas who also influence the course of events and subsequent decisions made by governments. Second, the ARAMCO historians were subsidised by an oil industry which, by the very nature of the political and economic system of the Arabian nation, dealt almost exclusively with the Saudi family whose influence was ubiquitous.

Furthermore, diplomatic historians directed their attention to more readily observable events such as conferences, treaties and questions of policy rather than to the more subtle questions of why and how a decision was made and the consequences of specific policy. The chronological listing of dates, the recitation of anecdotes and the contents of diplomatic missives do not suffice as historical explanation when political initiatives must be made with regard not only to foreign relations but also to immediate and long-term domestic influences. These influences encompass not only events such as natural disasters, in which individuals cannot intervene but only react in an effort to minimise the consequences, but also events in which individuals stimulate the process of decision making, whether directly or indirectly, by virtue of such factors as religious beliefs, social customs, economic incentives and resource utilisation.

The result of much scholarship about Arabia has been to romanticise Abd al-Aziz b. Abd al-Rahman Al Faisal Al Saud as a ruler who created an empire out of desert sand and established order where none had previously existed. Proclaimed King of the Hijaz, Najd and its Dependencies by 1926 and King by 1932 of the Kingdom of Saudi Arabia, of which the boundaries and new nation status had international recognition, Abd al-Aziz was perceived by the West as a progressive ruler. The discovery of oil and the revenues which accrued during the 1940s lent substantive credence to this 'kingship'. This is not to lessen the outstanding achievements of this man, but it is to say that the events which led to the founding of the Saudi state must be seen in a broader context. In creating his distinctive brand of order, he was considerably helped by the events which coalesced at that time.

It is important to make the distinction that, while the history of the Al Saud helped to shape Arabian history, Arabian history is not to be thought of solely in terms of Al Saud history. In order to understand the role of the Saudi family in the emergence of Saudi Arabia as a geopolitical entity, one must look not only at the policies of an individual man or family group, but beyond to see them as products of their culture and as innovators within it. The social, economic, political, military and religious factors must also be examined *vis-à-vis* the geographic environment and the historical chronology of the Arabian Peninsula as a whole. These factors formed a complex of variables which in the early twentieth century were to affect the course of Saudi Arabia's internal unification and the conduct of her foreign policy. Further understanding of her social and political evolution is to be found through research into the role of international powers during the post-World War I mandate period in which the modern Middle East state system was created. This period was especially significant as the artificial concepts of 'nation-state' and 'boundary', creations of Western industrialised society, were innovations to Middle Eastern cultures at the time. Although introduced by mandate powers as administrative concepts directed to the goal of more efficient governmental organisation, they became realities of far-reaching consequence when imposed on indigenous traditional sociopolitical systems. The early development of Saudi Arabia and the direction of both her domestic and foreign policy were to a considerable extent direct responses to enforced observance of these concepts as applied by the mandate powers in the newly formed countries bordering Saudi territory.

The original intent of this study was to focus solely on the physical delineation of Saudi Arabia as a nation-state: the purposes and actual decision making of the mandate powers in boundary delimitation, the effect of fixed borders on indigenous populations, and the response of Arab leaders to the new political environment. However, as research continued, three important observations were made. Even though previous studies had treated the subject of boundary delimitation and nation-state formation, they had concentrated on political diplomatic histories and had neglected the tremendous social, political and economic realignments stimulated by foreign intervention and, in consequence, inter-Arab relations during the war and post-war periods. Second, it was not sufficient to discuss the effects of boundary delimitation and almost useless to speak of nation-state formation without understanding the factors which were traditional influences within the Arabian Peninsula prior to European intervention. My final and most important realisation was that a study of Central Arabia could not be approached with the same assumptions as those with which scholars approached studies of Palestine, Syria, Mesopotamia and Egypt. These particular areas were dominated by agricultural, commercial and urban structures which regarded nomadic tribes as a threat to their prosperity. By contrast, the geography of Central Arabia favoured a flexible continuum between the extremes of nomadic pastoralist and settled merchant/agriculturalist communities. So unique were the conditions in inner Arabia that alliances between badu and settled populations were frequently made against other similar alliances. Continued research only produced more questions to which Western scholarship could provide no answers. Why, for example, did the Arab leaders in the early 1920s express their dislike of formal boundary delineation and yet by the late 1920s were not only requesting formal boundaries, but demanding their enforcement? Saudi expansion is taken for granted in all histories, but how did this family legitimise its exclusive claim to rule over such diverse social groups as were found in Central Arabia? Saudi success cannot be adequately explained simply by reference to military capability or qualities of statesmanship.

Although my interest in the creation of Middle Eastern boundaries and its implications did not decrease, I discovered that an equally fascinating study was to be found in the transformations occurring within Arab societies at that time. These were not, however, mutually exclusive subjects. Indeed, the acceptance by Arab leaders of fixed European-style boundaries coincided in the case of Central Arabia with a steady progression of social and political transformations under Saudi tutelage which were designed to enhance their exclusive claim to political authority. This acceptance of fixed borders was to reach a climax, quite literally, with the suppression of the last major internal opposition to Saudi rule on the borders of Iraq, Kuwait and Saudi Arabia in 1930.

It also became evident that any attempt to understand the evolution of Saudi Arabia as a geopolitical entity necessitated an interdisciplinary approach. Thus I found myself led into a labyrinth of questions which, like the answers, were eventually found to be inextricably linked. With reference to Central Arabia, the following questions presented themselves. What were the 'frontiers' of its ecological environment? How did the inhabitants of Central Arabia define their daily and seasonal activity spatially? What effects did this have on their patterns of settlement and their patterns of social, political and economic organisation? Among the diverse groups in Arabia, where did the limits of an individual's political, social and religious identity diverge or overlap and how were relationships between these groups regulated? Why were alliances able to form between badu and settled groups? Why were the Al Saud able to establish their authority across numerous tribal groups, settled and nomadic populations, and rival amirates and shaikhdoms? With reference to the Al Saud themselves, how did they perceive their own political identity and how did they utilise their authority? What were the implications when Abd al-Aziz first called himself Amir, then Imam, and finally proclaimed himself *malik* or King?

Throughout this analysis I have used the concept of political identity in two contexts. The first is specifically concerned with the way the Al Saud perceived their political identity as a family. What were the historical antecedents which motivated their political behaviour? How did they perceive authority relative to their Arab and Islamic heritage, relative to the numerous social groups in the Arabian Peninsula, and relative to foreign powers? The second context concerns the evolution of political identity among the peoples of Central Arabia—nomadic and settled—during the first three decades of the twentieth century. This involved realignments in their traditional patterns of allegiance and shifts in the movement of trade and populations as the Saudis further sought to centralise their political control.

This study has been organised in two parts. The four chapters comprising Part I provide a general foundation necessary for any analysis of Central Arabian affairs. Chapter 1 seeks to investigate the shifting social and ecological balances of the interior of the Peninsula in so far as these variables form a back-cloth which affected the course of Arabia's development during the early decades of the twentieth century. Historically, for example, it has been a general tendency to conceive that many areas of the Middle East, such as the Arabian interior, were composed of 'desert' and 'sown' communities, portrayed as antithetical groups in conflict. However, until recently, it has not often been recognised that the political, economic and social contacts between nomadic pastoralist and settled merchant/agriculturalist communities were numerous and the consequences of their contact far-reaching. This means that they cannot satisfactorily be studied as mutually exclusive cultural areas. Moreover, the methods employed by those social groups for the utilisation of resources and control of access to them greatly affected the nature of their interaction as well as the exigencies of their own social organisation. Although all nomadic groups within the Peninsula were organised as tribes and in tribal confederations and the majority of settled inhabitants were also associated with tribal groups, the implications of tribal affiliation, when used as an instrument of political control, have not been adequately studied. Political power and rights of usufruct over land and water resources as regulated by tribal authority in the desert were vital in the subsequent formation of tribal alliances over large territories. This is especially evident when one considers that access to the urban centres such as al-Riyad and Hail could only be obtained by traversing tribal boundaries. Such facts help one to appreciate the difficulties faced by any political contender in Arabia, especially one seeking to legitimise his authority across the particularisms of tribal affiliation and to establish the centralised functions and authority of government.

Chapters 2, 3 and 4 of Part I provide a framework within which to understand the evolution of political identity in Saudi Arabia—that is, the development of collective identity in a society characterised as highly segmentary. The first of these chapters is concerned with the role of the Al Saud within Central Arabian politics. From the time of the recapture of their ancestral capital in 1901/2 and continuing through the 1920s, Al Saud political authority found itself challenged from three sources. One threat emanated from European intervention in the Middle East, ostensibly for protection of the mandates; the second from Arab powers bordering Saudi territory, who either feared Saudi expansion or coveted extension of their own authority at Saudi expense; and, finally, internal dissension resulting from numerous strong tribal groups who recognised no authority other than their own blood relationships, and from rival 'city-states' which competed for the allegiance of nomadic tribes and urban areas. Excepting the blood bonds of the tribes, political authority in Arabia was characterised primarily as one of shifting balances. It was here that Abd al-Aziz as political leader of the Al Saud faced his most necessary task, that of cutting across tribal authority patterns and the power of so-called 'city-states' to establish the Al Saud as legitimate rulers. He did so by affirming his family's claim to hereditary leadership of an area which it had held with only two major interruptions since the early 1700s. He stressed that Saudi leadership had specific obligations and rights of authority over the traditional tribal and urban leaders because the Al Saud represented both an Arab and a lawful Islamic government. These claims were strengthened by the support he received from the alliance dating back to the mid-1700s of the Al Saud with the family of Al Wahhab, founders of a religious movement the aim of which was to revive the perceived original purity of Islam. That the union of religion and politics became a powerful force is illustrated by the fact that the great majority of Central Arabia's settled inhabitants had come to identify themselves during the previous two hundred years as *muwahhidun*, hereafter referred to as Wahhabis.

The intention of Chapters 3 and 4 has been to highlight certain aspects of Saudi rule. The first of these concentrates upon the Ikhwan or 'brethren'. These were badu whom Abd al-Aziz encouraged to settle in agricultural villages which also functioned as religious military centres. The Ikhwan were militant adherents of the Wahhabi movement and underwent daily religious instruction. It was the Ikhwan which enabled the Al Saud successfully to challenge patterns of tribal authority and to expand and establish the validity of Saudi political claims. The last chapter of Part I is concerned with taxation—that is, the establishment by the Al Saud of Islamic taxation in place of the system of levies organised by the badu tribes which had increased tribal divisions and had enhanced the authority of tribal shaikhs. These Islamic taxes gave further force to the Saudi claim that they represented a lawful Islamic government. Some 'inferior tribes' such as the Awazim were freed by Abd al-Aziz from paying the traditional badu tribute to 'noble tribes' and instead were obliged to pay *zakat* to the Al Saud. The subject of taxation is important because it indicates yet another move in Central Arabia towards the centralisation of authority and the way in which the Al Saud perceived themselves as political leaders. Part I is therefore concerned with the geography of Central Arabia and the social, economic and political relationships of its inhabitants. Within this context, it explores the foundations of Saudi claims to political authority; the religious and social implications of the Wahhabi movement; the transition from a hierarchical system of dependent places to the development of central government functions and authority; and the recognition, however superficial, by diverse groups that they now shared a common identity, or rather were bound by certain common interests irrespective of their other associations.

Between the years 1914 and 1926 Saudi authority continued to expand until its physical growth was checked by foreign intervention. Meanwhile, the internal transformations which had been occurring under Saudi guidance began in the mid-1920s to threaten the very existence of Saudi rule. Both challenges—foreign intervention and internal dissent—culminated in disputes during the late 1920s on the boundaries separating Saudi Arabia from her northern neighbours of Iraq and Kuwait and, to a lesser extent, the boundary of Jordan in the north-west. The establishment of these boundaries and the disputes which surround them comprise Part II of this study.

While Saudi Arabia was not included in the mandate settlement, she nevertheless was directly affected by the political manoeuvring of her Arab neighbours which were either mandated or protected territories of the British. The effects of the formation of these boundaries and nation-states were ubiquitous and irreversible, posing serious problems for indigenous populations. The boundary disputes are explored in Part II, both in their formal-legalistic sense and in their ramifications, as first Arab politicians, and later the local populations, were forced to recognise the limitations of Western-style borders and, concomitantly, to realise that, even if only in facade, they were assuming the external characteristics of a nation-state in the Western sense.

These boundaries became the source of friction and, sometimes, armed conflict in the 1920s and are of special importance because the disputes surrounding them help to illustrate the dichotomy between European and Arab perspectives of political and social traditions. The consequences of this dichotomy, only partially bridged today, were and remain sources of difficulty in the Middle East as a whole. Moreover, the specific boundaries mentioned above are important in understanding Saudi political identity, because it was on the northern frontier, in confrontation with Western powers, that Abd al-Aziz experienced the first effective limitations upon his authority and, therefore, a limit to the physical extent of the Saudi state. It was also here that Abd al-Aziz, in the late 1920s, used the Western concepts of 'boundary' and 'nation-state' successfully to undermine his strongest opponents within the central plateau area of Arabia, to overcome local particularisms and to establish the Al Saud as the predominant power and himself the first king of what is now referred to as the Kingdom of Saudi Arabia. The acceptance of fixed Western-style borders was to mark the end of one transitional period: the move from a hierarchical system of dependent places to the development of central government functions and authority. This also included the levelling, theoretically at least, of political, social and religious divisions.

After 1930 a protective curtain shrouded internal events of the country although political control was exercised much as it had been previously. The presence of non-Arab foreigners was carefully controlled and the reins of political authority and the process of decision making were kept tightly in the hands of the Al Saud. Religion and politics remained intertwined, each providing the justification for the other. The Al Saud regarded themselves as participants in both Arab and Islamic tradition. By substituting Islamic ideals for the bonds of tribal membership, they created the basis for a broader framework of allegiance patterns and succeeded in establishing their legitimate right to rule in spite of the barrier of tribal and urban loyalties. They therefore claimed the physical territory of all tribes which had declared allegiance to them.

Al Saud 'kingship' is more realistically viewed in this study as a myth created by Abd al-Aziz, supported by the Western world, and only *de facto* a reality. He had a number of opportunities which other amirates of the Arabian interior had not had nor, indeed, even contemplated in earlier centuries. The decline of Ottoman authority placed him in a position to form a series of alliances which, with some exceptions, were in time to become enduring. The opening of the Suez Canal, the increasing presence of foreign interests in the surrounding littoral areas, and the availability of Western technology produced not only new problems, but new political tools. World War I brought the realisation that a new world was on the doorstep. Offers by the British of subsidies and military assistance allowed Abd al-Aziz to fill his treasury, pay his army and secure the allegiance of rival shaikhdoms and amirates. His use of the Wahhabi movement allowed him to transcend tribal and urban particularisms to create a nation-state. The Ikhwan, set up on the same rationale, provided him not only with an army but with a police force. Formal recognition by international powers went far to legitimise his rule in a new world guided by new rules. New economic opportunities to exploit gold and oil resources were presented in previously unimportant and uninhabitable areas. The authority that Abd al-Aziz claimed was not fleeting, as had been the case of tribal shaikhs in the so-called 'city-states' of previous centuries. It was an authority strengthened and enhanced at a moment when a number of factors made political expansion and stability possible. The following chapters explore more fully the factors which were influential in the geopolitical formation of Saudi Arabia and in the evolution of political identity between 1901 and 1932.

PART I

Internal Factors Influencing the Evolution of Political Identity in Central Arabia

1

Shifting Balances: Interaction of Social and Environmental Factors

Many readers will have chosen this book solely with the intention of understanding the origin, history, and nature of the Saudi ruling family. One cannot understand the nature of any political authority in Central Arabia, Saudi or otherwise, unless first viewing it in its geographical and ecological context. Indeed, to omit this type of analysis would be to neglect one of the major determining factors of political behaviour in Central Arabia and one which has been neglected in studies of this region to date. For this reason it is essential that the reader develops from this chapter some understanding of the significance of water and grazing resources, land utilisation, and patterns of settlement—to whatever degree of detail he may wish—before proceeding to the succeeding discussions.

The Kingdom of Saudi Arabia, *al-mamlaka al-arabiya al-saudiya*, occupies over 90 per cent of the Arabian Peninsula. In the early twentieth century Saudi territory was divided into four regions—al-Hijaz, Asir, al-Ahsa and Najd—which reflect natural geopolitical segments that remain useful for the purpose of this study. It was in Najd that the Al Saud and Al Wahhab families, representing hitherto separate political and religious domains, made a concerted effort to obtain effective influence over a number of amirates[1] striving to maintain their separate political autonomy. Occupying the vast exterior of Arabia, Najd had no access to the coastal areas except through al-Hijaz or al-Ahsa. Enclosed by the virtually impenetrable al-Nafud, al-Dahna and al-Ramla sand deserts in the north, east and south, and extreme in its climate and geography, Najd evolved a cultural area distinct from the more urbanised regions of Palestine and Syria and Mesopotamia.

The success of the Al Saud was principally a consequence of their understanding of badu[2] culture, a life-style which was so encompassing in its economic, political and social significance in Najd that its usage here eclipses the terms 'nomadic pastoralists' or 'transhumance' which more narrowly describe human adaptation to ecological factors. Although nomadic tribes were also present in Palestine and Syria and Mesopotamia, they were always dominated by powerful urban structures, in contrast to Najd. Here urban areas and badu were enmeshed in a mutually beneficial relationship, although the badu had always maintained their status as powerful independent military tribes. It is notable that, even though the Al Saud were urbanised and identified in many respects with the interests of townspeople, their perspective remained badu and that for many years Abd al-Aziz maintained a roving *majlis* rather than centralise either the functions or location of his 'court'. Moreover, it was a custom that members of ruling amirates in Najd, even if settled in an urban area, were none the less sent at an early age to be raised in the desert by those badu tribes renowned for virtues of pride, fierce independence, nobility and military prowess. In this way, Abd al-Aziz spent part of his youth with the Al Murra tribe near the Arabian Gulf.

The focus of the present chapter is directed to those factors of decisive influence in Najd life: the geographic isolation; the ecological conditions and the dependence of the population on water and grazing resources; the solidarity (*asabiya*) of tribal structure; the lines of division inherent in a region characterised by numerous militarily independent tribes and competing urban areas; and the interdependence of urban and nomadic communities. All of these factors contributed to prevent foreign interference and to deter the formation of a central state apparatus even by internal Arab forces. Just as the Ottomans had realised that their control, limited to settled areas, would always be tenuous, so Great Britian realised that blockades and bombardment of coastal towns would be ineffectual threats to a Central Arabian power. Diplomacy became the best strategy for foreign powers seeking to pursue their own ends in Najd. Even Al Saud authority, which had been well established in the southern districts of Najd since the 1700s, encountered staunch opposition from both nomadic and settled elements. In order to establish the authority of his family throughout Najd, Abd al-Aziz was forced to eliminate traditional elements which emphasised the authority of the desert tribal shaikhs and the independent and competing power of the settled amirates while simultaneously substituting others which enhanced his own claim to legitimate rule. The following sections concentrate upon those elements in the sociopolitical climate of twentieth-century Najd which were the foundations upon which the Wahhabi movement[3] and the Al Saud were equally dependent and by which they were also threatened in their bid for political control.

Environmental Factors, Resource Utilisation and Patterns of Land Settlement

The most notable feature of Najd, the vast region in the interior of the Arabian Peninsula, is its geographic isolation. Unlike the more mountainous regions of igneous and metamorphic rocks along the western edge of the Peninsula, Najd in its wider sense is an uplifted plateau-shield area with an outlying scarpland, composed predominantly of a suite of alternating sedimentary structures. This is in strong contrast to the great mountainous region of al-Hijaz, literally meaning 'the barrier', which adjoins Najd to the west and runs 950 kilometres from north to south. This latter region was and still is characterised by a strong urban orientation. Water supplied in the piedmont zone, notably on the eastern side, enabled wells to tap groundwater supplies and settlements to be formed. These settlements were centres for caravan trade and nomadic supply bases over several thousand years. Their inhabitants functioned as traders and provided services during pilgrimage for the Holy Cities of Mecca and al-Madina, neither of which could provide sufficient basic necessities for its population.[4] Even the nomads in al-Hijaz profited from its urban orientation. They raided caravan traffic so frequently that the leaders of urban settlements were obliged to sanction the tribes and, if possible, force from them tribute or other contractual relationships as in the time of the Prophet Muhammad. Al-Hijaz, unlike Najd, was characterised by political continuity, having been ruled traditionally for many centuries by families claiming descent from the Prophet. Although they were later forced to acknowledge Ottoman suzerainty, these descendants remained the nominal authority until their final defeat in 1925 by the Al Saud.

Najd is surrounded on its three remaining sides by virtually uninhabited desert. In the south lies al-Ramla, one of the largest uninterrupted stretches of sand and one of the least inhabited areas of the world. For this reason al-Ramla (or al-Rimal), literally meaning 'the sand(s)', is better known to the West as al-Rub al-Khali or The Empty Quarter.[5] The fact that no European entered al-Ramla until Bertram Thomas did so in 1930, and that little other information was gathered about it until recent oil exploration, may give some indication of its harsh environment. Rainfall is rare and periods of up to ten years can be remembered when no rain fell at all. The only people to frequent the area were badu from Oman and southern Arabia who skirted the fringes of the desert.[6]

Extending north from al-Ramla is a long thin arc of reddish sand called al-Dahna, varying from 15 kilometres to 80 kilometres in width. This otherwise arid corridor of sand is underlain with impermeable formations which prevented further infiltration of water so that seasonal wells could be established. This region fell largely into the *dira* of the Mutair tribe, who utilised its temporary grasses in the spring. There were no permanent wells or settlements in al-Dahna. Anyone who wished to reach Najd from the Gulf coast had to cross this desert, a hazardous caravan journey of no less than two days.

Al-Dahna continues in a north-western direction until it merges into the great basin of sand known as al-Nafud, which stretches 325 kilometres north to south and 490 kilometres east to west. Rainfall and other water sources are so unreliable that only in a few isolated areas and on the desert fringes where water is retained in impermeable substrata does one find that permanent habitation was possible. There is, however, abundant desert vegetation which was utilised by the nomads after winter rains and in the spring. In their annual migrations the northern Shammar, Zafir and Muntafiq tribes skirted eastern al-Nafud, the Shararat and Anaza (al-Ruwala branch) in the north, and the Anaza (Bishr branch) and southern Shammar in the south. The only inhabitants of this formidable region during summer were the Suluba and Awazim, the former specifically renowned for their exceptional desert skills.

Central Arabia, unlike al-Hijaz, was not dominated by the interests of an urban structure reliant upon trading; neither was it, like the surrounding arid deserts, inhabited predominantly by nomadic tribes who alone were able to utilise its scarce water resources. Oasis settlements which could support large settled populations and which had strong links with the powerful nomadic tribes had long been a feature of Najd. Estimates at the beginning of the twentieth century indicate that the settled population of major cities such as al-Riyad numbered 8,000, Buraida 7,500, Hail 3,000, and Unaiza 10,000-15,000.[7] These major oases functioned in varying degrees as agricultural, mercantile and manufacturing centres as well as the crossroads of trans-peninsular caravan routes. Associated with the oasis settlements and urban centres were a number of subsidiary villages and nomadic tribes, giving rise to the creation of a hierarchy of central place functions and an actual if indistinct formation of districts. The central places provided a variety of functions, market and service, which they offered in exchange for other goods or services. Moreover, nomads in Central Arabia frequently owned agriculture in the urban areas, thus further reinforcing this integration. It is evident that the so-called 'desert' and 'sown' communities freely interacted to such an extent that complicated networks of social relations—tribal, governmental, religious, military, economic—evolved in consequence.

Estimates for the population of Saudi Arabia as a whole support the above statement and are open to further interpretation. In the early 1920s the population was thought to be approximately 1,500,000, of which one-quarter were nomads, one-half were agriculturalists, and the remaining one-quarter were involved in occupations associated with urban life, such as crafts or shopkeeping. If one excluded the areas of al-Hijaz, Asir and al-Ahsa, where the highest population densities were concentrated in a few urban centres, then the nomadic population of Najd could be considered to be as high as one-half. This amazing figure is substantiated by Lorimer whose estimates were frequently as high as that for individual regions such as, for example, Jabal Shammar, al-Washm and al-Arid as well as by a 1962/63 census taken by the Saudi government.[8] Uncertainty arises from these statistics, however, because of the fact that nomads are stationary only during summer when they must stay near wells and, even during this period, estimates must remain conjectural.[9]

Despite the high ratio of nomadic to fixed populations, there is no evidence in the literature which indicates that badu tribes tyrannised the settled areas of Najd, even though the most powerful nomadic tribes numbered over 30,000 members each. It was more frequently the case that the settled populations within individual districts of Najd were at enmity with one another. This situation greatly contrasted with settled life in al-Hijaz where badu often disrupted commerce and in the east where the predominantly nomadic tribes of the Bani Khalid had even been known to control the settled oases of al-Ahsa and al-Qatif which, numbering over 60,000 and 20,000 inhabitants respectively at the turn of the century, were much more populous than the settled areas of Najd.

It is well known that during the millennium preceding the twentieth century, and even today, there existed, throughout the Arabian Gulf littoral and into Central Arabia, amirates ruling settled and nomadic populations. The amirs were sometimes able to control areas of considerable extent by virtue of their tribal alliances. As the alliances shifted, so too did the extent of central authority. What is less well understood about Central Arabia is the nature of the relationships between the various amirates or between the municipal centres and their fringe areas. It is the economic, social and political history of these fluctuating territorial units that is more properly Arabian history in its fullest sense. Although the orientation of settled and nomadic groups in Najd might be expected to be antagonistic, there were two reasons—natural resources and social organisation—which ensured that they would be mutually supportive.

It is to water resources that our immediate attention is directed because they constituted the primary factor which determined patterns of land utilisation in Central Arabia and decisively influenced social organisation. It will be recalled that the eastern regions of the Peninsula are composed of numerous sedimentary structures dipping gradually to the north and east. In Central Arabia uptilting of these structures produces a series of plateaux and west-facing escarpments which align themselves north to south. The most prominent escarpment and, indeed, the dominant feature of southern Najd is Jabal Tuwaiq, 950 kilometres in length and rising up to 500 metres above its surrounding plain (cf. Figure 1.4). There are two parallel mountain ranges, Aja and Salma, which in northern Najd form the famous region of Jabal Shammar. Cutting across these escarpments and running north-east to south-west across the grain of this region are a series of well-developed *wadi* systems or 'valleys' (cf. Figures 1.1. and 1.2). Because of the availability of water in these *wadi*s, they were literally the ancient thoroughfares, caravan routes and centres of tribal activity. Permanent settlements also depended upon these same sources in order to secure sufficient water for crops and human needs. Such

Figure 1.1: The Arabian Shield and Major Wadis *of Central Arabia*

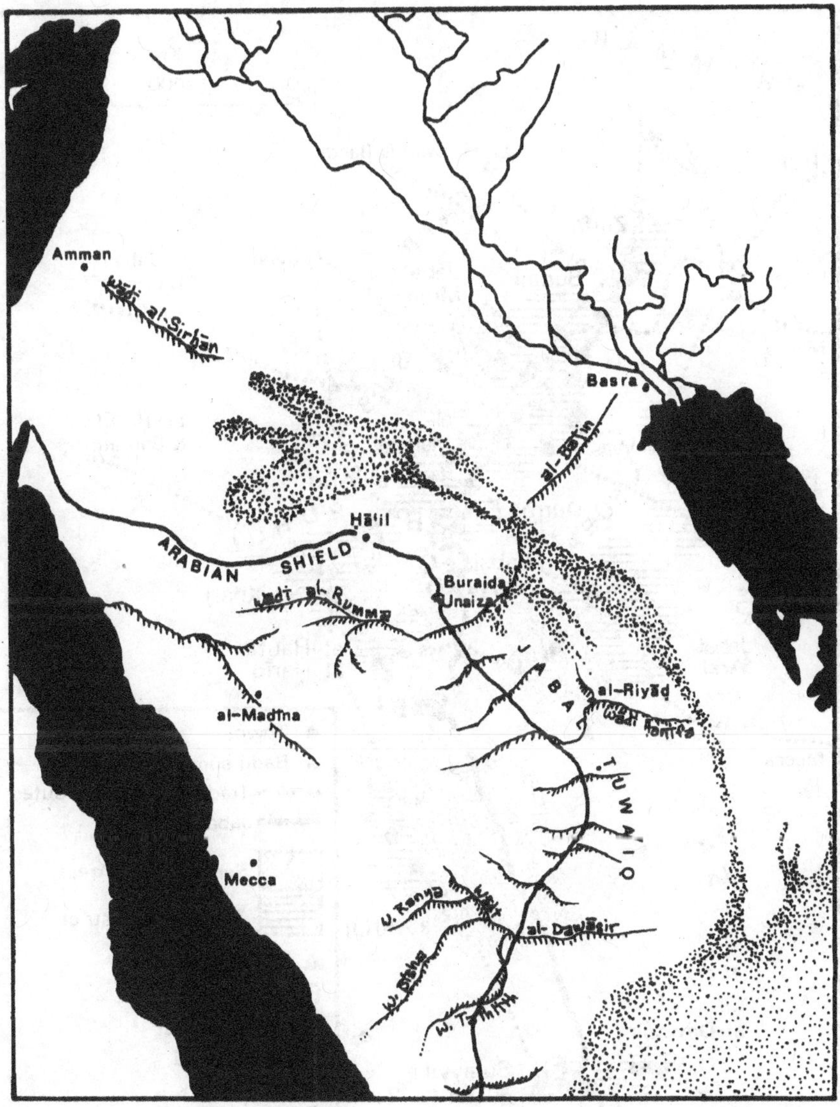

Figure 1.2: Districts and Tribes in Central Najd

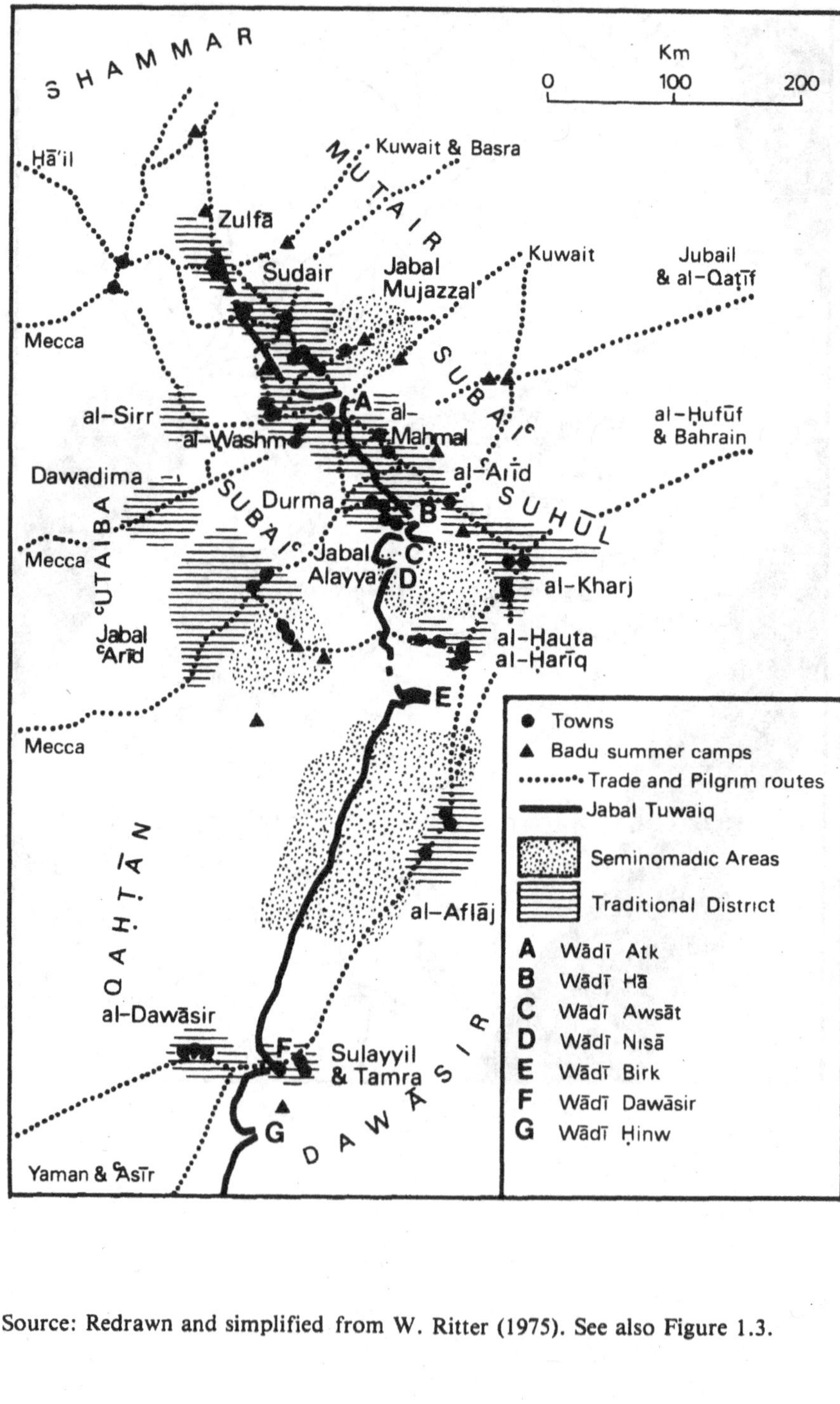

Source: Redrawn and simplified from W. Ritter (1975). See also Figure 1.3.

was the economic potential and strategic location of certain *wadis* that great political prestige accrued to tribes or settlements able to control them. Thus the Wahhabi coreland of southern Najd is seen to be situated around the base of Jabal Tuwaiq and along the numerous *wadis*, particularly Wadi Hanifa and Wadi Sudair, which traverse its slopes.

Before proceeding any further, it will be useful to outline the geopolitical divisions of Central Arabia so that the relationships between water resources and their utilisation can be more clearly understood. Central Arabia has traditionally been divided by the people themselves into three distinct regions: northern Najd or Jabal Shammar, al-Qasim and southern Najd. Southern Najd will hereafter be referred to simply as Najd because this area was identified by the people as Najd in its narrowest sense. Najd was the coreland of Saudi and Wahhabi strength. Jabal Shammar frequently rivalled its southern neighbour of Najd in political control, while al-Qasim, lying as an intermediary between the two, vacillated in its allegiance as expediency dictated. It is of note that the people of Jabal Shammar and al-Qasim were far enough north to devote as much of their trade to Syria and the cities along the Euphrates in Mesopotamia as they did to the coastal areas in the east and west. Najd, however, traded predominantly with al-Ahsa and Kuwait across the sands of al-Dahna.

The exact size and number of districts in Najd has varied through the years because of fluctuating political and economic conditions. In the minds of the inhabitants, political control was a function less of territory than of socio-economic links and kinship. As a result, certain districts were completely engulfed by their neighbours while others succeeded in establishing and maintaining an identity of their own. The regions most prominent in Najd affairs in recent centuries can be roughly subdivided into three groups: (1) al-Sudair, al-Arid, al-Aflaj, al-Mahmal, and the three interconnected districts of al-Hariq, al-Hauta and al-Kharj lying generally between Jabal Tuwaiq and al-Dahna towards the east; (2) al-Dawasir between Jabal Tuwaiq and the desert to the south; and (3) al-Washm lying to the west of Jabal Tuwaiq (cf. Figure 1.2). The more heavily populated settlement pattern evidenced along the eastern flank of Jabal Tuwaiq may perhaps be explained by the different patterns of drainage on the dip-and-scarp of Jabal Tuwaiq. The more gradual gradient in the east considerably eases problems of water collection and utilisation. The steep valleys on the west increase the potential for damage, soil erosion and flash flooding.

All of these districts are characterised by low precipitation, extreme temperature ranges, high evaporation, flash floods and absence of perennial rivers. The higher mountains such as those in Jabal Tuwaiq receive more rainfall than the lowlands, although most areas do not exceed 150 millimetres annually (cf. Figure 1.3). While the northern regions of Jabal Tuwaiq, which are also the most populous in Najd, have been recorded as receiving 200 millimetres of precipitation, this decreases to 100 millimetres in al-Kharj and 50-70 millimetres in al-Aflaj.[10] The rainy season (Najd colloq. *wasm*), generally occurring between the months of October and April in several cloudbursts and intermittent showers, is

Figure 1.3: Mean Annual Precipitation in Saudi Arabia

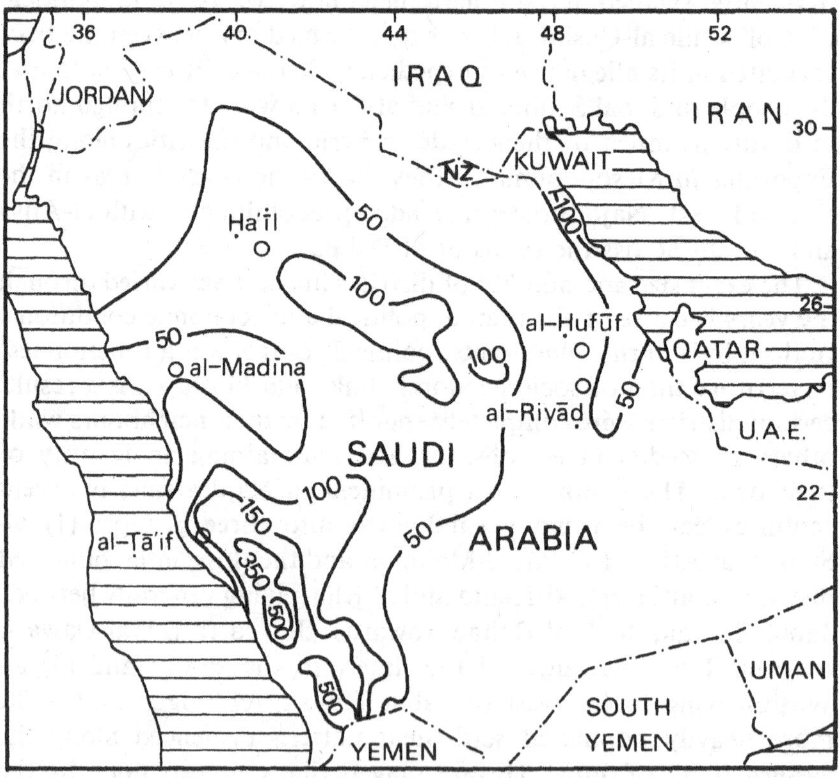

Source: Redrawn and simplified from P. Beaumont (1977).

unpredictable and Arab historians and travellers have recorded periods of drought lasting several years. While this was less serious for the oasis settlements relying upon groundwater supplies, it did affect cultivators dependent upon flood waters (*sail*, pl. *suyul*) and the badu who were frequently forced, during years of drought, to join settled communities in Najd or migrate to the Arabian Gulf where they undertook other occupations.[11]

In addition to the difficulties created by the unreliable and low rates of precipitation, populations also had to endure extremes of temperature. Mean monthly figures in al-Riyad have been recorded at 45°C for August and 3°C for January. Many other areas record temperatures as high at 50°C during the summer heat (*qaiz*). This is directly related to the high evaporation figures for Saudi Arabia, 3000 millimetres *per annum* from open water surfaces. The higher rates of evaporation also cause greater quantities to be required by men and animals as a result of fluid loss.[12] Frosts, sometimes snow, and biting winds are not unknown during winter in the regions around Jabal Shammar and, except in the southern districts of al-Aflaj and al-Dawasir, frost occurs throughout Najd, limiting the growing season and consequently causing grapes, apricots and peaches to be raised in the higher valleys in preference to citrus fruits and certain vegetables.

Although Central Arabia is arid, the nomadic and settled populations devised numerous techniques to utilise groundwater and surface runoff. The sandstone, dolomite and limestone formations of the eastern Peninsula contain tremendous volumes of groundwater gradually moving through confined aquifers towards the eastern shores of the Gulf where it is released under pressure as artesian springs (cf. Figure 1.4). Oasis settlements, such as al-Ahsa and al-Qatif, grew up around these fresh water springs which were capable of supporting large populations.[13] These same artesian springs occur around the island of Bahrain—its name, not without reason, means 'the two waters'.[14]

There are, however, only a few free-flowing springs (*ain*, pl. *uyun*) and no perennial streams in Najd itself so that groundwater was obtained only by the laborious task of lifting from wells (*qalib*, pl. *qulub*, *qulban*, *aqliba*) either by animal or human labour. Thousands of wells are scattered across Arabia, principally along *wadi* beds and depressions where water is concentrated in alluvial deposits and in the groundwater of the outwash zones along the base of upland areas.[15] There were, however, very few locations

Figure 1.4: Confined Aquifers of Central and Eastern Arabia

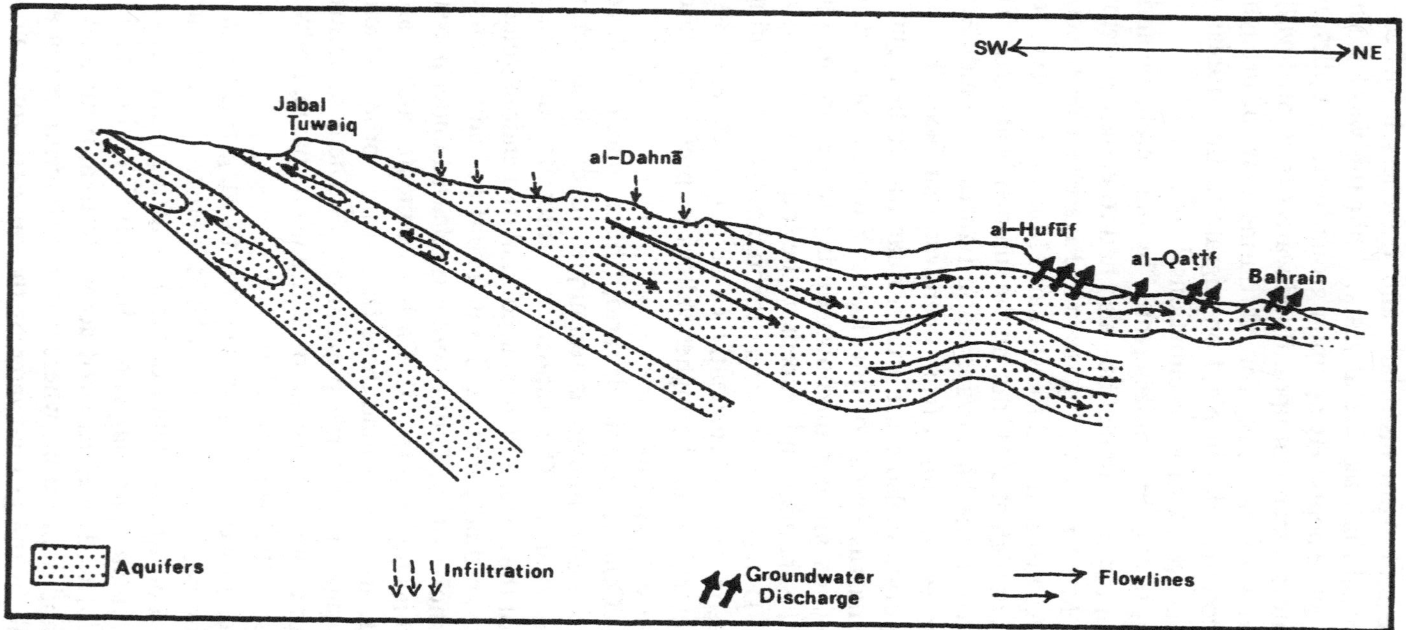

Source: Redrawn and simplified from P. Beaumont (1977).

where groundwater was sufficient to support sedentary communities. Three to four metres of water duty *per annum* are required for permanent irrigation. During the hot summer season and drought years wells were heavily relied upon for supplying increased human and animal needs. If draught animals could be afforded, they were kept almost continually busy lifting water for irrigation which, in turn, meant growing fodder crops.[16] During drought years, most crops had to be sacrificed to keep alive the date palms the importance of which in Najd was equal only to that of the camel. Although it requires more water than other crops, the date palm, like the camel in comparison to other animals, is the most tolerant of high levels of salinity and the date is therefore one of the most dependable staples in Najdi diets. Soil salinity is always a problem around settlements. The fringe areas of the settlements and the irrigation ditches, which also function as drainage basins, continue to accumulate salt residues resulting from evaporation. Moreover, underground water supplies become increasingly saline towards the eastern regions of the Peninsula. Some wells are so brackish that only camels can drink from them, afterwards supplying their badu owners with milk. In the past the Wahiba badu who range through territory in Oman were renowned for their diet consisting solely of camel milk and dates.

Another source of groundwater was the *falaj* (pl. *aflaj*), best known as *qanat.*[17] They were found only in the districts of al-Kharj and al-Aflaj whence the latter district probably derived its name. Some still function although archaeological evidence indicates that their origin dates back to pre-Islamic times. In this irrigation system mother wells were located in the aquifers and then a nearly horizontal channel, sometimes several kilometres long, was tunnelled back to them to bring water to sites favourable for settlement (cf. Figure 1.5). The complex water utilisation system that the *falaj* represents could only be sustained as long as political and social organisation remained strong. During the last two centuries, the *aflaj* of Najd were always reported to be in varying states of disrepair.[18]

Not infrequently water was also obtained by digging a metre or so in the sand along *wadi* bottoms to reach the water-table. This was possible because the sandy depressions where water tended to collect had only a low capillary rise and acted as a poor heat conductor, so that little moisture was subsequently lost by evaporation. Badu and small camping groups utilised such water

Figure 1.5: Cross-section of Falaj *(Qanat)*

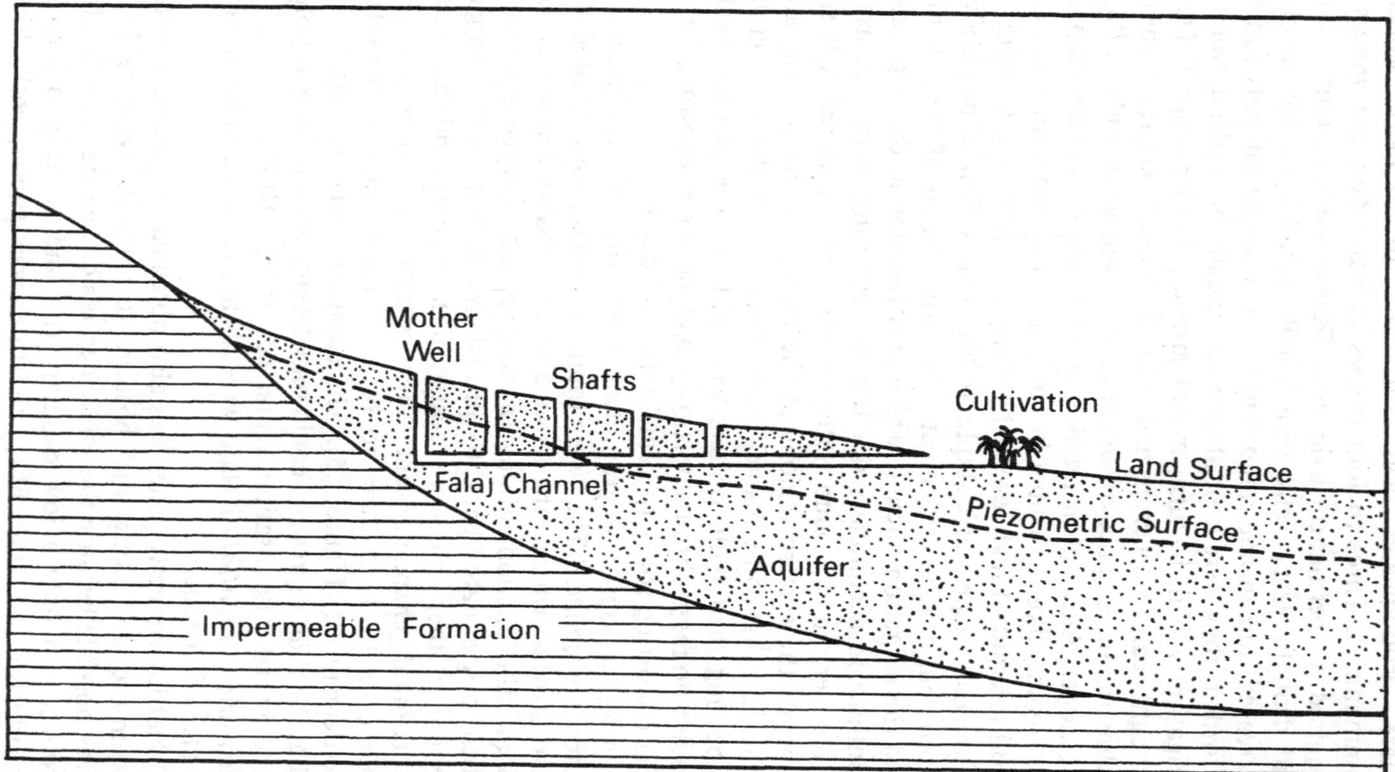

Source: Redrawn and simplified from J. Wilkinson (1977).

supplies until wells or oasis settlements could be reached. It may be noted that the names of many settled areas in Arabia were prefixed with the word *rauda* which literally means 'a moist hollow where natural vegetation grows' or simply 'a garden'. The plural of *rauda* is *riyad* after which the capital of Saudi Arabia, al-Riyad, was appropriately named for its extensive date plantations, a welcome green sight after days spent on a dry and desolate journey across the desert of al-Dahna.

There are also reported instances of what are referred to as 'natural wells' (*dahal*, pl. *duhul*), some one hundred of which were scattered between al-Dahna and Summan, a rock desert to the east of al-Dahna. These were underground caves, perhaps solution pools, entered by natural rock fissures sometimes running distances of thirty to forty feet.[19] Apparently the water was pure rainwater but was difficult to obtain. This method, as with that of digging in the sand, yielded only one skinful (*qirba*, pl. *qirbat*, *qirab*) of water. These *duhul* were all well known by travellers across al-Dahna who had to carry their water with them and by the Mutair tribe who frequented this region.

In addition to underground water sources, rainwater was also utilised by Najd populations. Late rains often provided summer grazing and in several areas, such as the district of al-Washm, cultivation was possible without resort to irrigation. Furthermore, flood waters recharged groundwater and provided an important means of irrigating fields by diversionary channels. Lateral seepage from perched water in major sand dune formations or *nafud*s also gave rise to accessible water and soils on their edges which could be exploited. If the soil was clay, then crops were planted; if sandy, then dates were grown for food and tamarisks for timber.[20]

The technology employed in utilising these water resources produced three general settlement patterns. These were organised around (1) wells and *falaj*es, (2) diversionary channels built to redirect flood waters to terraces along *wadi*s, and (3) controlled deposition of soil and rainwater from *wadi*s in the bajada or zone of coalescing outwash fans. Wells at average depths of 5-20 metres ensured supplies during the summer and in dry years, but only a few areas were fortunate enough to depend solely upon wells. Irrigation of terraces and delta regions by runoff was both efficient and, if controlled properly, had the added advantage of depositing silt valuable for agriculture.[21] In exceptional instances this allowed isolated farmsteads (*qasr*, pl. *qusur*) to scatter themselves across flat silt plains. Varying combinations of these methods of water utilisation were found in all districts. Al-Arid and al-Dawasir, for example, largely relied upon well irrigation while the districts of al-Sudair, al-Washm, al-Aflaj, and al-Kharj relied heavily on flood water as an irrigation technique. All of these different irrigation techniques were utilised in Zulfa, a major town in al-Sudair.

As has been seen, agricultural production was limited by the availability of water and fertile soils as well as by the technical and labour-intensive means of exploiting it. Only 0.2 per cent of Saudi Arabia is currently under cultivation because of water shortages and over 80 per cent of these cultivated areas must be irrigated (cf. Figure 1.6). All dry land farming is in the south-west. Because of the scarcity of water and the energy required for its utilisation, it was a commodity that had to be consumed largely in agricultural pursuits. Approximately 85 per cent of farms even today are less than 1.6 hectares, so that agriculture basically provides only for subsistence needs.[22]

The extensive areas where water was not sufficient to support permanent settlements did not, however, remain unutilised. Nomadic pastoralists organised into autonomous tribes and sub-units adapted themselves to utilise marginal resources in those regions too dry to offer any other alternative life-style. Centuries of nomadism in Central Arabia evolved efficient adaptive techniques to environmental conditions, and these in turn regulated social relations between badu tribes and between nomads and sedentaries.

At this point it is necessary to provide a more exact definition of the term 'nomadic pastoralism'. The term can be misleading because it actually includes within its meaning a diversity of adaptive techniques. Numerous attempts to develop a classification system of nomads have resulted in schemes based upon the listing of 'material' and 'non-material' culture traits and in the frequently used categories of 'nomad' and 'semi-nomad', the latter expression indicating anything intermediary between camel-herders and completely sedentary agriculturalists. These studies have been unable to reveal the tremendous variability, or rather flexibility, shown by individual groups to challenges in their environment. There were few tribes in Arabia which were purely nomadic—that is, those which herded only camels. Nomads might herd sheep, goats, camels, or any combination thereof and may additionally have owned land in settled areas or tended isolated stands of date palms.[23] The issue is further complicated by the realisation that,

Figure 1.6: Cultivated Land in Saudi Arabia

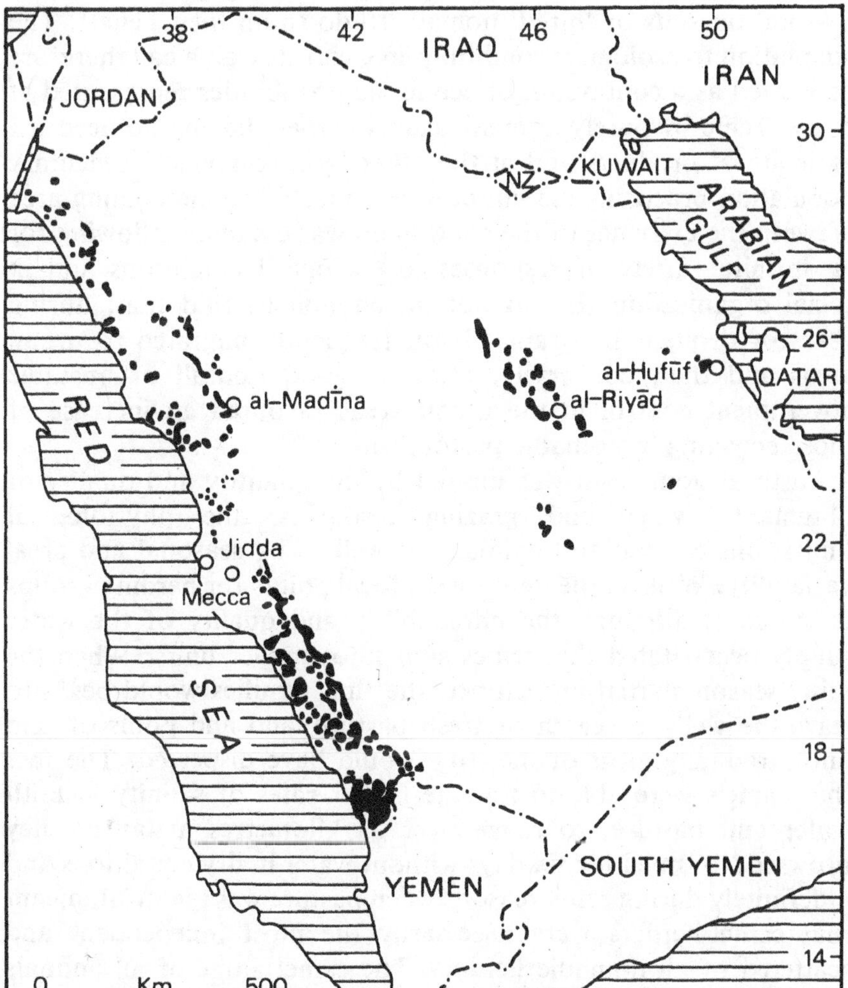

Source: Redrawn and simplified from P. Beaumont (1977).

although agriculture was the primary economic occupation among Arabia's settled population, many people did engage in subsidiary pastoral pursuits or 'hired' nomads to do so on their behalf. The adaptation to ecological conditions in Central Arabia can therefore be viewed as a continuum of economic possibilities represented at one extreme by purely nomadic camel-herders having no need for agricultural products and at the other by a completely sedentary population practising agricultural pursuits.[24] The intervening area between the extremes of the continuum was dynamic, allowing for an infinite variety of responses to ecological conditions and in social organisation. It was not uncommon to find that, during years of drought in Arabia, badu frequently migrated to urban areas and that, conversely, years of good rainfall or unstable government control in the urban areas favoured an increase of those engaging in nomadic pastoralism.

Pastoral nomadism was limited by the quantity and quality of obtainable water and grazing resources, the physiological limitations of men and animals, as well as by seasonal and areal variability. Wells in the desert were focal points for herding groups in summer, although the unreliability and quality of the water supply necessitated that tribes split into smaller units. When the rainy season started in October, the first families would begin to leave the wells in search of fresh pasture land and pools of rain until gradually most of the tribe would have dispersed. The fact that camels were able to tolerate higher rates of salinity in both water and pasture, to range over 25 kilometres a day as they browsed, to travel for six days without water in dry conditions and indefinitely during rainy reasons when pasture was plentiful, meant that camel-herders were necessarily the most independent and scattered of all nomadic herders. The camel alone of all animals provided milk and butter, meat, hides and transport. It was not without reason that these camel-herding tribes were the strongest and most warlike in Arabia, who by condition and necessity fiercely defended their tribal grazing territory or *dira*.

While it was man who limited the full adaptive capabilities of the camel, it was the presence of sheep and goats which limited the extent of territory that could be utilised by man. Both of these animals, sensitive to water deprivation and high rates of salinity, restricted herding to more permanent watering sites. If a tribe was mixed-herding—that is, herding some combination of goats and sheep as well as camels—then part of the tribe would be forced to remain at permanent watering sites or near the frontier of settlement to supply the needs of goats and sheep while another group would disperse to the desert to seek the best pasture land for the camels. The al-Ruwala tribe in north-western Arabia referred to this period of permanent encampment as *ma yusharriqun* or 'not going east' and as *yugharribun* or 'going west', which indicated that they were moving towards permanent wells on the western fringe of the desert. During the rainy season, they dispersed once more. Their term for this, *yusharriqun*, literally means that they were 'going east' into the desert.[25] This range of adaptive techniques by the nomad made for a continuity of land utilisation between permanent urban settlements and desert areas (cf. Figure 1.7).

Irrespective of the variety of adaptive life-styles or even of the interaction between groups, the inhabitants of Central Arabia perceived that members of their society fell into one of two main categories: *hadar*, those who were permanently settled, and *arab*, those who lived in movable tents (*bait al-shaar*).[26] Among the

Figure 1.7: Continuum of Land Use

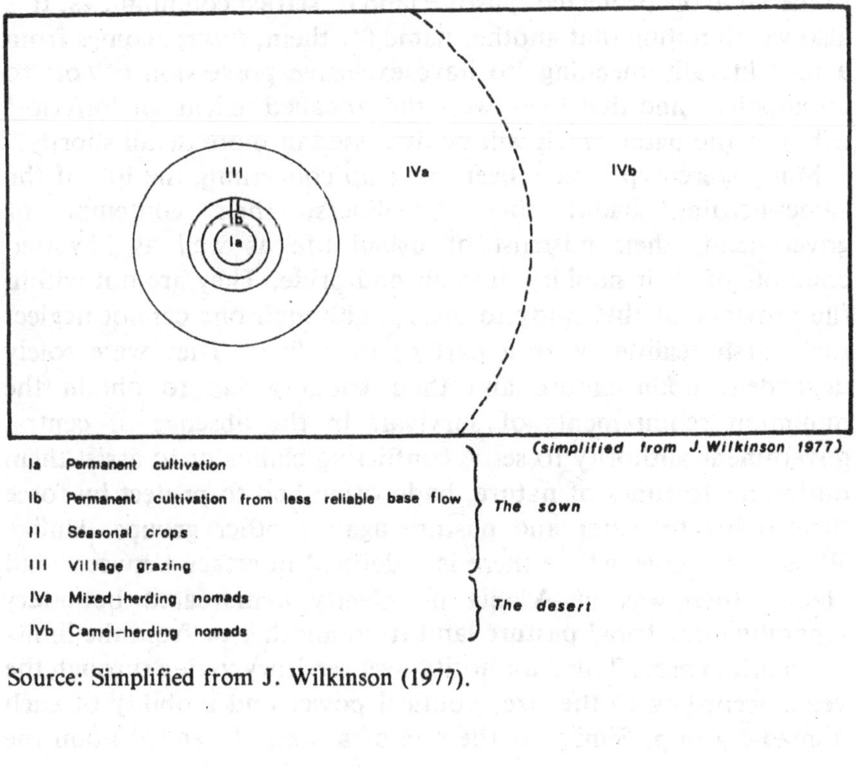

Source: Simplified from J. Wilkinson (1977).

hadar were distinguished those known as *qarawiyun* (sing. *qarawi*) or 'villagers', who remained permanently settled in towns pursuing urban occupations, and those who tended both livestock and agriculture, known as *rua* (sing. *rai*) or 'shepherds'. They left their towns during the rainy season to graze and water their flocks in the *hima*, 'protected pasture land of the town', returning in spring to harvest crops. The *arab* similarly made distinctions among their own kind. There were the camel-herding tribes who were recognised as badu by their long and continued association with the desert for more than ten months of a year and there were the herders of sheep and goats. The latter lived throughout the year in the *bait al-shaar*, but remained on the desert fringe because of the needs of their flocks. In northern Arabia these nomads were referred to as *shawawi* (sing. *shawi*) and they were often found in close proximity to the urban areas of the Euphrates. They were also known as *arab al-dar* or *ruhm al-dira*, that is 'relatives of the *dar* (variant of *dira*)' or 'kinship of the *dira*'.[27] This reference to *dira* is important to note in that it explicitly indicates that they were in some way related to the grazing territory of nomadic tribes and not to the *hima* or 'protected' pasture land of settled communities. It is also worth noting that another name for them, *hukra*, comes from a root literally meaning 'to have exclusive possession of' or 'to monopolise' and that these were the so-called 'client' or 'inferior' tribes of the badu which will be discussed in more detail shortly.

Many stereotypes have been built up concerning the life of the camel-herding badu: their unruliness, their contempt of government, their mistrust of urban life as well as idealised concepts of their nobility, honour and pride. They are not within the province of this study to discuss although one cannot neglect that harsh realities were a part of their lives. They were solely dependent upon nature and their tribal group to obtain the minimum requirements of survival. In the absence of central government authority to settle conflicting claims or to assist them during misfortunes of nature, badu often had to protect by force their rights to water and pasture against other groups. Unlike Western societies where there is a defined interface between land claims, there was in Arabia no clearly demarcated boundary separating one tribal pasture land from another or from the limits of an urban area. Tribal authority over territory varied through the years according to the size, political power and mobility of each nomadic group. Similarly, the size of a *hima* depended upon the ability of a settled group to defend it. The largest *hima* in al-Qasim was at Unaiza which had a protected area of 3,500 square kilometres.[28] An average tribal *dira* has been estimated to be approximately 55,300 square kilometres, although larger ones were known to exist, particularly if water and pasture resources were poor or if camel-herding was being practised.[29]

Contrary to accepted belief on the matter, the badu did not wander aimlessly in the desert. A regular pattern of tribal movement evolved, defined by availability of water, quality of grazing, ecological limitations of humans and animals, acknowledged systems of territorial rights among tribal groups and proximity of urban areas. Over centuries certain territories became identified as belonging within the sphere of a particular tribe's control. *Dira* in fact comes from a verb root which is translated as 'to turn; to revolve, rotate; to roam, wander about' and which has obvious associations with badu life. As a noun, *dira* may therefore be translated as the pasture land in which a tribe circulates in search for *al-haya*—that is, water and grazing or 'the life'. *Dira* may also be translated quite literally as 'homeland' (cf. Figure 1.8).[30]

Badu rights of ownership and usufruct over grazing and water resources varied between different regions in the Middle East. In one area rights to wells might have been specifically guarded while territory was freely grazed by all. Depending on ecological conditions and social organisation, the reverse situation or some variation might also have been found.[31] In Central Arabia land and water resources were not owned in the sense in which individuals in Western nations own property, that is, rights to which are legally embodied by a title deed the legitimacy of which is upheld by legal institutions organised and operated through a central state apparatus.[32] Rather, there existed among badu tribal groups specific and recognised rights of usufruct over water and pasture within a tribal *dira*. Such rights were held by customary law to belong to the tribe as a whole and not to individuals. Families might cultivate a piece of territory within the domain of the tribe's authority, but generally this right existed only in so far as the land remained under cultivation or the tribe had previously organised a rotation system for its utilisation. Nomadic tribal groups also maintained wells within the *dira* to which all members of the tribe had right of access. To designate these rights of usufruct, each tribe placed its *wasm* or brand on camels, wells and other personal property.[33] This was also true of smaller tribal units, as, for

Figure 1.8: Approximate Location of Major Tribal Grazing Diras

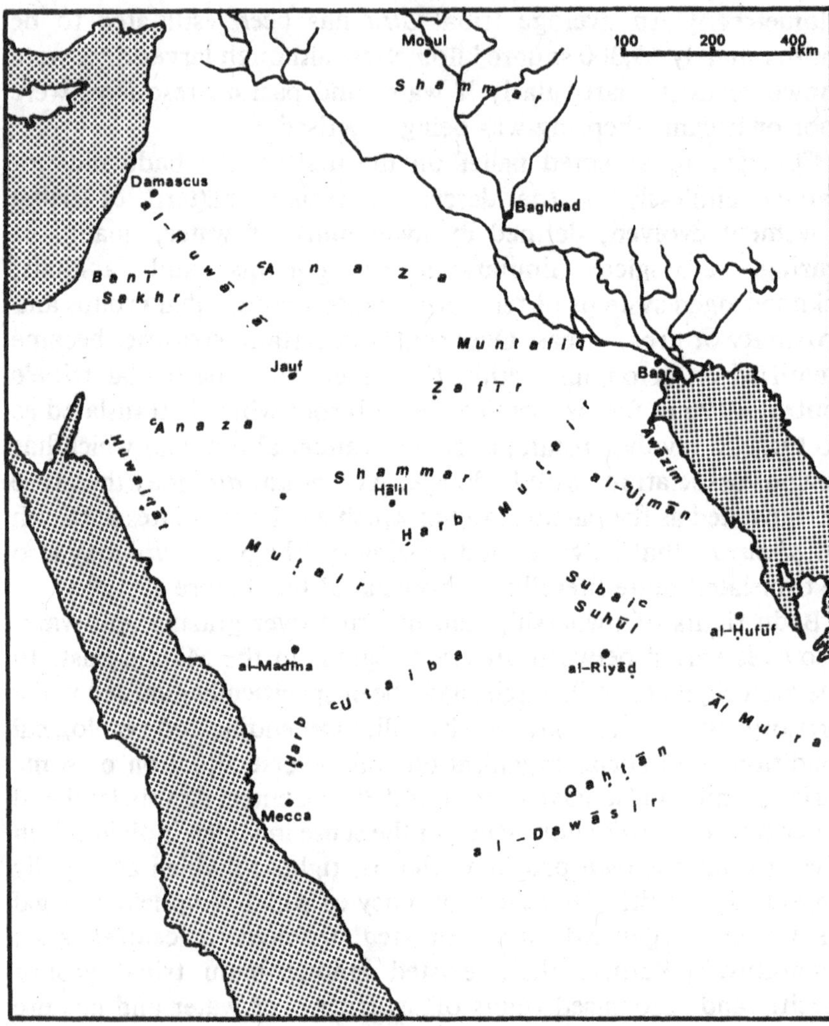

example, when a scattered herding group might excavate its own wells during summer, claiming sole right of ownership against strangers.

Just as a central government is forced to maintain its political strength, so too tribes had to be able to substantiate their political claims with force when necessary. The tribes of greatest nobility and prestige in Najd were also those tribes which were militarily the strongest and most independent. The sphere of a tribe's influence was clearly recognised even though most of the Najd landscape—consisting of sand, loess, gravel and lava fields—appears to those uninitiated to the desert as featureless and uninhabited. No fixed boundaries existed nor was it practicable to expect, given the nature of political and social organisation, that boundaries would be an effective way of organising relations between groups. Along the fringes or both *dira*s and *hima*s, there existed areas of overlapping interests with resultant outbreaks of inter-tribal fighting. The ability to protect rights to territory was affected by the strength of a tribe or settled area as well as by seasonal variability when tribes were either dispersed or gathered together. It can also be easily imagined how years of drought resulted in the movement of nomadic tribes outside their *dira*s as they sought sustenance for themselves and their flocks. In this way *dira*s have been known to shift gradually over the centuries from south to north although this process normally occurred at such a slow pace that it was not readily visible and did not alter an individual's perception of his tribe's authority within certain territorial limits.

The Influence of the Tribal Segmentary System upon Political and Social Organisation in Central Arabia

In the preceding pages we discussed how environmental variables affected patterns of settlement, resource utilisation and, to some extent, the influence they in their turn have had on the adaptive life-styles of badu and *hadar*. There remains, however, the complex problem of social organisation within Najd. Despite constant conflicts characterising a land of extreme adaptive life-styles, alliances between badu and *hadar* sometimes led to the formation of powerful amirates under the control of either badu shaikhs or settled amirs. What then enabled the nomadic tribes to act as a concerted group? How could their military strength and numbers eventually be united with the *hadar* under the leadership of a central authority such as that of the Al Saud?

Initially, it was the tribal system which structured the social, economic and political activity within Najd, even though urban structures gradually tended to break down tribal affiliation among the settled population. It was the tribe on which all individuals depended for their survival and within the framework of which all aspects of their lives were patterned. It was the vehicle by which they pressed for sanctions against other members of their tribe or against other tribal groups. The structure of the tribal system—perceived kinship—was one of the most powerful bonds which every individual inherited upon birth, irrespective of government, religion or race. It would not be difficult to discuss at some length kinship, tribal genealogies, and their impact upon life within the *bait al-shaar*. The present discussion, however, concentrates only upon those aspects which enable the reader to understand how the structure of tribal life provided a vehicle for the development of the Wahhabi movement and the formation of a larger state structure.

The foundation of the tribal system in Central Arabia was patriarchal—individuals identified themselves as *bani al-amm* (lit. 'sons of the paternal uncle'), tracing descent from an eponymous ancestor, whether real or fictitious. As the colloquial phrase *amama al-azim min khwala* (gram. *al-amam azam min al-khawal*) expresses, it is the paternal blood relationship, *amam*, which takes precedence over that of the maternal, *khawal*, and which forms the *ahl* or kinship group of most immediate assistance to an individual. Moreover, *amama asaba wa khwala arham* (gram. *al-amam asaba wa al-khawal arham*) explicitly states that *asabiya* or tribal solidarity and strength are derived from *amam*, while *khawal* quite literally provides the wombs which keep the tribal blood lines pure.[34] It is because women maintained the purity of the kinship group that a female child from a noble tribe was forbidden to marry a man from an ignoble tribe and, conversely, females of ignoble tribes were not received in marriage by one of the noble tribes. Ideally, girls were engaged at a very young age to their *walad amm*, 'paternal uncle's son'.

The Arabs believe that all tribes were originally descended from one of two ancestors, Qahtan or Adnan, who respectively represented a division between the southern and northern Arabs of the Peninsula. In isolated regions like Central Oman such formalised genealogies still have some meaning, although for practical purposes the tracing of genealogies in other regions presents difficulties. Many recorded genealogies have disappeared and great tribal migrations have occurred whereby some tribal groups split into smaller units while others amalgamated either by forming alliances (*hilf*, pl. *ahlaf*) or gradually assimilating their client tribes (*mawali*). Furthermore, tribes have sometimes adopted new names in order to claim an association with a stronger tribe or because the name by which they were originally identified fell into disuse.

Although all Arab genealogists concur that two factors—kinship and nobility—govern tribal relationships, there are conflicting opinions concerning the actual composition of tribal groupings. The tribal network itself has been divided theoretically into nine successively larger groupings—*raht* (*arhat*), *fasila* (*fasail*), *ashira* (*ashair*), *fakhdh* (*afkhadh*), *batn* (*butun*), *qabila* (*qabail*), *shab* (*shuub*) and *jumhur* (*jumahir*). If possible, these were traced to their 'root', *jidhm*, that is Qahtan or Adnan. Variant classification systems have reduced the number of these categories. Hamza, who gives one of the most complete classifications of tribes within Saudi Arabia and therefore will be referred to in this study, has developed five categories and designated an English equivalent: *raht*, family; *fasila*, clan; *fakhdh*, division; *batn*, group; *qabila*, tribe. Thus he gives the example that the Al Shalan family or *raht* belong to the *fasila* al-Mirid from the *fakhdh* al-Ruwala from the *batn* Dana Muslim of the *qabila* Anaza.[35] The *shab* (lit. 'people') and *jumhur* (lit. 'collection') were the tribal confederations.

The tribe is then a segmentary structure which becomes increasingly remote to the individual as it branches, but which nevertheless binds him in a very real sense to the family tree. Factional strife, such as that occurring from time to time in the Al Rashid of Jabal Shammar or between branches of the Al Saud, was inherent in a segmentary tribal structure, particularly when political hegemony was being sought over large regions containing other tribes as well as numerous settled areas. When threatened, however, by external trouble, the lineages recognised themselves at the broadest level of identification as members of the same tribe and united for their mutual benefit.[36] This sense of tribal solidarity, *asabiya*, formed a network of mutual obligations among tribal members and with their client tribes that effectively became a form of nationalism. Ibn Khaldun, the fourteenth-century Arab historian, noted that genealogies do not have to be accurate to be effective for, although 'a pedigree is something imaginary and devoid of reality', its authenticity cannot be denied by man as long as lines of descent remain clear enough to be a cohesive force.[37] Only tribes bound together in this way were able to live in the desert because *asabiya* functioned as an alternative to the urban structure, restraining internal dissension and uniting segmentary units for their mutual defence and protection.

Najd tribes did not recognise status differentials among members of the same tribal grouping although such differences structured all patterns of social interaction between tribes. The formation of social status categories was determined by two factors—descent and occupation—perceived by the tribes as the basis of nobility. Tribes of greatest nobility were those which were acknowledged to be of pure descent, *asil* or *sharif*. They also tended to be larger, more nomadic and militarily independent than other tribes. Among these tribes in Najd were the Harb, Shammar, al-Dawasir, al-Ujman, Al Murra, Mutair, Anaza and Utaiba. Those unable to trace their original descent from ancient Arabian tribes, but which were large and sometimes powerful nomadic tribes, comprised the Awazim (clients of al-Ujman and the Shaikh of Kuwait), Zafir, Rashaida (clients of Mutair), and Shararat (clients of the Amir of Jabal Shammar). They were considered as inferiors by the *asil* tribes. A third level which was differentiated consisted of so-called 'despised' tribes, such as the Hutaim and Suluba, which were clients of the more noble tribes with which they frequently travelled. The Hutaim did, in fact, pay the *khuwa* protection tax to the Amir of Jabal Shammar as well as to the Harb, Anaza and Shammar badu. The Suluba, known in Najd as *khaluwa* or 'solitaries', rendered tribute to all the major tribes scattered throughout Arabia,[38] although, unlike the Hutaim, the Suluba had not become settled.[39] Tribes of lesser nobility never inter-married with the *asil* tribes which continually held them in low esteem.

To combat the vagaries of environment and politics, alliances between different tribal groups were formed on the same rationale as kinship. Reciprocal obligations and rights evolved which were strictly regulated by tribal customary law and considered to be as morally binding as those of true kinship, although the content of these contractual relationships varied considerably according to the status of tribes involved, their specialised adaptation to the environment, and the geography of the territories they inhabited. Failure to fulfil these obligations was tantamount to failing one's own family, bringing disgrace upon the tribal group as a whole. Examples of such alliances in Najd were (1) Harb, Mutair (Ilwa), al-Ujman; (2) Mutair (Bani Abdillah), Utaiba; (3) Zafir, Shammar, Awazim; and (4) al-Ujman and Al Murra.[40] Depending upon the extent of the alliance, rights to commercial transactions, access to pasturage, political neutrality or military protection were granted in exchange for goods and services, promises of reciprocal military aid, or direct monetary payment.[41]

Payment of *khuwa* or 'brotherhood tax' entitled an ignoble tribe to military protection against hostile tribes and supplied a mechanism whereby any disputes with the patron tribe could be settled without recourse to bloodshed. This was accomplished by the principle of extended family relationships. Usually a tribal group obtained an *akh* in another tribe who then was regarded as their 'brother' with the responsibilities thereby implied. Carl Raswan, a traveller in Arabia during the early twentieth century, related an instance in which the 'Sulkan', a tribe in tribute to the al-Ruwala, was seeking redress for a wrong on the basis of this time-honoured custom of *khuwa*. The 'brother' was effectively the guarantor of his tribe's misdeeds against those from whom he accepted *khuwa*. In this particular case the *akh* was obliged to find and recover missing camels.[42]

Khuwa was also collected from settled areas on the same principle—that is, whoever collected *khuwa* was bound to protect those from whom it was collected. The ideological implications involved in this transaction were far-reaching, both in the way it came to be honoured in customary law and in that it represented an extension of tribal authority. *Khuwa* was not necessarily collected or paid by individuals, but rather by tribal groups or settlements. Payment of *khuwa* was recognised as acceptance of a more powerful political authority, literally a tribute.

> A weaker tribe has to recognize the supremacy of a stronger one and pay it a special tax, which is known as *ḫûwa* [*khuwa*]. The Rwala [al-Ruwala] collect the *ḫûwa* from all the Htejm ['despised' tribe of Hutaim] as well as from the inhabitants of various villages. The stronger the government (i.e. a central urban government), the fewer the villages which pay them the *ḫûwa*. Al-Zerjitejn, Tudmor, As-Suḫne, Kowm, and Aṭ-Ṭajjibe

> regularly deliver *ḫûwa*. Every settlement and every tributary tribe has among the Rwala its brother, *aḫ* [*akh*] or *ḫawi*, to whom it pays annually . . . . The *aḫ* is bound to restore to the settlement all the property which his fellow tribesmen have stolen from it. The basis of *ḫûwa* is *ḳûwa* [*qūwa*], force. Those who are strong compel the numerous settlements to raise *ḫûwa* for them. Those who have no *aḫ* must rely on the drawn sword, *sejf ṭâjel* [*saif ṭā'il*]. Those who receive the *ḫûwa* must protect those who give it to them, or, as the Rwala say: 'He who eats a young goat must protect its mother, *alli jâkol al-ğedi jaḥma ummeh* [*man yā'kul al-jidī yaḥma ummahu*].'[43]

Since it was impossible for anyone to enter the *dira* of another tribe without risking his life or property and because hundreds of tribal *dira*s were scattered across the Arabian Peninsula, movement and trade would have been severely restricted without customary law to regulate inter-tribal relationships. In many cases, however, geographic variables influenced the content of these relationships. The region which was historically known as the Trucial Coast provides a valuable comparison to Najd in regard to the nature of these tribal alliances. The smaller size of tribes, the less numerous urban areas and the availability of alternative means of livelihood, such as pearling and fishing in the Arabian Gulf during summer months, created a situation whereby Trucial tribes frequently intermingled, as, for example, when some had to traverse another tribe's territory in order to reach the coast. The inevitable conflict which arose from their interaction in maritime activities was regulated by a variety of contractual relationships controlled by élite families in the Arabian Gulf. These relationships developed to such an extent that certain tribal groups, such as some sections of the Manasir, recognised the paramount authority of the ruling family of another tribe called the Al Bu Falah. By contrast, the large size and military autonomy of the *asil* or 'noble' tribes in Najd usually led either to the formation of large tribal confederations between the *asil* tribes or to the extension of military protection to the ignoble tribes in exchange for *khuwa*.

To summarise, the tribe is an interlocking segmentary system that naturally forms economic and military units. The sense of *asabiya* that binds the tribal members in a set of reciprocal rights and obligations, the nature of authority vested in shaikhs and the ability of tribes to ally with alien tribes by extending an artificial, although realistic, rationale of kinship make the tribe a potentially valuable political and military tool.

The kinship group of most immediate assistance to the individual, however, is his *ahl*, 'family' or 'people'. An *ahl* is generally thought to comprise descendants to the third generation, ascendants to the third generation and descendants of the latter to the third generation. Variant interpretations, however, are found, as in the case of the tribes of Al Murra and al-Ujman, which include ascendants to the seventh generation within their *ahl*.[44] The underlying concept of the *ahl* is crucial to those whose life is solely regulated through the principle of tribal affiliation, for it is the *ahl* on whom a man is most immediately dependent and to whom he is in turn bound by obligations. A man's *ahl* seeks to protect him from injustice, concomitantly accepts responsibility for his misdeeds and clears the family's name if disgrace should befall it.[45]

Certain issues, however, were either unable to be settled by the *ahl* or concerned larger tribal units. Political authority had then to be vested in leaders who possessed a legitimate right to arbitrate and direct the activities of individual tribal segments. In Arabia this authority was traditionally held by a shaikh (*shaikh*, pl. *shuyukh*) whose influence at each level of the segmentary system helped to form natural economic and military units of protection. It was the responsibility of the shaikh to co-ordinate and, if need be, sanction other activities of tribal members for the common weal.

The position of shaikh was hereditary within a particular family, but was not necessarily passed from father to son. Consultation among the elders of a tribe led to selection of the paramount shaikh, who was chosen for the qualities of nobility, skill in arbitration, *hazz* or 'good fortune', and leadership which had earned him the confidence of the tribe. In polite address, the paramount shaikh was referred to as *shaikh al-shuyukh* or 'shaikh of the shaikhs'. Unlike rulers whose office is sacrosanct irrespective of their excesses or incompetence, a shaikh maintained his position only in so far as his leadership continued to fulfil the expectations of his tribe. A shaikh constantly sought and was given the advice of other shaikhs, and his *majlis* (lit. 'sitting session') was open to any member of the tribe who could freely express his views. For these reasons badu society has been frequently described as democratic.

One of the primary tasks of a shaikh was to lead the *qaum* or 'military fighting force' of his tribe in war. Thus references to the *qaum* al-Ruwala, *qaum* Ibn Shalan (paramount *shaikh* of the

Shalan *raht* of the al-Ruwala *batn*), and *qaum* Ibn *fulan* ('so-and-so') identified the fighting forces which were relied upon during any military situation. The shaikh rallied his forces behind a tribal banner and with a *nakhwa* or 'war cry' which invariably called the tribe's attention to their genealogical descent and kinship obligations.[46] The word *nakhwa* is, in fact, derived from the Arabic root *akh* or 'brother'. Thus, for example, the Al Murra *nakhwa* was *ana awlad bishr* or 'I am one of the sons of Bishr'[47] and al-Ujman called out *jarash al-hadid wa ana ibn al-ujman* or 'Pounder of iron and I am the son of the al-Ujman'.[48] Frequently a virgin was chosen for the honour of accompanying the men in battle where, loosening her hair and upper clothing, she would exhort the *qaum* of her tribe to greater feats of courage in defence of tribal honour.[49]

Badu chiefs in Central Arabia were also addressed by the title of shaikh, although urban leaders and even badu shaikhs who had managed to gain control over settled areas became known as amirs (*amir*, pl. *umara*). Here the element of territoriality became coupled with that of government for these amirs possessed *imara*, 'power' or 'authority', over districts of mixed populations containing badu and *hadar* as well as numerous tribal groups. This diversity meant that, in order to be effective rulers, the amirs had to seek neutrality by dissociating themselves from their tribal origins even though it was still important that they were considered to be of noble descent. Unlike tribal shaikhs who led with the consent of those governed, the amirs ultimately maintained their *imara* by threat of force. Neither the badu shaikhs nor the amirs sought to express their authority in religious terms; their leadership was purely secular.

The political structure of Najd, even in the settled areas, was to a great extent influenced by the tribal segmentary system and the nature of authority held by the shaikhs. The absence of a peasant class bound to the land and incorporated into the urban structure, such as was found in Egypt, Palestine, Syria and Mesopotamia, meant that the Ottomans and later the British found the prospect of establishing their control in Najd very daunting. The Ottomans had found that murdering tribal shaikhs produced no positive results, as men were always available to fill their position. They eventually adopted the policy of settling paramount badu shaikhs in urban areas under Ottoman control or, alternatively, establishing rival branches of a ruling family as paramount leaders so that internecine struggles weakened the tribe. British policy was to choose a potentially powerful leader, establish good relations with him and support him against all other claimants even to the extent of providing military assistance. Neither the Ottomans nor the British found these policies of much help in Najd because of environmental difficulties. Both found it sufficient to attempt to control the littoral areas of the Peninsula. Abd al-Aziz and previous Saudi rulers realised the important role of both shaikhs and amirs in their successful efforts to unite the Najd tribes and urban areas. They replaced the amirs of settled towns with their own trusted governors (*hakim*, pl. *hukkam*), frequently members of the Al Saud, forced tribal shaikhs to settle in al-Riyad under their surveillance and maintained tight control over rival claimants among the Al Saud. If tribal shaikhs could be controlled, the Al Saud found that the tribes themselves could be controlled. Pelly, who travelled through Arabia in 1865/66, reported that the Al Saud were finding it difficult to control the Suluba tribe because this ignoble tribe had no chiefs of its own and its members wandered throughout Arabia attaching themselves as clients to various tribes.[50] Therefore, if the Suluba was to be converted to the Wahhabi faith and Saudi allegiance, then it had to be done by persuading individuals rather than the tribe.

Abd al-Aziz faced the same problem as did an amir—that is, the establishment of his legitimacy among badu and *hadar* populations of mixed tribal groups—although his methods deviated considerably from established custom. While he claimed noble pedigree for the Al Saud by virtue of their blood links with the Anaza tribe, his family had been settled inhabitants of Najd ever since the fifteenth century when they had migrated to Central Arabia from the Arabian Gulf. It may be noted with some interest that the Najd tribes did not generally refer to Abd al-Aziz as shaikh and the polite address of *al-shuyukh* or *shaikh al-shuyukh* was only employed by the people of al-Hijaz or visitors to Najd. The badu frequently referred to him as Abu Turki, 'father of Turki', as the traditional custom has generally been to call a man after the name of his eldest son. After his early battles to unify Central Arabia, Abd al-Aziz was referred to as *amir najd wa rais al-ashair* or Amir of Najd and Chief of its Tribes.[51] It may also be noted that Abd al-Aziz, unlike badu shaikhs, attempted to establish the hereditary rule of his sons by having tribal leaders swear allegiance to his nominee.[52] Although hereditary rule met with continued opposition from the Najdis and even members of the Al Saud themselves, the British government readily agreed to this stipulation as early as the Anglo-Saudi Treaty of 1915. Article II of a treaty concluded between the Ottomans and Abd al-Aziz in May 1914 had also provided for the Ottoman Wilaya of Najd to be inherited by the sons and grandsons of Abd al-Aziz.

As will be seen in later chapters, Abd al-Aziz significantly altered the status of the tribes and their traditional patterns of authority. He sought to establish his authority across tribal groups by eliminating those elements of tribal custom which enhanced the authority of the shaikhs and emphasised the bonds of kinship to the exclusion of all else. For this reason he released the Awazim from payment of *khuwa*, thus theoretically freeing them of their inferior status. In this way he gained a loyal fighting force while weakening the larger tribal confederations. Like the tribes, the *nakhwa* of Abd al-Aziz made reference to his kinship group, as, for example, *ana ibn faisal* ('I am the son of Faisal'), *ana ibn muqrin* ('I am the son of Muqrin', a distant ancestor), *ana akhu nura* ('I am the brother of Nura', his favourite sister).[53] However, as he succeeded in gathering the tribes into the Wahhabi fold as Ikhwan or 'brothers', their tribal *nakhwas* were abandoned for those of the faith: *khayyal al-tauhid ahl al-tauhid!* ('Riders of Unity! People of Unity!');*sabi al-tauhid! akhu man ta Allah!* ('Youth of Unity! The Brother of those who obey God!'); and *habbat habub al-janna! wain anta ya baghiyaha?* ('The winds of Paradise have blown. Where are you, oh Baghay?'—i.e., those who have forsaken the Sharia, the sacred laws of Islam).[54]

Development of Central Authority

Tribal affiliation became a powerful political tool, particularly when it linked the interests of nomadic and settled populations. What has only been briefly mentioned is that the majority of people in Najd, nomadic and settled, identify themselves with some tribal group.[55] This pattern goes back a long way and is even further accentuated today. Over 80 per cent of the Najd population presently identify themselves with some tribal group. Many nomadic tribal members had transferred their animal stock to some other form of wealth within the urban structure—land, shops, wells or mercantile enterprises—eventually abandoning nomadism, becoming settled and functioning as middlemen between their nomadic brethren and the urban community.[56] Some districts were dominated by a particular tribe, such as, for example, the Dawasir tribe who were found throughout Najd although chiefly in the districts of al-Aflaj and al-Dawasir, where they formed the majority of both badu and *hadar*. This was also true of the badu and settled members of the al-Ujman in al-Ahsa and Kuwait, the Shammar of Jabal Shammar, the Harb in al-Qasim and al-Arid, the Mutair in al-Qasim and the districts of al-Washm and al-Arid in Najd, the Utaiba and Anaza of al-Qasim, the Qahtan in the districts of al-Sudair and al-Arid in Najd, and the Subai throughout the districts of Najd. Of all the Central Arabian tribes, only the Zafir remained fully nomadic, while the Bani Tamim, formerly a nomadic tribe, settled permanently throughout Najd, al-Qasim and Jabal Shammar, engaging primarily in agricultural pursuits.

More recent population statistics support the supposition that there were strong links between settled and nomadic members of the same tribe.[57] Since the early twentieth century, there has been a general depopulation of many villages which were pure farming communities in al-Sudair, al-Washm, al-Aflaj, al-Hauta and al-Hariq as people migrated to the capital, al-Riyad. There has been, however, a population increase in districts such as al-Kharj and al-Dawasir, which have traditionally been known to contain a high proportion of settled tribal members, because badu who were encouraged to settle did so among related tribal groups.

The social structure of urban environments manifested the segmentary nature of the tribal structure. Cities of the Peninsula were frequently divided into quarters which reflected tribal, religious and occupational divisions as well as stages in the growth of a settlement. Unfortunately, very little information is available about the social composition of these quarters which would enable us to understand the relative importance of each of these factors. It is possible, however, to make certain generalisations. Perhaps due to the larger concentrations of people and the diverse origins of immigrants on the eastern shores of Arabia, settlements of al-Ahsa oasis were primarily segregated along religious lines, between the Shiite and Sunni divisions of Islam. Central Arabia, in contrast, was composed mainly of indigenous elements who were Sunni, and in Najd who were almost entirely Sunni Wahhabis, so that religion was seldom a divisive factor in these settlements. The larger cities such as Unaiza, Buraida and al-Riyad were composed of various large quarters, many of which were surrounded by defensive walls. Although the social composition of these quarters is not generally known, it is reported that, at least in Unaiza, each possessed its own war banner, suggesting that those quarters were not differentiated simply by their time of settlement or by trade occupations. The variety of goods available in the *suqs* and the clothing of the inhabitants provided evidence that the larger cities were commercial centres in contact with external regions. By contrast, the smaller villages were mainly agricultural and obtained supplies from larger urban areas in close proximity. Like the larger settlements, these villages were composed of clusters of settled tribal groups and were generally separated by crops or date plantations. Those that were not members of a tribal group were immigrants from Iran, Syria, Egypt or the Gulf. They functioned as mercenaries or traders, never acquiring any political authority as a social group. Records of travellers through Central Arabia tend to show that some groups, especially those of low social status such as Bani Khadir, remained completely segregated. In other quarters and settlements a particular tribal group sought to dominate the rest, as did the Dawasir in all the districts of southern Najd. Similarly, a rivalry continued unabated in Buraida between the ruling houses of the Bani Tamim and Anaza tribes until the Al Saud finally imposed their control over all.[58] In the very small districts where two or three tribal groups were present, it was frequently the case that one tribal group rented or share-cropped land from another or that whole settlements were tributary to a larger urban centre or badu tribe.

The duplication of urban areas with similar service functions in close proximity and the development of quarters within the same settlement illustrate the influence of tribalism on settlement patterns in Central Arabia. Laila, Saih, Rauda and Kharfa were four villages in al-Aflaj district separated on average by no more than six kilometres. While all contained members of the Bani Khadir, which was one of the most inferior tribes, not one other tribal group was duplicated in any two of the villages. The Huqban and Mubarak Dawasir were found in Rauda; the Ammar Dawasir at Saih; the Ajlan, Buras, Hamdan, Hijji, Jibarin and Widain Dawasir in Laila; and the Ghaiyithat Dawasir in Kharfa. The Saqar Ashraf were found in Laila and the Hamid Ashraf in Saih while the Anaza were found only in Rauda.[59] There were other examples of the duplication of trading centres which were utilised by different nomadic groups: al-Riyad and Diriya of al-Arid; Huraimila and Sudus of al-Mahmal; Hariq and Hilla as well as Yamama and Dilam of al-Kharj; Ghatghat and Muzahimiya as well as Shaqra and Marat of al-Washm; the two towns of Zulfa as well as Harma and Majma in al-Sudair; Buraida and Unaiza in al-Qasim; and al-Hufuf and Mubarraz in al-Ahsa.[60]

To view either the settled or nomadic populations of Central Arabia as isolated, self-sufficient ecological adaptations or as static, defined phenomena is misleading. Both were part of a network of shifting ecological conditions and political alliances. The majority identified themselves with a tribal group. Moreover, the populations were often bound by a series of mutually beneficial economic exchanges, the importance of which cannot be underestimated in assessing the nature of political control and social life in Najd.

The variety of products and services which were being used, sold or traded by the badu and urban groups in Najd during the late nineteenth and early twentieth century was astounding. In the villages and oasis dwellings, there existed an abundant variety of fruit and vegetable produce: peaches, apricots, lemons, figs, dates, gourds, melons, grapes, corn and legumes. Spices, meat, milk, butter, eggs, yeast, wheat and other grains were available. Coffee and incense were brought from southern Arabia and Palgrave even reported the presence of American tobacco. Ostrich feathers, bricks for towers, silver swords, copper coffee pots, cauldrons for cooking, textiles, walking sticks, locks and bolts, lamps, charcoal, firewood, jewellery, pottery and medicines were also available. Irrigation devices, wells and cisterns were built and maintained. Although this list is far from complete, these products were none the less indicative of a tremendous organisation of merchants, weavers, locksmiths, free farmers, herders and share-croppers, tax collectors, religious and military personnel, blacksmiths, falconers, traders, shaikhs, slaves, medical men, midwives and ruling élites. The badu, for their part, were able to supply the urban areas with camels, sheep, goats, horses and subsidiary products such as wool, meat, hides and even butter made from bones of the camel and cakes made from their hooves.[61] The badu also tended settlement livestock during hot summer months when water was too expensive in the settlements[62] and provided military protection to the urban centres in exchange for other goods and services.

The actual movement by badu expressly for the purpose of trading was called by them *musabala*. The markets were usually permanent ones in large urban areas although occasionally temporary ones were arranged at fixed intervals and places. Central Arabia was literally intersected by the roads of the nomads, pilgrim and caravan routes where commercial transactions took place over tremendous distances.[63] The badu were known to make annual journeys to al-Hijaz, cities along the Euphrates and the Arabian Gulf where exchanges of news, goods, services and even populations occurred.

There was, however, a basic conflict between desert badu and urban *hadar* over rights to land and resources. To ensure their survival the badu had to be prepared to defend their rights of usufruct over grazing and water resources from encroachment by farmers. On the other hand, large urban areas had to be able to guarantee the free movement of goods and people through their boundaries or district territory. Unless this freedom was established, neither trade nor state formation was encouraged. The eventual supremacy of the badu in certain regions is testified by the presence of numerous small abandoned settlements. With more powerful settlements, the badu were forced either to come to a *modus vivendi* wherever possible or to acquire dominance over those areas with weak central authority without weakening their pastoral base. The unique circumstances found in Central Arabia, which have been discussed previously, favoured alliances between badu and *hadar* groups against similar coalitions. This was the first step, albeit tenuous, in geopolitical formations leading towards a state structure.

The numerous economic, social and political links between settled and nomadic communities led to the evolution of a protector-client relationship which had strong legal and ideological implications.[64] Large urban areas were geographically, economically and socially much better equipped to obtain control over extensive territories containing other settled and nomadic tribes, although there are several points which must be stressed. Irrespective of the strength of urban settlements in Najd, they had no economic monopoly over desert dwellers; they functioned as suppliers to the badu and were supply points for caravans. If trade declined, so too did the settlements. It was obviously to the advantage of the *hadar* to establish friendly relations with the badu, particularly the strongest tribes, because the latter presented a constant threat to the settlements and to the caravans while they journeyed between urban areas. Friendly relations with urban areas were also to the advantage of the nomads who found a market for their livestock, obtained otherwise unavailable supplies, notably dates, and extended the political and economic authority of their tribe.[65] As long as the relationship remained mutually satisfactory, there was an impetus for both badu tribes and urban centres to maintain these links.

Before the formation of the present Saudi state, authority was recognised by an enforced tribute by settled or nomadic groups upon other settled and nomadic groups, who expected protection both from those who collected the tribute and from potential enemies. It is reminiscent of the patron-client protection scheme of the mafia which kept its client safe and the economic competition in the area low. Tribute could be collected either from strong urban governments or from badu tribes.

Tribute collection by badu tribes was generally limited to the control of settled areas in close proximity to their *dira* and never achieved the extensive control of which the large urban settlements were capable. Musil related the following incident of tribute collection in a settled area by the al-Ruwala tribe of the Anaza confederation around Wadi Sirhan in northern Arabia.

> Prince an-Nûri eben Šaʻ lân [Ibn Shalan] had entered the territory of the settlers . . . . The camp was no sooner pitched upon the fields of the Naṣîb settlement than it was visited by the elders of the various adjacent villages, who came to pay fealty to the Prince and to invite him to dine with them. In the afternoon streams of camels, donkeys, and asses kept arriving laden with gifts of wheat, barley and flour for the Prince and other chiefs. It was the tribute [*khuwa*] by means of which the settlers purchased protection and safety from the Arabs.[66]

Although tribute collection by nomadic tribes has been recorded previously, it is not usually realised that badu tribes in Central Arabia frequently owned crops in these settled areas and hired share-croppers who retained part of the produce while ceding the greater part to the badu as rent.

> On Sunday the chiefs of the settlements of Eṭra and Čâf came to greet the Prince and render him tribute. They had brought

> five camel loads of dates. In these settlements the princely family of Šaʻlân owned more than five hundred date trees, which the settlers leased for one-fifth of the net profits, getting one-fifth of the fruit themselves and the owner four-fifths.[67]

It was not uncommon that a *badawi* (sing. of *badu*) would sometimes establish his family in an urban area, eventually identifying his interests with those of urban life as much as with his tribe. While maintaining his livestock, he also invested wealth in agricultural and commercial interests. He firmly established his control in the settlement and later over other desert tribes with the assistance of a personal militia. Musil recorded a conversation with Nawwaf b. Nuri Al Shalan, the ruling family of the al-Ruwala, in which Nawwaf actually proposed such an action.

> Why, Mûsa [Musil], with the help of Allâh, could I not found a dominion there like that which Eben Rašîd [Ibn Rashid] had founded? If I took possession of the oasis of al-Gowf [al-Jauf], I could establish myself there with a picked band and, by prudent words, with arms and gold, in a short time I could subjugate the entire northern population of Arabia. Let Eben Saʻûd rule in the south.[68]

Raswan related the same incident after, in fact, it had occurred. It exemplifies one way in which these tribute states began to develop.

> Moreover, this attack on Jauf was a reversal of tribal policy. From of old the Ruala [al-Ruwala] had peacefully traded with that oasis, bartering their camels, wool, cheese, and butter for dates, barley, salt, coffee, tent fittings, camel saddles, and textiles. Suddenly, and quite against the old Sheykh's intentions, Nauaf conceived the scheme of monopolizing that trade for himself and occupying the oasis as a strategic stronghold from which to dominate Northern Arabia and the caravan routes to Nejd.[69]

There is ample evidence of these tribute states, whether controlled by settled or nomadic leaders, in the writings of Musil, Philby, Burckhardt, Pelly, Rihani, Doughty, Guarmani and other visitors to Central Arabia during the last two centuries. The last five hundred years witnessed a succession of powerful urban-badu alliances that were the beginnings of central place systems. Among those recorded in recent centuries were Hail, al-Riyad, Buraida and Unaiza. The Al Saud themselves originally gained influence through one such tribute state in the 1700s which was controlled from the urban centre of Diriya.

The Al Rashid of the Shammar tribal confederation were originally a nomadic family which had settled in Hail, capital of Jabal Shammar. Strategically situated as the most southerly of a long series of wells which ran north to Iraq, Hail allowed the Al Rashid to become great entrepreneurs by monopolising trade that had formerly gone from Kuwait through al-Riyad to Mecca. Ibn Rashid was able to force tribes either to ally themselves with him militarily or to pay him tribute. In this way he expanded the commercial links of Jabal Shammar, controlling all the trade and caravan routes to Egypt and Mecca from the Arabian Gulf. His realm of control extended north to Palmyra, west to al-Jauf and to Buraida and Unaiza in al-Qasim where he made alliances against the Al Saud, and south as far as al-Madina. The population of Hail increased by between five and ten times during a period of fifty years, principally because of an influx of immigrants: craftsmen, businessmen, soldiers and marginal individuals.[70]

The population of Hail became highly heterogeneous; tribal loyalties became subordinate to the economic interests of the urban community as a whole; and state and commercial interests were considered as one. Hail developed into a class-oriented town with soldiers, slaves, shopkeepers, artists and merchants, as well as an administrative system consisting of accountants, supply officers and administrators and a court retinue of advisers, executioners, standard bearers and others necessary for the functioning of the Amir's palace.[71] Hail even had diplomatic connections with Damascus and Istanbul. All disputes and economic affairs were referred to the ruler. All foreigners and their business affairs were controlled by the court, and passports were issued on the authority of the Amir for travel through territory controlled by his tribal alliances. He forced payment of *zakat* tax,[72] confiscated rival lineage property and established garrisons along the pilgrim routes. Unlike the customary law of the badu whose sanctions were dependent on the moral solidarity of the tribe, the Amir now ruled with the assistance of police unrelated by kinship over numerous different social groups.

While these so-called 'tribute states' might initially have been supported by the ruler's blood relations, his role as Amir required him to be an arbitrator between different social groups which had no inherent reason for their continued support of him other than the quality of his rule or the force he employed. Initially the Al Rashid were supported by their own Shammar. When their authority was well established, their rulers began to separate from their 'equals in birth', that is fellow badu tribesmen, and to eliminate other rival branches within the family. Eventually the associations of the Al Rashid with the urban population and their own increasing strength forced them to identify themselves more closely with the urban population while suppressing the badu elements of the Shammar. This policy forced Rashidi authority to depend increasingly on mercenary and slave groups rather than on the badu for protection.[73] They were essentially a private militia.

> To secure the state and his own life the head chief, or prince is compelled to maintain a strong body of mercenary soldiers—almost always negroes—who, having no relatives among the settlers or nomads, are able to give effect to every order of their lord and to protect him against all enemies, since they know that their own fate is linked with his. The mercenaries are, therefore, the most hated and feared people in the entourage of a prince.[74]

The conflict within these geopolitical formations, as Rosenfeld has pointed out, was the continued development of the central urban area in relation to its periphery. As long as the area paying tribute saw the central commercial centre grow without benefit to the outlying areas, there was little reason to support it against any other shaikh or political authority. Every nomadic tribe and settled area chose either to continue payment or to withdraw from the tribute system. Therefore every ruling dynasty, settled or nomadic, was under pressure to maintain a monopoly of tribute collection and a stable environment conducive to exchange relationships. This was important because the urban rulers were burdened with the support of their private militias both in the field and at home. When funds were not available in the 'state treasury', the pay of the militia had to be stopped. Numerous examples in literature show that lack of funds resulted in the sudden dispersal of an army, some levies returning to their respective homes and others engaging in small forays for personal plunder. When Britain stopped its subsidy to the Hashimite King Husain after World War I, he in turn was forced to end his subsidies to the tribes. The result was an immediate increase in inter-tribal raiding and tribal defection to other political authorities, primarily the Al Saud, which undoubtedly played a significant part in the eventual Hashimite defeat in 1925 by the Al Saud.

A state based on tribute collection was forced to re-create itself annually by forcing populations on its periphery to pay tribute. The badu in particular had few real interests in fixed production or agriculture and few, if any, vested interests in the continuance of one specific urban area relative to any other. The Harb and Utaiba tribes constantly harassed the periphery of Rashidi authority just as the al-Ujman and Utaiba tribes harassed Saudi authority. Given the gradual weakening of central authority or the emergence of a potentially more profitable urban centre, the badu quite easily shifted their allegiance. This was no less true of settled populations dependent on trade. The urban populations did not hesitate to migrate if the deviation of a trade route caused a decline in the commercial activity of their settlement. Arabia had witnessed for centuries the shifting power balances among these states based on tribute collection. Just as the Al Saud in the nineteenth century had given way to the emergence of the Al Rashid, so the latter in turn were forced to succumb to the increasing authority of the Al Saud in the twentieth century from their new capital of al-Riyad.

The formation of the Kingdom of Saudi Arabia began much in the same way as that of the Al Rashid. Each firmly established and identified itself within an urban structure from which it extended its military and political influence over the desert. It utilised slaves and mercenary groups and established military quotas among the badu. The Al Rashid and initially the Al Saud were forced to reassert their authority each year by tribute collection in exchange for which they organised the means of military protection by levies of townsmen and badu not necessarily related to them.

The differences between the Al Rashid and Al Saud, however, are just as striking. The Al Saud had migrated in the fifteenth century to Najd where they had always been members of a settled community, whereas the Al Rashid had first been shaikhs of a powerful tribal confederation and only later became amirs of settlements serving as rallying points and markets for the tribes. Among other differences, which will be discussed in subsequent chapters, the Al Saud legitimised their control over diverse settlements and tribal groups and established the exclusive right of the state to political authority and taxation by asserting their own rights as Islamic rulers.

In the twentieth century Abd al-Aziz succeeded in establishing his authority and ultimately that of the Al Saud more effectively than had any shaikh or amir in Arabia, primarily because of his understanding of three factors: tribal networks, Islam and foreign intervention. He was also able to implement policy determined by these factors. As has been seen, kinship bonds and customary law provided valuable vehicles for political and military control as well as regulating inter-tribal relations irrespective of the social status of a tribe. The need to break down the patron-client relationships among the tribes and between the badu tribes and settled areas in order to establish exclusive political control by the Al Saud led Abd al-Aziz to stress the equality of men under Islam and to eliminate status differentials between tribes. Through the Wahhabi movement of Islam, which began two centuries earlier under the auspices of the Al Saud, state and religion were joined to foster a common ideology among the population, giving religious-legal sanction to the authority of the Al Saud. Territorial expansion was justified by the religious belief that it was the duty of all true Wahhabis to carry the message of Islam to all peoples who were non-Muslim 'infidels' and even 'innovators' within Islam. The following chapters explore more fully the specific foundations of Saudi authority and the way in which the conversion of badu tribes to the Wahhabi movement reinforced their identification with the Saudi state.

Notes

1. Amirate or 'princedom' is translated from the Arabic *imāra* (pl. *imārāt*) which implies 'power' or 'authority'. An amir, from the Arabic *amīr* (pl. *umarā*), is a secular ruler of an amirate. The position of amir in Arabian society is hereditary even though it is frequently contested between members of the same family. In Najd these families, originating from either settled or nomadic populations, ruled areas of varying extent from an urban centre or fortified palace. This led Philby to refer to the amirates of Najd as 'city-states', a misleading analogy to that phenomenon in Medieval Europe and, *a fortiori*, ancient Greece.

2. Although Western literature often uses the expression 'bedouin' to describe the nomadic pastoralists of desert lands (*bādiya*), this text retains the Arabic term *badu* (sing. *badawī*) by which the nomads of Arabia referred to their own life-style.

3. The Wahhabis derived their name from the founder of the movement, Muḥammad b. 'Abd al-Wahhāb. This term was derisively coined by opponents of the movement although the name became common usage even in Arabia. The

Wahhabis referred to themselves as *muwahhidūn* or *ahl al-tauhīd* to signify their belief in the 'oneness of God'.

4. See Fred McGraw Donner, 'Mecca's Food Supplies and Muhammad's Boycott', *Journal of the Economic and Social History of the Orient*, 20 (1977), pp. 249-66.

5. These sands have acquired many other names although they are less well known. Pelly reported that the Arabs also called the area Ramlat al-Khālī or 'Sandy Wastes'.

6. See Wilfred Thesiger, *Arabian Sands* (Longmans, London, 1959).

7. These estimates are to be found in J. G. Lorimer, *Gazetteer of the Persian Gulf, 'Omān, and Central Arabia*, 5 vols (Gregg International, Farnborough, 1970), under the principal articles in question. Note that population estimates, especially for a land such as Najd which was still uncharted and hostile to foreigners within the grasp of our memories, are necessarily open to debate. In his estimates of a settled population, Lorimer appraised five persons to each house. The figures for badu were obtained by calculating reputed tribal fighting strengths to be two-sevenths of the tribe.

8. While Ritter in his work conducted in 1970 and published in 1975 (Wigand Ritter, 'Central Saudi Arabia', *Wiener Geographische Schriften 43/44/45 Beiträge zur Wirtschaftsgeographie*, 1 (1975), pp. 205-28,) states on p.206 that the 'number of nomads remains a matter of pure conjecture', he estimated the nomadic population to be approximately 20 per cent in the Wahhabi coreland of Najd. This still remains an amazing figure when it is considered that the population of al-Riyad was swollen by reason of recent oil wealth, immigrant labour forces and its position as capital of a modern nation. If its population were excluded, the nomadic population of Najd would be 30 per cent of the total estimate. It can also be assumed that there were more badu eighty years ago than there are now.

9. It was for this same reason that Turkish troops sought to subjugate the badu by attacking them at their wells in summer and that Middle Eastern governments chose this same season to collect taxes from the badu.

10. Ritter, 'Central Saudi Arabia', p. 211.

11. The towns and villages of the oases of al-Qaṭīf and al-Aḥsā were highly heterogeneous, having received immigrants from many neighbouring lands. They included smaller factions of tribes—'Awāzim and Rashā'ida centred mainly in Kuwait; Dawāsir, Sahūl, Muṭair, Subai', 'Utaiba and Qaḥṭān from Najd; and Manāṣir from areas south of Qaṭar—who entered al-Aḥsā during their seasonal migrations to supplement their pastoralism or to escape drought conditions. The Dawāsir, for example, came to the coast to fish and for annual work as pearl-divers and sailors. These immigrants did not displace the al-Aḥsā tribes, but sometimes became rulers of settled groups on the coast, such as the 'Anaza or 'Utūb dynasties in Kuwait, Qaṭar, al-Qaṭīf and Bahrain.

12. Peter Beaumont, 'Water and Development in Saudi Arabia', *Geographical Journal*, 143 (1977), p. 44.

13. Lorimer reported that al-Ḥufūf, the largest town of al-Aḥsā, contained forty springs in its environs. The population for the whole province was estimated at 101,000 while the nomadic population, numbered at 57,000, was over one-half of the total population.

14. Al-Baḥrain originally designated the whole of Eastern Arabia and was so used in classical Arabic sources.

15. Two *wādī*s running east to west along the Bādiyat al-Shām contained almost continuous lines of wells that were literally used as highways between regions. The first ran north-west from al-Jauf along Wādī Sirḥān towards the Ḥaurān mountains of Syria and the second ran south-west from Karbalā to Ḥā'il, capital of Jabal Shammar. This was also true of Wādī Ḥanīfa and Wādī Sudair in Najd and Wādī al-Miyā in al-Aḥsā.

16. Many Arabian explorers have described the lift method by which camels, donkeys, or cattle moved backwards and forwards on an inclined area, filling and emptying containers of water. Because of the formation caused by radiating paths trodden from the centre of the larger wells, they were referred to as 'star wells'. See Sir John Bagot Glubb, *War in the Desert: An R.A.F. Frontier Campaign* (Hodder and Stoughton, London, 1960), p. 177, for a photograph of these wells.

17. J. C. Wilkinson, *Water and Tribal Settlement in South-East Arabia: A Study of the Aflāj of Oman* (Clarendon Press, Oxford, 1977), pp. 97-121.

18. Lewis Pelly, *Report on A Journey to Riyadh in Central Arabia (1865)* (Oleander Press, Cambridge, 1977), p.49.

19. In al-Kharj and al-Aflāj there also exist numerous limestone solution hollows, surface and underground. Some measure up to depths of 50 metres, thus providing natural water storage cisterns (H. R. P. Dickson, *The Arab of the Desert: A Glimpse into Badawin Life in Kuwait and Sa'udi Arabia* (George Allen and Unwin, London, 1972), pp. 428-30, and Pelly, *Report on A Journey*, p.57).

20. The *athl* or tamarisk was planted not only for firewood, but to stop the continued encroachment of sand towards settled areas. 'Unaiza, one of the two major cities of al-Qaṣīm, set about stabilising its sands by planting over 75 square kilometres of *athl*. Its importance lay in the fact that it needed to be watered only the first year following planting and thereafter relied upon rain and phreatic water supplies (Ahmed A. Shamekh, *Spatial Patterns of Bedouin Settlement in al-Qasim Region Saudi Arabia* (University of Kentucky Press, Lexington, 1975), p.97). Centuries of overgrazing left most areas depleted of vegetation, especially around urban areas and caravan routes where brush and wood were collected for fuel. In the absence of other fuels, dried camel dung was sometimes used.

21. Wādī Ḥanīfa and Wādī Sudair had almost continuous chains of wells and villages along their banks in contrast with other areas of Najd which were either desolate of habitation or evidenced numerous abandoned settlements. It has been hypothesised (Ritter, 'Central Saudi Arabia', p.213) that the density of settlement in these two *wādī*s was due to the quantity of alluvial deposits or loess the relatively small grain size of which allowed larger volumes of water to be stored. In many other areas, erosion carried away these deposits, leaving only gravel or sand, which perhaps explains the concern expressed by settled populations in preventing washouts and the presence of numerous abandoned villages. Louis P. Dame, 'Four Months in Nejd', *Moslem World*, 14 (1924), p.356, makes reference to the old buildings of the village of Dar'iya, the home of the Al Saud family, built on cliffs to the west of Wādī Ḥanīfa: 'The banks of the Wady [*wādī*] are built up with heavy stones, for occasionally the water overruns its banks and causes a great deal of destruction to the splendid gardens and terraced wheat fields on either side.'

22. Beaumont, 'Water and Development', p.43.

23. Alois Musil, *Arabia Deserta* (American Geographical Society/Oriental Explorations and Studies no. 2, New York, 1927), pp.109-10; and R. E. Cheesman, *In Unknown Arabia* (Macmillan, London, 1926), p.215.

24. See Douglas L. Johnson, *The Nature of Nomadism: A Comparative Study of Pastoral Migrations in Southwestern Asia and Northern Africa* (Department of Geography Research Paper no. 118, University of Chicago, 1969).

25. Alois Musil, *The Manners and Customs of the Rwala Bedouins* (American Geographical Society/Oriental Explorations and Studies no. 6, New York, 1928), pp.44-5.

26. *Bait al-sha'ar* literally means 'house of hair' in reference to the fact that these tents were constructed either from sheep or from goat hair.

27. Dickson, *The Arab of the Desert*, pp.108-9; and Musil, *The Rwala Bedouins*, p.45.

28. Shamekh, *Spatial Patterns of Bedouin Settlement*, p.70.

29. Dickson, *The Arab of the Desert*, p.47.

30. See Musil, *The Rwala Bedouins*, pp.77-8. Three tribal maps are in Carl R. Raswan, 'Tribal Areas and Migration Lines of the North Arabian Bedouins', *Geographical Review*, 20 (1930), pp.494-502, and are especially interesting as they illustrate the overlapping quality of tribal *dīras*.

31. Roman wells dug along the Nile valley close to Alexandria are such an example. They had been built so long ago that because 'no particular tribe or individual could claim to have made the wells in the first instance, and as numerous other wells existed in the immediate vicinity, consequently no claims to ownership were put forward' and therefore these wells were freely used by all nomadic tribes (Austin Kennett, *Bedouin Justice: Law and Customs Among the Egyptian Bedouin* (Frank Cass, London, 1968), p.94). See also J. C. Wilkinson's 'Islamic Water Law with Special Reference to Oasis Settlement', *Journal of Arid Environments*, 1 (1978), pp.87-96, in which he points out that the Islamic rights to private property (*mulk*) do not extend to grazing, fire or water—three things which men hold in common.

32. Peter Gubser, *Politics and Change in Al-Karak, Jordan: A Study of a Small Arab Town and its District* (Oxford University Press, London, 1973), illustrates the difficulty of tribes in Jordan understanding the concept of land ownership. After the arrival of the British in Transjordan, a land registration programme was begun in which all families were told to register their land on a particular day. It was not realised or else it was ignored that the land was tribal land and that the individual families did not own land in the Western sense, but only the rights to cultivation. People were to register whatever land they currently held in possession. Certain tribal shaikhs, such as the Majaly family of al-Karak, realised the importance of these land deeds and they obtained huge tracts of land at little or no cost from families who did not understand the concept or the rights inherent in these land deeds—that is, that rights to land could be owned and that title of ownership could exist in a deed.

33. The *wasm* of 'Abd al-'Azīz, for example, was  placed on the right thigh of the camel; the *wasm* on the camels he confiscated from the Ikhwan after their rebellion was  (Dickson, *The Arabs of the Desert*, pp.419-28).

34. Musil, *The Rwala Bedouins*, pp.46-7; and Dickson, *The Arab of the Desert*, pp.114-16.

35. A *faṣīla* may also be referred to as *'ashīra* or *badīda*, and a *raḥṭ* as *'ā'ila*. See Fu'ād Ḥamza, *qalb jazīrat al-'arab* (Maktaba al-Naṣr al-Ḥadītha, al-Riyāḍ, 1388 (1968)), pp.133-235, for a detailed list of tribes and their classifications in Central Arabia.

36. It is of note that, in inter-tribal and inter-lineage warfare, wives of the defeated were married to the victors in a symbolic but highly political act. 'Abd al-'Azīz himself took wives from many tribes. Although often the marriage was dissolved shortly thereafter, he successfully cemented numerous political relationships in this way. The former wife received an allowance and the honour which accrued to such a marriage. If any offspring resulted, they were brought to al-Riyāḍ after they had reached a certain age to be raised in the palace of their father.

37. Ibn Khaldun, *The Muqaddimah: An Introduction to History* (Routledge and Kegan Paul, London, 1967), pp.91-122.

38. Lorimer, *Gazetteer*, pp.681-3, 1658-61.

39. Ḥamza, *qalb jazīrat al-'arab*, pp.134-5.

40. Dickson, *The Arab of the Desert*, p.48.

41. Pelly, *Report on A Journey*, p.67.

42. See Carl R. Raswan, *Black Tents of Arabia: My Life Among the Bedouins* (Hutchinson, London, 1935), pp.66-7. The concept of a 'brother' was an important element in customary law and its benefits have often been recorded by travellers to

Arabia who were extended the 'brotherhood' or protection of a tribe.

43. Musil, *The Rwala Bedouins*, pp.59-60.

44. Dickson, *The Arab of the Desert*, p.115.

45. A shaikh of the Muṭair explained that the original concept was that the obligation to seek retribution or, alternatively, to accept blood money for a man's murder devolved upon the victim's *ahl* (ibid., p.114). This is common to all Central Arabian groups and is absolutely basic.

46. Musil, *The Rwala Bedouins*, p.50; and Wilkinson, *Water and Tribal Settlement*, pp.174-5.

47. Khair al-Dīn Ziriklī, *shibh al-jazīra fī 'ahd al-malik 'abd al-'azīz*, 3 vols (Maṭābi' Dār al-Qalam, Beirut, 1390A (1970)), pp.651-2.

48. Dickson, *The Arab of the Desert*, p.48.

49. Julian Morgenstern, *The Ark, the Ephod, and the 'Tent of Meeting'* (Hebrew Union College Press; Cincinnati, 1945), pp.15-27, 55-71.

50. Pelly, *Report on A Journey*, p.29.

51. Ziriklī, *shibh al-jazīra fī 'ahd al-malik 'abd al-'azīz*, pp.649-50. This signature is also found in personal correspondence from 'Abd al-'Azīz to Captain Shakespear: W. H. Shakespear, *Private Papers Collection* ('Journal of a Trip via Central Arabia to Egypt', memoranda, letters, photographs) in the possession of Major-General J. D. Lunt, Oxford.

52. Dickson, *the Arab of the Desert*, p.117.

53. See also Ameen Rihani, *Ibn Sa'oud of Arabia: His People and His Land* (Constable, London, 1928), p.325.

54. Ziriklī, *shibh al-jazīra fī 'ahd al-malik 'abd al-'azīz*, pp.651-2.

55. Shamekh, *Spatial Patterns of Bedouin Settlement*, p.43.

56. Ahmed (in Cynthia Nelson (ed.), *The Desert and the Sown: Nomads in the Wider Society* (University of California Institute of International Studies, Berkeley, 1973), pp.75-96) has written a monograph entitled 'Tribal and Sedentary Elites: A Bridge Between Two Communities' in which he explores the nature of a relationship in which settled members of a tribal group who possess religious and economic power act as mediators for badu members of their same tribe and thereby acquire political power in just such an arrangement between members of the same tribe.

57. W. Ritter, 'Central Saudi Arabia', *Wiener Geographische Schriften 43/44/45 Beiträge zur Wirtschaftsgeographie*, 1 (1975), pp.220-3.

58. Rihani, *Ibn Sa'oud of Arabia*, p.305.

59. See Lorimer, *Gazetteer*, under specific articles.

60. Ritter, 'Central Saudi Arabia', pp.223-5; and Ḥamza, *qalb jazīrat al-'arab*, pp.74-5.

61. Rihani, *Ibn Sa'oud of Arabia*, pp.293-4.

62. Sometime during the summer months in Kuwait Town the residents went into the hinterland to graze their animals at wells because water in the towns was so expensive. They also 'hired' this work out to the nomads of the surrounding desert so that over the years close ties were established between the two communities. During World War II they even joined together in smuggling operations, to their mutual benefit.

63. See Lorimer, *Gazetteer*, under specific articles.

64. See Henry Rosenfeld, 'The Social Composition of the Military in the Process of State Formation in the Arabian Desert—Part I', *Journal of the Royal Anthropological Institute*, 95 (1965), pp.75-86.

65. J. C. Wilkinson, 'Problems of Oasis Development' (School of Geography Research Paper no. 20, Oxford University, 1978).

66. Musil, *Arabia Deserta*, p.353.

67. Ibid., p.109.

68. Ibid., p.110.

69. Raswan, *Black Tents of Arabia*, p.24.

70. See Henry Rosenfeld, 'Social Composition of the Military', and 'The Military Force used to Achieve and Maintain Power and the Meaning of its Social Composition: Slaves, Mercenaries and Townsmen—Part II', *Journal of the Royal Anthropological Institute*, 95 (1965), pp.174-94, for a more detailed discussion of Ḥā'il's transformation into a thriving commercial centre.

71. S. S. Butler, 'A Journey into Unknown Arabia, in 1908, living as, and with, the Bedouin', travel diary.

72. See Ch. 4.

73. The slave trade has been engaged in this part of the world for centuries and continued well into this century. 'Abd al-'Azīz gave Philby a slave who had been a member of his household and whom Philby eventually married. Philby also described the scenes in which new Ford cars arrived in Sa'udi Arabia and 'Abd al-'Azīz's personal bodyguards—all Negroes—mounted the running board of the King's car. The mercenaries were largely fugitives and adventurers from eastern Najd and descendants of Turkish-Egyptian army deserters from Ibrahim Pasha's expedition.

74. Alois Musil, *Northern Najd* (American Geographical Society/Oriental Explorations and Studies no. 5, New York, 1928), p.303.

2

Al Wahhab and Al Saud: 'Church' and 'State'

Saudi history has been much discussed in Western sources owing to Saudi territorial expansion and the outstanding oil wealth accumulated in more recent decades. There is little dispute over the historical facts although it is unfortunate that there has been almost no interpretative scholarship regarding the political identity of the Al Saud or their relationship with Central Arabian populations and with other Arab leaders. It is often assumed that the Al Saud originated from the badu of Najd, but the truth is quite different. The earliest traceable ancestors of the Al Saud are known to have immigrated to Najd from al-Qatif in al-Ahsa during the fifteenth century. The first settlement associated with them, Diriya, was located in Wadi Hanifa, fifteen kilometres north of al-Riyad, an urban area already well established. Although the Al Saud proudly claim to be related to the great Anaza tribal confederation of northern Arabia, their primary interests lay with those of urban populations from the moment of their arrival in Najd and even prior to their departure from al-Ahsa. The first goal of the Al Saud, ever since the eighteenth century, was the union of urban areas under a single political authority. It was only in the twentieth century that they were able to initiate a deliberate policy aimed at the eventual settlement of the badu who were an indispensable element in any scheme of political expansion and consolidation in Arabia.

Another misconception about Al Saud history is that the family was always the predominant political force in Central Arabia. There is, in fact, little historical reference to them until the eighteenth century when, at some date prior to 1720, the eponymous founder of the Al Saud, Saud b. Muhammad b. Muqrin, began his brief rule. Upon his death, he was succeeded by his son Muhammad with whom most historians of the Al Saud begin their narrative. The exact vicissitudes of the family are not relevant here, but it is significant that its fortunes so far increased in the years prior to the rule of Muhammad b. Saud that it started to call itself an amirate, one among many in Central Arabia, and the ruler was referred to by the title Amir of Diriya. These years were marred, however, by internecine strife and even a brief period when the family's hold on the amirate was usurped by the Bani Khalid of al-Ahsa.

The subsequent development of Saudi history after Muhammad b. Saud can conveniently be divided into three major periods: the initial period from 1745 to 1818, the intermediate period from about 1824 to 1885, and the present period beginning in 1901. Each period was characterised by Saudi political expansion so extensive that it spread its influence throughout the Arabian Peninsula and as far north as Baghdad and Damascus; and each was separated by the curtailment of Saudi authority by other political forces such as the Ottoman Porte or the Al Rashid of Jabal Shammar. One common element links all of these periods and fundamentally distinguishes them from the Saudi rule of previous years and from other amirates and shaikhdoms of Central Arabia. This was the effective union of political/military organisation and religious ideology which began when Muhammad b. Saud, Amir of Diriya, and Muhammad b. Abd al-Wahhab, founder of the Wahhabi movement of Islam, formed an alliance in 1745, further strengthened by frequent inter-marriage between the Al Saud and Al Wahhab.

Much has been written about Saudi history in the twentieth century, but the concentration on factual material rather than analysis has obscured the significance of the Wahhabi movement and its role in understanding the political behaviour of the Al Saud. Although little is understood about the Al Saud and Al Wahhab alliance, it is none the less viewed by historians more as a justification than as a motivation for Saudi actions. The following quotation from a letter written by Abd al-Aziz b. Abd al-Rahman Al Saud on 24 Rajab 1346 (17 January 1928) to the British Political Agent in Bahrain is unique in that it is one of the few statements from a Saudi ruler openly reflecting the motivations and domestic problems of his administration. It illustrates his acute awareness of the difficulties of controlling a segmentary society and the role of religion in solving this problem.

> The Government that has been established in this wide desert, which with its power, brought all forces that are in it under its control and managed its administration by the virtue of the social teachings of the religion, and made all the desert tribes within the lands under our control obey our orders in a manner that cannot be compared with (that of any other Government) in the world towards nomad tribes and the best proof of this is the state of peace which is spread all over our kingdom and which makes us to boast and say that there is no similar thing to be found in any country in the world (will not be a weak one). A Government which by its own force made its authority firm in this vast country.[1]

The failure of modern histories to deal with this union of religion and politics, as well as with the nature of the social organisation in Central Arabia, has left serious gaps in our knowledge. While no one can doubt that the Al Saud were forced into negotiations with the British out of political necessity in the early twentieth century, there is no indication in the source literature of their attitude to their new Christian ally. Indeed, the Saudi attitude to the Ottoman Empire and the Khalifate remains ambiguous. Military campaigns against British, Ottoman and other Arab leaders have been fully recorded, but there has been no attempt to understand these in the light of Saudi attitudes to their Arab and Islamic heritage.

This chapter is concerned with the origins and tenets of the Wahhabi movement and its influence on Saudi political identity, and particularly with Abd al-Aziz in the twentieth century. Wahhabiism has clearly influenced all aspects of social, economic and political life in Saudi Arabia, particularly in Najd where it was conceived and nurtured. Almost from the beginning, it was given strongest support from the Al Saud whose political authority was, in turn, given the sanction of religious validity. The Wahhabi *ulama* gave explicit approval to the hereditary rule of the Al Saud; and the Islamic belief that all men are equal within the *umma* gave credence to the Saudi policy of eliminating tribal particularisms and urban rivalries to establish its own paramount authority. As a number of reference works already exist, this study will not follow an historical chronology, but will rely heavily on footnotes to support textual statements.

The Wahhabis: Inheritors of a Radical Tradition

Little is known about the Wahhabi movement from direct sources. There were no printing presses in Central Arabia until this century, so most Wahhabi works were transcribed by hand. Some tracts were later printed in India[2] and also in Mecca after its conquest in the 1920s by the Al Saud. Western travellers such as Niebuhr, Palgrave, Burckhardt, Guarmani, Doughty, Philby and Rihani indirectly provide us with some information. References also exist from people in Damascus, Baghdad and Cairo with whom the Wahhabis either traded or came into contact during periods of expansion. The following sections have utilised these sources in order to present the origins, fundamental beliefs, and consequences of Wahhabi doctrine for political and social life in the Peninsula.

The movement was begun by Muhammad b. Abd al-Wahhab. He was born in 1703/4 in al-Uyaina in Najd where both his father and grandfather were Hanbali *qadis*. Trained from an early age in Arabic and Islamic texts, he received further instruction in al-Hijaz, Basra and al-Ahsa. Throughout his travels, Ibn Abd al-Wahhab was struck by the accretions which Islam had experienced to its detriment since the eighth century and which were leading to decadence among the people of the Peninsula. He was further confronted by many pre-Islamic customs which remained in daily life and which he became determined to eradicate.[3] When he returned to Najd, he joined his father at a new home in al-Huraimila where he formulated the basic tenets of his beliefs. His extreme doctrines, however, placed his life in jeopardy and he was forced to return to al-Uyaina. There he reinstituted Islamic law to punish an adulteress with stoning and to destroy venerated trees and tombs which he considered objects of non-Islamic tribal customs. The influential Bani Khalid in al-Ahsa were sufficiently disturbed by these acts to press the ruler of al-Uyaina to expel this zealot. Thus, in 1744, Muhammad b. Abd al-Wahhab found refuge in Diriya, the Saudi home.

The Wahhabi movement has not been a static phenomenon during the last several hundred years, although it can essentially be seen as a revival of the purity of early Islam and as a reform movement which in the twentieth century would oppose the presence of non-Muslim powers and corrupt Islamic governments in the Peninsula. The little that has been said about the Wahhabis has generally been limited to a list of their acts: destruction of tombs and minarets, intolerance of smoking and wearing of fine adornments, and their merciless slaughter of enemies. Many reports have been so exaggerated as to obscure any understanding of their beliefs.

The Wahhabis, as Abd al-Aziz himself frequently told visitors to Najd, adhered to the Hanbali school of law or *madhhab*. This school, the fourth and last of the orthodox Islamic *madhhab*s, had its origins in the writings of Ahmad b. Hanbal who was active in the early ninth century in Baghdad. During the following century his teachings were codified and for a while enjoyed a popularity never regained until they were revived in modern times by the Salafi and Wahhabi movements. While Wahhabi doctrine itself is based more on the teachings of Hanbali jurist Ibn Taimiya, its origins cannot be isolated from the radical tradition of Hanbalism. Hanbalism marks a deliberate stage in the distinction between state and religion in Islam, one which classical Islam did not make. Ibn Hanbal had denounced in varying degrees *ilm al-kalam*, 'scholastic theology'; *qiyas*, 'analogical reasoning'; *ijma*, 'consensus'; *aql*, 'reasoning'; and any other accretion which gave too much leeway to the interpretation of the Quran and Sunna and which affected the original purity of Islam. In the view of the Hanbali followers, the obligations of Islam derived solely from the Quran and Sunna and everything else was *bida* or 'innovation'. They did not oppose the Khalifa or the Abbasid *dawla*, but they believed that Islam would be more truly preserved by Islamic religious bodies independent of the Khalifa or his political interests. It was the duty of the *ulama* to interpret the Quran and of the *umma* to adhere to the precepts of Islam, but they were no longer bound solely to Khalifal authority. According to Hanbali belief, it was the duty of Muslims to have patience even with tyrannical rulers rather than to cause *fitna* or 'civil disturbance'; however, the duty of obedience ceased when the ruler disobeyed God's law. In such a case an individual must refuse the will of the ruler, just as Ibn Hanbal did at the *mihna* of Mamun over the issue of *khalq al-Quran*.[4]

Taqi al-Din Ahmad b. Taimiya and his disciple, Ibn Qayyim al-Jauziya, active in the fourteenth century, were the best-known exponents of Hanbalism and more influential to Wahhabi thought than the earlier Hanbalis, although their teachings are not considered typical of the school itself.[5] While not accepting *ijtihad*, 'independent reasoning', Ibn Taimiya rejected *taqlid*, 'the uncritical acceptance of faith', and sought to reach fresh interpretations of Islamic law. His teachings had three major implications for Wahhabi thought. The first concerns Ibn Taimiya's view of state and religion in Islam. Ibn Taimiya felt that the *ulama* were responsible for preserving the divine law. No one should follow the authority of any single individual and, by logical extension, this included the Khalifa. A government was considered Islamic by virtue of the support it gave to Islam and to the *umma*; it was perfectly legitimate to accept the rule of anyone who followed the Sharia. This had profound implications for Wahhabi ideology. The Wahhabis accepted the Al Saud as a legitimate and hereditary Islamic government and, notably, had referred to them as Imams ever since the mid-eighteenth century. Their rule was so absolute that in 1803/4 and again in the twentieth century the Wahhabis even attacked the holy territory of al-Hijaz and ousted the descendants of the Prophet, hitherto both considered sacrosanct by all Muslims, on the orders of the Saudi Imamate.

Second, Ibn Taimiya sought to find a pure Islam, untainted by the developments of later centuries. Like Ibn Hanbal before him and the Wahhabis after him, Ibn Taimiya turned to the Quran and Sunna as the basis of divine law. Any accretion after the initial pristine years of *salaf*, the first three generations of Islam, was considered *bida* or 'innovation'. The unfortunate result has been that Ibn Taimiya is frequently portrayed as a fanatical heretic who opposed philosophers, Sufis, theologians and the practices of saint worship and of shrine and grave cults. This is, however, a misrepresentation. At the core of Ibn Taimiya's and Wahhabi ideology was the emphasis on *tauhid*, the Doctrine of the Unity of God. No one could be a good Muslim without accepting the absolute and ultimate authority of God in every aspect of life. It was an error to believe that the true perfection of the soul (*kamal al-nafs*) or the ability to say 'I am Muslim' was to be found only in the knowledge of God. There must also be love of God (*mahabba*), performance of the prescribed rituals, and submission. Ibn Taimiya did not oppose either *qiyas* or philosophy when they were based on the Quran and Sunna and when not considered absolute methods of understanding divine law.[6] Contrary to all generally accepted opinions, recent scholarship has shown that Ibn Taimiya was in fact a Sufi of the Qadiriya Order and had even been invested with the Sufi cloak or *khirqa*. He rejected *ittihadiya* or the 'mystical unity with God' of the Sufis, but orthodox Sufism was acceptable if it was based on revealed law. Sufi *ilham* or 'inspiration' and *irada* or 'seeking of God' were also considered completely consonant with orthodox Islam under this prohibition.[7]

Ibn Taimiya's abhorrence of saint worship and of shrine and grave cults became the third element of importance in Wahhabi doctrine. It was a logical development of the doctrine of *tauhid*. All these practices, including the celebration of festivals or *iqtida*, were classed as intercession between God and man because they verged on idol worship.[8] All were considered *shirk*—that is, 'polytheism' or 'the association of anyone or thing with God'. They were thus seen as shifting faith from the creator to the creature, obliterating the distinction between God and man.[9] Ibn Taimiya's writings and those of the Wahhabis were frequently directed against *shirk* and any *bida* which encouraged *shirk*.

There is evidence that a general orthodox revival had been building up since the 1700s in the outlying areas of the Ottoman Empire. A number of reform movements developed, such as the Sanusi[10] and Wahhabi, which condemned the moral laxity and corruption of religion. Many of these movements were also disturbed by the non-Arab and non-Muslim influences that were gradually increasing in India, the Middle East and North Africa. They aimed to restore the initial purity of Islam by abolishing customary law or *hukm al-mana*, literally 'the provision of protection', and exclusively enforcing Islamic law. Many rejected *ijma* and *qiyas* as they returned solely to the Quran and Sunna as sources of Islamic law. *Jihad*, which had generally been reinterpreted in Sufi ethics as 'to strive' or 'to endeavour', was elevated to an importance it had not had since the early community of the Prophet. These movements viewed themselves as defenders of the faith. *Jihad* was directed not only against non-Muslims, but also against Muslims whose decadence had weakened Islam, in the same way in which the Khariji, Azraqi and Ibadi movements had been compelled to become sectarian movements in early Islam and to take violent action against other Muslim 'dissenters' who opposed them. Many were agreed on two fundamental principles: *istirad*, 'legalised political murder', and the right of any believer who is morally and religiously irreproachable to lead the Islamic community if he is chosen by consensus.

The Wahhabi *Dawa*: Social and Political Implications

There are two theories as to the origin of Wahhabiism or *al-wahhabiya*. The first is that it was a derogatory term current in the countries bordering territory under Saudi dominion which were the first to fall victim in the late 1700s to the proselytising zeal of the Wahhabi *mujahidun* or warriors. A second theory, more generally accepted, traces the first known reference of *al-wahhabiya* to a book called *al-ṣawā'iq al-ilāhīya fī al-radd 'alā al-wahhābīya* or *The Divine Thunderbolts in Refutation of Wahhabiism* written by Shaikh Muhammad b. Abd al-Wahhab's brother. Ironically, the name Wahhabiism has come to be the most widely accepted term of reference for the religious movement even though the Wahhabis despised its elevation of a man, albeit their founding father.[11]

The Wahhabis called themselves *ahl al-tauhid*, People of Unity, or *muwahhidun*, Those who Profess the Doctrine of the Unity of God. They referred to their movement as *al-dawa al-najdiya*, The Najd Call; *al-dawa ila tauhid*, The Call for Tauhid; and simply *al-dawa*, The Call. This term reveals much about the Wahhabis for it was a 'summons, convocation, or missionary call' to all Muslims to unite for a return to the purity of early Islam. The Wahhabis have been frequently labelled Kharijites or a 'fifth *madhhab*' because the reform they sought was so extreme in its intolerance of other Muslim groups that they were viewed as secessionists and even as heretics until their political successes of this century. In their writings the Wahhabis frequently refuted these two labels which they considered unlawful departures from Islam. The use of the term *dawa* indicates that they considered themselves a fully orthodox Islamic movement.

It is said that when Shaikh Muhammad b. Abd al-Wahhab returned to Najd after his religious study, his thinking had been strongly influenced by what he considered to be the decadent social conditions which he had found in the Peninsula. Wahhabi religious texts, Saudi historians and poets of the *dawa* have frequently mentioned that highway robbery, prostitution, murder and plunder were indeed prevalent prior to the Wahhabi *dawa*.

> Know that the people of Najd—nomad and settled—before the Shaikh al-Islam [Abd al-Wahhab]. . . were in the *jāhilīya* [ignorance characterized by the pre-Islamic period]. Islam had

> become almost unknown. Evil, corruption, *shirk*, and *kufr* were widespread in towns, villages, cities, and among the desert and the sown. Idols and images were widespread. The people had abandoned *zakāt*.[12]

Shaikh Muhammad b. Abd al-Wahhab sought to eliminate all paganistic rituals and to eradicate all forms of popular Islam which were responsible for the disunity of the *umma* just as the Prophet Muhammad, eleven centuries earlier, had sought to eliminate or to endow with a new significance all paganistic rituals. The main principles of Shaikh Muhammad b. Abd al-Wahhab's *dawa* was the fundamental principle of the Prophet 'There is no God but Allah'. Temporal authority was legitimate only in so far as it conformed to divine law and sought to eliminate *fitna* or 'civil disturbance' within the Islamic *umma*.

There were three important concepts formulated within Wahhabi doctrine which subsequently had great influence upon the social life of the Peninsula. The first concept relates to the internal composition of the Islamic community and the other two to the relationship between *al-wahhabiya* and the external world. The Shaikh, fully consonant on the first point with Islamic thought, taught that membership in the *umma* took precedence over any other social bonds and that therefore all men within the *umma* were equal. The importance of this belief for Wahhabiism lay in the unique composition of Central Arabian society. From Chapter 1 it will be recalled that approximately three-quarters of the total population of Central Arabia, both nomadic and settled, identified themselves as belonging to a tribal group. There was frequent conflict between alliances of the desert and sown communities against other such alliances and there was a considerable amount of social stratification and, hence, friction between tribes. To believe that all men are equal and to set up the methods to equalise any existing differences in such a society was bound to have extensive ramifications, as the events of the early twentieth century proved, when Abd al-Aziz freed the 'inferior' tribal groups, abolished customary law and the inter-tribal system of levies and supported a policy of settling nomadic elements under his supreme temporal authority.

The Al Saud and the Wahhabi shaikhs utilised this concept of equality as a political tool to control the badu whom they believed were pernicious and constituted a major cause of disunity among the communities of Najd. They had to be shown the straight path of Islam, by force if necessary.

> The strongest binding force is love of God and hatred of all that is not. God has made it a duty for the *mu'minīn* [believers] to manifest enmity to the *mushrikīn* [polytheists] among the *kuffār* [unbelievers] and the *munāfiqīn* [hypocrites]. Badu tribes are known for their hypocrisy. God has commanded the believers to carry on *jihād* in word and deed and has threatened them [the *kuffar*, *mushrikun*, *munafiqun* and badu tribes] with killing.[13]

At another time the Shaikh was asked whether 'the customs of the ancestors of the desert'—that is, the customary law of the badu—could be termed as *kufr* or 'unbelief'. His response was direct and simple: 'Anybody who makes a judgement other than by the book of God is a *kāfir* . . . All *ṭāghūt* [those who appeal to or worship idols] are *kāfir*.'[14]

These statements point to a decided bias against the life-style of the badu who were thought to prefer customary tribal law rather than God's law for settling disputes and to employ pre-Islamic rituals in their daily lives. It would not be unfair to say that the Shaikh felt that the towns offered a greater sense of social cohesiveness and less of a tendency to anti-Islamic practices. Anything conducive to *fitna* was repudiated. The security of the *umma* was sacrosanct, and therefore it is not difficult to understand the importance Shaikh Muhammad b. Abd al-Wahhab placed on unity and equality. Those who joined *al-wahhabiya* were called Ikhwan or 'brothers', irrespective of their tribal origin, occupation or race. All Ikhwan shared equal rights and equal responsibilities with the *umma*.

The remaining two factors—*balad al-muslimin* and *hijra*—which were important in Wahhabi thought emphasise the social and cultural exclusiveness of the Wahhabi *umma* to the external non-Muslim world and, as will be seen later, to other Muslim groups. Islam categorised the world into two major divisions: *dar al-islam*, House of Islam (also *balad al-muslimin*, Country of the Muslims); and *dar al-harb*, House of War.[15] As is evident from the names, anyone who is not within the *dar al-islam* must be in the *dar al-harb*—that is, liable to *jihad* or 'holy war' and subject to the laws governing Islamic warfare. There is much that has already been written about this, but it can briefly be said that most Islamic movements have tended to reinterpret such concepts much less radically.[16] The Wahhabis, however, chose not only to interpret them in their most literal sense, but also to include within the *dar al-harb* those Muslims who, they believed, were 'unlawful'.

The last factor, *hijra* or 'emigration or departure', has received little or no attention from scholars, except to note that the Ikhwan settlements were called *hijra* (pl. *hijar*) which, they presumed, symbolised the journey of the badu from a nomadic to a settled life-style. This is, however, only a partial answer because the *hijra*, one of the most distinct features of *al-wahhabiya*, was an incumbent duty on all Muslims and had long-ranging social and political implications. It was, in fact, said to be one of the pillars of the religion, *al-hijra rukn min arkan al-din*. 'There has been a rise in chaos, and *kufr*, and *shirk*, and threats to the foundations of Islam and *tauḥīd*. I was right when I said that the *hijra* was one of the pillars of Islam.'[17]

Hijra has two specific meanings. The first is obvious. It is obligatory for all Muslims 'to emigrate from every country in which *shirk* and *kufr* are apparent. The person there is not free to claim his freedom from *shirk* or to claim his religion. He believes their *kufr*.'[18] If one is able to claim one's religion in the *dar al-harb*, then immigration to the *balad al-muslimin* is desirable, but not compulsory.[19]

It may be noted that the term *hijra* has had a similar significance at other times in Islamic history. The Muslim calendar begins at the date when the Prophet Muhammad left Mecca and went to al-Madina. This date officially became known as 1 Muharram A. H.—that is, *Anno Hijirae* or Year of the Migration. Those who followed him to al-Madina were known as *al-muhajirun* or The Immigrants, an association of great prestige in future years; and al-Madina became known as the *dar al-hijra*, House of the Hijra. After the conquest of Mecca it became a duty to immigrate to al-Madina. It will be recalled that Shaikh Muhammad b. Abd al-Wahhab's journey from al-Uyaina to a refuge in Diriya was also called *al-hijra*, a choice of words that cannot be taken as coincidental. Just as al-Madina had provided sanctuary for the new religion of Islam and its Prophet, Diriya offered refuge and a sanctuary from which to spread the message of an Islamic revival.

The terms *hijra* and *dar al-hijra* have also been employed by other reform movements in Islam. Nafi b. al-Azraq, leader of the

Azraqi, professed that only he was deserving of the support of true Muslims. His followers were known as *muhajirun* and his camp as the *dar al-hijra*. The utilisation of such terms by reform movements like the Azraqi and Wahhabi indicates that a departure from the Islamic community was considered necessary in order to fashion a new and purer society.

The second meaning which the Wahhabis ascribed to *hijra* other than 'emigration' was the *hijrat al-muhramat*. This was the 'abandoning of all sinful things forbidden by God and the Prophet Muhammad'.[20] These forbidden things are clearly spelled out in Wahhabi religious texts and will be discussed shortly. For the present it is enough to stress the enormous religious and political implications of *hijrat al-muhramat*. *Hijra* implied a transition from one life-style to another; a break from the past and the submission to Islam; a rejection of customary law and the acceptance of God's divine law in all aspects of life; and a renunciation of tribal bonds of loyalty in favour of membership in the Islamic brotherhood. The following questions by the Ikhwan and the answers by their Wahhabi shaikhs show their concern about the status of badu tribes, and their own relation to *hijra* and to those who separate from Islam.

> This concerns those who go out into the desert with their property but who intend to return to the town. Is he regarded as an *'āṣī* [rebel] or not?
>
> We do not call him a rebel against God and therefore he is not subject to judgement. It is not considered *ma'ṣiya* [sedition or rebellion]. He is considered a *muhājir* [immigrant] if he has the intention of returning to his homeland and to the *hijra* with his brothers and therefore he cannot be considered in *ridda* [apostasy] or *ma'ṣiya*.

> What about those who sell their house and go to the desert without the intention of returning even if he is a confirmed Muslim and obeys all its laws and loves the Muslims?
>
> He can be considered as committing *ma'ṣiya* after his *hijra* and he would be subject to the *hadith* recorded by Ibn Abū Hātim regarding those who separated from the community and he is subject to the laws regarding separation from *al-muslimīn al-jamā'a* [the Muslim concourse]. He has not committed *kufr* or *ridda*, but he is an *'āṣī* [a rebellious Muslim] although he has

faith. He must not be treated severely. He shall not be regarded as among the *murtaddīn* [apostates].

What is the law concerning him after he has settled, then he goes to the desert and commits many *kufr*?

This person is a *murtadd* and has left Islam. Previously he was living with his brothers and listening to sermons: The Qur'ān would establish a case against him because he has denied his former membership in the Islamic community and has done things which showed the evil in his heart. He has shown hatred and turned from the lawful duties of the Sharī'a. Righteous repentance should be obtained from him.

What is said concerning the *hijra* of the *mushrikīn* [those practising *shirk*] of the badu and the *ḥaḍar*? Is there between the badu of Najd and others among them like the 'Anaza and the Ẓafīr and those who are allied with them from the north and south that which is concealed from responsible people [i.e., true Muslims]?

The *hijra* is one of the most pious duties of religion and one of the most virtuous. This is the reason for the well-being of the religion of the worshipper and the retention of his faith.[21]

Widely interpreted, the concept of *hijra* had tremendous implications for Saudi political policy, particularly in regard to the nomadic tribes, as will be seen in Chapter 3. It was obviously preferable to be in the *dar al-islam* and, while it was felt that some of the desert dwellers[22] did keep to the law of Islam and avoid bloodshed and plunder, the inference was that it was much more difficult to do so. The settlement of the badu in *hijar* not only satisfied the Wahhabi religious shaikhs but also functioned to increase the political control of the Al Saud.

Tauhid and *Shirk*: Major Tenets of the Wahhabi *Dawa*

The central tenet of the Wahhabi *dawa* concerned *tauhid* or the doctrine of the unity of God. *Tauhid* literally means 'unification' which theologically relates to the 'oneness' or 'unity' of God in all its literal and abstract senses. The Wahhabis distinguished three categories of *tauhid: tauhid (wahdaniya) al-rububiya*, unity of

Lordship; *tauhid (wahdaniya) al-uluhiya*, unity of the divinity; and *tauhid (wahdaniya) al-asma wa al-sifat*, unity of names and attributes, which structured many of the beliefs and actions of the Wahhabis.[23]

The recognition of *tauhid al-rububiya* is common to all Muslims, although its definition in Wahhabi texts went far to validate their claim of exclusive righteousness in contrast to other Muslim groups. All Muslims must recognise the absolute and unique lordship of God and His deeds above everything, inanimate and human, in the world. God is the omnipotent lord of creation, forbidding the attribution of divine powers to anyone but Himself. God created humans from nothing; He sustains all things; He is known by His signs and His creations which surround us, such as the day and night and the sun and moon; and He alone is deserving of worship. All affairs of daily life should be referred only to the Quran of God and the Sunna of His Prophet. The Wahhabis believed that many people abused this because they did not look to God, but only sought a lord. This was not Islamic and the Prophet justly fought them and outlawed them and their property even if they claimed to be Muslims.[24]

The *tauhid al-uluhiya* is sometimes referred to as Practical Tauhid or *tauhid al-amali*. It includes all the daily rituals, beliefs and acts of faith, and strivings in love, fear, hope and trust in God. Stated differently, it is the unity of God as seen in the deeds of His followers in the things that they lawfully have to do. It is the submission to Islam, to God's word and guidance, and to all which that entails. For all devout Muslims there were three incumbent principles: knowledge of one's Lord, His religion, and His Prophet—*marifa rabbihi wa dinihi wa nabiyihi.*[25] The *tauhid al-uluhiya* based this knowledge on the five traditional pillars of Islam: *shahada*, prayer, fasting, *zakat* and pilgrimage. It included belief in God and His omnipotence, His angels, the revealed books and the Last Judgement. A good Muslim must identify Muhammad b. Abdullah b. Abd al-Mutallib b. Hashim as the last of God's Prophets who was sent to all mankind, although all must realise that Muhammad was only a man. At all times a Muslim must act in full conformity with God's commands and in full cognisance of God's judgement.

Finally, the unity of God is seen in the names and attributes of God. The Wahhabis were anthropomorphic, interpreting quite literally every passage in the Quran which referred to God and His attributes. Anyone who was a 'backslider' in one of the names of God was to be condemned by all righteous Muslims.

In the collections of Wahhabi writings the extensive expositions concerning *tauhid* were equalled only by their vehement condemnation of *shirk*, 'polytheism' or 'the association of anyone or anything with God', and, to a lesser extent, *kufr*. In the earliest Suras, *kufr* meant 'the concealing of (or being ungrateful for) God's blessings',[26] but later it came to signify unbelief or infidelity.[27] Those who practised *shirk* were called *mushrik* (pl. *mushrikun*); those practising *kufr* were the *kafir* (pl. *kafirun* or *kuffar*). Discussions of *tauhid* frequently revolved around the topic of *shirk* in particular, because it was a concept which stood in complete opposition. A good teaching method was not simply to recite the various meanings of *tauhid*, but to define it by stating what it was not. The importance of *shirk* for Wahhabi ideology and for political life under periods of Al Saud rule is illustrated by a letter written by Abd al-Aziz (I) b. Saud probably sometime around 1800.

> From 'Abd al-'Azīz b. Sa'ūd to whoever sees this from among the people of Mukhalāf Āl Sulaimānī, particularly the sons of Sharīf Ḥamūd—Nāṣir, Yaḥyā, and their brothers, and sons of their brothers and likewise the Ashrāf of Banī al-Na'mā and all Ashrāf of Tihāma. May God help them see the light and reject the *shirk*. The burden of this letter is that the Sharīf Aḥmad b. Ḥusain al-Falqī came to us and he saw our opinion of him and the accuracy of this became known to him. After this he supplicated that we should write to you about doubt disappearing from him. You know the religion of Islam does not accept anything else other than Him [Allah]. Know that God sent Muḥammad after his other apostles and guided him to complete a perfect religion and the law. The greatest of all that is the sincerity in the worship of God who has no partner—the refutation of *shirk*.[28]

It will be recalled that the Wahhabi *dawa* laid particular stress on the first part of the *shahada*, namely 'There is no God but Allah'. God alone deserved worship, without intermediaries.[29] To pray, supplicate for divine assistance, sacrifice, vow, submit, show humility, genuflect in prayer, fear, hope, or express wishes to anyone but God, however small the departure, was to commit an act of *shirk*. There are three types of *shirk*—major, minor and hidden.[30] The major *shirk*, punishable by hell (*al-nar*), can be divided into four categories: *shirk al-iddia*, 'praying other than to God'; *shirk al-niya wa al-irada wa al-qasd*, 'seeking after worldly possessions by intention or will'; *shirk al-taa*, 'obeying leaders who are themselves in *shirk*'; and finally, *shirk al-mahabba*, 'loving other than God'. The minor *shirk* is more a sin of hypocrisy or doubt, *al-riya*. If a Muslim wishes to meet his God, he is admonished to do good deeds and to avoid this *shirk*. The hidden *shirk* is 'even more hidden than an ant on a black background in the dead of night'—that is, it is committed unknowingly or unintentionally and may be forgiven by God.

While the *kuffar* are despised in Wahhabi eyes, they are not to be regarded with as much abhorrence as the *mushrikun* who, knowing the *sirat al-mustaqim* or 'straight path', have denied *tauhid*. There were, however, a number of people who fell under the term of *kuffar* and who deserve mention because of the religious and political ramifications of such a label in the twentieth century. They included those who likened anything to God's creation, who said their religion was from Gabriel, who set the religion of *kufr* over that of Muhammad, who hated or scorned Islam, who practised sorcery, who helped the *kuffar* against the Muslims, who did not deny to the unbeliever his unbelief, who did not swear loyalty to the *imam al-muslimin*, who lived by a non-religious order rather than by a religiously sanctioned order, who lived in a land of *kufr* when they could have immigrated to *balad al-muslimin* and, finally, those Muslims who either assisted or defected to *kuffar* in active opposition to the Muslims.[31]

The above descriptions of *tauhid*, *shirk* and *kufr*, which have been based on collections of Wahhabi texts, do not seem at first to be so distinct from descriptions of other Islamic groups, and there are Quranic verses which support many of the Wahhabi beliefs. Many other Wahhabi writings are innocuously addressed to regulations regarding the mundane but essential affairs of daily life: divorce, marriage, buying and selling, alms, usury and public sanitation. A further review of their literature, however, reveals several points of interest. There is a considerable, even extreme, importance placed on the meaning of *tauhid* and *shirk*, the communal obligations of Muslims in regard to obedience to a legitimate political authority, and the political implications of *zakat, hijra, jihad, fitna* and types of secession from Islam. There are also lengthy discussions concerning which religious scholars and Islamic groups are to be included, or rather excluded, from the true Islamic community.

The criteria underlying Muhammad b. Abd al-Wahhab's doctrines led the Wahhabis to view themselves exclusively as the truly guided Islamic community. In one of the early letters of Muhammad b. Abd al-Wahhab, he pointedly quotes the Prophet as saying that there would be seventy-three Islamic sects formed, of which only one would survive. When asked which one, the Prophet had replied, 'Those who are like me and my Companions on the Day of the Last Judgement'.[32] The narrow limitation of what were to be valid criteria for religious interpretation and the literal understanding of the Quran and Sunna texts led to a strict conservatism in the Wahhabi movement. The road to the knowledge of faith for Abd al-Wahhab included only the Quran, six collections of the *hadith*—especially al-Muslim and al-Bukhari—and two collections of *tafsir* or 'interpretations' by Ibn Kathir and al-Baghawi.[33] The Wahhabis did not accept *taqlid* and *qiyas* as unquestionable methods of interpretation, but later they reinstituted *ijtihad* and accepted the *ijma* of the first three generations of Islam. It was this stress on the purity of the early Islamic community that led to the Wahhabi emphasis on *bida*, 'innovation', both in a material and in a non-material sense, as a method of evaluation. Anything that deviated from the Quran and the Sunna was *bida* and therefore unlawful.

In their search for the knowledge of Islam, the Wahhabis emphasised the exclusive nature of the pure Muslim community which, by implication of textual interpretation, was as important an element of *dawa ila tauhid* as any acts performed by individuals towards that end. The whole idea of obeying God as a collectivity was stressed in Wahhabi texts.[34] Loyalty to the *umma* superseded all other social bonds and all who joined *al-wahhabiya* were significantly called *ikhwan* or Brethren. When the idea of membership in an exclusive and rightly guided movement is coupled with the extreme emphasis on *tauhid* and the broad inclusive definition of *shirk*[35] that the Wahhabis held, the consequences are not unpredictable. The major *shirk* included such acts as votive offerings, participation in certain festivals, saint and tomb worship, supplicating for intercession or help from anyone but God[36]—even the Prophet himself—and the erection of *qubbas* or domes over mosques, many of which were practised to a greater or lesser extent by most Muslims. Anyone who was guilty of even the most insignificant transgression was labelled a *mushrik*, however much he might profess himself to be a good Muslim, and was liable to be censured by the Wahhabis. Many Shiite and Sunni communities received this appellation.

The Wahhabi *Dawa* in Poetry

There is more than a little evidence that the Wahhabi *dawa* evolved under different phases of Al Saud rule in response to the social and political climate of the Arabian Peninsula. The general dissatisfaction concerning conditions in Najd has been expressed not only in Wahhabi writings and historical works, but can also be found in poetry. The first poetry praising the Shaikh appeared as far away as Yaman recited by Muhammad al-Sanan. Later, when an unstable political void had been created in Najd and eastern Arabia because of the Egyptian conquest of 1818, another poet, Ibn Musharraf, appeared in al-Ahsa. He described the anarchy and terror that reigned among the people and asked why the torch of unity was dead. Two other poets, Sulaiman b. Sahman, who defended the ideals of his fellow Arabians against the foreign penetration, and Ibn Uthaimin, who wrote of the political struggle between Abd al-Aziz (II) Al Saud and his enemies in the Peninsula during the early twentieth century also appeared.[37]

Altogether these three poets produced more than 13,000 verses in which are discerned three key subjects: *tauhid*, attributes of *kuffar* and Muslims, and the political and social situation. *Tauhid* occupies the place of most importance in the poetry of Ibn Musharraf and Sahmān who both use the technique of repetition so much so that their copious works can be condensed to a few lines. Sahmān in particular mentions *tauhīd* in 42 *qasīdas* or over 5,431 verses. Ibn Musharraf lived at a time when no printing presses existed and in eastern Arabia where the atmosphere was heavily influenced by a large Shiite population who were against the Wahhabi *dawa*. Sahmān, a contemporary of Abd al-Aziz b. Abd al-Rahman Al Saud, lived in an equally turbulent period when he was to witness the re-establishment of the *dawa* and the unification of the Peninsula under new political forces.

As in the Wahhabi religious texts, the central theme of *dawa* poetry was *shirk* and the attributes by which one is identified as a *mushrik* or a *kafir*. Similarly, the poetry stressed the value of *hijra* and the need to cleanse the Peninsula of its decadence.[38] This poetry can be seen to be as much a reaction to foreign interference and a consequence of social disunity as it is a theological statement, as Bakri Shaikh Amin, who has studied the poetry of the Arabian Peninsula, has noted.

> There is no doubt that those who do not rule according to the revelation of God are like those who submit to the Ottomans even though in outward respects they are believers. It [expressions of the Wahhabi *dawa* in poetry] appears really that it is an attack on Ottoman rule.[39]

This statement is further supported by the following quotation from a collection of Wahhabi writings which attributes *fitna* or 'civil discord' in the Arabian Peninsula specifically to the Ottomans and Egyptians.

> Among those who helped him [Shaikh Muḥammad b. 'Abd al-Wahhāb] in the *da'wa* were the Imām Muḥammad b. Sa'ūd and his children and his brothers. They got stronger and killed those who were against them . . . . All the people of Najd and the Jazīra —badu and settled—entered and bound themselves to this religion. The Islamic *da'wa* was observed along with its laws and duties. They remained in peace and safety. Suddenly a fateful punishment from around them occurred which was the result of rebellion . . . . The *fitna* [sedition] which came to them was the sedition of Turkish and Egyptian soldiers and its helpers and supporters. The Islamic order was scattered. The *munāfiqūn* [hypocrites] now declared their belief and returned to *shirk* and *kufr* . . . . This is temporary *kufr* and not original *kufr*. They should be treated like the people of the *ridda*, but they are not completely *kufr* because some kept to the duties and laws of Islam. Also some *kuffār* were among the lawful. They did not leave the *milla* [Islamic community].[40]

As has been indicated, unity of the *umma* was sacrosanct. This unity was believed to be strongest under a true Islamic ruler to whom all Muslims should submit. The Al Saud had been given the stamp of legality by the Wahhabis and, moreover, their continued opposition to foreign powers earned them a permanent place in the poetry of the *dawa*. Ibn Musharraf praised Faisal b. Turki Al Saud while Sahmān and Uthaimin praised Abd al-Aziz b. Abd al-Rahman Al Saud. A Saudi Imam was variously termed the *imam al-huda*, Imam of Guidance; *amir al-muslimin*, Amir of the Believers; *imam al-muslimin*, Imam of the Muslims; *imam al-islam*, Imam of Islam; and *husam al-din*, Sword of the Religion.[41] The Saudi leaders were eulogised for their nobility and faith, and because they raised the banner of *jihad* against foreign domination and impurities of the religion. From the destruction of Diriya in 1818 to the unification of Central Arabia under Abd al-Aziz, most historians restricted themselves to the wars of the *umara*, 'amirs', although the poets of the *dawa* continued to praise the Saudi amirs and urged them to cleanse the Peninsula of its flaws and to save all true believers. Shaikh Muhammad b. Abd al-Wahhab was seen as the architect of the *dawa*, the Al Saud as the engineers, and the people of Najd received special praise for their continued support and propagation of *al-wahhabiya*. One traveller in Arabia, in fact, was told that all people outside Najd were in the *balad al-kuffar* or the Country of the Unbelievers.[42] The home district of the Al Saud, al-Arid, was noted to have the most fanatical and devout Wahhabis, and its *ulama* were considered the most uncompromising and severe.

The Wahhabi *Jihad* Against *Shirk* and *Kufr*

The preceding sections have been devoted primarily to a discussion of some of the major tenets of Wahhabiism. It now remains to be seen how these theological concepts were translated into actual behaviour patterns with social and political consequences. All of the literature on Central Arabia in the last three centuries has recorded the extreme antipathy shown by the Wahhabis to foreigners, Shiites and certain non-Wahhabi Sunni Muslims. This same literature has shown that the term *jihad*, loosely translated in the West as 'holy war', was in current usage among the Wahhabi Ikhwan of Najd. Unfortunately, this term has been used more often for emotive effect rather than with scholarly intent, so that any understanding of this phenomenon and its peculiar manifestations in Central Arabia has been obfuscated. This section concentrates on the relation of *jihad* to Wahhabi doctrine in order that the historical events of the early twentieth century, especially those motivated by Arab and Islamic ideals, may be understood as emanating from and justified by a system of beliefs, logical and consistent within itself.

Jihad has frequently been translated as a 'holy war', by which is meant 'a military war sanctified by religious rationale'. This definition, however, emerges from a more fundamental and abstract concept which means 'to endeavour, strive, exert' and only in its most narrow sense means 'to struggle or wage a holy war'. It is easy to see that these definitions are not mutually exclusive. Ideally, a Muslim should strive for spiritual enlightenment in all his activities, not the least of which is war; conversely, a person may figuratively wage war with such non-military weapons as words. A Muslim may therefore 'strive' in both an abstract and a concrete sense throughout his daily life. As a member of the Islamic community, he struggles for an internal spiritual reform in the path of God against the profane aspects of his human existence while at the same time waging an external struggle against those who oppose his goal or the well-being of his religion. It is precisely this abstract quality, inherent in the verb *jahada* and its derivatives, that has resulted in variant interpretations of the same Quranic verse.[43] Ibn Taimiya, who influenced Wahhabi thought, also recognised this duality of meaning.

> It [*jihad*] includes all kinds of worship, apparent and hidden, because it takes in the love of God, sincerity to him, trust in him, surrendering of the soul and property to him, patience and abstinence, remembering the name of God, and all kinds of actions. It includes all activities . . . by a person or by the *umma*.[44]

Although some groups in Islam, such as the Ahmadi, as well as modern apologists deny the legitimacy of *jihad* as a military struggle, theoretically it was considered an incumbent duty for individuals and for the *umma*, as Ibn Taimiya also noted above, until everyone could be counted as within the *dar al-islam*. In the earliest Suras of the Quran tolerance by the Muslims of other social groups had been encouraged, but this gradually changed so that fighting was permitted if the Muslim *umma* was attacked, and then Muslims were allowed to fight so long as it was not one of the four sacred months of Islam. Eventually, Muslims were not only allowed but encouraged to attack, irrespective of previous limitations.[45] Obviously the duty of *jihad* was curtailed after the dissolution of the Muslim Empire into independent Islamic states around the tenth century. It continued, however, to be recognised by individual Islamic sects as one of the pillars of Islam, its performance considered as meritorious as fasting and prayer.

A warrior, *mujahid*, who dies for the cause of his religion is given ample reward by God. He is known as a *shahid*, 'witness, martyr', and accorded great honour on earth and in *al-janna* or Heaven. The Quran states that when such a person dies, having striven with his wealth or his person, he is immediately admitted to Heaven, circumventing both the interrogation by the two angels and the fires designed to test his righteousness.[46] Ibn Taimiya states that the 'death of the martyr for the unification of all people in the cause of God and for his word is the happiest, best, easiest, and most virtuous of all deaths'.[47] The Wahhabis believed that *jihad* alone would be able to rid the Peninsula of its ignorance and moral decay. Death in these battles offered the greatest means of obtaining happiness. Those who fought the *mushrikun* were rewarded[48] while 'those who abandon *jihad* and involve themselves in *fitna* please the devil with this deception'.[49]

Jihad is most often thought to be directed against non-Muslims, although the Wahhabis generally directed their antipathies against so-called apostates or secessionist sects from Islam. They frequently quoted the Quranic sayings: '*Fitna* is a greater sin than *killing*'[50] and 'Fight them until there is no dissension and religion belongs entirely to Allah'.[51] *Fitna* may be considered simply as a 'civil disturbance' or more strongly as a 'doctrinal difference or schism which endangers the unity of Islam'. Every man guilty of *bida* or 'innovation' in the religion, whether of a non-material or of a material nature, may also be regarded as an instigator of *fitna*. Muhammad b. Abd al-Wahhab felt that *fitna* was a great threat to the unity of the religion and he abjured all his followers that 'an oppressive Sultan [ruler] was better than continuous *fitna*' in order that the *umma* would at least remain united.[52] The earlier discussion of *tauhid* and *shirk* showed that he included many groups, even Sunni Muslims, as *mushrikun* liable to *jihad*. A passage quoted earlier from the Wahhabi texts states that it was an incumbent duty for the believers to wage war against *kuffar*, hypocrites and badu tribes known for their hypocrisy even though many tribes already considered themselves Muslims. In another epistle entitled 'Is Mecca a Country of *Kufr* or Not?', the Wahhabi

Shaikh Hamad b. Atiq condemned the two Holy Cities of Islam for *shirk*.

> Praying to the *ka'ba* or to prophets and saints; harlotry; usury; and the various types of oppression and ignorance of the Sunna are *bid'a* against the Qur'ān and are to be found in the land of *shirk*. Even the person of meanest intelligence knows that this country is judged to be condemned as a land of *kufr* and *shirk* especially if they [its inhabitants] show hostility to the people of *tauḥīd* and are doing their best to eliminate them from the lands of Islam . . . . This *shirk* does not come from the people of the town. It is said that this comes from pride or ignorance . . . . *Shirk* remained because of 'Amr b. Luḥayy.[53]

Abd al-Aziz also expressed a similar opinion regarding the *mushrikun* of Mecca which is quite startling.

> Why, if you English were to offer me one of your daughters to wife, I would accept her, making only the condition that any children resulting from the marriage should be Moslems. But I would not take of the daughters of the Sharif or of the people of Mecca or other Moslems whom we reckon as *mushrikîn*. I would eat of meat slain by Christians without question. Ay, but it is the *mushrik*, he who associates others in worship with God, that is our abomination. As for Christians and Jews, they are 'people of the book'.[54]

Jihad against believers can be divided into three categories—*murtadd* (pl. *murtaddun*) or apostates, *baghi* (pl. *bughat*) or 'dissenters', and *al-muharib* (pl. *muharibun*) or 'secessionists'—which are of relevance here. The *jihad* against apostasy or *al-ridda* includes all those who as individuals or groups turned their backs on Islam, separating themselves from it although not necessarily with the intention of joining the *dar al-harb*. A *murtadd* must either return to Islam or suffer the consequences of *jihad*. *Bughat*, however, are dissenters although they do not renounce the authority of the Imam. As long as they do not attack the head of the Muslim *umma*, the Khalifa or Imam, they remain in the *dar al-islam* but are still liable to *jihad* in order that the unity of the community may be maintained. The *baghi* is not liable to death, nor his property to confiscation.[55] The *muharibun* are those who commit disorders or desert from the Islamic community and they may be punished by death, crucifixion, amputation of hands and feet or banishment. Punishment of each category is determined according to the individual case and to the school of Islamic law which sits in judgement.

The Wahhabis, however, took an uncompromising, radical and indiscriminating attitude to these categories. Any Muslim who, for whatever reason, fell into conflict with their interpretation of Islam or challenged their authority was generally considered to be a *kafir murtadd*, and was liable to the severest sanctions, although these were not clearly defined. During the years 1910 to 1930 the Wahhabis, particularly the Ikhwan, advanced from Central Arabia towards the peripheries of the Peninsula. Utilising large-scale hit-and-run tactics against the badu and pitched battle against fortified towns, the Ikhwan brought large geographical areas under the administrative control of the Al Saud and the religious imperatives of *al-wahhabiya*. They demanded the unequivocal payment of *zakat* in order to seal the allegiance of these populations to Najd authorities. Those refusing *zakat* payment were liable to *jihad* despite the fact that in many cases they were Sunni Muslims.[56] In Central Arabia, *zakat* essentially became a contract, sanctified by religion, between the people and the state. The government became God's representative on earth and, hence, refusal to pay *zakat* was tantamount to rejecting Islam and its legal representatives on earth. Moreover, Ikhwan frequently treated these people as unbelievers and did not hesitate to kill them. Because they firmly believed that the reward of a warrior slain in battle was *al-janna*, they attacked with little regard to life or limb and the consequent death toll sometimes numbered thousands. The following extracts from Muhammad b. Abd al-Wahhab's son, Abdullah, deserve to be quoted at some length because they succinctly state the religious rationale for much of the political activity of the Ikhwan during the twentieth century.

> *Battling with any sect of Muslims who deny the obligations of the Sharī'a.*
>
> Contemplate the words 'God have mercy upon you' and what the statement contains because it is this which has influence. Visiting places and the domes over tombs found in many countries are the greatest *shirk* which the polytheists perform.

There are many *mushrikūn* because of al-Lāt, al-Uzzā, and Manāt and they are among the greatest of the people of *shirk* because they perform the deeds of the polytheists and observe their path identically. Contemplate his words 'The *shirk* takes possession over most souls because of the manifestation of ignorance and the concealment of *'ilm*! . . .'

Shaikh Taqī al-Dīn [Ibn Taimiya] was asked about the battle of the Tatars and the observance of the two *shahādas* when they [Tatars] claimed to be followers of the principles of Islam. He said all sects who constantly refuse the obligations of the revealed laws of Islam, either from those people [Tatars] or from others, must be fought [by true Muslims] until they observe the divine law even though they may utter the two *shahādas* and observe some of the laws just as Abū Bakr with the Companions fought those who refused to pay *zakāt* . . . . Ten precepts were established from the Prophet concerning the secessionists and the order to go out and fight them and he [the Prophet] said about them that they were the most evil of creation: 'You will despise your prayers with their prayers and your fast from their fast'. It is known that mere refuge in Islam without observation of its laws does not mean that you may fail to go out and fight because it is an incumbent duty until all of the religion is invested in God. There should be no *fitna* [sedition]. When religion applies to something other than God then fighting is obligatory. Whichever sect refrains from some of the prayers, or obligatory duties, or fasting or *hajj*, or the obligation of prohibitions—wine, fornication, gambling, adultery, and all that is forbidden—or they refuse the duty of the *jihād* against the *kuffār* or the imposition of the *jizya* tax upon the People of the Book or anything else concerning the obligations of the religion, then they are a *kāfir* for there is no excuse for anybody to deviate. Verily, you must fight dissenting sects even if they admit to it [to be Muslims], and I know that the *'ulamā* do not dispute this point. The only disagreement concerning the dissenting sect is when they declare a deviation to some precepts such as the dawn prostrations or the call to prayer and so forth.

As for the obligations and what is forbidden, there is no argument among the *'ulamā* about fighting over these tenets as they are not to be regarded in the same way as the *bughāt al-khārijīn* concerning [their opposition to the authority of] an Imam or the *khārijīn* concerning its submissiveness like the people of Syria with the *amīr al-mu'minīn* 'Alī b. Abū Ṭālib. Those people are dissenters against obeying an appointed Imam in order to get rid of his rule, but those whom we have talked about are actually rebels against Islam in the same way as those who refuse [to pay] *zakāt* like the *khawārij* whom Abū Ṭālib fought. Therefore there was a difference in his method of fighting the people of Basra and Syria and his fighting of the people of Nahrawān. The real dissenters are those who have dissented from Islam and refused the *zakāt*. His method with the people of Basra and Syria was rather like the way of a brother to another brother, but to the real *khawārij* it was otherwise. Texts which have come down from the Prophet have established what the *ijmā'* of the Companions decided concerning the fighting of Abū Bakr with those who refused *zakāt* and 'Alī's fight with the *khawārij*.[57]

Battling of those persistent backsliders after investigations have proved he is a backslider.

Contemplate the first and last words and contemplate the words concerning one who worships a prophet or a saint saying 'Oh my lord, help me'. If he asks to be granted repentance and if he repents, then it is alright, but if not he must be killed. You will find him clearly an unbeliever in the *ahl al-shirk* and you must kill them after they ask for repentance and after a further case has been established against them. Those who excessively praise a Prophet or a pious man and make him some kind of divinity which means that he has reckoned this [him] as God and he seeks him in worship and in prayers, and in fear and in glory, and in extolling. If he claims he does not want anything but intercession, this is what the first *mushrikūn* sought . . . .

If a sacrifice is made to any other than God, it is *muḥarram* [forbidden]. If one said *bismi'llāh* [in the name of God] before the sacrifice and pronounced it as a hypocrite and if these people were *murtaddūn*, their sacrifice would not be acceptable . . . There is joined in this sacrifice two forbidden things and this is what they do in Mecca and other places in regard to killing.

Observe the words that anyone in the *umma* who sacrifices to anyone but God is a *kāfir murtadd* [an unbelieving apostate] and his sacrifice is not permitted because he has included two forbidden acts: he is a *murtadd* and he has worshipped someone but God.[58]

It must be stressed that the Wahhabis saw themselves not only as truly guided Muslims, but also as participants in a social movement so revolutionary that it demanded a complete reinterpretation of social values. The form of monotheism which it stressed affected every aspect of social life, including major changes in patterns of settlement, acceptance of political authority, regulations of daily life, and economic exchange relationships. As adherents themselves of one of the four orthodox *madhhab*s, the Wahhabis were paradoxically forced to break the existing unity of the *umma*, resorting even to armed force against other Muslim groups, in order to open the door for reform activity and recreate a new social order as they saw it. Both as a religious movement and in its implications for other aspects of life, the extreme position of *al-wahhabiya* caused it to become a symbol for all analogous movements in modern Islam. In the last two centuries, its stance on lawful political authority and Islamic governments led it to direct many of its activities against non-Arab, non-Muslim and especially 'unlawful' Islamic leaders. This was to have serious consequences for the development of Saudi Arabia and neighbouring governments in the twentieth century, as will be seen in Part II in the discussion of Saudi Arabia's boundary disputes with Iraq and Kuwait.

Imara and *Ilm*: The Alliance of the Al Saud and Al Wahhab

In 1744 Muhammad b. Abd al-Wahhab found protection in Diriya under the ruling Amir, Muhammad b. Saud, thereafter forming with him an alliance sealed on the same oath as that which had allied the Prophet and the people of al-Madina.[59] The Shaikh promised that political success would reward the Al Saud if they remained true to the principles of *tauhid*; Muhammad, for his part, agreed to accept the responsibilities of an Islamic ruler. Although Muhammad b. Abd al-Wahhab himself was deeply involved in all aspects of religion, war and politics, his descendants have become more generally renowned for their involvement in religious affairs, while the Al Saud have firmly established their control in the political arena.

This separation of temporal power (*imara*) and religious authority (*ilm*) is not, however, clearly defined. In the period preceding the alliance, Saudi leaders styled themselves as shaikhs (*shuyukh*) or amirs (*umara*), titles with no religious significance. During Muhammad b. Saud's rule, however, the Wahhabi *dawa* was articulated and the succeeding years were characterised by wars of religious intent. Anyone accepting Saudi authority was a Muslim; anyone resisting was a *murtadd* and liable to *jihad*. Saudi leaders were hereafter known as Imams, a title which had implicit rights among Muslims with regard to obedience to lawful Islamic authorities and to divine law, as will be seen. They called their state an Imamate.[60]

Frequent inter-marriage between the Saud and Wahhab families further strengthened the alliance, although its benefits proved to be particularly advantageous for the Al Saud. Traditionally, members of the Al Wahhab have been accorded an almost automatic prestige because of their descent from the Shaikh and because the family has produced a number of well-known religious scholars since his death. The descendants of Muhammad b. Abd al-Wahhab have, in fact, become known as the family of Al Shaikh. The respect associated with the Al Wahhab, however, is limited in the sense that the family never held *imara* or temporal authority. When the Shaikh died in 1792 his family was bankrupt, whereas the personal wealth of the Al Saud was tied to the public treasury until 1933. After the death of Muhammad b. Abd al-Wahhab the family acted only as advisers to the government and religious leaders, generally remaining a conservative force within the country, in contrast to the Al Saud who, bridging the world of temporal and religious authority, were forced to confront the realities of domestic and foreign problems, thus becoming a more liberal force. Many of the reigning Al Saud could boast that they were descendants on their mothers' side of the Al Wahhab and were thus inheritors, albeit by birth alone, of whatever prestige was associated with them, while on their fathers' side they came from an outstanding lineage of politicians and warriors.

It is understandable that a movement so pragmatic, fundamentalist and dogmatic as *al-wahhabiya* did not develop any political theory. There is almost nothing in the Wahhabi religious texts concerning questions of temporal authority, such as the office of Imam, statecraft, political theory of the Islamic state or practical issues of government. While the supportive role of the Al Saud in the initial revival of the purity of Islam is acknowledged, their hereditary accession to the Imamate seems to be taken for granted. The Wahhabis directed their concern to the immediate problems of daily life, such as marriage, divorce, taxation, usury and public sanitation; and to the exposition of their doctrine, particularly *tauhid*. These were logical concerns for a young community anxious to emphasise its identity. A few basic precepts formed the foundation from which certain political conclusions were inevitable.

Whether as the Imam of the Muslims, Imam of Islam or Amir of the Believers, a Saudi ruler was not simply a secular authority, but ostensibly the representative of God and His divine law on Earth. His position as Imam was therefore given religious validity and, as earlier sections have indicated, the Wahhabis believed the Imam to be legitimate only as long as he continued to support the Islamic community. Within the objectives of Islamic law, the authority of an Imam over the Islamic community was absolute and, although he might delegate responsibility, he retained the powers of veto, the negotiation of foreign relations, the sanctioning of members of the community and the arbitration of disputes. The unity of the community was of paramount importance even if its cost was obedience to an unjust Imam; moreover, the Wahhabis believed that there was no community without the Imam. Most important, the Wahhabi Imam acknowledged the incumbent duty of *jihad*, for the organisation and execution of which he was entirely responsible. The following extract from Wahhabi texts is significant. *Jihad* here specifically refers to those who had left the Islamic community rather than signifying a war against infidels.

> There is no Islam except in congregation and there is no community except the Imamate . . . . You know that the affairs of the Muslims cannot be managed unless there is an Imam. It cannot be said that religious goals are completed unless they are in conformity with the Islamic pillars. The rules of the Qur'ān do not appear except to the congregation and the Imamate. There will be no Sharī'a except this one. Whoever knows the lawful foundations, knows the necessity of people and their need for religion . . . . They [Muslims generally] persevered and carried out the *jihād* with every Imam as it has been recorded in the tenets of the people of the Sunna and of the necessity of going out against those who had left the community and their

persons and property were lawful . . . . *Jihād* goes with every Imam and that is well-known and is one of the pillars of Islam and this cannot be denied.[61]

The Wahhabi community did not elect the Imam; the Imam, ever since Muhammad b. Saud, chose his own successor who was called the *wali al-ahd* or, literally, The One to Whom the Covenant is Entrusted. Traditionally, it seems that the Imam retained the actual sovereignty of the state while delegating the command of military forces to his designated successor, usually a son or brother. Thus Muhammad b. Saud entrusted the military command to his son Abd al-Aziz (I), as Abd al-Aziz (I) later did to Saud (II), and Saud (II) to Abdullah (I). In the nineteenth century Turki appointed Faisal to this position and, upon Faisal's accession to the Imamate, he appointed Abdullah (II). Abd al-Aziz (II) in the twentieth century returned from exile to reconquer al-Riyad and, although he retained the actual authority of the Saudi state, his father, Abd al-Rahman, was the Imam. When they were old enough Abd al-Aziz's sons, Saud and Faisal, frequently represented their father in military campaigns while he remained in al-Riyad.

Each Saudi leader was officially installed in the Imamate after tribal and urban leaders had sworn an oath of loyalty, *baia*, to him. The *baia* was also required of other members of the Al Saud in order to minimise any potential disagreement over succession.[62] Unfortunately, this was not always possible and there were periods when internecine strife, termed *fitna* by the Wahhabi shaikhs, left the Saudi state vulnerable. During the late nineteenth century the Imamate of Abdullah (II) b. Faisal was successfully challenged by his brother, Saud (II) b. Faisal, ultimately leading to the downfall of the second major period of Saudi rule. The following letter from Shaikh Abd al-Latif to the Ikhwan is quoted at length because it gives an insight not only into this period of time but, more importantly, into the attitudes of the Wahhabis generally to the authority of the Imam and the Imamate and to the legitimacy of Al Saud rule.

I have been the subject of much imposition and curses. People are complaining of *fitna* [sedition] and the first of these things is the separation of Sa'ūd from the Muslim community and his going out against his brother [Imam Abdullah]. We have sent out a refutation to him . . . Qur'ānic and Prophetic sayings all forbid his actions and those who helped him [Saud]. Muḥammad b. Faiṣal [brother of Saud and Abdullah] is imprisoned [by Saud because he supported Abdullah]. 'Abdullāh has escaped and his relatives and his *anṣār* [supporters] have left him . . . . Sa'ūd came to us and with him were the al-'Ujmān and al-Dawāsir and the people of Far' and al-Ḥarīq and al-Aflāj and the people of the Wādī. We, however, are few and weak. There is not in our town anyone who would reach forty fighters.[63] I went out to him and did my best and I defended the Muslims as far as I could. Among those who were the evil doers were the shameless townspeople who had urged him [Saud] to do that [i.e., rebel]. They were imputing *kufr* to a number of the heads of our town. Some of the badu announced their association with 'Abdullāh b. Faisal. Let God guard us from *fitna* and be kind to us. He [Saud] entered it [the town] after a pledge . . . . He came in possession of the *wilāya* [government] by conquest. His orders were valid. There had to be obedience to him. His good orders had to be obeyed like it has always been by the people of learning through the ages. His *kufr* was not proven to me so I walked in the footsteps of the *ahl al-'ilm* [people of learning] and took them as an example in the obedience to leave the *fitna* and all the evil that has happened to the religion and the world.

Whoever finds this difficult then let him refer to the books of *ijmā'* such as Ibn Ḥazm and Ibn Hubaira and those of the Ḥanbalites and others. I did not think this would be concealed from anyone who had the least sense. It is said that an oppressive Sultan is better than a continuous *fitna*. As to the Imam 'Abdullāh, I advised him as already mentioned. After he [Saud] came and repulsed the partisans of 'Abdullāh, he [Abdullah] came back from al-Aḥsā. I reminded him of the advice I had given him and recited verses from the Qur'ān. I advised him to keep a long distance from his enemies and the enemies of his religion, that is *shirk, ta'ṭīl*,[64] and *kufr*. He showed repentance and sorrow. Sa'ūd's affairs grew weak and he went with a small portion of the Āl Murra and al-'Ujmān and 'Abdullāh achieved a victory which consolidated his *wilāya* over what had been decided from the Ḥanbalites . . . . Then we were afflicted with Sa'ūd who came to us a second time. You have already heard of his victory over 'Abdullāh and his troops so that he [Abdullah] passed through the district defeated. He could not get refuge with anybody. I feared the desert people and I quickly wrote a letter to Sa'ūd seeking safety for the people of the town [because they had accepted Abdullah?] and to stop the desert people bothering them. I myself started repulsing the badu with a small number of the townspeople hoping to please God. He [Saud] entered the town and 'Abdullāh went north. Victory was again with Sa'ūd and in his hands and the rule goes with its defects.

After the death of Sa'ūd the raiders came. Among them were the wandering badu and the oppressive *ḥaḍar*. We feared there would be conflict, atrocities, and the shedding of blood in the *ḥamūla* of Āl Muqrin [ancestral name for the Al Saud] with the absence of 'Abdullāh. I did not give him the *bai'a* nor even write to him. Those who were with him were evil. Each man who mentioned him [Abdullah]. feared for himself and his goods. Would it be good to leave the Muslims to be plundered by the evil nomadic badu and be taken prisoners of war when they did, in fact, talk about plundering al-Riyāḍ before the pledge of loyalty? Would they not be more evil and oppressive than 'Abd al-Raḥmān [youngest brother of Abdullah, Saud, and Muhammad; father of King Abd al-Aziz (II)]. It is not possible to turn them back. Who can imagine that I and people like me are able to repulse that with my weakness and lack of authority....

Who knows the fundamentals of religion and *fiqh* and what can he achieve from good deeds and the repulsing of evil ones? One does not talk on a high plane with stupid and senseless people. We only talk to judges and muftis and those who are concerned with doing good to people in general and protecting the Sharī'a. Good things will not be achieved by those who are just waiting as it would to those who it is a duty to obey only the Imamate.

It happened that the *ḥamūla* of Āl Sa'ūd had hostility, enmity, and hatred amongst them. Each one reckoned his own precedence for the *wilāya*. We were expecting every day a *fitna* and every hour a trial. Ibn Jilūwī went out from the town and he killed Ibn Ṣunaitān. It fell to me to interfere in the attempt of 'Abd al-Raḥmān to make peace and to leave the *wilāya* to his brother, 'Abdullāh. My effort did not achieve that although I had done a lot of that effort during the period of his governorship until four days before 'Abdullāh arrived when he

> [Abd al-Rahman] agreed to put forward 'Abdullāh and remove himself seeing that he [Abdullah] has the right, and is more appropriate because of age, and his Imamate is older as well. When Imam 'Abdullāh arrived in our place, I strove that Muḥammad b. Faiṣal would go out to his brother and would come with an *amān* of safe conduct for 'Abd al-Raḥmān and his people and the people of the town. In spite of all my efforts, when I went to greet him, suddenly there were the Far' and the *jāhil* of the desert. Those hypocrites with him were asking him to plunder our *nakhl* [date palms] and our goods, but I saw a change in him and sadness. After this he showed nobility and lenience. His repentance was true, . . . he showed me humility, and I swore him upon the book of the Sunna.[65]

The attitudes concerning the Imam and Imamate in Abd al-Latif's letter are not strict rules reasoned through or compiled by the Wahhabi shaikhs. They are rather opinions expressed by the leading scholars which arose as circumstances necessitated third-party arbitration. It is clear from this letter that the Wahhabis understood *fitna* to mean 'secession from' or 'disorder in' the Islamic community. *Fitna* was to be avoided whatever the cost. Thus Saud was given the oath of allegiance by the Najd leaders and *ulama* after he had successfully taken the Imamate by force, even though he was initially condemned for his actions against his brother, Imam Abdullah. When Saud died and Abd al-Rahman attempted to claim the Imamate, he was encouraged to return the leadership to the eldest brother, Imam Abdullah, because Abdullah 'has the right, and he is more appropriate because of age, and his Imamate is older', and, no doubt, because another period of *fitna* was envisaged.

The Al Saud placed tremendous importance on the right of the Imam to choose his successor irrespective of periods of *fitna* within the family itself because the validity of their rule could most easily be rationalised on the basis of hereditary rights. Moreover, the Al Saud were acutely aware that their claims to political authority over Central Arabia specifically and Muslims generally were closely linked with the success of the Wahhabi *dawa* and its support of their hereditary claims, as Abd al-Aziz himself was to express.

> I, Ibn Sa'oud, what do I want? Two things are essential to our State and our people, two fundamental things: religion and the

rights inherited from our fathers. To these add two things, which are deemed essential in these days: right relationship with the foreigner and right understanding among ourselves.[66]

Abd al-Aziz included the last two factors because the twentieth century had created a unique historical context. The expansion of Saudi authority into Muslim areas unsympathetic to Wahhabi doctrine and, in particular, the conquest of al-Hijaz produced outcries from Islamic communities throughout the world who feared the administrative control of a Wahhabi Imam over the two Holy Cities of Mecca and al-Madina. This must undoubtedly have been a major factor in Abd al-Aziz's decision to abandon the title of Imam in favour of Sultan and later of King,[67] titles which reflected a series of political contexts leading to the emergence of a 'nation-state'.

As has been mentioned previously, Abd al-Aziz has been variously referred to as Abu Turki by the badu, Ibn Saud and *shuyukh* by non-Najdis, and Imam, especially by the people of Central Arabia. During his period of expansion and consolidation in the early 1900s he was called the Amir of Najd and Chief of its Tribes (*amir najd wa rais al-ashair*). It was said, however, that he did not like the title amir because he was then equated with all other amirs of towns and small regions. He preferred the title *hakim* or 'governor'. On 22 August 1921 he was proclaimed Sultan of Najd, a secular title subsequently changed in 1922 to Sultan of Najd and its Dependencies after he had annexed Jabal Shammar and the Amirate of Aid in Tihama. When al-Hijaz fell in 1926, Abd al-Aziz took the title of King of al-Hijaz, and became King of al-Hijaz, Najd and its Dependencies on 19 January 1927. He called for the unification of his country on 22 September 1932, turning it into the Kingdom of Saudi Arabia, and four days later he was proclaimed King of Saudi Arabia. It is noteworthy that the Arabic word *mulk* not only means 'supreme authority, power or sovereignty', but it is also the same word used to indicate 'right of possession, tenure or ownership'. *Mulk* is derived from the verb root *malaka*, meaning 'to exercise authority' and 'to take possession of', from which the word *malik* or 'king' is derived. The relationship of the two ideas seems to indicate that a ruler possesses rights of authority over his subjects. However, *mulk* belongs only to God and he alone gives *mulk* to earthly rulers. The term *malik* was used in the Quran only in reference to foreign rulers and its subsequent use by Muslim rulers was regarded as a form of rule contradictory to Muslim political theory. Because it was also reminiscent of pre-Islamic days, there was a traditional resistance to its adoption and, generally, it occurred only when the Khalifate was breaking down.

It is remarkable that Abd al-Aziz was proclaimed King of Saudi Arabia—the first king in Central Arabia—when earlier he had heavily criticised Grand Sharif Husain who had proclaimed himself King of the Arabs, a title subsequently reduced in scope to King of al-Hijaz. No other leaders in the Peninsula had independently made such a declaration unless, as later with King Faisal of Iraq, they were supported by Western powers. In this regard it is of particular note that the British encouraged such a policy while the French, who had abolished their own monarchy, wanted nothing to do with either the title or the man in their mandated territory of Syria following World War I. The Al Saud could hardly hope to have the legitimacy of their Imamate recognised by the diverse independent groups that comprised the Islamic world, and it is interesting that the Saudi rulers today never publicly refer to themselves as Imams. They also realised that the presence of non-Arab foreigners with tremendous political and military strength was inceasingly affecting the course of Arabian affairs. The Al Saud were therefore forced to validate their rule within Central Arabia by virtue of Wahhabi doctrine and to secure international recognition by emphasising the historical rights of their family as Arab and secular rulers and not as Wahhabi Imams. It is notable that in all treaties with the Ottomans and the British, Abd al-Aziz insisted that one of the first provisions should be the recognition of his family's historical rights and his own right to choose a successor.[68] Moreover, he was to claim that

> the territories of Najd and the Badawin world have extended as far north as Aleppo and the river Orontes in north Syria, and included the whole country on the right bank of the Euphrates from there down to Basra on the Persian Gulf[69]

and that these territories, having been formerly under Al Saud control, were now his by virtue of his hereditary rights.

The Date Palm, the Sword and the Profession of Faith

The date palm, the sword and the *shahada* or Profession of Faith are frequently represented on Saudi Arabia's flag and on other government emblems. They are symbolic of social organisation, politics and religion—separate but interlinked considerations for every Saudi ruler since the mid-eighteenth century. The numerous tribal groups, the competition for scarce resources and the strong military alliances of badu and urban populations militated against the formation of a centralised political authority which the Saudis had been striving to create.

Two major tasks confronted the Arab rulers. First, the social bonds of the tribes, extending from nomadic groups to settled inhabitants, had either to be broken or made subsidiary to another and greater loyalty which would attract the allegiance of all the tribes. The second task was to establish authority over the badu whose nomadic life-style prevented any permanent control being operated by a central government and who saw no reason to suppress any of their activities in order to support a larger state structure. Amir Abdullah of Transjordan attempted to explain to the British this dilemma confronting many Arab rulers of the Middle East.

> 1. Raiding as viewed by tribes is legitimate and the existence of each tribe within the limits of their natural boundaries gives them the right to raid any other tribe outside their boundaries.
>
> 2. Bedouin Arabs . . . took the leadership of their tribes to raid the other when quarrels between them were declared, because those tribes are in fact the soldiers of Bedouin Amirs.
>
> 3. When one of them conquers the other, the tribes of the vanquished commit themselves to the victorious Amir and unite with him and then will attack with him that Amir who had been their previous chief in their country and would not mind capturing that chief and his family. This is what happened when Mohamed Ibn Rasheed conquered all Nejd and captured Al Saud and the very same thing happened recently to Al Rasheed at the hands of Ibn Saud [Abd al-Aziz]. Such is God's law in Jazeera [Arabian Peninsula].[70]

What Amir Abdullah referred to as 'God's law in Jazeera' was something of which the Al Saud themselves were acutely conscious. During Pelly's visit to al-Riyad in 1866, he engaged in a series of conversations with Faisal b. Turki Al Saud, then the current Saudi ruler, who spoke at one meeting about 'the physical and political position of Arabia; explaining its great want to be rain. If only rain would fall agriculture would be possible, and the tribes might be rendered sedentary'.[71] Abd al-Aziz b. Abd al-Rahman Al Saud would be equally concerned in the twentieth century with rendering the tribes sedentary because, as Abd al-Aziz himself was to say, 'the trouble with the Arab is that he will not do anything in which his own interest is not paramount'.[72] A badu owed loyalty only to his tribe; a tribe owed loyalty to none but itself. Abd al-Aziz explained to the British that ruling nomadic groups had no parallel in European experience, precisely because the mobility of nomadic tribes meant that they could not be held accountable for their actions and because the badu, who did not have any vested interest in membership of a larger state structure, could withdraw their support at any time.[73]

> His family, he said, had been in Najd from time immemorial and had for centuries ruled over it without interference from outside. He himself was an Arab Chief whose views on matters of policy naturally differed from those of European Powers. Bedouin tribes are not concerned in weighing the merits of different Governments as they live as nomads, and when oppressed move off to another locality.[74]

Abd al-Aziz had also explained to the British that the badu 'are the friends of a weak Government, which lets them do as they please', particularly if they were paid an allowance. The badu, he said, only feared a powerful government. 'Draw the sword in their face and they will obey; sheathe the sword and they will ask for more pay.'[75] The first part of this statement was no doubt an oblique reference to Ottoman authority which had allowed badu to continue their traditional *ghazzus* as long as they did not encroach on the settled areas. The Ottomans thus effectively remained in control of urban areas, such as the oases in al-Ahsa, while the badu continued to disrupt the countryside, preventing economic growth and political stability.[76]

Each period of Saudi rule had initially directed its 'proselytising zeal' against urban areas and, only after some success, to the badu tribes. Abd al-Aziz, in the twentieth century, was true to this pattern. When he recaptured al-Riyad in 1901/2 and al-Ahsa in 1913, his forces were almost entirely composed of townspeople. It was not until 1916 that he began to utilise badu forces on a large scale; the Ikhwan, the militant adherents of the Wahhabi movement chiefly responsible for Saudi territorial expansion in this century, were badu. It was a tactically sound policy to gain control of the urban areas first, not only because they were militarily easier to capture and control, but also because they would later provide a framework for economic expansion and political stability. It was in their interest to support a state structure which provided a stable environment for trade through the establishment of administrative bodies and a legal system to organise exchange relationships.

Principally through the Wahhabi movement, Abd al-Aziz and previous Saudi rulers had been able to transcend tribal and urban loyalties while still using their social structure as a basis for political manipulation. Membership in the Islamic community theoretically served to equalise any social differentials and, as the tribes embraced the Wahhabi *dawa*, they accepted the Imamate of the Al Saud, a lawful state validated by Islam. This gave the Al Saud more temporal authority than the shaikhs and amirs, but Abd al-Aziz's alliance with many of the badu remained tenuous. He was to compare his alliance with the badu to the alliance of America with Europe—that is, the political alliance of a strong power with a weak one which exists at the time to fulfil specific purposes.

> America is the mother of weak nations, and we Arabs are of them . . . . A man of good sense needs but a suggestion—point the way to him, and that is sufficient . . . . It is sufficient, what America has done—what she said to the small oppressed nations—what Wilson said in her name. And the man of good sense is he who strives for himself and profits by the striving . . .
>
> I liken Europe to-day to a great iron door, but there is nothing behind it . . . . It would be strange if she [America] continued as the partner of Europe . . . . I say, that partnership of America and Europe to-day is like my partnership—the partnership of Ibn Sa'oud—with the Bedu of the North.[77]

If the Al Saud had relied upon religion to validate their authority, they did not confuse it with political expediency. The partnership of Abd al-Aziz with the badu was clearly designated by the former as one of political/military convenience. When the Ikhwan forces, composed mainly of badu tribes, began to rebel against Saudi authority in the late 1920s, Abd al-Aziz threatened them not with religion but with force, asking 'Are there not a number of you upon whose fathers' and grandfathers' necks my sword and that of my fathers and grandfathers made play?'[78]

> You people of Nejd—I do not mean by the people of Nejd those who have made a covenant with the word of God, but those who may belong to those backsliders or debauchers or those who may have associated with them or agreed to their ideas—you all know that we are your masters and descendants of your masters and that, by the will of God and the word 'unity' and the sword we are your Kings.[79]

The backsliders were those who rejected the benefits of the government—that is, the Imamate of the Al Saud—and therefore rejected Islam. Theoretically, this included all political opponents. Anyone who did not accept the legal verdict of the *ulama* and return to the allegiance with Abd al-Aziz was subject to a strict chastisement, the chastisement of the *kafir murtadd*. Even though religion sanctioned Saudi actions, it was not confused with political behaviour. This is made evident in a conversation recorded with Abd al-Aziz. When the Saudi ruler was asked whether he considered it 'a religious duty to wage war against the *mushrekin* to the end of making them Unitarians', Abd al-Aziz gave the following reply.

> 'No, no', he straightway replied, striking the carpet twice with his staff. And he continued: 'Take Al-Hasa [al-Ahsa], for instance. We have there thirty thousand of the Shi'ah, who live in peace and security. No one ever molests them. All we ask of them is not to be too demonstrative in public on their fête-days. Rest assured . . . . We are not as some people imagine us.'

Then the question was rephrased and Abd al-Aziz was asked whether he considered it 'a political duty to fight the *mushrekin* till they become religious'.

> Politics and religion are not the same. But we the people of Najd desire naught that is not sanctioned by religion. Therefore, if religion sanctions our desire, the political measures we adopt for its realization must be lawful. If politics fail, then war. And everything in war is permissible.[80]

A half-century earlier, when Pelly visited Imam Faisal Al Saud, Faisal told him, 'There is always a distinction between religious and political warfare. When the question is one of religion we kill everybody, but in politics we make exceptions.'[81] It is not, however, clear under what circumstances political behaviour in Central Arabia was religious or political. During the rule of Abd al-Aziz warfare was simply directed to the establishment of his hereditary rights even though he justified his actions with religion. Potentially powerful opponents like the Al Rashid or other members of the Al Saud were not killed, but remained under surveillance at al-Riyad where they were free to participate in the daily affairs of the *majlis*. Many men who had formerly been independent rulers were given positions of trust in the government. It is significant that, until Abd al-Aziz came to rely primarily on Ikhwan forces, there was no wholesale massacre of populations like those which later characterised the warfare of the Ikhwan in the al-Khurma and Turaba dispute in 1918, the invasion of al-Hijaz in 1924 and the extensive raids against the northern frontier in the 1920s. Women, children and the elderly, who were normally exempt in such disputes, were indiscriminately killed by the Ikhwan; and it has been recorded in numerous histories that Abd al-Aziz himself was horrified by the brutality of these attacks and was later forced to clamp down on such activities. This suggests that, although religion sanctioned Saudi political activity, it was not carried to its most logical extreme. The Al Saud, particularly Abd al-Aziz in the twentieth century, acted as a moderating force on the religious movement although dependent upon it to support Saudi rule.

Neither the Al Saud nor the Wahhabi shaikhs gave prolonged serious thought to the interaction of politics and religion except as the need arose. Abd al-Aziz said, and no doubt sincerely believed, that 'we . . . desire naught that is not sanctioned by religion' at the same time that he was saying 'by the will of God and the word "unity" and the sword we are your Kings'. If any discrepancies occurred, they were conveniently dismissed. No political theory of the Islamic state was ever created by the Wahhabis; nor was its absence ever bemoaned. Although the line separating political and religious motivations was frequently as fine as a razor's edge, this was of no consequence except when it interfered in the daily functions of the government, such as when *fitna* occurred amongst the Al Saud.

Religion and Politics in the Twentieth Century

How did the political and religious factors discussed in the earlier sections of this chapter influence Saudi political behaviour and their attitudes towards other Arab and non-Arab leaders? The Al Saud have generally been represented as pro-British and anti-Ottoman prior to World War I. A closer analysis reveals a more complex picture. The Al Saud, under Abd al-Aziz's leadership, did not recapture their ancestral home, al-Riyad, until 1901/2 and were forced to spend the next twelve years before the war consolidating their position. In 1912 the British concluded a treaty with the Turks which recognised Ottoman authority in Najd even though the Saudi ruler was in *de facto* control of this territory. The last Ottoman troops in Central Arabia had been evicted in 1906 under local pressure generated by the Al Saud. Abd al-Aziz had continued to consolidate his control after this date and, prior to World War I, had sought assurances of British help against the Ottomans. Historians have viewed this as an indication that he was anti-Ottoman. There were, indeed, many reasons why the Al Saud should oppose Ottoman rule. Foremost among them was the fact that Ottoman rule would reduce the Saudis to vassal lords, a position not likely to be accepted by a family who could say 'we feel ourselves a King every inch'.[82] The Al Saud had also harboured antipathies to the Ottoman Khalifate who had instigated Muhammad Ali's conquest of the Saudi Imamate in 1818. This had led to the deportation of the family to Egypt and the beheading of the Saudi leader in Constantinople. Subsequent Ottoman control, which had continued in al-Ahsa until 1913 when Abd al-Aziz reconquered what he felt was his hereditary right, was considered harsh. The Ottoman policy of supporting one ruler and then another had formerly kept the unity of the Arabs fragmented, but later was a source of alienation against the government. Along the fringe areas of the Ottoman Empire, a loose confederation of Arab rulers, disenchanted with Turkish authority, had begun to unite under leaders like Abd al-Aziz. Abd al-Aziz was quoted by Captain Shakespear, Political Agent in Kuwait, as having remarked that he opposed the Ottomans because they were corrupt and had subverted the Khalifate; at another meeting, he said that he could not oppose the Ottomans indefinitely because they outflanked him on both the west and the east, forcing him to request help from the British.

The reality, however, seems to be that the Al Saud did not prefer Great Britain to the Ottoman Porte, but merely saw the former as a convenient vehicle to secure the rights of their family as a ruling élite. This is supported by several facts. First, when Abd al-Aziz was refused any help by the British prior to World War I, he began to negotiate with the Ottomans because he knew he was not yet strong enough to resist them alone. A treaty, unratified because of the outbreak of the war, was found in Basra, which confers on Abd al-Aziz the Turkish title, Wali of Najd. The treaty was dated 4 Rajab 1332 (15 May 1914). Article II contained the Ottoman recognition of Saudi hereditary rights.[83]

While many people have denied the importance of this treaty or Abd al-Aziz's knowledge of its contents, the evidence is to the contrary. Before the negotiation of this treaty, Abd al-Aziz wrote to Shaikh Mubarak Al Sabah of Kuwait agreeing to submit to the Ottoman Porte 'if the matter which will guard my rights is granted'—undoubtedly a reference to his family's hereditary rights which were, in fact, secured in the treaty.

> In agreeing to approach (Kuwait) I have obeyed your instructions as regards obedience and submission to our Government [Ottoman], but you know well with what contempt and disdain the officials of Government have treated me, and you have seen the patience with which I have submitted to their conduct all these years notwithstanding that I never once experienced anything from them which does console me. And now, Heaven be praised, I am in a position to do great things even as far as Iraq, were it not that I do not wish to be the cause of (further) decline to the Government and additional revolt on the part of the Arabs.
>
> Now I have recovered my own country as you are witness Oh Mubarak; and it was you who went to Hassa [al-Ahsa] with a force to protect me and afterwards betrayed me, you and the

soldiers! I ask you, is it or is it not correct what I say about all the difficulties which have been brought upon me by the officials and the submission and patience which I have shown? As to your urging me now to submission to the Government—I did not disobey you formerly that I should do so now, so if the matter which will guard my rights is granted and I and my affairs secure protection—then submission will certainly be incumbent upon me.[84]

It is evident that Abd al-Aziz had no reservation about negotiating with either the British or the Ottomans. His primary goal was to secure the rights of his family to rule in Central Arabia. While he might sincerely feel that the Ottomans had subverted the Khalifate and were corrupt, it is clear from his letter that he was submitting to Ottoman authority as he had done in the past and also that he wished to avoid fragmenting the Arabs.

When the war broke out, Abd al-Aziz agreed to support Great Britain although it is a fact that the British blockades of Ottoman territories were broken several times by caravans coming from Central Arabia. Abd al-Aziz denied knowledge of these caravans, but it is difficult to believe that he was not aware of them. Once he remarked that 'England is of Europe . . . and I am the friend of the Ingliz, their ally. But I will walk with them only as far as my religion and my honour will permit . . . .'[85] It is doubtful whether his attitude differed substantially during the first three decades of this century. Just as his partnership with the badu had been one of political and military convenience, so too must his partnership with the British be regarded. In a speech in 1930 he expressed his attitude towards the British in even more vehement terms.

An Englishman came to a Bedouin of Irak during the World War and said to him: 'I will give you one guinea if you kill this dog.' The Bedouin killed the dog. He said to him: 'I will give you two guineas if you skin it.' He skinned it. Then he said to him: 'I will give you three guineas if you eat its meat.' The Bedouin ate the dog. After that the Englishman said: 'This is how we have conquered you, Oh Arabs!'[86]

The Al Saud also intensely disliked the Hashimite family who had allied themselves with Great Britain. A long-standing rivalry had existed between the two families which was to re-emerge with the Arab Revolt in 1916 and the armed struggle at al-Khurma and Turaba in 1918, and culminate in the Saudi capture of al-Hijaz in 1924. It was felt by the Islamic world generally that the Hashimite/British alliance was anti-Islamic, especially since it was directed against the Ottomans who had held the Khalifate. The struggle of the Al Saud against Al Hashim was seen in Najd as a nationalist cause leading to the freeing of the Arabs and Islam from corrupt forces. The Hashimites and Husain's pretensions as King of the Arabs were viewed as an individual affair leading only to the elevation of crowns and thrones.[87] This is supported by a letter written sometime after early June 1916 by Abd al-Aziz himself to Ali Haidar who had been offered the Amirate of Mecca by the Ottoman Porte after its previously appointed Grand Sharif Husain had proclaimed the Arab Revolt. Ali Haidar viewed the Sharifate as legally belonging to his branch of the family and, even though he was only able to reach al-Madina and later was forced to retreat to Damascus, his legitimate claim to the Sharifate was clearly recognised by Abd al-Aziz, as the following translation of this letter illustrates.[88]

In the name of Allah, The Beneficent, the Merciful.
Praise only be to Allah!
To His Highness, the Grand Sherif and Amir of Holy Mecca, Sherif Ali Haidar, the Respected.

May God make you victorious. I have had the honour to receive your kind letter. Everything that is at present happening in Arabia is known to me, and I am aware of your appointment to the Throne and Holy See of Mecca, and your recognition as such by His Majesty, The Caliph and Amir el Muslimen. I realize also that your acceptance of this high honour is not prompted by personal ambition, nor by a desire for material advantage, but by your zeal and fidelity to Islam in order to improve the conditions of all Muslimen. You have raised your Standard on behalf of Islam against Hussein and his sons, who have transgressed the Law of the Holy Prophet.

The family of Hussein have produced nothing but injury and discord by their rebellion against the Caliph of Islam and his government, but there is no power greater than the power of God. The permission given by Hussein for the entry of Christians into the Holy and Sacred Places is just one of his transgressions against Islam, and will eventually cause his downfall. His behaviour is utterly against the spirit of Islam, and contrary to the faith of the Arabs. His rebellion against his own Caliph shows his evil will. He desires independence at any cost and for this he will indulge in every kind of intrigue among the peoples of Arabia, inciting them against each other to serve his own interests. Those whose interests are identical support him. The present important situation requires much consideration by the Government of Your Highness. The intrigues of Hussein and his sons have provoked no little irritation among my own tribes, and I have informed both your Highness and the Government officials of these undesirable activities that are taking place.

Today, I am under the orders of the Turkish Government and prepared to do anything you desire, but we require further supplies of ammunition. At the moment the position of Sherif Hussein is one of little importance, and we can easily defeat him if further supplies are made available. These we await with the instructions of Your Highness. The Arabs are now gathering here, and this is the best moment for any movement to take place.

(Signed) Abdul Aziz Sa'ud,
Governor of the Country of Nejd

After the war ended, the political situation changed. The Ikhwan and Abd al-Aziz constituted an increasingly powerful force, while King Husain was becoming a liability for the British. In correspondence sent from the American Consulate in Beirut to the United States Secretary of State there is a long memorandum included from Bearer of Passport No. 354536, presumably Ameen Rihani, about his attempts to unite the Arab leaders of the Peninsula.[89] Rihani asked Abd al-Aziz if he would recognise the Khalifate of Husain if the latter recognised Abd al-Aziz as the political leader of Arabia. Rihani did not receive a reply until news had also reached him about the Ikhwan conquest of al-Taif. In his reply, Abd al-Aziz had agreed to Rihani's suggestion on condition that the Islamic world also accepted this conquest. Rihani concluded that Abd al-Aziz had already planned the defeat of al-Taif to ensure that Husain would not hesitate to agree to the political leadership of the Al Saud. Later, when Abd al-Aziz was asked whether he would accept the authority of another Arab leader if the Arabian Peninsula could be united under a Pan-Islamic movement, he categorically replied, 'We know ourselves, and we cannot accept the leadership of others'.[90]

Several points can be enumerated. While Abd al-Aziz was reluctant to oppose Ottoman rule before the war, he at all times insisted on his rights as an independent Arab and Islamic leader and on the hereditary rights of the Saudi Imamate (see Appendix for further information about the Al Saud prior to World War I). After the conclusion of the war, Abd al-Aziz was in an increasingly strong position to oppose both the British and the Hashimites. He proceeded to exile the Hashimites, formally annexing al-Hijaz and incorporating it within the Kingdom of Saudi Arabia in 1932. The Al Saud placed paramount importance on retaining their rights to political rather than religious authority, as was especially evident when Abd al-Aziz relinquished the title of Imam to his father while using the secular title of Sultan and, later, King in order to facilitate his accession to the leadership of al-Hijaz.

Notes

1. India Office Records, *Political and Secret Department Separate Files 1902-1931*, L/P&S/10 (henceforward abbreviated to IO L/P&S/10): IO L/P&S/10/1235, letter from 'Abd al-'Azīz to the British Political Agent Bahrain, 24 Rajab 1346 (17 January 1928).

2. The Wahhabi doctrines were transplanted to India by Saiyid Aḥmad who adopted them in 1822/3 while on pilgrimage. After returning to India, he took the title of Khalifa and established a city near Patna, obtaining followers in Bombay and Calcutta. It was essentially a movement to re-establish Muslim authority and he advocated *jihād* against the Sikh cities. His views were so radical that both the Sunni and Shi'ite communities dissociated themselves from Wahhabi doctrine in 1870. Other than Central Arabia, India was the only area where Wahhabi doctrine found a fertile area for expansion.

3. Many travellers during the last several centuries have mentioned the prevalence in Najd of superstitions and pre-Islamic customs: star worship (Lewis Pelly, *Report on a Journey to Riyadh in Central Arabia (1865)* (Oleander Press, Cambridge, 1977), p. 59); belief in demons and jinns (Ḥāfiẓ Wahba, *Arabian Days* (Arthur Barker, London, 1964), pp.60-2); attitudes to eclipses (R. E. Cheesman, *In Unknown Arabia* (Macmillan, London, 1926), p.263); and Louis P. Dame, 'Four Months in Nejd', *Moslem World*, 14 (1924), p.355); protection of crops from the evil eye (Cheesman, p.91); and camel sacrifice over revered graves (Carl R. Raswan, *Black Tents of Arabia: My Life Among the Bedouins* (Hutchinson, London, 1935), pp.110-11). Many badu tribes had *nakhwas* based on ancient tribal totems and transported a *markab* on their travels which was believed to contain its tribal spirit or God (Julian Morgenstern, *The Ark, the Ephod, and the 'Tent of Meeting'* (Hebrew Union College Press, Cincinnati, 1945)). Moreover, the Central Arabian populations, including 'Abd al-'Azīz himself, were firm believers in the interpretation

of dreams (H. R. P. Dickson, *The Arab of the Desert: A Glimpse into Badawin Life in Kuwait and Sa'udi Arabia* (George Allen and Unwin, London, 1972), pp.329-35). Ibn Ghannām, the Sa'udi chronicler, also referred to the presence of pre-Islamic customs.

4. See Ira M. Lapidus, 'The Separation of State and Religion in the Development of Early Islamic Society', *International Journal of Middle Eastern Studies*, 6 (1975), pp.365-85.

5. King 'Abd al-'Azīz, in fact, tried to obtain in 1927 the permission of the Ḥanbali *qāḍīs* in Saudi Arabia to utilise elements of Ibn Taimīya's thoughts if they were more in accordance with the Quran and Sunna (Joseph Schacht, *An Introduction to Islamic Law* (Clarendon Press, Oxford, 1964), p.87).

6. George Makdisi, 'The Tanbīh of Ibn Taimīya on Dialectic: The Pseudo-'Aqīlian Kitāb Al-Farq', in Sami A. Hanna (ed.), *Medieval Middle Eastern Studies* (E. J. Brill, Leiden, 1972), p.293. See also Henri Laoust, *Essai sur les doctrines sociales et politiques de Takī-d-Dīn Aḥmad b. Taimīyah, canoniste ḥanbalite* (Imprimerie de l'Institut Francais d'Archéologie Orientale, Cairo, 1939).

7. See George Makdisi, 'Ibn Taimīya: A Ṣūfi of the Qādiriya Order', *American Journal of Arabic Studies*, 1 (1973), pp.118-29.

8. See Muhammad Umar Memon, *Ibn Taimīya's Struggle Against Popular Religion: With an Annotated Translation of his Kitāb iqtiḍā' as-sirāt al-mustaqīm mukhālafat aṣḥāb al-jahīm* (Mouton, 1976).

9. This explains the burial practices of the Wahhabis. When King Faisal was assassinated in 1975, he was buried in an unmarked grave because the erection of any tomb or shrine, however small, would be *shirk*.

10. See E. E. Evans-Pritchard, *The Sanusi of Cyrenaica* (Clarendon Press, Oxford, 1973).

11. Bakrī Shaikh Amīn, *al-ḥarakat al-adabīya fi al-mamlaka al-'arabīya al-sū'ūdīya* (Dār Ṣādir, Beirut, 1972), pp.42-58.

12. Shaikh 'Abd al-Raḥmān b. Ḥasan b. Shaikh al-Islam Muḥammad b. 'Abd al-Wahhāb, *majmū'at al-tauḥīd al-najdīya* (edited by Rashīd Riḍā) (Al-Manar, Cairo, 1346 A (1927)), p.136.

13. Shaikh Sulaimān b. 'Abdullāh b. al-Shaikh Muḥammad b. 'Abd al-Wahhāb, *majmū'at al-tauḥīd* (as in note 12), p.178.

14. Shaikh 'Abd al-Laṭīf b. 'Abd al-Rahmān b. Ḥasan, *majmū'at al-rasā'il wa al-masā'il*, 3 vols (edited by Rashīd Riḍā) (Al-Manar, Cairo, 1344 A -1349 A (1925-30)), vol. I, p.422.

15. There was also a third category, *dār al-ṣulḥ* or House of Peace (or Conciliation), although only a few nations were classified in this way because of special treaties the Prophet had negotiated with them.

16. See Majid Khadduri, *War and Peace in the Law of Islam* (Johns Hopkins Press, Baltimore, 1955).

17. Shaikh 'Abd al-Laṭīf b. 'Abd al-Raḥmān, *majmū'at* (as in note 14), III, p.80.

18. Shaikh 'Abd al-Raḥmān b. Ḥasan b. Shaikh al-Islam Muḥammad b. 'Abd al-Wahhāb, *majmū'at*, II, p.135.

19. Shaikh Ḥamad b. Nāṣir b. Mu'ammar, *majmū'at*, I, p.581.

20. Shaikh 'Abd al-Raḥmān b. Ḥasan b. Shaikh al-Islam Muhammad b. 'Abd al-Wahhāb, *majmū'at*, II, p.134.

21. Ibid., pp.132-4.

22. The following question and answer in the Wahhabi texts define the term badu:

> As for the badu, if they have their people and property with them and they follow their pastures and water from territory to territory should they be treated like the traveller?

> I would not recommend them as either settled or travellers, but if they had the intention of settling so long as pasture is in it, or if they intended to dwell there from time to time, or settled where there was water then they are dwellers and are subject to the laws of residences (*aḥkām al-iqāma*) and, therefore, they are not permitted the status of travellers . . . . If they moved to find pasture or water and there was two days journey of travel between water, then they would be reckoned as travellers.

(Shaikh 'Abdullāh b. al-Shaikh Muḥammad b. 'Abd al-Wahhāb, *majmū'at*, I, pp.250-1.)

23. Shaikh 'Abd al-Raḥmān b. Ḥasan, *majmū'at al-tauḥīd*, pp.156-7.
24. Ibid.; and Amīn, *al-ḥarakat al-adabīya fī al-mamlaka al-'arabīya al-su'ūdīya*, p.52.
25. Shaikh al-Imam Muḥammad b. 'Abd al-Wahhāb, *majmū'at al-tauḥīd*, p.124.
26. Suras 16: 57, 85; and 30:33.
27. Sura 74:10.
28. Muḥammad Kurd 'Alī, *al-qadīm wa al-ḥadīth* (Al-Maṭba'at al-Raḥmānīya, Cairo, 1343A (1925)), pp.165-6.
29. Shaikh al-Islam Muḥammad b. 'Abd al-Wahhāb, *majmū'at al-tauḥīd*, p.115.
30. Shaikh 'Abd al-Raḥmān b. Ḥasan, *majmū'at al-tauḥīd*, pp.158-9; and Amīn, *al-ḥarakat al-adabīya fī al-mamlaka al-'arabīya al-su'ūdīya*, p.53.
31. Amīn, pp.76-8.
32. Kurd 'Alī, *al-qadīm wa al-ḥadīth*, p.158.
33. W. F. Smalley, 'The Wahhabis and Ibn Sa'ud', *Moslem World*, 22 (1932), p.237; and Fazlur Rahman, *Islam* (Weidenfeld and Nicolson, London, 1966), p.199.
34. Shaikh al-Imam Muḥammad b. 'Abd al-Wahhāb, *majmū'at al-tauḥīd*, pp.128-30; Shaikh 'Abd al-Raḥmān b. Ḥasan b. al-Shaikh Muḥammad b. 'Abd al-Wahhāb, *majmū'at al-tauḥīd*, pp.161-2; and Shaikh 'Abd al-Laṭīf b. 'Abd al-Raḥmān, *majmū'at*, III, pp. 170-1.
35. Smalley, 'The Wahhabis and Ibn Sa'ud', pp.238-9, states that the Wahhabis had four classifications of *shirk*: (1) *al-'ilm*, 'ascribing knowledge to others but God'; (2) *al-taṣarruf*, 'ascribing power to anyone but God', (3) *al-'adāt*, 'praying, taking oaths, or performing other acts for or by the dead'; and (4) *al'ibādāt*, 'worshipping anyone or thing but God'.
36. Thus Ibn Musharraf, a poet who praised the Wahhabi *da'wa*, requested Imam Faiṣal b. Turkī to destroy *'ain najm*, hot sulphur springs in al-Aḥsā, because people went there for a cure and not to God. This was considered a great *shirk*. See also Amīn, *al-ḥarakat al-adabīya fī al-mamlaka al-'arabīya al-su'ūdīya*, pp.72-7, for a detailed list of various theological groups and scholars which the Wahhabis believed were practising *shirk* or *kufr*.
37. Ibn Musharraf was born in al-Aḥsā where he also died in 1868 (1285A). Sulaimān b. Saḥmān was born in 1852 (1269A) in al-Saqqa in the province of Abhā in 'Asīr and died in 1930 (1350A). Ibn 'Uthaimīn was born in 1853 (1270A) in al-Salamīya in al-Kharj and died in 1943 (1363A). See Amīn, *al-ḥarakat al-adabīya fī al-mamlaka al-'arabīya al-su'ūdīya*, pp. 59-97, for further information about the poets and literature of the Wahhabi *da'wa*.
38. In support of their interpretation of the *hijra* in Islam the Wahhabis frequently recited Sura 5:44-47.
39. Amīn, *al-ḥarakat al-adabīya fī al-mamlaka al-'arabīya al-su'ūdīya*, p.79.
40. Shaikh 'Abd al-Raḥmān b. Ḥasan b. al-Shaikh Muḥammad b. 'Abd al-Wahhāb, *majmū'at*, II, pp.136-7.
41. Amīn, *al-ḥarakat al-adabīya fī al-mamlaka al-'arabīya al-su'ūdīya*, p.85.
42. Dame, 'Four Months in Nejd', p.360.
43. Suras 9:72; 22:77; 29:5; and 49:14.

44. Ibn Taimīya, *al-siyāsat al-shar'īya* (Dār al-Kutub al-'Arabīya, Beirut, 1966), p.106.

45. Suras 8:40; 9:22; and 2:190-4, 216-19. See also Ibn Taimīya's '*jihād al-kuffār . . . al-qitāl al-fāṣil*', in *al-siyāsat al-shar'īya* (1966), pp.102-22.

46. Suras 9:19-22; 48:5-7; and 61:10-14.

47. Ibn Taimīya, *al-siyāsat al-shar'īya*, p.106.

48. Muḥammad Mughairabī Fatīḥ al-Madanī, *firqat al-ikhwān al-islāmīya bi najd au wahhābīya al-yaum* (no publisher listed, 1342A (1923)), p.35; and Shaikh 'Abdullāh b. al-Shaikh Muḥammad b. 'Abd al-Wahhāb, *majmū'at al-tauḥīd*, p.248.

49. Shaikh 'Abd al-Laṭīf b. 'Abd al-Raḥmān, *majmū'at*, III, p.62.

50. Sura 2:217.

51. Sura 8:39.

52. Shaikh Sulaimān b. Saḥmān, *majmū'at*, III, p.70.

53. Shaikh Ḥamad b. 'Atīq, *majmū'at*, I, pp.742-6.

54. Smalley, 'The Wahhabis and Ibn Sa'ud', p.243.

55. Khadduri, *War and Peace in the Law of Islam*, pp.74-82, 147-52.

56. Ibn Taimīya, *al-siyāsat al-shar'īya*, p.108, states that *zakāt* is an incumbent duty and refusal to pay incurs *jihād*; see also Suras 9:1-11; 22:39-40; and 40-60. See also Ch. 4 for a detailed explanation of the religious and political implications of *zakāt* payment, collection and dispersal.

57. Shaikh 'Abdullāh b. al-Shaikh Muḥammad b. 'Abd al-Wahhāb, *majmū'at al-tauḥīd*, pp.247-50.

58. Ibid., pp.242-4.

59. See George Rentz in Derek Hopwood (ed.), *The Arabian Peninsula: Society and Politics* (George Allen and Unwin, London, 1972), p.56.

60. Ibn Bishr refers to Muḥammad b. Sa'ūd as Imam in 1753. Ibn Ghannām refers to Muḥammad's rule as an amirate and first uses the title of Imam when he refers to Muḥammad's son, 'Abd al-'Azīz (Khair al-Dīn Ziriklī, *shibh al-jazīra fī'ahd al-malik'abd al-'azīz* (Maṭābī' Dār al-Qalam, Beirut, 1390A(1970)), pp.34-5).

61. Shaikh 'Abd al-Laṭīf, b. 'Abd al-Raḥmān, *majmū'at*, III, pp.170-4.

62. H. St John B. Philby, *Sa'udi Arabia* (Ernest Benn, London, 1955), p.77, notes that it was Muḥammad b. 'Abd al-Wahhāb who issued orders to the provinces to pledge their loyalty to 'Abd al-'Azīz (I) Āl Sa'ūd's son, Sa'ūd, as the future ruler.

63. The number forty is a general reference in Najd to an unknown quantity. Many sources have disputed the number of people involved in 'Abd al-'Azīz's conquest of al-Riyāḍ and, interestingly, all estimates are forty or close to it.

64. *Ta'ṭīl* is a theological concept which denies God all his attributes as opposed to *tashbīh* which is the anthropomorphisation of God.

65. Shaikh 'Abd al-Laṭīf b. 'Abd al-Raḥmān, *majmū'at*, III, pp.69-73. It should be noted that most of the Wahhabi texts are addressed to the 'Ikhwan'—that is, those Muslims who are Wahhabis. It is not a reference to the military/religious settlements of twentieth-century Sa'udi Arabia the inhabitants of which were known as Ikhwan.

66. Ameen Rihani, *Ibn Sa'oud of Arabia: His People and His Land* (Constable, London, 1928), pp.39-40.

67. Ibrahim al-Rashid, *Documents on the History of Saudi Arabia*, 3 vols (Documentary Publications, Salisbury, North Carolina, 1976): vol. II, pp.146-50, 'Official Title of Ibn Saud', dispatch of US Consul, Aden, 7 November 1927, with enclosures; and vol. III, pp.133-6, 'Kingdom of Hejaz and Nejd and its Dependencies Changes Name to the Kingdom of Saudi Arabia', dispatches of US Chargé d'Affaires, London, and US Consul, Aden, 29 September and 12 October 1932. See also Ziriklī, *shibh al-jazīra fī 'ahd al-malik'abd al-'azīz*, pp.649-51.

68. Rashid, *Documents on the History of Saudi Arabia*, vol. III, pp.174-9, 'Appointment of Prince Saud as Lawful Successor to King Ibn Saud as Ruler of the

Kingdom of Saudi Arabia', dispatch of US Consul, Aden, 31 July 1933. Gary Troeller, *The Birth of Saudi Arabia: Britain and the Rise of the House of Saud* (Frank Cass, London, 1976), pp.248-9, 'Translation of Treaty between Ibn Saud and the Turks', 15 May 1914. See Aḥmad 'Abd al-Ghafūr 'Aṭṭār, *ṣaqr al-jazīra*, 7 vols (Maṭba'at al-Ḥurrīya, Beirut, 1972), pp.405-7, for the Arabic version of 'Abd al-'Azīz's treaty with the Ottoman government; and see also C. U. Aitchison, *A Collection of Treaties, Engagements and Sanads Relating to India and Neighbouring Countries* (vol. XI) (Kraus Reprint, Nendeln/Liechtenstein, 1973), pp.206-8, 'Treaty between the British Government and the Ruler of Nejd, El Hassa, Qatif, etc.—1915'.

69. H. R. P. Dickson, *Kuwait and Her Neighbours* (George Allen and Unwin, London, 1968), p.272.

70. IO L/P&S/10/1241, letter from Amir 'Abdullāh to Lieutenant-Colonel Cox, British Resident, Transjordan, 25 January 1930.

71. Pelly, *Report on A Journey*, p.49. King 'Abd al-'Azīz also noted the importance of water when he said that flock size was doubled when there were good rains (Rihani, *Ibn Sa'oud of Arabia*, p.223).

72. Rihani, *Ibn Sa'oud of Arabia*, p.39.

73. See Henry Rosenfeld, 'The Social Composition of the Military in the Process of State Formation in the Arabian Desert' and 'The Military Force used to Achieve and Maintain Power and the Meaning of its Social Composition: Slaves, Mercenaries and Townsmen', *Journal of the Royal Anthropological Institute*, 95 (1965), pp.75-86 and 174-94.

74. IO L/P&S/10/385, memorandum of an interview with Ben Saud ['Abd al-'Azīz] on 15-16 December 1913, from A. P. Trevor, Political Agent Bahrain, to the Political Resident in the Persian Gulf, Bushire, 20 December 1913, T.806.

75. Rihani, *Ibn Sa'oud of Arabia*, p.75.

76. When Britain ended its subsidy to King Ḥusain, he was forced in 1923 to discontinue subsidies he had been giving to the badu tribes throughout World War I and afterwards. The result was that many tribes began to raid pilgrim caravans bound for Mecca which hitherto had been regarded as sacrosanct. Many other tribes deserted to Sa'udi forces in the latter's conquest of al-Ḥijāz which began the following year (Sir Reader Bullard, *The Camels Must Go: An Autobiography* (Faber and Faber, London, 1961), p.128).

77. Rihani, *Ibn Sa'oud of Arabia*, pp.44-5.

78. IO L/P&S/10/1243, speech of King 'Abd al-'Azīz to the chiefs of the 'Utaiba tribe, reported in *Umm al-Qurā* and included in dispatch from W. L. Bond to the Secretary of State for Foreign Affairs, 30 July 1929; and Rashid, *Documents on the History of Saudi Arabia*, vol. III, pp.73-7, 'Speech of Ibn Saud', dispatch of US Consul Beirut, received 19 July 1930, with enclosures.

79. Ibid.

80. Rihani, *Ibn Sa'oud of Arabia*, pp.234-5.

81. Pelly, *Report on a Journey*, p.47. During the first decade of the twentieth century, 'Abd al-'Azīz was forced to suppress challenges to his authority which often emanated from his own family. The Al Hazān and the 'Arā'if were members of the 'Anaza and relatives of the Al Sa'ūd. Little is known of Al Hazān except that it was powerful in al-Ḥarīq and had, in fact, been responsible for a series of civil disturbances and the deaths of two important shaikhs. 'Abd al-'Azīz was eventually able to defeat Al Hazān. The 'Arā'if, however, claimed closer kinship to 'Abd al-'Azīz, being sons of Sa'ūd b. Faiṣal, 'Abd al-'Azīz's uncle on his father's side. The term *'arā'if* is used by the badu for camels lost during a raid and subsequently recovered in a counter-raid which, indeed, reflects the fact that some of the 'Arā'if were later reconciled to the authority of 'Abd al-'Azīz. Although 'Abd al-'Azīz obtained no decisive victory, the 'Arā'if left Najd to take refuge with Grand Sharif

Ḥusain in al-Ḥijāz, with the al-'Ujmān tribe in al-Aḥsā, and in Qaṭar. This association of the 'Arā'if with Arab leaders allied to the British later caused great difficulty in Sa'udi-British relations. For obvious reasons, 'Abd al-'Azīz forbade the time-honoured custom of *dakhāla* or 'taking refuge', particularly if those taking refuge were his political opponents. It is remarkable that many of these early opponents later became trusted members of 'Abd al-'Azīz's government. Those who did not reconcile themselves to his leadership were generally exiled to other Arab countries. For further information about these conflicts see 'Aṭṭār, *ṣaqr al-jazīra*, II, pp.374-91.

82. Pelly, *Report on A Journey*, p.50.

83. See note 68.

84. IO L/P&S/10/385, letter from 'Abd al-'Azīz to Shaikh Mubarak Āl Ṣabāḥ, 16 April 1914, included in sub-enclosure in enclosure no. 3, from Lieutenant-Colonel W. G. Grey, Political Agent Kuwait, to the Political Resident in the Persian Gulf, Bushire, 22 April 1914, no. C.-15.

85. Rihani, *Ibn Sa'oud of Arabia*, p.46.

86. Rashid, *Documents on the History of Saudi Arabia*, vol. III, pp.73-7, 'Speech of Ibn Saud', dispatch of US Consul Beirut, received 19 July 1930, with enclosures.

87. Madanī, *firqat al-ikhwān al-islāmīya bi najd au wahhābīya al-yaum*, pp.45-52.

88. Princess Musbah Haidar, *Arabesque* (Hutchinson, London, 1948), pp.92-3. This is further confirmed by a letter sent from Sharif 'Alī Ḥaidar to the President of the United States (Rashid, *Documents on the History of Saudi Arabia*, vol. I, pp.42-9).

89. Rashid, *Documents on the History of Saudi Arabia*, vol. II, pp.22-43, 'Efforts of Ameen Rihani to Bring about Peace between Ibn Saud and Prince Ali', dispatch of US Consul Beirut, 23 September 1925, with enclosures.

90. Rihani, *Ibn Sa'oud of Arabia*, p.236.

3

The Ikhwan: Badu answer the Wahhabi 'Call to Unity'

When Abd al-Aziz captured al-Ahsa in 1913, his army consisted almost entirely of *hadar*, the settled merchants and agriculturists of Central Arabia, as Captain W. H. Shakespear, Political Agent in Kuwait, reported.

> he [Abd al-Aziz] issued orders for a general mobilization of his troops (i.e. townsmen and villagers as distinct from the nomad Bedouin, who do not count for much). This mobilization only called up a small proportion of the available fighting strength of each village—some 30 per cent was my estimate after many enquiries—but even then Bin Saud had anything from 5000 to 7000 well-armed and mounted men ready to his hand. The military efficiency of Bin Saud's arrangements will be realized when it is understood that some of the villages are nearly 150 miles from Riadh [al-Riyad], that the mobilization was practically complete within a fortnight, and that 1000 men were despatched and posted in the coast villages . . . within the first week.[1]

This pattern was to change entirely during the succeeding decade. Beginning with the al-Khurma-Turaba dispute of 1918/19, the Al Saud were dependent primarily on badu contingents called the Ikhwan for all their major campaigns of territorial expansion: the capture of the mountain area of Asir in 1920, Hail in 1921, Jauf in 1922 and al-Hijaz in 1925. The Ikhwan, who reportedly numbered 150,000 fighting men alone, are the subject of this chapter. Although they were both a military and a police force, they followed the teachings of Muhammad b. Abd al-Wahhab and, as a consequence, underwent transformations in the economic and social aspects of their lives unfamiliar to any other badu group of the Arabian Peninsula.

The Origins of the Ikhwan

Two factors—the segmentary structure of tribal organisation and the status differentials between tribes—made it difficult for any political contender in Najd to secure the allegiance of the numerous tribes. It will be recalled from previous chapters that the badu tribes were forced to submit to Saudi authority only after the allegiance of the urban areas was secured. The reason was that the allegiance of the settled people was more dependable while the loyalties of the badu quickly vacillated in response to the political fortunes of individual rulers. It will also be recalled that Pelly was told by the Imam Faisal Al Saud in 1865/66 that the greatest political problem in Najd was the lack of rain which prevented agriculture and the settlement of tribes. Imam Faisal also indicated that the only way the tribes could be controlled was through the tribal shaikhs and, if Pelly cared to visit the jail, he would see seventy tribal shaikhs imprisoned.[2] Abd al-Aziz realised, in the twentieth century, that he confronted the same problem, but also that the badu were a powerful military force if means could be found to control them.

> The Arabs of the North . . . are heavy of foot and stolid; the people of Najd are quick, light, wiry . . . . The *zelul* [riding camel] of the North is strong but slow; that of the South is fast, although he has not so much enduring power. But the people of Najd are like the Bedu in hardship and adversity . . . . Especially the Najdis of the South—we are like our Bedu in this . . . .The people of Al-Qasim are traders and are not, therefore, so hardy and brave as the people of al-'Ared [al-Arid, the home district of the Al Saud] or the Bedu of the Kharj country. There in the south are the hardest and most truculent of the Bedu; the Benu Murrah and the Dawasir are savages. In their quarrels they thrust their *jambiyah*s (daggers) into each other, and draw them out exultantly . . . and lick the blood. They are madmen in the fight. Bravery is something common among the lowest of them.

> In the days of peace they come to us for everything—food, clothes, money. But in times of war the poorest and meanest among them makes not a demand. It is a shame with the people of Najd to ask for anything when we are at war or on a *gazu*. They gather up their own . . . . Our little serves much during war.[3]

Although the Al Saud had encouraged Wahhabi doctrine among the badu ever since the mid-1700s, it was not until the beginning of the twentieth century that Abd al-Aziz actively began to Islamise the badu population, in the sense that policies of control—economic, social, military and religious—were institutionalised by a central authority. It is not clear, however, whether this was a process of his own initiation or whether it already existed and only later came to his attention. There is evidence to support both cases.[4] Lieutenant-Colonel H. R. P. Dickson, Political Agent in Kuwait, stated that Abd al-Aziz personally told him that it was only after he recovered al-Ahsa that the Ikhwan came to his attention.[5] There is, on the other hand, a letter from Amir Abdullah, King Husain's son, to Abd al-Aziz dated 23 Shaban 1337 (1919), in which he stated: 'If you [Abd al-Aziz] wished well to the Muslims as you claim, then return those whom you commanded to sell their cattle and to build houses . . .'[6] Neither statement gives final confirmation as to whether or not the Saudi leader initiated the movement. It was undoubtedly Abd al-Aziz's close association with the Ikhwan after 1913 which has obscured, probably forever, its exact origins, although no one disputes that he became the absolute spiritual and secular leader of the Ikhwan after this date.

It is interesting to note that W. G. Palgrave, who travelled through Central Arabia in 1862 and 1863, recorded that there was a Wahhabi revival in the mid-1800s following a severe outbreak of cholera and that Imam Faisal founded in 1855 a group of twenty-two 'zealators' called *meddey'yeeyah*, possibly the *muttawwiun* of whom more will be said, to eradicate any practices contrary to Wahhabi doctrine.[7] Palgrave provides an extensive description of these Zealators which shows that they possessed many characteristics identical to those displayed by the Ikhwan and *muttawwiun* of the early twentieth century. All persons who were found smoking, wearing gold or silk, singing or playing musical instruments, or who were lax in their religious observances were punished with a long cane carried by the Zealators for such purposes—the *muttawwiun* were to act in the same way in the twentieth century. The style of dress for both was simple and, with the exception of the cane, no weapons were carried. It seems very probable that during the late 1800s there existed, at the very least, an incipient and extremist movement based on Wahhabi doctrine, although to what degree it was extant by the late 1800s or early 1900s is not known.

The Ikhwan: Equality of All Men in Islam

It was reported between late 1912 and early 1913 that some Najd tribes were selling their horses, camels and personal wealth in the markets of Kuwait and elsewhere just prior to the time that Abd al-Aziz was utilising townsmen in his capture of al-Ahsa.[8] These were the earliest, if not the original, badu tribes to sell their possessions and settle in co-operative, agriculturally oriented colonies called *hijra* (*hujra*, pl. *hijar*, *hujar*). They referred to themselves as *ikhwan* or 'brethren' as did all badu who, irrespective of their tribal origins, pursued a similar course in Central Arabia during the following two decades. All of the Ikhwan, as the movement became known, recognised the Al Saud as holders of a lawful Islamic Imamate and Abd al-Aziz as the Imam.[9]

The terms *ikhwan* and *hijra* symbolised Ikhwan attitudes not only to the new movement, but also to the life which they had abandoned. It was shown in Chapter 2 that Muhammad b. Abd al-Wahhab and other Wahhabi *ulama* believed that the life-style of the badu contributed to the chaos and social decadence of the Peninsula. *Shirk* and *kufr* were apparent in all aspects of their lives and, moreover, tribal solidarity (*asabiya*) tended to distract an individual's attention from the true path of Islam. The Wahhabi *dawa*, begun in the mid-eighteenth century to revive the initial purity of Islam, became in the early twentieth century a reform movement designed to eliminate social inequalities and moral laxity and to unite all men in one community—the Islamic *umma*. Just as the Prophet Muhammad made 'brothers' or 'allies', *ikhwa*, among his supporters who came from unrelated kinship groups, the term *ikhwan*, literally translated as 'brothers', represented a new equality among men. The second term, *hijra*, also has religious significance. As mentioned previously, the Wahhabis believed that the *hijra*, 'emigration or departure', was one of the pillars of Islam.

It had two specific meanings: emigration from any land of *shirk* and *kufr* and the abandonment of all things forbidden by Allah and the Prophet Muhammad. Not only did the badu depart for new homes, but they abandoned a way of life in favour of Islam for, as the badu said, *al-din hadari* or 'the religion is a sedentary religion'.[10]

The social and political implications of Islam as a uniting force are obviously great in a region like Najd where there were over one hundred tribes. That it was successful is evidenced by a statement made by one of the Ikhwan in 1924 to a traveller in Buraida, al-Qasim, that everyone outside Najd was in the *balad al-kuffar* or Country of the Infidels.[11] Abd al-Aziz clearly understood that an Islamic movement such as the Ikhwan was an ideal way to undermine the tribal shaikhs and legitimise his own claims to political authority by emphasising the Arab and Islamic heritage of the Al Saud. He implemented this idea to advantage by declaring that all so-called 'inferior' or client tribes were henceforth independent and exempt from the payment of *khuwa* to their patron tribes.[12] Two such tribes were the Awazim, who were freed from the al-Ujman and given modern weapons, and the Suluba, who were given their own war banners.[13] Now all tribes were to pay Islamic *zakat* to the Al Saud and, in so doing, recognise them as constituting a lawful Islamic government.

The Ikhwan, the Imamate of the Al Saud and Wahhabi Doctrine

The Ikhwan now recognised the authority of three persons or groups previously alien to them: the Imam, the *ulama* and the *muttawwi* (pl. *muttawwiun*). As the temporal head of the Islamic community, the Imam was responsible for negotiating relations with foreign powers, declaring *jihad* and directing all daily affairs of the people. He was, however, responsible to the *ulama* who, as the guardians and interpreters of divine law, could intervene in his decisions.[14] The *muttawwiun*, literally meaning 'those who obey or volunteer', were the only authorities in direct contact with the *hijras*. They were sent out to convert and teach the badu the basics of Wahhabi doctrine. These were generally the most illiterate and intolerant of all Wahhabis and, well known and hated as religious police, they were the men who publicly flogged all persons who were caught smoking, wearing fine adornments or procrastinating in their religious duties. They were also responsible for the collection of *zakat* for the central government.[15] The tribal shaikhs thus lost their importance as sole arbiters in the affairs of their tribe and became important because they now acted as intermediaries between their tribes and the central government in al-Riyad.

Interviews conducted in 1972 among men who had been Ikhwan in the early *hijras* of al-Qasim asked what factor was most important in determining their decision to abandon nomadism for an Ikhwan *hijra*. The overwhelming answer was that religion was the most important factor in 83.8 per cent of the *hijras*, the hard life of nomadism was a factor in only 2.7 per cent and the amenities of settled life in only 5.4 per cent of the *hijras*. Special factors comprise the remaining per cent, but underlying these was the encouragement of the nomads to settle under the strong central authority of the Al Saud.[16]

Whatever the origins of the Ikhwan, two letters provide evidence that, at least by 1914, they had completely accepted the Imamate of the Al Saud and were adhering to Wahhabi doctrine. These letters were addressed to the Ikhwan from Abd al-Aziz and the Wahhabi *ulama* after a conference had been held in al-Riyad. They chastised the Ikhwan for excesses in their religious zeal and reminded them of their duties as good Muslims, to avoid too narrow an interpretation of the Wahhabi texts and to refer disputatious matters to the *ulama* and to the Imam. The conference apparently was convened to settle internal dissent arising from what appears to have been the first major conflict over religious affairs among the Ikhwan, non-Ikhwan badu and urban populations. Notably, it was the Ikhwan and the *muttawwiun* who were singled out for criticism. The first letter written in 1332 ▲ (1914) is from Abd al-Aziz.[17]

> It is not unknown to me that your ancestors took *nahb* [plunder which is not allowed in Islam] and deviated from the Sharī'a . . . Keep to the Holy Book and its teachings, the Prophet, and his Companions . . . We follow the right path . . . and not those who deny [Islam] . . . we take refuge from deviationists . . . . Those who attended this assembly have heard the '*ulamā* without intermediaries . . . . You have seen innovation and evil spread because people have strayed from the right path . . . . The '*ulamā* carry on the heritage of the Prophets . . . here you have the statement that we are attached to the Qur'ān and in the branch of Aḥmad b. Ḥanbal.

The second letter, written by the most important Wahhabi shaikhs, is addressed to all the Ikhwan of the *hijra*s on 10 Dhu al-Qada 1332 (1914).[18]

> We renew the call to religion . . . . Avoid evil, differences and deception . . . . People fell into ways against their religion . . . . In view of this, we must return . . . . Among the causes of the different splits in religion [presumably within Najd itself] . . . there were those who so hated the Ikhwan they attributed to them disagreements, vanities, and doubts. Among them were those whose aim was good, but who were not learned. Then there were those who appeared among the common people whose aim was in learning in order that they could attract followers to themselves [*muttawwiun?*]; the aim of these people is bad. You must be careful of them. When those in power among the *'ulamā* realized the dissension in the matters of religion, he [Abd al-Aziz] wanted to convene a conference and have everyone attend who had the slightest opposition or doubt in any matter concerning religion in the presence of their *'ulamā* and prominent men so that the truth and the evil would become clear. The Imam would ask each of them these questions which the ignorant had raised in regard to religion:
>
> Does one apply the term *kufr* [infidelity] to the desert [*badu*] Muslims who are firm in religion and who carry out the command of God? Do you reject him or not?
>
> Was there a difference between the first settled people [*hadar*] and those badu *hijra*s established recently?
>
> Was there a difference in the blood sacrifice of the badu whose way of life and belief was that of the Muslims and in the first settlement of the badu *muhājirūn* [the 'emigrants' from desert to settled life] now?[19] Was it a difference between *ḥalāl* [that which is permitted] and *ḥarām* [that which is forbidden]?
>
> Did those who leave the desert have permission to transgress against people who had not abandoned the desert in that they struck them and forced them to abandon the life of the badu? Is there anyone who would desert another be it a badu or an urban dweller unless it is clear that he had committed *kufr* or some action which necessitates that he should be deserted except when he has the permission of his guardian or his governor?
>
> Is there a difference beween wearing the *'iqāl* and the *'imāma* [the Ikhwan distinguished themselves from other Najdis by their

style of dress] which differentiates those who wear it and their belief?

Our answer to all these questions is that they are all against the Sharī'a. God did not command them and neither did his Prophet. Nothing follows an answer to them except false statements. [Emphasis mine.] He who repents his errors is excused, but, if he continues and is stubborn, he must be chastised publicly among the Muslims until he mends his ways. Therefore, whoever commands [the Ikhwan leaders] and denies [this] or whoever transgresses without the command of those in charge of affairs and the legal government—if he would be going against the Sharī'a—then his ways are not the ways of the Muslims. We must then ask God to judge him . . . . We hope God shows fortune and makes it propitious for us and you to follow the same path.

There are three features which stand out in these letters. First, the Wahhabi *ulama* are clearly supportive of Abd al-Aziz and warn the people that anyone who disobeys the lawful government is, in fact, contravening the Sharia. The transgressor will be punished publicly and judged by God. Second, Abd al-Aziz and the *ulama* are sufficiently in control to convene a conference in which they not only issue commands but expect obedience. Finally, the questions contained in the second letter indicate that the Ikhwan and the *muttawwiun* were adopting an extreme religious stance which both Abd al-Aziz and the *ulama* opposed.[20] Each of these questions indicates that the Ikhwan were perceiving themselves as Muslims on the true path of Islam. The badu who had not settled in *hijra*s were apparently being forcibly 'converted' by the Ikhwan, although not by the orders of Abd al-Aziz or the Wahhabi shaikhs, who both condemned these actions. It also appears that there was some antipathy between the Ikhwan and the *hadar*, although it is not explicit what form this took.

In 1916 the fanaticism, which the government and the *ulama* had tried to eradicate in 1914, had broken out again. Although there is little information about this conflict, Abd al-Aziz reportedly sent a new group of religious scholars, less extreme in their views, to replace the earlier teachers who had caused the trouble.[21] This fanaticism of the Ikhwan was a characteristic which continually reappeared and, as will be seen in Part II, it was their exclusive sense of identity and their literal interpretations of the Wahhabi texts which led them to rebel against the Imamate of the Al Saud itself during the late 1920s.

It should be emphasised that not all Wahhabis, nor all badu, were members of the Ikhwan who, even within Najd, were an exclusive religious-military movement. The Ikhwan distinguished themselves from other Wahhabis by the simple way in which they dressed, avoiding affectation or concern in material affairs. They were easily identified because they wore a band of white cloth rather than the traditional black rope or *iqal* to hold the Arab head-dress in place. They refused to address non-Ikhwans, frequently crossing roads in order to avoid any encounter with them. It has also been reported that when they went to urban areas, they would stuff their nostrils and ears with material in order to prevent breathing or hearing any infidelity. They described their pre-Ikhwan days as the *jahiliya* or 'state of ignorance'—that is, the pre-Islamic period.

Site Selection in the Early Ikhwan *Hijras*: Tribal and Geographical Influences

Many writers have estimated the number and size of the Ikhwan settlements, but the lack of any primary source material means that these estimates remain in the realm of speculation. There is, however, enough information from which broad generalisations can be made and will be stressed in the next several sections of this chapter.

The most important feature of these Ikhwan *hijras* was that the tribal idea remained intact and, even though a single settlement might be composed of several tribal groups, each retained its traditional shaikhs. Shamekh, who has written the only study which concerns itself with *hijra* composition and patterns of badu settlement, noted that a single branch of a tribe (*fakhdh*) represented an average of 86 per cent of the total population in each of the 37 *hijras* he studied. He also noted that in al-Qasim there was a distinct separation between the *hijras* of the Bani Salim and Bani Amr divisions of the Harb, who settled in the north and south respectively.[22]

There are two major reasons for the association of tribes with *hijra* settlement. First, the Ikhwan were obviously knowledgeable of the tribal territory within which they had lived a nomadic existence. Sites were chosen for settlement because of favourable geographical factors: arable land, sufficient grazing and a reliable water supply. Although the earliest nomads sold their livestock before settling, they were encouraged by Abd al-Aziz after 1915 to retain their livestock wealth because the purely agricultural *hijra*s had no source of income while learning the practices of cultivation, other than government subsidies. It is therefore not surprising that the Ikhwan settled near permanent water supplies and grazing in their own tribal *dira*s with which they were already familiar and which they knew to be reliable. Second, when tribes settled in their own tribal territory, they minimised potential conflicts arising from differences in tribal membership or status. Even though Abd al-Aziz had theoretically freed the non-*asil* tribes, it is unlikely that this made any practical difference to their perceived status by the *asil* tribes who never regarded them as worthy of inter-marriage.[23] Furthermore, as had always been true in the past, there was undoubtedly an impetus for affiliated tribal groups to maintain territorial cohesion, particularly in the larger and wealthier tribes, such as the Mutair, Harb, and Utaiba.

Shamekh briefly mentions that *hijra*s were assigned to the tribes as free land grants by the central government.[24] He also states that only in a few instances did the government make land purchases—in areas where date palms, for example, had been previously owned.[25] Unfortunately, he does not give any evidence to support these statements and I have found only two other references to land grants. First, Rihani mentions that each *hijra* was assigned a *hima* or protected territory for its own use.[26] Madani, the second reference, states that a tribe was allotted a particular *hijra* after representatives from that tribe requested a site from the government.[27]

There is nothing in any of the references that clarifies whether or not these were land grants of a specified size. Several factors lead me to assume that they were not. First, most of the tribes settled within or near their own tribal *dira*s; second, tribal shaikhs selected the settlement site; third, some members of nomadic tribes did not join the Ikhwan; and, finally, environmental factors varied between sites. Shamekh states that the mean area of each *hijra* was 1023.8 square kilometres. He personally admits that there were certain variables—size of tribe, number of settlers, prestige of tribe and quality of site—which determined the area allotted by the government.[28] It seems more likely that the Al Saud acknowledged the founding of each settlement and gave it full support, but that a *hijra* reached its own optimum size as determined by the above factors.[29]

Number and Population Size of the *Hijras*

The exact number and population size of the Ikhwan settlements are not known, although Habib and Shamekh, who both were able to interview some of the early Ikhwan settlers and to visit the sites, estimate that there were over 200 *hijras*.[30] Habib specifically identified 222.[31] These settlements were generally clustered in the central and northern parts of Najd where there was sufficient water and arable land (cf. Figure 3.1). In al-Qasim settlements were situated east to west along Wadi al-Rumma. There were also a few isolated settlements scattered along the extreme western, northern and south-eastern frontiers of Saudi-controlled territory.

The settlement of the badu in the immediate years after 1912 appears to nave been slow. It increased considerably after the successful Ikhwan campaigns against Jabal Shammar in 1921 and al-Hijaz in 1925. Shamekh ascertained from interviews with the Ikhwan from early *hijras* in al-Qasim that there were only seven settlements founded between 1913 and 1920. This number increased to nine between 1921 and 1925 and to 21 between 1926 and 1930.[32] As will be seen in Part II, the years 1928 and 1929 marked the height of Ikhwan strength, as well as their rebellion against the Saudi authority. It is significant that, after Abd al-Aziz crushed this rebellion in 1929/30, no new *hijras* were established in al-Qasim until 1942 when the reasons for nomad settlement were economic rather than religious. This was presumably true for other areas of Central Arabia as a result of new controls by the central government and the desire of the Ikhwan to be on the side of the winner—that is, the side of the Al Saud.

The population size of these Ikhwan settlements, individually and collectively, has been a subject of the most intense and varied speculation. Shamekh notes that population size in any given settlement was determined by environmental factors, but that the optimum size of most *hijras* was generally 1,500 persons.[33] Assuming that a few of the *hijras* were significantly larger, Shamekh estimates that the mean population for the 37 *hijras* in al-Qasim was 2,593 during the 1920s.[34] Habib's interest in the Ikhwan

Figure 3.1: Clustering of Pre-1930 Ikhwan Settlements

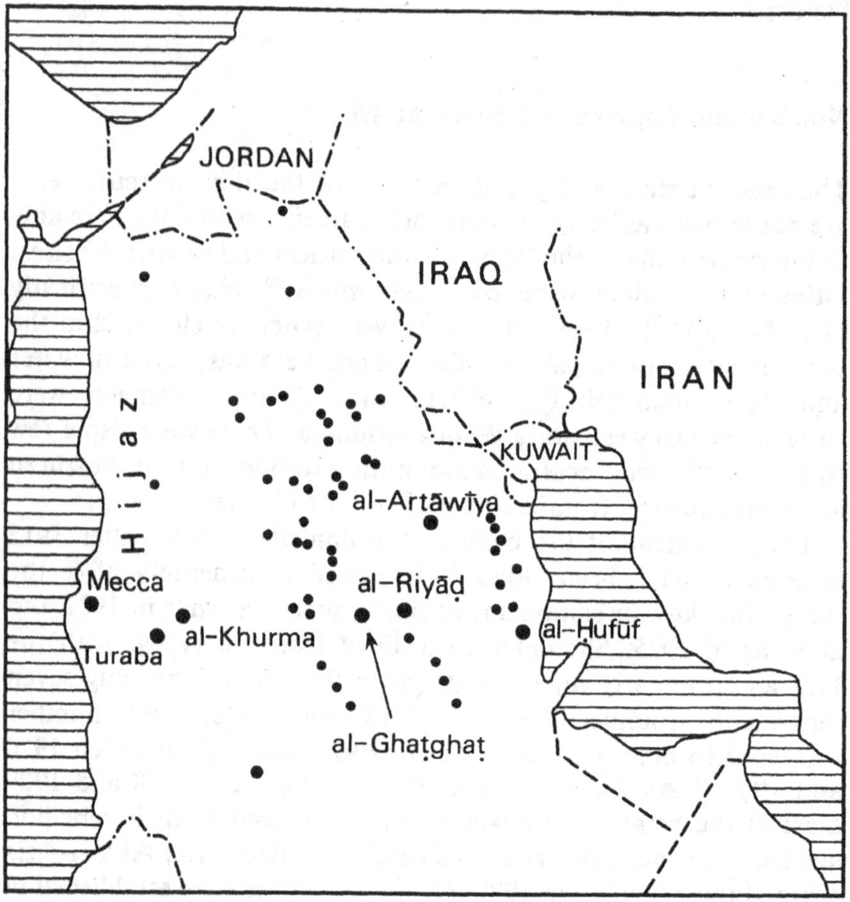

as a military force led him to compile the most extensive lists available on the *hijras*, their associated tribes and their potential fighting strength, even though his final estimates, by his own admission, are only conjectural. Relying on records from British Political Agents, travellers in Central Arabia, Arab writers such as Attar and personal interviews with former Ikhwan warriors, Habib states that a reasonable estimate of the Ikhwan, excluding women and children, would be 150,000 after 1926.[35]

Two of the first, if not the original, Ikhwan settlements were al-Artawiya and al-Ghatghat. Their names brought fear throughout the Peninsula because they were the largest and most fanatical of the Ikhwan settlements and because their leaders, Faisal al-Duwish (Mutair) of al-Artawiya and Ibn Bijad (Utaiba) of al-Ghatghat, were famed for their military exploits and their strict attention to Wahhabi doctrine. It was not without reason that Ibn Bijad was also known as *sultan al-din*, the Sultan or Power of the Religion. Individual estimates for the populations of al-Artawiya and al-Ghatghat have ranged as high as 35,000 and 10,000 respectively. Habib estimated, on the basis of a house count calculating seven persons in each home, that more accurate figures would be 10,000 to 12,000 for al-Artawiya and 3,500 to 4,000 for al-Ghatghat.[36] It should be emphasised that Habib made his count approximately forty years after Abd al-Aziz destroyed al-Ghatghat for its participation in the Ikhwan rebellion. Nor does he take into account any tent dwelling which may have been pitched outside the cities. Concerning the latter of these two points, it is particularly interesting to note that, when Cheesman visited the Al Murra *hijra* in Jabrin during 1923/24, he noted that most of the Ikhwan had remained in their tents and that even the Amir had not yet moved from his tent to the building provided for him.[37]

Organisation and Daily Life in the *Hijras*

Since the principal reason for settling was Islam, it was only natural that the mosque—unadorned and with the low square minaret typical of Wahhabi design—became the focal point of the Ikhwan *hijras*. The town square, containing the central market and stables, was nearby. Mud-brick houses, with adjoining walls, were tightly compressed around the mosque and town square and it is perhaps not surprising that the former badu referred to this area as the *jamsha*, literally 'dry mud', unlike the *hadar* who always called it simply 'the town'.[38] The Ikhwan houses were austere two or three-room structures, each generally provided with its own well so that the women had no need to go to a public one.[39] Tents, still used by the former badu as dwellings, surrounded the *jamsha*. Many of the *hijras* were enclosed by a wall and guard towers, outside which lay the cultivated areas. This was a common defensive measure employed by many of the settled areas of Central Arabia the inhabitants of which retired each night from their fields to protection behind the city walls.

Life in the *hijras* was highly regimented and the chief instrument of control and organisation was the mosque. The Ikhwan, men and women, were obliged to be present in the mosque for the five daily prayers and sermons, sometimes lasting two hours each. The Imam of the mosque took the attendance of all those who were late or absent and, after the sermon, he went to their house to determine the cause, marking their shoes with a special sign to indicate their laxity. These persons were required to explain their behaviour before the Imam if they were absent once, the governor (*hakim*) if twice, and a convocation of the people if thrice.[40] Harrison, who travelled to al-Riyad during the earliest years of the Ikhwan settlements, recorded his impressions in 1918 of this daily regimentation. Although al-Riyad was not an Ikhwan *hijra*, the severity of Wahhabi discipline was, none the less, in evidence.

> In this city men live for the next world. Hundreds are studying in the mosques to go out as teachers among the Bedouin tribes. It is the centre of a system of religious education that takes in every village of Central Arabia, and imparts the rudiments of an education to much the larger part of the male population of the towns. Great efforts are being made now to educate the Bedouins. Many pray five times a day in Riyadh. In the winter the roll is called at early morning prayers and also at the service in the late evening. Absentees are beaten with twenty strokes on the following day. In the summer, duties in the date gardens and elsewhere are considered a valid excuse for praying at home. Only a few years ago a man absented himself for some days from all prayers and was publicly executed for so doing. It is safe to say that there is one city on earth where men are more interested in the next world than they are in this one. Late dinners are unknown. The evening meal is eaten one hour before sundown that there may be time for religious reading and exhortation before going to bed. That is the regular programme in the house of the great chief [Abd al-Aziz] himself.[41]

The Wahhabi teachers constantly stressed to the Ikhwan the importance of one's daily life. A good Ikhwan was to concentrate on his deeds (*ibadat*)—that is, all of his daily actions including those which were not religious in orientation—engaging in productive activity for himself and the community. Although they became formidable military troops, as will be seen in a subsequent section of this chapter and in Part II, the Ikhwan were supposed to devote their time to agriculture. Farms were apportioned by the tribal shaikhs to individual families in the hope that the settlements could eventually become self-supportive. Wheat and date palms were the primary crops. Vegetables and fruit provided a subsidiary crop when water was not too saline. The former badu, unfortunately, had no prior experience with agriculture or the problems of irrigation and it was frequently several years before they developed the necessary skills. Cheesman reported in 1923/24 seeing only small patches of wheat being irrigated in the Jabrin *hijra*;[42] and Dame, who travelled through parts of Central Arabia in 1924, commented on the poor quality of Ikhwan cultivation in the areas he visited.

> We saw some Ikhwan towns too, but their work of cultivation is the poorest I have ever seen. Some sowing is usually done by Bedouins between little hills, but there is not proper preparation of land, weeds are frequently left in, and, of course, no weeding is done after the seed has been sown.[43]

It is not unexpected that the difficulties of agricultural life which the Ikhwan encountered contributed to a continuation of nomadism. Shamekh estimates that in the *hijras* of al-Qasim the mean ratio of people engaged in semi-nomadism was 37 per cent of the total population.[44] Not only was this life-style an efficient use of resources, but it provided them with a supplementary and, in some *hijras*, a primary souce of income.

There were also a number of other occupations practised in the settlements: masonry, metal working, policing and teaching.[45] There were undoubtedly simple stores selling basic goods and people involved in the organisation and maintenance of the irrigation systems and buildings. Additionally, there were people who assisted the central government as tax collectors, messengers, or with military functions. Some of the non-*asil* tribes also specialised in occupations normally regarded as inferior: transporting goods and collecting firewood.

Administration in the *Hijras*

As already stated, after the tribal members became Ikhwan the tribal shaikhs lost the complete authority which they had previously exercised. The shaikhs were frequently to be found in al-Riyad where they underwent special indoctrination in Wahhabi tenets. While there, they pledged, as representatives of their tribes, *baia* or the 'oath of allegiance' to the Saudi Imamate. Many of these shaikhs remained in al-Riyad, no doubt as guarantees of their tribes' loyalty and, if troops needed to be gathered quickly for battle, as intermediaries between the central government and the tribes.

The administration of the *hijras* was under the direct control of an *amir* and *hakim*. The *amir* was elected by the *majlis al-shura* or Consultative Assembly and confirmed by the Imam to whom he was directly responsible. It was his duty to see that any decrees of the Assembly were fulfilled. The *hakim*, on the other hand, was responsible to the *shaikh al-islam*, the head of the Wahhabi *ulama*, and he dealt with any matters that had to be settled by Islamic law.[46] They were both concerned with the *bait al-mal* or 'Islamic treasury'—that is, the collection of taxes and the distribution of subsidies.[47]

The Ikhwan as a Military Force

Prior to the Ikhwan, Abd al-Aziz, like his ancestors in the preceding century, depended on regular conscriptions of badu and *hadar* to compose his army.

> Their military arrangements were entirely administrative; and the mobilisation of their armies was based on registers, in which the obligations of every town, village and tribe to supply men, camels and horses for the various kinds of muster were duly recorded and fully understood by those concerned. In principle arms and ammunition were supplied by the State, when necessary, but the mustered men had to bring their own camels (in some cases two men to one camel) or go afoot, while horsemen had special inducements. In fact every serving man was, as it were, paid out of the proceeds of his service; in that

> when booty was captured from the enemy, one fifth of the whole was allotted to the State Treasury, and the rest was divided among the troops in the proportion of one share to the camel-riders and footmen and two to the cavaliers.[48]

The quotation at the beginning of this chapter concerning Abd al-Aziz's mobilisation of troops for the capture of al-Ahsa is typical of the process described above by Philby. The formation of the Ikhwan was, by 1914, to change not only the composition of the army but the organisation, tactics and even the rationale for which battles were fought. After 1920 Abd al-Aziz's army was almost entirely Ikhwan, and it is said that there was not a single 'sedentary' person who took part in the campaign against al-Hijaz.

Colonel H. R. P. Dickson reported in 1929 that Abd al-Aziz's forces were divided into three categories: regulars, *arab* and Ikhwan.[49] Dickson described the regulars [*sariya*, pl. *saraya*] as paid mercenaries who received a monthly wage and were generally *hadari*s or townspeople. Because they were reliable, they were frequently utilised as garrison forces in places such as al-Ahsa and Hail, as messengers and as guards in transporting the tax collections.[50] They acted under the specific command of Abd al-Aziz in contrast to the *arab* and the Ikhwan who were under the immediate orders of their shaikhs. The *arab* were non-Ikhwan badu, allies of Abd al-Aziz, who acted as scouts or reserves to the main Ikhwan force. The Ikhwan, however, became the most formidable fighting force of the Al Saud from the time of the al-Khurma and Turaba dispute of 1918/19. It was solely through their efforts that Saudi authority expanded into Jabal Shammar, Asir and al-Hijaz. They also made extensive damaging raids into Transjordan, Iraq and Kuwait during the 1920s. Dickson described their tactics as follows:

> when they attack, they have a regular drill which consists of dismounting from their camels and horses, and advancing shoulder to shoulder infantry fashion, and in several lines. Their boast is that they never run nor are tempted to sheer out of the fight as ordinary Bedouins do when on horseback. If an 'akhu' [brother] is slain, his place is immediately taken by another. There is no pause in the forward progress . . . their motto is 'move swiftly and secretly to your objective, when there, attack on foot' . . . . A regular reserve is always maintained in rear to

> reinforce where necessary. Such manoeuvres as dawn attacks, night attacks, flank and rear attacks . . . are regularly understood and practised.[51]

The success of the Ikhwan can be attributed to a number of factors. First, they were highly mobile and armed with modern weapons. Second, as former badu, they had hardened themselves to travelling for days with little to no food or water and were renowned for long stabbing raids and surprise dawn attacks.[52] The final factor was religious zeal. In battle they fought without fear of death, believing that all warriors slain in the cause of Allah immediately entered Paradise. Even though the Ikhwan often fought under the individual tribal banners, their war cries or *nakhwas*, as was seen in Chapter 1, extolled the virtues of Islam—especially their Wahhabi Call to Unity. Their wars were *jihads* and they called themselves the *ahl al-tauhid*, People of Unity. In battle, they frequently killed everyone, including women and children, believing that they alone were the representatives of a pure Islam. The booty from these raids was called *ghanima*—that is, 'booty which is lawfully allowed to be taken in Islam'. Its division was according to Islamic law; four-fifths was divided among the warriors and one-fifth went to the Islamic treasury.

The way in which the troops were mobilised remains largely unknown. Rihani reported that there were three types of mobilisation corresponding to the Turkish terms *nazam*, *radif* and *nafir*, although I have not seen these references made by either the Ikhwan or Abd al-Aziz.[53] There obviously must have been some communication between the Imam, the *ulama* and the *hijras* but, on the other hand, some Ikhwan raids seem to have originated without the knowledge of Abd al-Aziz or, possibly, of the *ulama*. Theoretically, a declaration of *jihad* would be issued by the Imam and the *ulama* through the *majlis al-shura*. Madani records that there were five main branches of the Ikhwan which were organised after 1921 to meet the changing military situation.[54] The first or north-east branch was headquartered at Lina and Umm al-Radma under its chiefs Ibn Jabril and Ibn Thunayan. The duty of this force was to protect the Iraq frontier, converting, if possible, the Anaza, Shammar and Zafir tribes to Wahhabi doctrine. Ibn Daghmi and Ibn Uqail were the chiefs of the north-west branch of the Ikhwan which was centred at al-Jubba—a site midway between Najd, Iraq, al-Hijaz and Syria. They were to control the territory between Maan and the Syrian Desert which included the tribes of the Bani Sakhr, al-Ruwala, Bani Atiya, al-Huwaitat and Shararat. Another branch was in northern al-Hijaz at Dakhna and Taima under the command of Ibn Nahait (or Nahit), whose primary concern was the control of tribes around al-Madina and Mecca. Khalid b. Luai at al-Khurma was chief of the fourth branch of the Ikhwan in southern al-Hijaz, controlling the roads east of Mecca and al-Madina. The fifth and final branch was led by Faisal al-Duwish from al-Artawiya, north of al-Riyad. Madani lists this as a reserve branch.

Although Habib feels Madani's classification may have some general validity, he believes that the Ikhwan followed their own leaders, particularly Duwish of al-Artawiya and Ibn Bijad of al-Ghatghat, to a much greater extent than was realised.[55] It should be pointed out that Habib based his opinions largely on interviews conducted with relatives or former assistants of Duwish who was later one of the major instigators of the Ikhwan rebellion against Abd al-Aziz and they were therefore more likely to emphasise the role of their own shaikhs than that of Abd al-Aziz with whom they had little contact. There are two further reasons which lead one to question Habib's criticism. First, he credits Duwish as being a more influential leader than Ibn Bijad. This is not supported by Attar, the India Office Records or Lieutenant-General Sir John Bagot Glubb; all three indicate that the control and influence wielded by Ibn Bijad were greater than those of Duwish until the latter half of the 1920s.[56] Second, Habib cites Madani's 'glaring omission' of al-Ghatghat. This could possibly be explained by the fact that this *hijra* was included within one of the other divisions. During the conquest of al-Hijaz, in 1924/25, Khalid b. Luai, whom Madani lists as the chief of southern al-Hijaz, was made the chief Ikhwan commander during the campaign. It is clear from historical accounts, however, that Ibn Bijad was equally important during this campaign and it was he who anticipated being appointed as Governor of al-Hijaz itself after the campaign was completed. Although Duwish was one of the commanders, he did not occupy a place of importance equal to that of Luai or Ibn Bijad. It was the colourfulness and daring of Duwish in the Ikhwan rebellion several years later which helped him to dominate our historical perspective, as will be seen in Part II.

Whatever the final answers to the problems presented above, it is clear that, in the process of becoming the main striking arm in Abd al-Aziz's forces, the Ikhwan were experiencing a number of theoretical and practical changes. Before the formation of the *hijras*, many of the badu had not known the correct Islamic prayers, did not sanctify their marriages by Islam, settled disputes by customary tribal law, engaged primarily in nomadism or semi-nomadism, and accepted the authority only of their tribes. The changes they experienced were reflected in new attitudes to political authority, to social status, to patterns of settlement, occupation and warfare, and to the arbitration of disputes.

Summary

In the preceding chapters it was shown that the alliance of the Al Saud with the Al Wahhab helped to establish the supreme political authority of the Saudi family as Arab and Islamic leaders over numerous tribes and urban areas which previously had been independent. The isolation of Central Arabia, the absence of any foreign influence, the alliance of badu tribes with urban areas, and the organisation inherent in tribal structure all facilitated the consolidation of Saudi authority.

During the first three decades of the twentieth century, political control began to be exercised as much in the countryside as in the cities for the first time in Central Arabian history. All tribes were theoretically considered equal in status and all men were brothers, as Abd al-Aziz said: 'We the people of Najd follow the Prophet, who recognized no differences in rank among Muslims.'[57] Thus, while tribal structure could act as a divisive factor, it was also employed as a valuable political tool. Inferior tribes were freed from paying *khuwa* to more powerful tribes as the Al Saud instituted Islamic taxation. The Saudis also declared unlawful those tribal customs which reinforced the authority of tribal shaikhs, such as *dakhala*, and tribal shaikhs were held responsible for crimes committed by their tribal members. Formerly, during poor seasons, tribes had moved across tribal boundaries to obtain water and grazing, and this practice had resulted in many conflicts. Abd al-Aziz, however, instituted a system whereby tribes had to ask permission from the central goverment to move out of their territory. Furthermore, badu began to settle in new towns, *hijras*, which functioned as religious, political, economic, administrative, educational and military centres. For many years these men,

Ikhwan, formed the core of the Saudi military. Administrative provinces were determined and governors appointed to carry out economic and social policies emanating from the central government in al-Riyad as the Al Saud continued to consolidate their control, validating their exclusive claim to political authority by their emphasis on their Arab and Islamic heritage.

This chapter has concerned itself primarily with the formation of the Ikhwan and their role in Saudi political expansion. In the late 1920s the Ikhwan openly rebelled against the Saudi Imamate. The origins of this rebellion are fully discussed in Part II. The next chapter, however, discusses one aspect of Saudi political control—taxation—and its significance both to the nature of Saudi authority and to the way in which the Ikhwan perceived a true Islamic government.

Notes

1. India Office Records, *Political and Secret Department Separate Files 1902-1931*, L/P&S/10 (henceforward abbreviated to IO L/P&S/10): IO L/P&S/10/385, memorandum from Captain W. H. Shakespear, Political Agent Kuwait, to Sir Arthur Hirtzel, Secretary to the Political Department of the India Office, 26 June 1914.
2. Lewis Pelly, *Report on A Journey to Riyadh in Central Arabia (1865)* (Oleander Press, Cambridge, 1977), pp.49-50.
3. Ameen Rihani, *Ibn Sa'oud of Arabia: His People and His Land* (Constable, London, 1928), pp.196-7.
4. John S. Habib, 'The Ikhwan Movement of Najd: Its Rise, Development and Decline' (PhD thesis, University of Michigan, 1970), pp.32-8 and 85-95, presents a detailed discussion of this contradictory evidence although his conclusion, that 'Abd al-'Azīz was the creator of the Ikhwan, is not supported by his analysis. It may be noted that there is only one Arabic source, *firqat al-ikhwān al-islāmiya bi najd au wahhābiya al-yaum* (no publisher listed, 1342 (1923)) by Muḥammad Mughairabī Fatiḥ al-Madanī, which is devoted entirely to the Ikhwan. Unfortunately, it does not deal with the origins of the movement and, because it was published in 1923, omits the later period when Ikhwan strength reached its height.
5. H. R. P. Dickson, *Kuwait and Her Neighbours* (George Allen and Unwin, London, 1968), p.149.
6. Aḥmad 'Abd al-Ghafūr 'Aṭṭār, *ṣaqr al-jazīra*, 7 vols (Maṭba'at al-Ḥurrīya, Beirut, 1972), pp.429-31.
7. William Gifford Palgrave, *Narrative of a Year's Journey Through Central and Eastern Arabia*, 2 vols (Gregg International, Farnborough, 1969), vol. I, pp.407-15, and vol. II, p.3. It might also be noted that Madanī, *firqat al-ikhwān al-islāmiya bi najd au wahhābiya al-yaum*, pp.26-8, refers to *mubashirūn* or 'missionaries' carrying the message of Wahhabiism into Jabal Shammar prior to 1910.
8. Sulaimān al-Dakhīl, 'al-arṭawīya au balad jadīda fī diyār najd', *Lughat al-'Arab*, 2 (1913), p.481.

9. Even though 'Abd al-'Azīz's father, 'Abd al-Raḥmān, formally retained the title of Imam, 'Abd al-'Azīz was recognised as the real head of the Islamic community.

10. Ahmed A. Shamekh, *Spatial Patterns of Bedouin Settlement in al-Qasim Region Saudi Arabia* (University of Kentucky Press, Lexington, 1975), p.46.

11. Louis P. Dame, 'Four Months in Nejd', *Moslem World*, 14 (1924), p.360.

12. Ch. 4 gives a detailed discussion of Abd al-'Azīz's substitution of *zakāt* in place of *khuwa*, the old badu levy paid by a client tribe to a stronger tribe which then promised them military protection. The implications of *zakāt* payment, collection and dispersal are also discussed within the context of Saudi Arabia.

13. H. R. P. Dickson, *The Arab of the Desert: A Glimpse into Badawin Life in Kuwait and Sa'udi Arabia* (George Allen and Unwin, London, 1972), p.572.

14. Rihani, *Ibn Sa'oud of Arabia*, pp.200-3. The leading Wahhabi shaikh in Najd was 'Abdullāh b. Muḥammad b. 'Abd al-Laṭīf b. 'Abd al-Raḥmān Al Shaikh until his death in 1920/21 (Madanī, *firqat al-ikhwān al-islāmīya bi najd au wahhābīya al-yaum*, p.20).

15. Under the reign of the Abassid Khalifa al-Ma'mūn, Baghdad was the centre of a number of uprisings so severe that *muṭṭawwi'ūn* or 'volunteers' gathered to protect the quarters of the city. One of the leaders of these groups was Sahl b. Salāma al-Anṣārī who enlisted followers after they agreed to uphold the Qur'ān and the Sunna and pledged allegiance, *bai'a* to him. He voiced slogans calling for all to obey the legal, moral and ritual teachings of Islam as well as to oppose its violation by others. His position was extreme, essentially denying the leadership of the Khalifa and undertaking to represent the interests of the *umma* himself. Although he was later stopped, his actions represented one of the first direct challenges to the authority of the Khalifate. One can compare Anṣārī to 'Abd al-'Azīz who, during the period between 1912 and 1920, opposed the authority of the Ottoman Khalifa and then the Al Hāshim in al-Ḥijāz. Like Anṣārī, 'Abd al-'Azīz claimed his position was legitimate.

16. Shamekh, who conducted the survey (*Spatial Patterns of Bedouin Settlement*, p.121), noted that none of these *hijras* was founded because of losses in livestock.

17. Both of the letters quoted here are found in Madanī, *firqat al-ikhwān al-islāmīya bi najd au wahhābīya al-yaum*, pp.35-40.

18. The Wahhabi shaikhs were 'Abdullāh b. 'Abd al-Laṭīf, Ḥasan b. Ḥusain, Sa'd b. Ḥamad b. 'Atīq, 'Umar b. Muḥammad b. Salīm, 'Abdullāh b. 'Abd al-'Azīz al-'Unqarī, Sulaimān b. Sāmḥān, Muḥammad b. 'Abd al-Laṭīf, 'Abdullāh b. Bulaihid and 'Abd al-Raḥmān b. Sālim.

19. *Muhājirūn* was also the word applied to those Meccans who were 'immigrants' to al-Madīna in order to follow the prophet Muḥammad.

20. See Ch. 2 for a more detailed discussion of Wahhabi doctrine, particularly its attitude to Muslims who were not Wahhabis and to non-Muslims, and to the way in which this affected political behaviour. There are a number of stories, however, which illustrate that 'Abd al-'Azīz was moderate in his own religious observances, such as the following story told to Ameen Rihani by one of 'Abd al-'Azīz's companions: 'We rode out of Al-Hasa . . .', he said, 'we were about twenty—and when we entered the Dahna Abd'ul Aziz took off his *ighal* and *gutrah* and put them in his saddle-bag. He then looked around and said: "There are no Ikhwan with us. He who has a good voice will now let us hear it." We started to sing, *wallah*! and Abd'ul Aziz was most pleased.' (Rihani, *Ibn Sa'oud of Arabia*, p.212.)

21. Ḥāfiẓ Wahba, *Arabian Days* (Arthur Barker, London, 1964), p.127.

22. Shamekh, *Spatial Patterns of Bedouin Settlement*, pp.123-4 and 282-6. Shamekh, a Sa'udi Arab, limited his study to the region of al-Qaṣīm although there is no reason to suspect that the composition of the settlements varied, particularly as tribal boundaries were not confined to the limits of any of the major regions such as

al-Qaṣīm. Shamekh divided his study into 'early *hijras*' or pre-1930 settlements and 'recent *hijras*' or post-1930 settlements. The recent *hijras* were differentiated from their earlier counterparts primarily because they were not founded for religious but for economic reasons.

23. Ibid., pp.113-14, in which is recorded the case of Muḍabra, a branch of the so-called 'despised' Hutaim tribe, who had been living an isolated existence in a mountainous region. It was only after 'Abd al-'Azīz established a strong central government that the Muḍabra chose to move down to the surrounding plains in 1921. They do not appear to have joined with any previously existing *hijras* nor did any other tribe choose to settle with them.

24. Ibid., p.125.

25. Ibid., p.120.

26. Rihani, *Ibn Sa'oud of Arabia*, p.194. All *ḥimās* were abolished by the Sa'udi government in 1953, presumably to encourage sedentarization (Shamekh, *Spatial Patterns of Bedouin Settlement*, pp.44, 71, 256). See also Frede Løkkegaard, *Islamic Taxation in the Classic Period with Special Reference to Circumstances in Iraq* (Branner and Korch, Copenhagen, 1950) for a more detailed discussion of the *ḥimā* system generally.

27. Madanī, *firqat al-ikhwān al-islāmīya bi najd au wahhābīya al-yaum*, p.34.

28. Shamekh, *Spatial Patterns of Bedouin Settlement*, p.125.

29. There exists only one reference to the fact that 'Abd al-'Azīz controlled the allocation of tribes in some of the *hijras*, but this only concerned those tribes recalcitrant to Sa'udi authority. Dickson, the Political Agent in Kuwait, reported that 'Abd al-'Azīz had said the al-'Ujmān had twice betrayed him and he hoped to bring them to the interior of Najd and distribute them among twenty *hijras* (Dickson, *Kuwait and Her Neighbours*, p.250).

30. Shamekh, *Spatial Patterns of Bedouin Settlement*, pp.108-9. See Habib, 'The Ikhwan Movement of Najd', p.111; pp.305-14 for an extensive compilation of Ikhwan *hijras*; and pp.245-53 for a list in English of the political and religious leaders of the *hijras* (originally from *Umm al-Qurā*, no. 208).

31. Habib, 'The Ikhwan Movement of Najd', p.112, identified a dominant tribe in 175 out of the 222 *hijras* he found. The tribes who had the largest number of *hijras* were Muṭair with 27; 'Utaiba, 25; Ḥarb, 38; Shammar, 23; Qaḥṭān, 11; and al-'Ujmān, 19.

32. Shamekh, *Spatial Patterns of Bedouin Settlement*, pp.109-13 and 169-70.

33. Ibid., p.117.

34. Ibid., p.130.

35. Habib, 'The Ikhwan Movement of Najd', pp.40-8. 'Aṭṭār, *ṣaqr al-jazīra*, pp.414-15, records the number of the tribes who were Ikhwan as follows: Muṭair, 40,000; Dawāsir, 7,000; Raqā, 14,000; Barqa, 8,000; al-'Ujmān, 15,000; Ḥarb, 30,000; 'Awāzim, 10,000; Al Murra, 10,000; and Shammar, 50,000.

36. Habib, 'The Ikhwan Movement of Najd', pp.96-109.

37. R. E. Cheesman, *In Unknown Arabia* (Macmillan, London, 1926), pp.250-1.

38. Shamekh, *Spatial Patterns of Bedouin Settlement*, p.160.

39. According to Habib, 'The Ikhwan Movement of Najd', p.102, women were not allowed in the public market and purchased any goods they needed near the mosque. Even a daughter of the former King Sa'ūd b. 'Abd al-'Azīz was forcibly prevented from entering the *sūq* of al-Arṭāwīya in March 1968. When Habib visited al-Arṭāwīya in the same year he found that women were still not permitted to speak in public and attracted the attention of other women by clapping their hands.

40. Madanī, *firqat al-ikhwān al-islāmīya bi najd au wahhābīya al-yaum*, p.41.

41. Paul W. Harrison, 'Al Riadh, The Capital of Nejd', *Moslem World*, 8 (1918), pp.418-19.

42. Cheesman, *In Unknown Arabia*, pp.250-1.

43. Dame, 'Four Months in Nejd', p.357.
44. Shamekh, *Spatial Patterns of Bedouin Settlement*, pp.138-43 and 274-81.
45. 'Aṭṭār, *ṣaqr al-jazīra*, pp.411-16.
46. Madanī, *firqat al-ikhwān al-islāmīya bi najd au wahhābīya al-yaum*, pp.41-2.
47. Ch. 4 is concerned with the substitution by the Al Sa'ūd of Islamic taxation for the system of tribal levies which operated prior to the firm establishment of Sa'udi authority. Habib, 'The Ikhwan Movement of Najd', pp.78-80, gives a detailed account of government subsidies. It may be said generally that they varied considerably according to the prestige of a tribe or individual, whether the King received military assistance from them, and other political and economic considerations. Payments might be made at specified times or only once, such as the offer of marriage money. Finally, subsidies were made in all forms: money, clothing, food or anything else which was needed or requested. 'Abd al-'Azīz, for example, made frequent contributions of seed and rice to the *hijras*.
48. H. St John B. Philby, *Sa'udi Arabia* (Ernest Benn, London, 1955), pp.194-5.
49. IO L/P&S/10/1243, letter from Lieutenant-Colonel H. R. P. Dickson, Political Agent Kuwait, to the Political Resident in the Persian Gulf, 2 September 1929.
50. Dickson's use of the term 'mercenary' does not, unfortunately, distinguish between townspeople who volunteered their services in lieu of tax payment or who were obligated to spend so much time each year in fulfilment of military service and those who quite literally were paid mercenaries, such as former Turkish soldiers. Until the Ikhwan, the townspeople were considered the most loyal of all troops because their interests were more closely allied to those of the ruling family. As will be discussed in Ch. 8, 'Abd al-'Azīz once again relied upon assistance from the townspeople when he crushed the Ikhwan rebellion. Nor does Dickson include the slaves who frequently accompanied 'Abd al-'Azīz as personal and trusted guards.
51. IO L/P&S/10/1243, letter from Lieutenant-Colonel H. R. P. Dickson, Political Agent Kuwait, to the Political Resident in the Persian Gulf, 2 September 1929. See also Habib, 'The Ikhwan Movement of Najd' for a detailed study of their battles, tactics, numbers and so forth.
52. Sir John Bagot Glubb, *War in the Desert: An R.A.F. Frontier Campaign* (Hodder and Stoughton, London, 1960).
53. Rihani, *Ibn Sa'oud of Arabia*, p.194.
54. Madanī, *firqat al-ikhwān al-islāmīya bi najd au wahhābīya al-yaum*, pp.43-5.
55. Habib, 'The Ikhwan Movement of Najd', pp.139-40.
56. Glubb, as a young officer at that time, was involved in protecting the southern Iraq frontier from the Ikhwan. He told me in an interview that he personally believed Ibn Bijād to be the most influential of all the Ikhwan leaders until 1926/27.
57. Rihani, *Ibn Sa'oud of Arabia*, p.46.

4

The Al Saud and Policies of Islamic and Non-Islamic Taxation

By the year 1927 a rift begun two years earlier between the Saudi government and the Ikhwan substantially widened and the latter began openly to criticise the sincerity of Abd al-Aziz's motives as an Islamic leader. One of their complaints concerned the taxes instituted by the Al Saud, other than *zakat* which they considered a lawful Islamic tax—*ma ahalla Allah* or 'that which God permits'. It is essential to examine the meaning of *zakat* and other taxes then current in Najd not only in order to determine the latent and manifest reasons for the Ikhwan complaint, but also because the protest against the taxes reveals something of the fiscal structure of the Saudi state and the difficulties that confronted Abd al-Aziz's administration. A study of the evolution of *zakat* tax—payment, collection and distribution—within the confines of Saudi authority also helps to illustrate the nature of the society in that tax is neither paid nor collected without an attendant set of mutual expectations and obligations.

As will subsequently be discussed, a unique development occurred in the evolution of *zakat* as a fiscal instrument when the Saudi government asserted that this tax amounted to a political tribute. Since the eighteenth century the first act of every Saudi ruler, after the successful defeat of urban areas or badu tribes, had been to demand *zakat*. Moreover, they claimed the allegiance of all who paid this tax, notwithstanding its collection by force, and, by extrapolation, they claimed all political rights accruing from that allegiance. It is important to examine the meaning of *zakat* in concrete terms, as well as the original concepts underlying its institutionalisation, before attempting to explain its manifestations within the Arabian Peninsula.

Islamic *Zakat*

In simplistic terms *zakat* is a form of alms giving incumbent only on Muslims, one of the five obligatory virtues or 'pillars' of Islam. During the early Khalifate period, with the rapid expansion of Islam and the establishment of governmental institutions, it evolved into a strictly regulated tax levied by an Islamic government on specific forms of property.[1] The sum was divided into eight portions: seven were distributed to seven categories of persons and the eighth portion was reserved *fi sabil Allah* or 'in the path of God'.[2]

Zakat originated in the earliest days of Islam from the simple beliefs that benevolence and justice were virtues, worldly possessions obfuscated the true purity of life, and giving was a pious deed. The verb *zaka* from which *zakat* is derived literally means 'to be just', 'to be good' and 'to be pure'. In the transition from the earliest Meccan Suras to those of the Madina period, the performance of *zakat* remained one of the chief virtues of Islam although its original meaning gradually came to mean 'gift' and 'alms' or 'charity'. Even in later periods of Islam, when *zakat* was considered chiefly as a 'religious tax', it never lost its fundamental associations with justice, piety, purity and, later, alms giving. Although the alms as such were important, it was the actual act of giving that alone was considered meritorious.[3]

It was inevitable that, in time, *zakat* as an institution would be influenced by the political and social environment. During the life of the Prophet himself, not only did the implicit meaning of *zakat* evolve, but there is evidence that its interpretation by nomadic and settled peoples differed. As mentioned previously, *zakat* was initially seen as a virtue relating solely to personal 'spirituality'. Later in Muhammad's life, however, while the act of giving remained paramount, importance also began to be attached to the recipient and to the general awareness that one was participating with fellow Muslims in a distinctly Islamic tradition. Furthermore, *zakat* seems to have been an individual contribution in the settled areas while in the case of tribal badu groups, lump sum payments were made. These were the result of agreements between the tribes and Muhammad which the former could scarcely have regarded as an Islamic alms tax. This is evidenced by two facts: many badu tribal groups considered these to be contractual agreements abrogated upon the Prophet's death and Umar, one of the four Righteous Khalifas, concurred with their opinion. It may be that the badu regarded the tax not as a contract between themselves and Allah, which would be unaffected by the death of a temporal leader, but rather as a contract between themselves and a political leader—a token of alliance or allegiance. It is noteworthy that the tax was taken as a lump sum payment from the tribal chief and not 'given' by individuals with 'pure intention'. Furthermore, it resembles other forms of taxation in Arabia among badu tribes quite outside Islamic tradition—taxes which did signify political associations. It is possible that the tribes saw an analogy between the Islamic *zakat* and the non-Islamic forms of tribal taxation with which they were familiar.

After the death of the Prophet, *zakat* underwent even more definite change as the early Khalifate regularised its payment and allocation. What had once been a voluntary and individual act of giving directly to deserving persons became for most people a tax that was assessed by a government collector known variously as an *amil, muzakki* or *arif*. The distribution was left entirely to government authorities and the category that was designated 'in the path of God' to receive *zakat* was broad enough to allow Islamic governments to appropriate the tax for their own political and military purposes, such as payment of non-regular Muslim troops who fought in a *jihad*. It is clear that the method of payment, collection and distribution of *zakat* would vary according to each individual or Islamic government which independently interpreted *zakat* according to its own needs and with regard to the school of Islamic law to which it adhered. This reason alone is sufficient to illustrate that *zakat* cannot be categorically defined because it was never a static concept or institution; any attempt to do so ignores the realities of institutional development and human participation in the process.

Contending that payment of *zakat* was equivalent to pledging allegiance to a temporal government, the Al Saud claimed the Buraimi Oasis and certain other territories which the United Arab Amirates had considered to be under their jurisdiction.[4] As justification of its claim, the Saudi government produced a document in 1955 entitled *ʿarḍ al-ḥukūmat al-ʿarabīya al-saʿūdīya:*

al-taḥkīm ma'a masqaṭ wa abū ẓabī , known in English as the *Sa'udi Memorial*. The position of the Saudi government concerning the implications of *zakat* taxation are succinctly stated in the following extracts which deserve to be quoted at length because of the light they throw on the political events of the 1920s.

> Of all the State activities tending to substantiate a claim of effective possession . . . those having the greatest probative value are the collection of taxes and the preservation of public security . . . . *zakāt* early became the chief general tax imposed on the Muslims. On him who has the right to collect it rests the corollary duty to protect those who pay it: no collection, as has been said, without protection (*lā jibāya illā bi ḥimāya*).[5]

> The Sa'udi Arabian government is and always has been a true Islamic government, founded firmly on the principles of the Sharī'a. As such, it has always taken *zakāt* from its subjects in the manner prescribed by that law . . . . the significant point . . . is the character of the *zakāt* as a true tax, implying on the part of the taxpayer an allegiance in secular as well as religious matters, and on the part of the government an assertion of temporal sovereignty. It is the view of the Sa'udi Arabian government that the paying and taking of *zakāt* implies precisely this . . . . Those who pay *zakāt* are devout Muslims, and the Imam has as his duty the protection of the Faith and the Faithful. Thus the payment of *zakāt* is an act which puts the tax-payers under the protection of the collector. In effect, this amounts to a sealing of allegiance through the joint performance of an obligatory religious act.[6]

The Saudi position was strongly criticised by many Westerners and by Arabs in a position to lose territory to the Al Saud. These criticisms were based on the fact that the concept of Saudi *zakat* was not a 'pure *zakat*'.[7] Although it is not the purpose of this study to discuss the relative merits of these arguments, the following discussion will show that even though the Saudi *zakat* was not a so-called 'pure' one,[8] it naturally embodied the fundamental and evolved concepts of *zakat* as well as incorporating elements of the 'desert' or customary law of the badu, and gives an insight into the nature of Saudi political authority.

Saudi Position on *Zakat*

Upon what grounds did the Saudis feel justified in claiming that payment of *zakat* was tantamount to a pledge of alliance or, more to the point, that payment gave the payee, in their view, a claim to the allegiance of those who paid the tax? What were the implications of such a claim? From a purist point of view, the Saudi claim regarding the implications of *zakat* payment would have to be rejected outright. For the moment, however, let us assume that *zakat* as it is found in the Arabian peninsula is a manifestation of the particular character of that society and, further, that Saudi *zakat* is not inconsistent either with the early Islamic concept of it or with the Islamic concept of government.[9]

Taking the Saudi position on *zakat* at face value, several observations can be made. First, payment and collection of the tax can be viewed as a contract analogous, in a way, to the individual's fulfilling his covenant with Allah. The contract in this case was between a Muslim government and its Islamic subjects. The government was empowered to make such a contract because it was an Islamic authority which belonged at once to the Islamic community or *umma* but ultimately to Allah. Second, after the tax had been paid the Muslim authorities had the duty to protect those who had paid it: a contract must be fulfilled by all parties signatory to it. As will be discussed, this concept of 'protection of those who pay' is strikingly similar to other forms of non-Islamic taxation such as the *khuwa* or 'brotherhood tax' found among the badu tribal areas of the Arabian Peninsula.

It is not possible to discuss any of these questions without understanding that the Quran and the Sunna laid down a system of moral rules for the guidance of activities between men and between men and God. Following Muhammad's death, divine legislation came to an end and the Khalifas became enforcers of the divine law, the authority that legitimised their own power.[10] The temporal leader of an Islamic government fulfilled part of his covenant with Allah by enforcing the latter's divine and ultimate authority on earth, just as every Muslim had his individual covenant with Allah. The nature of the sacred law implied that both temporal leader and every Muslim were in a contractual relationship with the Muslim *umma*. Loyalty to the *umma* superseded loyalties to any other social group. Governments and individuals within Islamic society had inherent rights by virtue of belonging to that society, both deriving their rights from their covenant with Allah. So great was the implicit belief in the authority of Allah, that the distinction between society and state in early Islam was vague.[11]

To return to the role of *zakat* in Islamic society, it might be argued that, in presenting alms, the average Muslim was not fulfilling a contract between himself and Allah or between himself and the Muslim *umma*, but was simply performing an act of personal purification or being virtuous. This was undeniably true at one level. However, if you were not a Muslim, the payment would not be possible. Furthermore, you would not be a Muslim if you did not pay it. Theoretically, alms were 'voluntary, disinterested and spontaneous', but in fact were 'obligatory and interested'—individually and societally.[12] Payment of *zakat* was tantamount to a declaration both of right and of obligation to defend Allah and the *umma*. A statement was issued in November 1936 by Shaikh Shakhbut b. Sultan, a former ruler of Abu Dhabi, re-emphasising the implications of *zakat*. The meaning is uncompromisingly clear—*zakat* signifies secular as well as temporal authority.

> To all people of Liwa who may see it: The bearer, Humaid bin Dahnān, is an agent for us and on our behalf to collect the *zakah* [*zakat*] due to us with you. Anyone who refuses him refuses us. This should be known to you.[13]

The Saudi assertion that *zakat* signified allegiance is not justified solely by an interpretation of the fundamental and evolved meaning of *zakat* (the transition from personal virtue to a covenant relationship), but also through its association with the essence of Islam implicit in such concepts as the *umma* and the nature of temporal authority based on the divine law of Islam.

The only claim of the Saudis that deviated from so-called pure *zakat* was their insistence that protection of those who paid the tax was an obligation on those who collected it. As is well known, Islamic influence after the death of Muhammad extended over three continents. Eventually, the Muslim world became fragmented and Islamic religious and governmental institutions evolved more in response to localised social and environmental conditions. The comparatively large ratio of badu to townspeople in Najd as distinct from other areas of the Arab world, and its isolation, were two factors that characterised this region. As has been seen in

Chapter 1, the nomadic and settled populations of Central Arabia had for centuries been evolving traditions for regulating intra- and inter-community relationships quite apart from any Islamic influences to which they were exposed.

Each individual was subject to the customary law of his tribe as administered by the shaikhs. This system of customary law served to regularise the shifting political and ecological relationships between tribes when there was no central governing authority and force was the predominant means of determining hierarchical authority patterns. *Khuwa*, a term derived from the same root as that of *akh* or 'brother', means 'a brotherhood tax' and was an important element of this customary law.[14] The following definition of *khuwa* by Lieutenant-General Sir John Bagot Glubb indicates the important role that *khuwa* played in regularising certain aspects of tribal and inter-tribal life.

> This was a household word all over Arabia before the 1920s. In the old days, the bedouins in the desert were completely independent. The Turks made virtually no attempt to control them. They regarded the desert as their country and they collected dues for safe conduct from anyone who crossed it. In addition, there were many routes which were partly desert like Amman to Maan, or up the Euphrates from Ramadi to Aleppo. Any merchant who wanted to take a caravan up these routes paid dues. The system was an elaborate one. *Khuwa* means brotherhood. The merchant would have a 'brother' in each bedouin tribe. He would contact his brother, pay the dues, and the brother would then send an escort to protect the caravan from molestation by his fellow tribesmen. He could only protect from his own tribe, so the merchant might also have a 'brother' in Shammar or Bani Sakhr or wherever he was going. Each of these would send an escort to protect the caravan from molestation by his fellow tribesmen. Secondly there were many agricultural villages along the edge of the desert who could be looted by the nomad bedouins. In order to live in peace, these villages also paid *khuwa* to the nearest bedouin tribe for protection. You could call it blackmail if you like.[15]

It will also be recalled from Chapter 1 that *khuwa* was given as tribute by settled or nomadic groups to a more powerful tribe. Its underlying concept is so strikingly similar to the 'unpure' aspect of the Saudi interpretation of *zakat* that it appears that the peculiar cast of *zakat* in the Central Arabian plateau arose from its association with customary law.

Both *khuwa* and *zakat* were based on the principle that an unwritten but valid contract exists between two parties: individuals and tribes were bound under certain circumstances to fulfil self-serving but mutually beneficial obligations. When a peripheral tribe paid *khuwa* to a more powerful tribe, it expected and received protection against any aggressor. Moreover, *khuwa* relationships between otherwise antagonistic tribes served to regularise a variety of everyday relationships, such as helping to restore stolen property and assisting the passage of goods and people across alien tribal territory. If a brother failed to fulfil his *khuwa* obligation it was considered a serious breach, dishonouring not only himself but his tribe.[16] He might even be ostracised from his blood group. *Khuwa*, unlike *zakat*, was not a sacred tribute, although both reflected the shifting socio-economic relationships in tribal society. The badu said of *khuwa* that 'Those who receive the *khuwa* must protect those who give it to them'. Expressed in similar fashion, the al-Ruwala, a powerful tribe in north-western Arabia, have a saying that, 'He who eats a young goat must protect its mother'.[17] Both phrases are strikingly similar to the quotation from the *Sa'udi Memorial* concerning *zakat* which states that there is 'no collection . . . without protection'.

The importance attached to the claim of *zakat* arose in the Buraimi dispute because the Al Saud wished to extend their territorial boundaries. By claiming the political allegiance of nomadic tribes, they expected to gain rights to tribal territory. The assumptions attached to *zakat* were the same in the 1920s as in the 1950s, although in the earlier years Abd al-Aziz was trying to consolidate his authority and create a strong central government over numerous powerful tribes as much as he was seeking to extend his territorial influence.

In the post-World War I period Western-style boundaries had been drawn across badu grazing *diras*, interfering with tribal access to resources and their *musabala*—the travelling to the markets of the larger towns in order to trade. Lengthy diplomatic negotiations were initiated between Saudi Arabia, Iraq and Kuwait to determine whose authority the tribes were under when they crossed the boundaries. Saudi Arabia maintained that collection of *zakat* was a symbol of legitimate authority irrespective of the physical location of the tribe. Thus, Abd al-Aziz was faced with the dual problem of preventing his tribes from moving across the border in summer and hence paying *zakat* to a foreign government,[18] and collecting *zakat* from Saudi tribes encamped in foreign countries. The conflict was further exacerbated by the Saudi claim of *zakat* from foreign tribes camped within Saudi territory.

'Unlawful' and Other 'Lawful' Islamic Taxes

After the initial expansion of Islam, lawful taxes were not sufficient to support the Islamic state and Muslim authorities were forced to seek additional sources of revenue which were considered unlawful by Islamic law. A review of the revenues, both lawful and unlawful, and the expenditures generally prevalent during Islamic history will provide a background for understanding similar issues which faced the Saudi authorities during the 1920s as they attempted to solve their economic, social and political problems.

The revenue of the Muslim *bait al-mal* or 'treasury'[19] can be divided into two categories. The first is *mal al-sadaqa*, 'wealth of alms', which is property housed in the treasury but the ownership of which is vested in those people who are due to receive it. *Zakat* was in this category. The second category was *mal al-muslimin*, 'wealth of the Muslims' or *huquq bait al-mal*, 'rights of the treasury', both distinguished from *mal al-sadaqa* in that they signified public funds of the *umma*. Allocation of funds in the *bait al-mal* was determined by the Imam.

The predominant revenue classed as *mal al-muslimin* during the early Islamic conquests came from *jizya* and *kharaj* taxes, collectively termed *fai*.[20] According to Sura 59:6-7, *fai* means 'what God has allowed to return to his Apostle' or that which has been 'returned' to the Muslims. Both *jizya* and *kharaj* were taxes levied against non-Muslims in territory under Islamic jurisdiction. *Jizya* was a poll tax levied on adult males of the *ahl al-dhimma*. The *ahl al-dhimma* were *ahl al-kitab*, People of the Revealed Book, such as Jews and Christians who had surrendered to the Muslim army without raising arms.[21] In return for his payment of *jizya*, the *dhimmi* was promised protection by his Muslim sovereign, the right to keep his property and a certain freedom of action in his private affairs. *Jizya* was usually a collective tribute given over by villages and districts. *Kharaj* was a tribute levied against the *dhimma* communities on the produce of their fields. This latter tax was especially important to the Umayyads during their period of expansion and to the Abbasids who collected tremendous sums. However, as people began to convert to Islam they gradually ceased to pay *kharaj* and substituted *ushr* or 'tithe' on their fields. Because of this continued loss in revenue, *kharaj* was made a permanent rent irrespective of the religious denomination of the landowner. However, this only slowed down and did not halt the attrition of lands subject to *kharaj*.[22]

Ushr, literally translated as 'one-tenth', was another tax considered legal, but it was generally contested by the people because it resembled *zakat* in regard to interpretations of taxation for both landed and movable property. This is shown by the fact that some legal scholars regard it as *fai* if paid by non-Muslims and others as *sadaqa* if paid by Muslims.[23] If Muslims and *dhimmi*s paid *ushr*, the former were absolved from paying *zakat* and the latter from paying *jizya*. The nature of *ushr* may have been further confused because it was present in Near and Middle Eastern pre-Islamic societies in the form of a sacred tithe or sacrificial tribute—political and religious.[24]

The final legal revenue of importance was *ghanima* (pl. *ghanaim*)—movable property including people captured in war from the unbelievers. This property was lawful Islamic booty distributed immediately after the conclusion of battle, troops receiving four-fifths and Allah one-fifth.[25] The distribution was strictly regulated according to the type of troop—cavalry or infantry—and to the equipment an individual provided for the battle.[26] The cavalry therefore received twice to three times as much *ghanima* as the infantry. In addition, a warrior had the right to appropriate the *salab* or 'equipment' of an enemy he had slain in battle. The one-fifth of *ghanima* reserved for Allah was *khums*, literally 'fifth'. Considered as *mal al-muslimin*, it was to be divided between Muhammad and his family, orphans, needy and travellers.[27] As will be shown later, this tax played an important role in Saudi Arabia during the days of the Ikhwan who claimed themselves 'rightly guided in the path of Allah' and therefore claimed all the property of those they had vanquished as *ghanima* or legal booty.

In addition to the revenues legally permitted to Islamic governments, there were revenues not expressly allowed by Islam, which had been introduced during the Umayyad Khalifate. These usually involved levies against commerce and were known as 'unlawful' taxes under the general term *maks* (pl. *mukus*). At that time an excise duty was placed on goods, often at the rates of *ushr* (one-tenth) or *khums* (one-fifth) of their value. The taxation generally took place at frontiers, ports and market centres on a variety of goods and numerous activities.[28] *Maks*, however, never lost its negative associations even though it became a regular form of taxation for many Islamic governments.[29]

Saudi Revenues and Expenditures

In the preceding discussion institutional policies regarding taxation were seen as direct responses to evolving social and environmental factors. These changes were especially highlighted by the subsequent fractionalisation of the Islamic world into autonomous authorities. Ostensibly, taxation policies were implemented within the framework of Islamic law, but independent government interpretations created an inevitable gap between theory and practice. Abd al-Aziz, like all Muslim rulers, was caught in the dilemma of needing to legitimise his rule in Islamic terms but at the same time facing problems of governing for which the Sharia alone did not provide guidance.

Until the mid-twentieth century, various governments of the Arabian Peninsula were economically poor. The little revenue that was collected from taxation went to support government and little or nothing was spent on public services. Part of the problem was the prevalence of what Shaikh Hafiz Wahba, who held many high ambassadorial and ministerial appointments in the Saudi government, summarised as 'autocratic and individual' systems of taxation.

> Whatever the system of government . . . it brought in little revenue, apart from the religious tax levied on agriculture and any dues that could be collected from the Bedouin. The smallest revenue of all was probably that of Kuwait, until, in 1897, Sheikh Mubarak ascended the throne over the bodies of his brothers. Until then the Sheikh had levied only a small tax on merchandise, this not being fixed by him but assessed by the population, who voluntarily recognized their duty to help him and his family in the duties of government and to remunerate

> him for their work. In addition, shopkeepers had to contribute towards the payment of the night-watchmen. Up to that time, in general, the Sheikhs of Kuwait had lived with their people as brothers.
>
> Taxation in Bahrein was similar, except that the rulers of Bahrein controlled larger possessions and a bigger and richer population. The rulers of Nejd, Saud and Rashid alike, derived their revenue from the religious tax on agriculture and cattle, from the pilgrim tax, and from the State's share of one fifth of the spoils of any Jihad or holy war.[30]

Taxation in these states was arbitrary in comparison to its institutional standardisation in modern nation-states. The élite ruling families in the Arabian Peninsula derived their income almost wholly from tax revenues. Among such families were the Al Sabah of Kuwait and the Al Rashid and Al Saud of Central Arabia. It was only much later, as their political links enabled them to pursue other economic activities, that revenues ceased to be the main undergirding of their expenditures. The public treasury and the private purse of the ruler were often synonymous and there was therefore no incentive for a ruler to reveal to the public what records, if any, did exist.

> Naturally these autocratic and individual methods of taxation did not usually involve the ruler in any consultations with his people, although sometimes an individual ruler might consult his leading citizens, their opinion being merely advisory. All revenues were treated as secret, and there were no budgets. The only records that existed were books in which revenue was entered along with expenditure, the latter covering merely the salaries of officials, personal servants and so on, nothing having been spent on public works, except in the Hejaz, before 1920.[31]

The difficulties inherent in an examination of the early financial affairs of these areas are obvious. During the first three decades of the twentieth century the Saudi treasury was synonymous with Abd al-Aziz's private purse and information about it remained secret. Such information as is obtainable comes primarily from three sources: observations made directly by foreign officials visiting Arabia, such as British political, intelligence or military officials;

statements made by Abd al-Aziz to foreign or Arab individuals; and historical works in the Arabic language based on secret official documents only now being published. Although the information is sketchy in certain areas, there is enough to shed light on the internal financial conditions of Saudi Arabia.

This discussion will deal with the following questions. What was the state of Abd al-Aziz's treasury in the early twentieth century? What were the revenues and expenditures? Were they consistent with Abd al-Aziz's claim as an Islamic leader? Were the Ikhwan justified in criticising Abd al-Aziz for his collection of certain taxes? A pertinent comment on the subject of revenues accruing to the Saudi state was made in a conversation in 1927 between Abd al-Aziz and the two Ikhwan leaders, Faisal al-Duwish and Ibn Bijad, when the latter complained about a temporary stoppage of their allowances. The answer of the Saudi leader was terse and has been recorded in official government documents: 'You both know that I [Abd al-Aziz] and the Āl Sa'ūd do not possess commerce or agriculture. From what source should I give you [the Ikhwan] your allowances?'[32]

This is a revealing statement in that it illustrates the economic difficulties of the Al Saud as a ruling élite, dependent on tax revenues for their support. Their wealth was not based on agricultural or mercantile enterprises, and neither did they constitute a great nomadic tribe tending camels and other livestock. Unlike the Gulf Shaikhdoms, they derived no revenue from fishing or pearling taxes. They did not capture the valuable agricultural and mercantile districts of al-Ahsa until 1913, northern Arabia until 1921, and al-Hijaz until 1924/25. As a ruling dynasty their revenue came primarily from taxes and later from sources such as British subsidies.

The lawful sources of revenue present in Najd and available to Abd al-Aziz were *zakat* and *ghanima*. *Khums*, one-fifth of *ghanima*, undeniably provided substantial revenues, especially during the mid-1920s, for Abd al-Aziz and for the Ikhwan who received four-fifths of the plunder. Several hundred raids were made by the Ikhwan, in which hundreds of thousands of camels, sheep and goats were taken. These raids were meticulously recorded by the Iraq, Kuwait and British authorities.[33] Significantly, the Ikhwan always referred to booty taken in raids as *ghanima* and never as *nahb* or 'plunder' which would signify non-Islamic booty taken from any people during *ghazzu* by the badu;

and they never protested against the levying either of *khums*, due to the Saudi government from *ghanima*, or of *zakat*.[34]

Khums and *zakat* seem to have formed the major part of the Saudi revenue, at least in the mid-1920s, as was evidenced by a letter sent from Duwish, the Ikhwan leader, to Shaikh Ahmad al-Jabir Al Sabah, ruler of Kuwait, during the Ikhwan revolt against Abd al-Aziz. Duwish declared that, if Ahmad would consent to be their leader, the Ikhwan would pledge their allegiance to him. Duwish then listed the revenue that would accrue to the Shaikh as it had previously accrued to Abd al-Aziz.

> Do not therefore be stingy with your new people and you [Shaikh Ahmad] will not want for wealth in this world, for such will indeed now come to you from three sources.
> a) In the form of salaries for Najd tribes hitherto received from the High British Government [by Abd al-Aziz].
> b) In the shape of *zakāt* from us the tribes.
> c) By means of our raids and attacks the one-fifth (*khums*) of which will be set aside for you.[35]

With regard to these three sources of revenues, it will be recalled that the British subsidy had been discontinued in 1924, and in any event had not been a significant sum. However, the large-scale raids of the Ikhwan provided tremendous revenue in the form of *khums* and had the additional benefit of ensuring that troops were always remunerated by division of the spoils even if the government treasury was depleted. The implications of *zakat* as regards the obligations and privileges of an Islamic government and its subjects have been discussed already, but how valuable was it as a form of revenue? It is unfortunate that there are no records available to indicate what percentage *zakat* constituted of the total revenue. However, collection of *zakat* could have potential benefits beyond the actual income derived from it. Remember that the Saudis claimed that payment of *zakat* was a declaration of a tribe's allegiance and with that allegiance went access to a tribe's territory and consequent strategic and economic rewards. During the mid-1920s Saudi tax collectors went to the Manasir tribe in what were then known as the Trucial States, offering *ikramiya* or an 'honorarium' to the tribes in exchange for their payment of *zakat*.[36] In some cases the *ikramiya* exceeded *zakat* in value. The collection of *zakat* was meant to form the basis of the Saudi claim over the Manasir territory.[37]

Just as Islamic governments had earlier been forced to depend on non-Islamic taxes for additional revenue, so too did the Al Saud. It has been shown earlier that these unlawful taxes in Islam were grouped under the general term *maks*. When the Ikhwan clashed with Abd al-Aziz over non-Islamic or 'despised' taxes, they used the term *maks* itself. Eventually, the Ikhwan categorically demanded that these taxes be stopped and Abd al-Aziz agreed that he would cease to levy *maks* in addition to *zakat*. However, he added that, if he did so, his gifts to them would have to stop.[38] It must be remembered that the Saudi government itself reflected many attributes of nomadic society: the Al Saud needed revenue not solely for their own purposes, but because they were expected to redistribute their wealth to retainers, guards and political supporters just as badu tribal leaders had done for centuries. Indeed, anyone who arrived at the Saudi door was entitled to gifts of food and sometimes clothing or other goods. Undoubtedly, hospitality was both a virtue and a simple political expedient, as the following story illustrates.

> He [Abd al-Aziz] was a great admirer of Mohammed Ibn Al Rashid, Emir of Ha'il, who at one time ruled the whole of Nejd and during whose reign, as a small boy, Abdul Aziz had been taken by his father to Kuwait in voluntary exile. He emulated Mohammed's example in generosity, and often told the following story about him. On one occasion an important Bedouin Sheikh was Mohammed Ibn Rashid's guest, and he treated him very well and on his departure presented him with a small gift. Also staying there at the time was a small Bedouin Sheikh whose chief occupation was leading his tribe in bandit raids in northern Nejd. To him Mohammed Ibn Rashid was even more attentive, presenting him with beautiful cloths and a very valuable gift. Questioned about this strange behaviour, he replied that the important Sheikh knew his responsibilities and wished to preserve his position, influence and wealth by being on good terms with the Rashids; therefore there was no need for the latter to buy his friendship. But the little man was like a bird who flew from tree to tree, and therefore very difficult to catch. So it was to the Rashid's advantage to cajole him into friendship, and the little they could give him in presents would

> be nothing compared with what it would cost them to send a punitive expedition against them.[39]

What were these non-Islamic or *maks* taxes implemented by the Al Saud? How important were they? The first reference to this form of taxation occurs in 1913 when Abd al-Aziz captured al-Ahsa and raised the customs duties.

> Abdul Aziz had had no experience of customs dues before he occupied Hasa, but on his conquest of that and Qatif he imposed taxes not exceeding 5 per cent on imported goods. These were farmed out to private individuals, as, until 1921, was the case with the taxes of Bahrein, which were farmed out to an Indian. The Nejdi customs dues were later organized by Sheikh Abdul Latif Al-Mindil, and the annual revenue from them then rose from £5,000 to £20,000. The customs revenues were later bought by a wealthy man in Qatif for £40,000 a year, and in 1920 for £72,000, the condition being made that there should be no commercial dealings with Kuwait. Later on, however, the system was again reorganized, and the custom of farming-out abandoned.[40]

Maks has often been referred to as a market tax and as such it was often levied against livestock and other produce in the Arabian Peninsula. However, the most important and telling economic event of these years was a growing dissatisfaction, beginning in the year 1916 and culminating in the demand by Abd al-Aziz for part of the customs dues from Kuwait. This demand was viewed by the ruling Al Sabah as payment of tribute and they refused to pay it. In retaliation Abd al-Aziz initiated an economic blockade of Kuwait in 1921, forbidding his tribes *musabala* outside Najd—the consequences of which are discussed in Part II.[41] When one realises the constraints of Islamic taxation as well as the fact that, unlike Western societies, no income tax was levied, it is obvious that custom duties and market dues must have formed an important part of a country's over-all budget.[42] Until 1913 Saudi Arabia had no ports and it was virtually impossible to collect import duty on the desert frontier between Najd and Kuwait, certainly not without co-operation on the part of the Kuwaitis. Even collection of custom duties within Saudi Arabia itself was hindered by the physical characteristics of the country.

> With the acquisition of El Hasa [al-Ahsa] by Ibn Saud in 1913, Nejd acquired a sea front, but the sea front in question contained no port of any real value, and the efforts made from time to time by Ibn Saud, with the assistance at intervals of His Majesty's Government, to secure that steamship lines such as the British Indian Steam Navigation Company should call at Ojair or at Qatif, or to develop Ojair, Qatif or Jubail, have proved abortive. In these circumstances a friendly understanding with the Sheikhs of Bahrein and Koweit on the question of customs and transit dues is of great and evident importance to the Ruler of Nejd. Agreement with Bahrein, on the basis of a transit duty of 2 per cent, was reached in 1920, after long discussion and much ill-feeling, with the assistance of the Government of India. Agreement with Koweit, which in 1923 levied a 4 per cent duty on imports and a further 4 per cent transit duty, has not yet been reached; and since 1920 Ibn Saud has in consequence maintained an embargo on trade with Koweit with the result that the prosperity of the Principality, as indeed of Qasim and Hail in Nejd, has been seriously affected.[43]

Colonel Biscoe, Political Resident in the Persian Gulf, reported a conversation he had had with Abd al-Aziz in which the latter stated that he was in serious financial difficulties and that these acted as the stimulus for his political intransigence towards Kuwait.[44] The importance of these custom dues in a budget was also illustrated indirectly by the ruler of Kuwait, Shaikh Ahmad, who complained to the British about the effects of the Saudi blockade on the Kuwait revenues.

> To such an extent has trade between Najd and Kuwait been interfered with [by the strictness of the blockade and the activities of Abd al-Aziz's forces near Kuwait Town] that my revenue has been reduced from its former figure by 70 per cent. This too has been brought about by Ibn Saud's siege operations which have been going on without interruption from the year 1340 [1920/21] to the present time [1929].[45]

An extraordinary form of *maks* was found in eastern Arabia, although not a great deal of information is available on it. Wahba briefly mentions that the 'populations of Hasa, Qatif and some parts of the Hejaz, who seldom participated in the actual fighting, had to pay a special War Fund Tax'.[46] Sadleir, the first European to travel across Arabia east to west, also mentioned that, at the time of his trip in 1819, there was a 'jahand' or war-tax being collected at al-Qatif: 'Jahand [*jihad*], or war-tax paid by villagers and townsmen, as not being liable to be called into the field. This is paid in cash and does not vary.'[47] It must essentially have been *jizya* charged against the non-Wahhabi population, perhaps the Shiites. It is interesting to recall the *khuwa* whereby all who paid were protected by a powerful warrior tribe and were not liable to contribute men to battle. According to Sadleir, the annual revenue from this 'jahand' tax equalled 20,000 G. Crowns. Although no name was given for it, a tenth of the produce of the fields—undoubtedly *ushr* or *zakat*—was also collected, the revenues amounting to 50,000 to 60,000 G. Crowns. A further 5,000 to 6,000 G. Crowns were collected from 'sea customs', and a further miscellaneous sum from fishing and anchorage fees.

It was precisely this reliance by Abd al-Aziz upon *maks* taxes that caused the Ikhwan to lodge a major complaint against their Imam. They felt that his action was a direct abuse of Islamic sacred law and eventually Abd al-Aziz temporarily stopped this taxation. However, when the Ikhwan complained about the simultaneous stoppage of their salaries, the Saudi leader countered that he had no financial reserve to cover the expenditure of his government without levying *maks*.[48] *Maks*, he said, provided for the allowances of the Ikhwan.

> I have advised my *wazīr al-māl* [finance minister] against levying *maks* as it is unlawful. Since my forbidding of *mukūs* my *bait al-māl* [treasury] is exhausted. In fact, the greater part of my wealth in my treasury was from *tutun* [tobacco] which the Hijazis use. Since *tutun* has become unlawful according to you [the Ikhwan leaders Duwish and Bijad] the levying of *maks* on that which is forbidden is an even greater sin. The result is that straitened means have fallen on me and you.[49]

After the capture of al-Hijaz in 1924/25 Abd al-Aziz had forbidden the sale of tobacco found in the warehouses. The Saudi economy must have been in difficulty, for only a year or so later he once again allowed the import and sale of a product despised in Ikhwan eyes and, moreover, imposed a *maks* upon it. Although the Quran did not mention any sanctions against the use of tobacco, its use might have been equated with that of alcohol which, according to Sura 5:90-2, was considered a creation of the devil. Among many Muslims there is a disagreement about whether alcohol is *muharram*, 'expressly forbidden', or merely *makruh*, 'hated'. According to Wahhabi doctrine both smoking and drinking were strictly forbidden. The Wahhabi Shaikh Abdullah Abu Batin was asked about the ban on tobacco and what form it took.

> As for tobacco, we see it should be banned for two reasons:
> 1) the obtaining of intoxicants . . . The Imam Aḥmad [Ibn Hanbal] narrates a *ḥadīth* showing the denial of the Prophet of drugs or things that make you go to sleep . . .
> 2) the smoke of tobacco is vile and it is hated by those who are not accustomed to it. Some *'ulamā* have stated that all obnoxious things should be forbidden to you and, without doubt, this is an obnoxious thing.[50]

Travellers to Najd have frequently noted that the purchase of tobacco was a clandestine affair and that it sold for very high prices. Anyone who was found smoking was publicly whipped or otherwise punished. It is therefore remarkable that, in levying *maks* against *tutun*, Abd al-Aziz came extremely close to alienating one of his most potentially dangerous opponents, the Ikhwan. This controversy was actually discussed at a congress convened in al-Riyad on 25 Rajab 1345 (January 1927) between Abd al-Aziz and the Ikhwan. Regarding *maks*, the congress issued the following *fatwa*, 'formal legal opinion', condemning the taxation. However, they refrained from an open break with Abd al-Aziz who was the head of their Muslim *umma*.

> Taxes, we have ruled, are completely illegal and it is the King's duty to remit them, but if he refuses to do so we do not feel it permissible to break up Moslem unity and revolt against him solely on this account.[51]

Another relevant piece of information regarding this tax is found in Attar, whose outlook is pro-Saudi and anti-Ikhwan. He claims that the *maks* was essentially *kharaj* and therefore permissible.

> Their [the Ikhwan] accusation was nothing, but it arose from their ignorance of Islamic rules concerning *kharāj* . . . . they

> allow the plundering of Muslims and their murder, but they forbid the *kharāj* which is taken for the benefit of Muslims and the elevation of Allah. That which is taken by the *ḥākim* [governor] in Islam is not all *maks*. Rather, it is the *kharāj* which is allowed to be taken in Islam. As for the *maks* which is forbidden in Islam, it is something which is taken from the Muslims without right.[52]

Although this quotation is meant to exonerate the Al Saud, it is generally indicative of an extreme Wahhabi attitude to Muslims who were non-Wahhabis and who were considered so far outside Islam as to be charged *kharaj*, a tax levied against non-Muslims. Although land remained theoretically taxable, even if sold to a Muslim (whether originally Muslim or converted), the *kharaj* had almost completely fallen out of use in the Muslim world. There is, however, another example of *kharaj* being levied by the Saudis in the preceding century.

> Because of the preoccupation of the Wahhabi Amir with the Hijaz in the years after 1803 [during the second major period of Saudi rule] Oman did not feel the full weight of Wahhabi power until 1808. Towards the close of that year a new *naib* or lieutenant, Mutlaq al-Mutairi, was sent to take charge of the outpost at Buraimi with a strong reinforcement of troops. His coming, according to the historian of the Ibadiya, Abdullah ibn Humaid al-Salimi, 'was a long and bitter punishment and a great calamity'. Shaikh Nasir ibn Abi Nabhan recorded that he made it lawful to shed the blood of the Muslims [i.e. the Ibadi], claiming that they were polytheists and calling upon the people to accept his doctrines. He records also that anybody who did not accept Wahhabism, their women and children were sent into captivity and their property was plundered. Another annalist puts it on record that true Muslims were treated as polytheists and made to pay the *jizyah* [poll tax] and the *kharāj* [land tax].[53]

It is tempting to make a comparison between Wahhabi beliefs and practices of the nineteenth and twentieth centuries, but with so little information it is dangerous. It can definitely be said, however, that Abd al-Aziz was charging *maks* which, strictly speaking, was decidedly non-Islamic, as the Ikhwan had charged. It is also undeniable that Abd al-Aziz needed the revenue of *maks* over and above that of *zakat*, just as most, if not all, Islamic governments have been forced to find other non-Islamic forms of taxation.

Another source of revenue for the Saudi state came from Great Britain's subsidy which began during World War I and was ended in 1924.[54] In addition, Britain made loans of both money and weapons to Abd al-Aziz. There is no information available as to the percentage of the total financial reserves formed by the subsidy, nor is there any information about any specific use to which it might have been put. Ostensibly, it began as a payoff for Saudi neutrality during the war, but the war soon left Central Arabia on the sidelines and the only Saudi efforts made to help the Allies were against the Al Rashid family of Hail who were pro-Ottoman. This family was not, however, to be eliminated from the competition for Arabian rule until 1921 when Shaikh Ahmad Al Sabah of Kuwait was asked by Abd al-Aziz to contribute money and supplies to the Saudi offensive against Hail. Eight years later during the Saudi blockade of Kuwait, Shaikh Ahmad complained that Abd al-Aziz had not yet returned his loan.

> He has strangled Kuwait and killed us, and this in spite of all we have done for him. He even now owes me 60,000 Reals in cash apart from the cost of untold food supplies sent him by me for the capture of Hail.[55]

Once again there is little to be concluded as there is no context in which to place this information. It cannot even be said that there is proof Abd al-Aziz was in need of money, even though he continually stressed his dire situation. It seems likely, however, that until the late 1920s this was indeed true, as his expenditure on military campaigns alone must have been the main debit in the Saudi budget from 1913 to 1930. Official salaries, public offices, hospitality to the community at large and support of his bodyguard and household were continuous, not intermittent, expenses. In addition, he had to provide for constant monetary support of his troops—Ikhwan, regulars or paid mercenaries, and *arab* or badu who were not Ikhwan.[56] There were also Ikhwan leaders and over sixty *hijar* which were constantly subsidised by Abd al-Aziz, monthly and yearly.[57]

Conclusion

As has been discussed in other chapters, the rule of an Islamic leader had sacred legitimacy and was to be tolerated despite his accession by force. Under Abd al-Aziz's instruction the Wahhabi movement continued to be encouraged and used as a political tool. Indeed, ever since the establishment of Saudi political authority in the mid-1700s, Wahhabiism never ceased to be associated with it and there were frequent inter-marriages between the Al Saud and Al Wahhab. This association gave a stamp of religious validity to Saudi rule.

Abd al-Aziz's claim to Islamic leadership is further evidenced by the fact that he strove to eliminate certain aspects of tribal customary law that enforced the authority of the tribal shaikhs. Predominant among these was the custom of *khuwa* which he replaced with the Islamic *zakat*. It will be recalled that a tribal leader who collected *khuwa* had an obligation to protect those who paid not because of a sacred obligation such as that associated with *zakat* but because of the obligation ensuing from a purely financial transaction and the sanction of tribal traditions. No tribal leader would collect *zakat* unless he perceived himself as an Islamic leader or wished others to recognise him as such. Abd al-Aziz constantly found himself torn between the need to preserve badu customs helpful to his own survival and the need to break those tribal customs such as *khuwa* which undermined his claim to a divine and predominant authority and which reinforced inter-tribal conflicts.

As the period of Abd al-Aziz's rule progressed, however, he found himself in serious financial difficulties and, like other Islamic governments before him, was forced to resort to non-Islamic forms of taxation. The noble or free badu of Arabia knew no taxation *per se* before the present Kingdom of Saudi Arabia. Revenue was derived from *ghazzus*, trade with settled areas, and tribute from weaker tribes. At the conclusion of a *ghazzu*, the shaikh or amir was entitled to a portion of the plunder. Tribute was always received from foreign groups with whom there were no common blood ties. While tribute was a source of wealth, its importance was undoubtedly more far-reaching. Access to pastures and wells belonging to other social groups provided greater flexibility in ecological relationships; and a larger base of extended non-kin associations provided military alliances in times of political strife. A tribal shaikh maintained his rule through the consent of those governed and by virtue of his qualities of generosity, bravery and justice.[58] Although he received nearly one-quarter of any booty from raids, he was expected to redistribute his financial reserve through hospitality to other members of the tribe and to aliens crossing the tribal *dira*.

While Abd al-Aziz found it relatively easy to inculcate his rule in the towns, his difficulty came from maintaining control over the nomadic elements. The Al Saud were not nomads nor did they associate their authority with any of the great desert tribes. Thus they could not rely on any powerful tribal backing as had the Al Rashid in northern Arabia who were supported by the Shammar tribe.[59] Abd al-Aziz's major problems were to stabilise caravan and pilgrim routes, secure an environment conducive to trade, institute a military police force for his disposal, establish his own control over independent self-governing tribes and secure a source of revenue for himself.

All of these problems were inextricably related and most were to be solved in the second decade of the twentieth century with the settlement of badu in the agricultural *cum* military communities or *hijar*. These settlements were undoubtedly a drain on the budget until the mid-1920s when large revenues were brought in from the Ikhwan *ghanima*. However, the British then began to claim restitution for these raids on behalf of their mandated territories, Transjordan and Iraq, as well as Kuwait, a territory under their protection, so that Abd al-Aziz was forced to confiscate the Ikhwan portion of *ghanima* and return it to the government of its origin in order not to alienate the British. *Zakat* was no longer sufficient to cover the fiscal expenditure of the Saudi state and Abd al-Aziz came to rely increasingly upon *maks* or unlawful Islamic taxes. This reliance and Abd al-Aziz's confiscation of the *ghanima* were two economic factors which served to bring the Saudi leader and the Ikhwan into open conflict in the late 1920s, as will be discussed in greater detail in Part II. It would not be until much later, in the middle of the century, that the Saudi state would again find a profitable and continuous revenue with the development of oil concessions.

Notes

1. *Zakāt* is liable to be paid on five categories of goods: crops planted for food; fruits, specifically grapes and dates; livestock; precious metals; and merchandise.

Tax on crops and fruit is paid at harvest at the rate of 5 per cent if the fields are artificially irrigated and 10 per cent if not. *Zakāt* paid on livestock is determined on the quantity and type of animal and is only liable to be paid if it grazed freely for one year without working. Crops and livestock are termed *ẓāhir* or 'openly visible' possessions and their value is determined by a government official. The last two categories are taxed at a rate of 2½ per cent, but only if they have been in a person's uninterrupted possession for one year. These goods are *bāṭin* or 'hidden' and determination of their value is left to the conscience of the individual. A person must possess more than a predetermined minimum of taxable property, *niṣāb*, before he is liable to be taxed (*Encyclopedia of Islam*, '*zakāt*', vol. IV, pp. 654-6).

2. According to Sura 9:60, the eight categories which are entitled to the proceeds of *zakāt* are the poor; the needy; those involved with collecting or distributing the tax; those whose hearts need to be conciliated, presumably for political reasons; the slaves; the debtors; 'in the path of God'; and wayfarers.

3. All Islamic governments were under the proscription that they could not include any *zakāt* which was stored in their *bait al-māl* or 'treasury' when calculating their own capital revenue. This was obviously because the lawful recipients of *zakāt* were the poor, the needy and so forth to whom it had yet to be dispersed. See Marcel Mauss, *The Gift: Forms and Functions of Exchange in Archaic Societies* (W. W. Norton, New York, 1967), especially Ch. 1, pp.15-16.

4. J. B. Kelly's book, *Eastern Arabian Frontiers* (Faber and Faber, London, 1964), contains the most complete version of the boundary disputes between Sa'udi Arabia, Masqat and the United Arab Amirates. However, in a private conversation Kelly admitted to this author that at the time of his writing the book he lacked access to certain important documents from the 1930s which were not declassified until the 1960s.

5. *'Arḍ ḥukūmat al-mamlaka al-'arabīya al-sa'ūdīya: al-taḥkīm ma'a masqaṭ wa abū ẓabī*, or *The Sa'udi Memorial*, 3 vols (1374(1955)), vol. I, Ch. VI, paras 37-8, pp.469-70.

6. Ibid., vol. II, Appendix B, Part 2, pp.295-6.

7. The criticisms would have been more powerful had they questioned whether force was a legitimate means of obtaining *zakāt*; whether the *zakāt* was still valid even if collected at intermittent periods; and what reciprocal protection—which the Sa'udis claimed was requisite on the government authorities in performance of *zakāt* —was given in return for payment of the tax? Finally, how does one determine allegiance if more than one Islamic authority claims the right to it?

8. The issue was unnecessarily confused by the Sa'udi claim that they had levied two *zakāts* simultaneously, the 'pure *zakāt*' and a 'tribute *zakāt*'.

9. Lieutenant-General Sir John Pasha Glubb stated in private correspondence with this author that 'the term *zikat* [*zakāt*] was not used in the northern Arab countries'. However, in another private conversation with an Iraqi, it was found that *zakāt* was present, but not as a government tax. Apparently, it was current only as one of the Islamic 'pillars' which individuals voluntarily decided to give or not.

10. Even if that leader acquired his position by force or was unjust, the Muslim community owed him their obedience because the unity of Islam was of paramount importance.

11. Majid Khadduri, *War and Peace in the Law of Islam* (Johns Hopkins Press, Baltimore, 1955), p.7, states that 'In the early Islamic conception society and the state meant the same thing; indeed the term state is not to be found in the Qur'ān, nor was it in vogue in Muḥammad's time. The Qur'ān merely refers to organized authority, which belongs to God (as the source of governing authority) forming part of the state; while society, whether it engulfed the state or constituted certain aspects of it, was the creation of man's needs to fulfill certain social functions.' Khadduri also points out that the modern Arabic word for state is *dawla* which did not become

current until the Abbasids. Initially they used the term to signify a 'new regime established by revolution' and, as their own regime became more stabilised, its usage evolved to mean 'organised authority'.

12. Mauss has persuasively argued in favour of this idea in *The Gift* (Ch. 1). He described alms as a 'result on the one hand of a moral idea about gifts and wealth and on the other of an idea about sacrifice'. Gifts to men and gifts to God have the same aim which is that of buying peace or securing salvation. This can only be achieved by association with one's communal group. Throughout history, the evolution of legal and religious thought leaves man as a representative of God's will on earth, particularly in the monotheistic religions of Judaism, Christianity and Islam. God's will is not fulfilled as long as the legal, social and religious proscriptions of life remain unperformed. *Zakāt* is a gift made to man in the sight of God and for God—a spiritual bond.

13. *United Kingdom Memorial* or *Arbitration Concerning Buraimi and the Common Frontier Between Abu Dhabi and Sa'udi Arabia: Memorial Submitted by the Government of Great Britain and Northern Ireland*, 3 vols. (1955), vol. I, p.68.

14. *Khuwa* was banned by 'Abd al-'Azīz undoubtedly because he relied entirely on the support of individual tribes and had to establish his own authority across tribal particularisms. *Khuwa* tended to reinforce status differentials between tribes (Ibn Khaldūn, *The Muqaddimah: An Introduction to History* (Routledge and Kegan Paul, London, 1967), p.111).

15. Private Correspondence from Glubb to this author.

16. In a society where unwritten rules bind so many actions upon which peace or stability is solely dependent, a man's honour and dignity are his most valued possessions equalled only by the virtue of generosity in a land harsh to give.

17. Alois Musil, *The Manners and Customs of the Rwala Bedouins* (American Geographical Society/Oriental Explorations and Studies no. 6, New York, 1928), p.60.

18. The collection of *zakāt* was not haphazard, usually occurring during the summer months when badu tribes were encamped on wells and could be more easily located.

19. The term *bait al-māl* literally means 'the house of wealth'. Although originally only a repository for goods and money awaiting redistribution to individuals, its function evolved during the early Khalifate to house money intended for public service projects for the community as a whole. Its officials were empowered by the authority of the Imam or religious leader of the community, who also remained responsible for the general functioning of the treasury.

20. There were also minor sources of legal revenue such as property of the apostates, deceased and unknown persons, as well as produce of mines and treasure troves.

21. The *ahl al-kitāb* who resisted were variously freed, enslaved or killed. Because polytheists and atheists were not considered *ahl al-kitāb*, they were only offered the choice of conversion to Islam or death.

22. In the later books of Islamic law, *kharāj* was discussed little or not at all, while regulations regarding *jizya* were still given in detail.

23. Presumably if *'ushr* was regarded as *ṣadaqa* (an alms tax generally synonymous with *zakāt*), then it was not allowed to be calculated as an asset of the *bait al-māl*. See Paul G. Forand, 'Notes on *'ušr* and *maks*', *Arabica*, 13 (1966), pp.137-41.

24. The following quotation from W. Robertson Smith, *The Religion of the Semites* (Adam and Charles Black, London, 1894), pp.245-6, discusses the relation of tithe and tribute and their religious and political implications: 'In antiquity tithe and tribute are practically identical, nor is the name of tithe strictly limited to tributes of one-tenth, the term being used to cover any impost paid in kind upon a

fixed scale. Such taxes play a great part in the revenues of Eastern sovereigns, and have done so from a very early date. The Babylonian kings drew a tithe from imports, and the tithe of the fruits of the soil had the first place among the revenues of the Persian satraps. The Hebrew kings in like manner took tithes . . . and the tribute in kind which Solomon drew from the provinces for the support of his household may be regarded as an impost of this sort. Thus the institution of a sacred tithe corresponds to the conception of the national god as a king, and so at Tyre tithes were paid to Melcarth, "the king of the city". The Carthaginians . . . sent the tithe of produce to Tyre annually . . . . This is the earliest example of a Semitic sacred tithe of which we have any exact account, and it is to be noted that it is as much a political as a religious tribute; for the temple of Melcarth was the state treasury of Tyre, and it is impossible to draw a distinction between the sacred tithe paid by the Carthaginians and the political tribute paid by other colonies, such as Utica.'

25. The division of *ghanīma* was so carefully determined that carpets were sometimes split in half and livestock killed and cut in pieces so that the division would be equal among all the participants of the battle.

26. According to non-Islamic custom, badu tribal chiefs also received a share from raids or *ghazzus*. 'In ancient Arabia the chief took the fourth part of the spoils of war . . . in Moslem theocracy the chief's fourth is changed to a fifth, payable to Allah and his prophet, but partly used for the discharge of burdens of charity and the like, such as in old times fell upon the chiefs.' (Smith, *Religion of the Semites*, pp.459-60.)

27. Suras 8:1, 41-2; and 59:6-10.

28. Many rulers attempted to improve their popularity by eliminating or reducing *maks* charges, but they slowly reappeared. Shaikh Ḥāfiẓ Wahba refers to these unjust taxes with the word *mathalin* or 'iniquities' and mentions that, when Shaikh Jābir Al Ṣabāḥ succeeded Shaikh Mubārak of Kuwait, 'he cancelled some of the taxes his father had introduced, and when Shaikh Salim succeeded in his turn, he reduced others' (Ḥāfiẓ Wahba, *Arabian Days* (Arthur Barker, London, 1964) p.66). Forand, 'Notes on *'ušr* and *maks*', pp.138-40, notes that occasionally *'ushr* or *'ushūr* became synonymous with *maks* because attempts were made to collect *maks* under the more laudable term of *'ušhr*. See also *Encyclopedia of Islam*, '*maks*', vol. III, pp.176-7, for a list of the various *maks* charges.

29. Forand, 'Notes on *'ušr* and *maks*', p.140.

30. Wahba, *Arabian Days*, pp.65-6.

31. Ibid., p.68.

32. Aḥmad 'Abd al-Ghafūr 'Aṭṭār, *ṣaqr al-jazīra*, 7 vols (Maṭba'at al-Ḥurrīya, Beirut, 1972), p.974.

33. One of the Ikhwan complaints against 'Abd al-'Azīz was that, when Britain demanded the restitution of the animals raided by them from Iraq, Kuwait and Transjordan, 'Abd al-'Azīz remanded the four-fifths share belonging to the Ikhwan and retained the one-fifth which was his own portion. See Sir John Bagot Glubb, *War in the Desert: An R.A.F. Frontier Campaign* (Hodder and Stoughton, London, 1960) for a detailed account of these disputes.

34. When Duwīsh revolted against 'Abd al-'Azīz, he claimed that the latter had turned his back on the true path of Islam; and then Duwīsh incited his Ikhwan to battle by claiming that he had seen much plunder in the Saudi camp. Significantly, the word he used for plunder was *ghanīma* or 'lawful Islamic booty', indicating that 'Abd al-'Azīz was no longer considered a lawful Islamic leader and it was incumbent to revolt against his authority ('Aṭṭār, *ṣaqr al-jazīra*, p.998).

35. India Office Records, *Political and Secret Department Separate Files 1902-1931*, L/P&S/10 (henceforward abbreviated to IO L/P&S/10): IO L/P&S/10/1243, letter from Faisal b. Sulṭān Āl Duwīsh, Ikhwan leader, to Shaikh

Aḥmad al-Jābir Āl Ṣabāḥ, Ruler of Kuwait, dated 17 Muharram 1348 (25 June 1929).

36. Kelly, *Eastern Arabian Frontiers*, p.41.

37. The Sa'udi tax collectors appeared in the Trucial States only twice in the early twentieth century—1926 and 1928—and not again until 1967. The first two occasions correspond to the beginning of the Ikhwan dissatisfaction and one wonders whether 'Abd al-'Azīz was anticipating a need for political, military or financial support from the Gulf region. See Kelly, *Eastern Arabian Frontiers*, for the history of Sa'udi incursions into the Gulf.

38. IO L/P&S/10/1240, memorandum from Political Agent Kuwait to Political Resident, Bushire, 14 December 1928, no. 507-S.

39. Wahba, *Arabian Days*, p.168.

40. Ibid., pp.66-7.

41. IO L/P&S/10/1245, India Office Memorandum, History of Koweit Affairs, 1908-1928, Paras.17, 36-8.

42. R. E. Cheesman, *In Unknown Arabia* (Macmillan, London, 1926), p.172, related an interesting conversation he had with 'Abd al-'Azīz in the early 1920s concerning custom duties although it is unclear to what tax 'Abd al-'Azīz himself was referring: 'The Sultan ['Abd al-'Azīz] asked if I had any news of the English elections, but I had none. I explained that the election was being fought on the one issue of Free Trade *versus* Protection. This started a discussion as to the amount of tariff charged in England, and my neighbour ['Abd al-'Azīz] settled the question by saying that it was one-fifth.'

43. IO L/P&S/10/1245, Indian Office Memorandum, History of Koweit Affairs, 1908-1928, Para. 36.

44. IO L/P&S/10/1245, 'Précis of recent correspondence regarding questions outstanding between Ibn Saud and the Sheikh of Koweit', compiled by J. G. Laithwaite, Private Secretary to the Secretary of State, 1 July 1930.

45. IO L/P&S/10/1243, letter from Shaikh Aḥmad al-Jābir Āl Ṣabāḥ, Ruler of Kuwait, to Lieutenant-Colonel H. R. P. Dickson, Political Agent Kuwait, dated 27 Safar 1348 (3 August 1929).

46. Wahba, *Arabian Days*, p.69.

47. George Foster Sadleir, *Diary of a Journey Across Arabia (1819)* (Oleander Press, Cambridge, 1977), p.53.

48. There is evidence that even during the early period of 'Abd al-'Azīz's rule he had no compunction about charging *maks*. Article 6 of the treaty drawn up between 'Abd al-'Azīz and the Ottoman government on 15 May 1914 provided that any deficit in the budget of Najd would be met from revenue on customs, posts, telegraphs and ports (Gary Troeller, *The Birth of Saudi Arabia: Britain and the Rise of the House of Saud* (Frank Cass, London, 1976), pp.248-9; and 'Aṭṭār, *ṣaqr al-jazīra*, pp.405-7).

49. 'Aṭṭār, *ṣaqr al-jazīra*, pp.974-5.

50. Shaikh 'Abdullāh Abū Baṭin, *majmū'at al-rasā'il wa al-masā'il*, 3 vols (edited by Rashid Rida) (Al-Manar, Cairo, 1344A-1349A (1925-1930)), vol. I, p.652.

51. Wahba, *Arabian Days*, p.136.

52. 'Aṭṭār, *ṣaqr al-jazīra*, p.974.

53. Kelly, *Eastern Arabian Frontiers*, p.55.

54. Beginning in January 1917, 'Abd al-'Azīz was receiving approximately £60,000 *per annum*. This was reduced in March 1921 to £25,000 and a final payment of £50,000 was made by the British for the year 1922/23. It is interesting that 'Abd al-'Azīz attacked al-Ḥijāz almost immediately upon the conclusion of this subsidy, undoubtedly motivated, in part, by the realisation that he no longer needed restraint in his relations with the British.

55. IO L/P&S/10/1243, Report, statement by Shaikh Aḥmad al-Jābir Āl Ṣabāḥ

included in report from Lieutenant-Colonel H. R. P. Dickson, Political Agent Kuwait, to the Political Resident in the Persian Gulf, Bushire, 20 June 1929, Confidential Correspondence no. 394.

56. Wahba, *Arabian Days*, p.168, records that in time of war 'Abd al-'Azīz discontinued his usual gifts to the badu because he felt 'that to be generous to a Bedou in wartime would at once make the latter suspect weakness'.

57. 'Aṭṭār, *ṣaqr al-jazīra*, pp.969-7̱0.

58. When Shaikh Ṣabāḥ al-Sālim Al Ṣabāḥ, the ruler of Kuwait, died in 1978, it was reported that he received an annual allowance of $27 million from the government which was intended to support 500 members of the ruling family and 600 persons in his service.

59. See Henry Rosenfeld, 'The Social Composition of the Military in the Process of State Formation in the Arabian Desert' and 'The Military Force used to Achieve and Maintain Power and the Meaning of its Social Composition: Slaves: Mercenaries, and Townsmen', *Journal of the Royal Anthropological Institute*, 95 (1965), pp.75-86 and 174-94.

PART II

External Factors Influencing Attitudes to Politics, Political Structures and Authority during the Post-World War I Mandate Period

5

Phenomena of 'Nation-State' and 'Border': Transition from Ottoman Territories to Modern Middle East State System

> As late as 1914, Syria and Iraq were mere geographic concepts; Jordan was the name only of the river and as a country not even a geographic concept; Turkey was a European misnomer for the Ottoman Empire. Egypt retained its distinct geographic identity but was *de facto* part of the British and *de jure* part of the Ottoman Empire. Arabia was a congeries of amirates, shaykhdoms, and tribal confederations among which the Saudi was one of the lesser. What was to become Israel was a Utopian dream in the minds of a handful of absentee Zionist enthusiasts. Only Iran and Afghanistan had had a political identity dating back several centuries.[1]

The situation described above is an accurate portrayal of geopolitics in the Middle East prior to World War I. After the defeat of the Ottoman Empire in the war, however, a vast area once under the control of the Ottoman Porte in Istanbul was divided into numerous geopolitical entities under European aegis and these divisions formed the basis of the Middle East state system as it is known today. In order to understand the political and social adjustments resulting from the actual physical delineation of these states, it is essential to return to events prior to and during the post-war period. The internal political identity of Saudi Arabia and its external political relations were directly influenced by these new geopolitical configurations.

The Arabian Peninsula under Ottoman Control and during World War I

During the period preceding World War I the Ottoman Porte had maintained its control in the Middle East although growing dissatisfaction within the Empire had facilitated a gradual incursion of European interests into Ottoman territories. Meanwhile, some individuals like Abd al-Aziz were able to establish networks of alliances and acquire considerable influence over indigenous populations. This was particularly true in fringe areas of the Empire—such as the interior of the Arabian Peninsula—which were of minor strategic and economic importance and where Ottoman influence had never been more than intermittent and tenuous.

In the Arabian Peninsula itself—that is, the area bounded in the north-east by the Arabian Gulf, in the south-east by the Indian Ocean, in the west by the Red Sea and in the north by what are now known as the Hashimite Kingdom of Jordan and Iraq—there were a number of natural geographic divisions separated by desert or mountain barriers. Roughly corresponding to these geographic divisions were ten major political subdivisions of 'Arabia', agreed by the Foreign Office and the India Office—namely, Hail, Kuwait, Asir, Yaman, Anaza, Trucial Coast, Masqat, Bahrain, Hadramaut and Najd.[2] The Offices also agreed that, with the exception of the Trucial Coast of Oman and the Anaza, who both recognised a number of political leaders, their policy would be to deal with each subdivision through one individual. A large proportion of the population in these areas was composed of tribes and confederations of tribes. The Anaza, for example, were listed as a major political unit because they were in fact a tribal confederation controlling a large geographical segment of southern Mesopotamia. Especially at the beginning of the war years, this and other similar lists reflected the spheres of British military and political interests in the area. Although these classifications represented, for the most part, natural geopolitical divisions, British policies during the war helped to intensify the divisions and, in some cases, to subordinate the political strength of one area to another. As the Ottomans had done previously, Britain followed the dictum of *divide et impera*, playing off one tribal leader against another, supporting weaker elements against the strong, and militarily subjugating others in an attempt to thwart opposition to its authority. In later years these territorial divisions formed the basis of the state system in the Arabian Peninsula.

Great Britain's primary concern with internal Arabian affairs before World War I was to protect its interests in India. In pursuance of this, from the time of its entry into Ottoman territories until the declaration of war, it supported the policy of a 'strong Turkey in Asia'. By recognising over-all Ottoman suzerainty, Britain hoped to prevent interference on the part of rival powers. Administrative officials in the Government of India described Great Britain's relationship with the Porte in a telegraph to the Secretary of State on 8 September 1913, saying that as long as the British were able to 'come to terms with the Turkish Government as regards their respective interests in the Persian Gulf they [the British] have nothing to fear from the Turks and every advantage to gain from friendly relations with the Porte'.[3] As an additional safeguard, the British government concluded a number of treaties from the 1790s onward with local authorities which occupied strategic inland or littoral positions adjacent to British communication routes with India—such as the amirates of the Arabian Gulf. In areas with potential strategic value, such as Kuwait, Yaman, al-Hijaz and Najd, it strove to establish and maintain friendly relations.

By the late 1800s, political unrest within the Ottoman Empire had become increasingly apparent. Moreover, the once successful policy of *divide et impera* was now uniting opposition to the Porte; people, even those in government service, were demanding reform. In the Arabian Peninsula itself, dissatisfaction with Ottoman rule was being openly expressed. Captain W. H. Shakespear, who was the British Political Agent at Kuwait and the first British representative to Abd al-Aziz, was prompted after extensive travel in the Arabian Peninsula to report to the India Office that 'throughout the country I was struck by the contempt with which the Arabs all regarded the Turkish Government, its troops and its civil officials'.[4]

As World War I approached, the British, aware that the Ottomans might ally themselves with Germany, sought support amongst dissatisfied individuals within Ottoman-controlled territory. Local leaders were approached quietly through men such as Storrs and Wingate who promised political and economic concessions in return for support of the war effort. The British gave unofficial support and later direct help to the Arab nationalist movements. The concept underlying these movements, that of an Arab as distinct from an Ottoman identity, was potentially a highly emotive issue for Middle Easterners and thus dangerous to the Ottomans who generally had tried to repress any racial, ethnic or religious attitudes considered to be divisive. The bitterness that resulted from these war agreements between Great Britain and various Arab leaders has been the subject of many other studies. The agreements were so vague that contradictory interpretations were inevitable. The Arab leaders concerned had anticipated independence and self-rule. Unknown to them, however, Great Britain had held a series of secret discussions with its allies, primarily France and Russia, the purpose of which was to divide all Ottoman territories into various 'spheres of influence' under direct British control following the war.

Although Britain won the war, these secret territorial agreements were modified as a result of the spread of Arab nationalism in many forms, such as numerous clubs and social groups which fought against foreign intrusion, the use of Arabic printing presses, the general world dismay regarding the failure of big powers to honour their war promises, and President Wilson's refusal on behalf of America to recognise the secret agreements of Europe. Eventually these territories were declared mandates, acquiring provisional international recognition under the guidance of a European 'parent'. Turkey was forced through the Treaty of Sèvres in 1920 to relinquish its sovereignty over all former territories, thus liquidating the Ottoman Empire and paving the way for a legal entry by the Europeans as mandate powers (cf. Figure 5.1). The United States Congress failed to pass an approval of these treaties, but dropped its criticism as it was unwilling to become involved in other commitments or to offend the Europeans with whom it had more important interests. The mandate powers were then free to intervene in Middle Eastern affairs without interference from an Ottoman middleman or fear of international sanction.

In the Arabian Peninsula the Middle East mandate powers—France and Britain—immediately turned their attention to the creation of borders and nation-states that would provide buffer zones along areas of potential long-term development. Geographic Syria, which included what is now known as Syria and Lebanon, went to the French. Palestine, Transjordan and Mesopotamia went to the British. Thus political interests crystallised into the geographic configurations visible on maps of

Figure 5.1: Liquidation of the Ottoman Empire

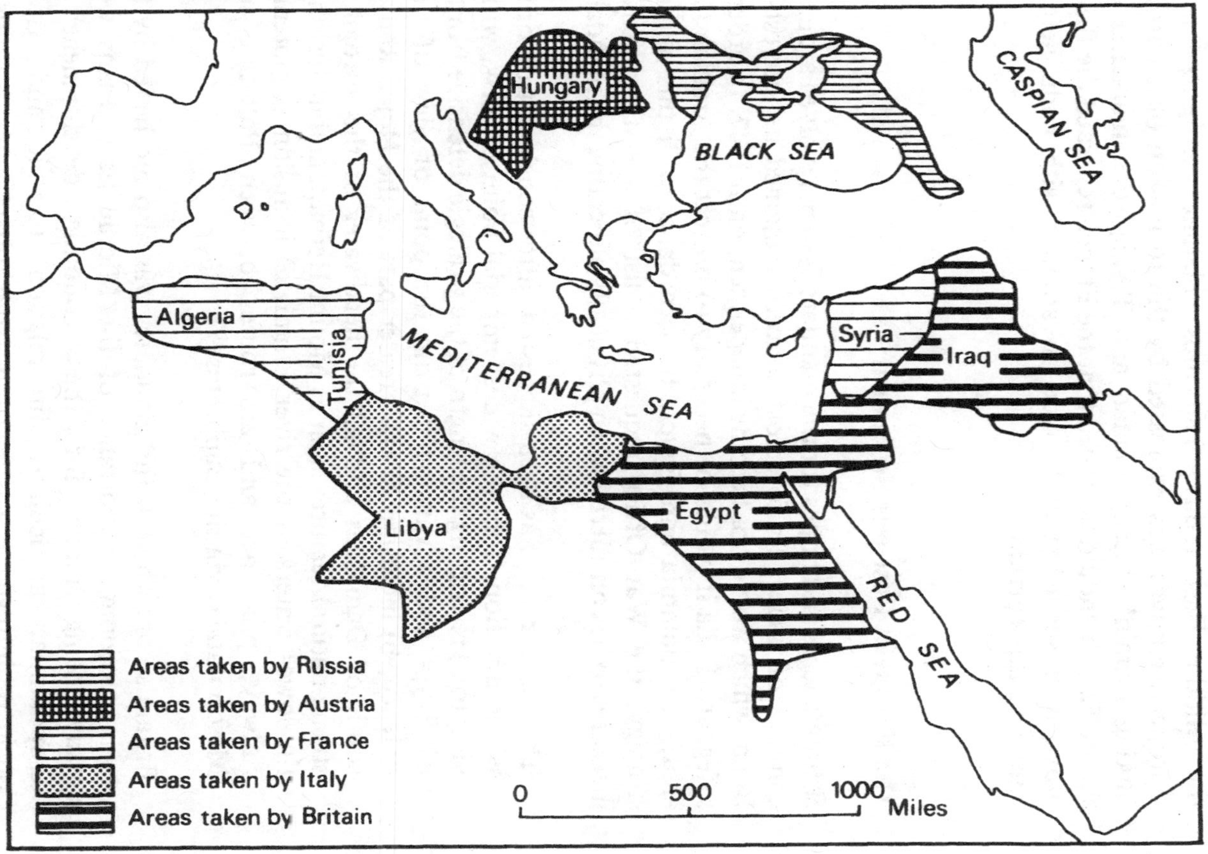

the Middle East today. The most blatant configuration of European motives was expressed by the formation of a corridor linking Britain's Mesopotamian and Transjordan mandates (cf. Figure 5.2). It should be added that the French regarded the British move with suspicion and made an attempt with badu help to eliminate this corridor.

The European Post-war Settlement

Britain's fears and hopes for the mandate system revolved around a complex of issues. Its foremost concern remained its interests in India, which would not become independent until 1947. In order to safeguard India it would be necessary to protect the Arabian Gulf area, Mesopotamia and Egypt. In accordance with this military strategy, the War Office requested a list of specific defensive measures to be considered when physically allocating the mandates.

> The frontier . . . has been suggested, after consideration of the whole question from the widest imperial point of view, with a view to a) restricting the length of the strategic defensive frontier of Egypt and advancing it from the point of view of their defence, b) inclusion of the greater part of the Hejaz Railway south of Damascus and all the headwater of the Jordan, c) strong natural features such as Mount Hermon and inclusion of the lower waters of the river Litani, d) inclusion of potential railway, pipe-line, and air routes between Palestine and Mesopotamia, via the Euphrates.[5]

Britain's concern with the mandates was also motivated by the growing economic importance of the Middle East. Plans were already being made for the economic development of Mesopotamia, particularly in relation to oil and grain. Considerable revenue was accruing from tobacco sales surplus to the cost of civic administration in Sulaimaniya. Supplies of oil and bitumen had been reported at Qaiyara just south-east of Mosul on the Tigris and revenues were expected from tobacco, corn and wood fuel in other areas. Mesopotamia was also regarded as rich recruiting ground for the military. The border eventually defined between Mesopotamia and Syria was the result of the rivalry

Figure 5.2: British Corridor Linking the Hashimites in Iraq and Transjordan

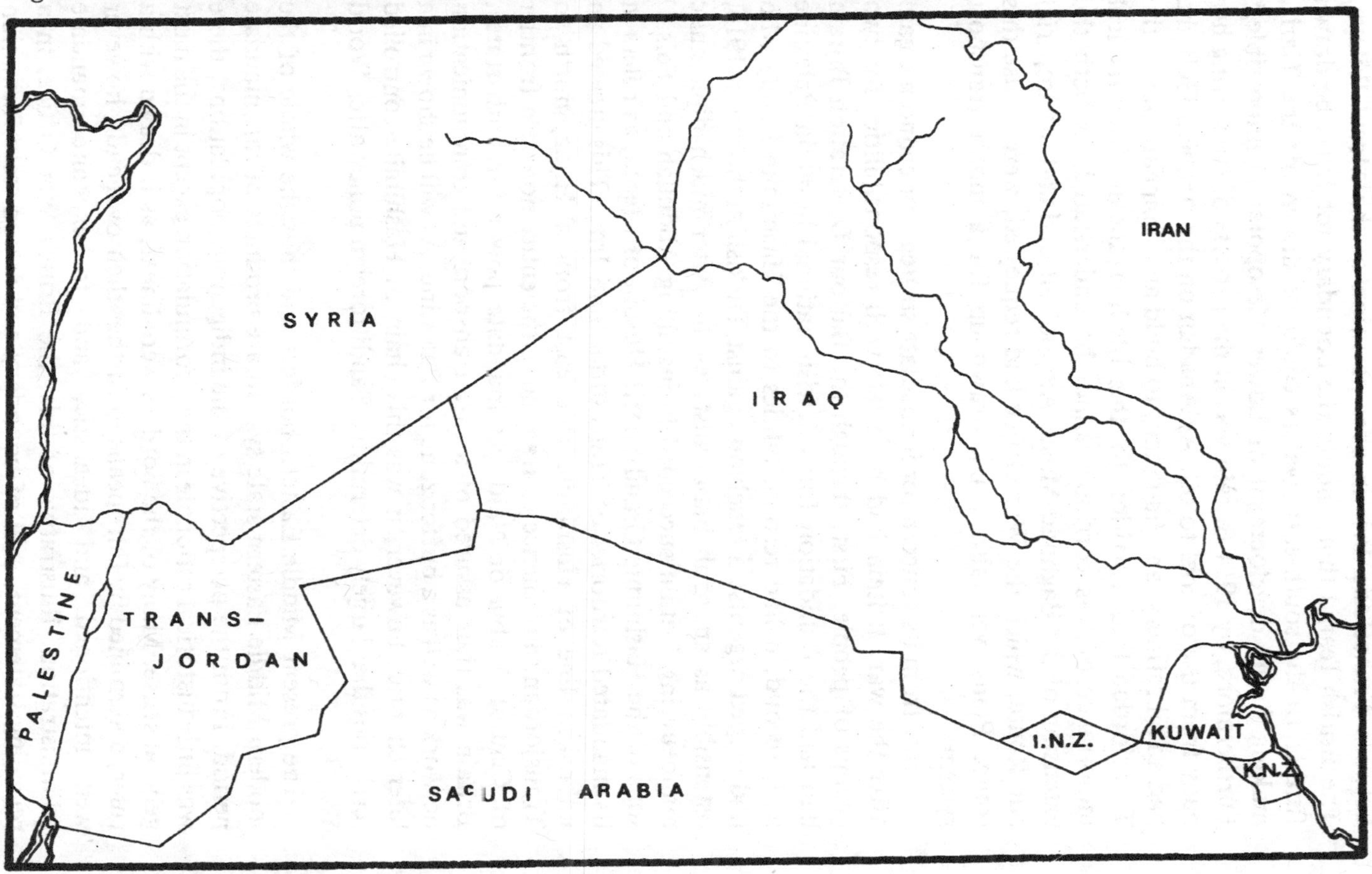

between France and Britain over partition of the Mosul Wilaya. The British feared that, should the boundary for Syria be drawn further to the south-east, waters could be drawn off the Tigris, making future development of Lower Mesopotamia impossible.[6] Furthermore, by 1914 Britain was in the process of converting her navy from use of coal to oil. At Abadan on the Arabian Gulf she had an oil refinery, and had plans to build an oil pipeline across the Transjordan-Iraq corridor to the Mediterranean. The tactical importance of this corridor cannot be understated, as both the extension of the Baghdad-Mosul-Aleppo railroad and the Imperial Air Route, which the War Office had requested, were to use this route. Plans were also being drawn up for a motor transport system.

Apart from its concern for immediate strategic or economic gain after the war, Britain had been left with responsibilities for two groups of people. First, through the Balfour Declaration Britain had laid the foundation for a Jewish national home in Palestine and, second, it had responsibilities to the Hashimite family who had helped organise a rebellion against Turkish authority in 1916, ostensibly as an Arab nationalist revolt. After much diplomatic manoeuvring Britain succeeded in installing Abdullah and Faisal, sons of the Hashimite Grand Sharif Husain of Mecca, as rulers in its mandated territories of Transjordan and Iraq. This created an unbroken line of Hashimite rule east from al-Hijaz, north to Transjordan, and thence to Iraq along the entire northern frontier of Central Arabia or Najd. As mandate power for both states, Britain was thus assured of a safe transport and communication network as well as a buffer zone for Palestine. As will be shown in a later chapter, however, it was this chain of Hashimite-controlled territories that largely determined Saudi foreign policy after World War I.

The present Middle Eastern borders and thus the whole of the modern Middle Eastern state system are products of this mandate period. From the perspective of the indigenous populations, there was little historical rationale in their formulation except in the most general sense. Many of the borders were linear, as if drawn with a ruler, determined by Europeans to further their own ends, however well intentioned and idealistic, and to expedite mandate administration. Illustrative of this, the British War Office, in a revealing statement, said of boundary and nation-state formation that it was a result of the 'best compromise between the requirements of imperial defence and the local claims of French, Arabs and Jews'.[7]

Phenomena of 'Nation-state' and 'Border'

The European post-war settlement also acted as an effective barrier to any scheme by Middle Easterners for unifying states on the basis of a wider Arab ideal. Arab nationalism had been maturing, but it had not yet developed the articulateness or the strength necessary to resist the mandates of Palestine, Transjordan, Syria, Lebanon and Iraq. Temporarily forestalled, Arab nationalists in Cairo, Baghdad, Beirut and Damascus planned for a future when they would take the reins of their government from the mandate powers. During the next twenty-five years, political activities were 'fully absorbed in the struggle against foreign rule within these particular boundaries'.[8] Individuals found themselves members of new geopolitical entities that had not existed previously and their perception of their identity as individuals and as social groups began to undergo a transformation. It is easy to understand that enforcement of fixed Western-style borders and state organisation had a tremendous effect on populations within defined territorial limits. Social groups which were once autonomous political units became subsumed to a larger governmental organisation with responsibilities for numerous diverse communities. Over time these social groups developed a sense of nationalism identifying, at least to some extent, with other groups in a common governmental system.[9]

The transformation that Middle Eastern populations underwent, as a result of the introduction of Western-type boundaries and nation-states, is incalculable. In the early decades of the twentieth century the spirit of state nationalism in the Middle East, except in Egypt, was virtually non-existent. After World War II and the major withdrawal of mandate powers, a struggle resulted within the new Middle Eastern nation-states as nascent local leaders sought to legitimise or to stabilise their own power, often by force, and as these new countries sought to maintain their independence from neighbouring states. In time these struggles were heightened by economic practicalities: the search for transport and communication routes that were vital to development; disparities in wealth that became more apparent with capital growth; intensifying conflicts between social groups; and new resources, such as oil, which were discovered in previously unclaimed and undesirable territory. Changing job markets and new opportunities created fluctuations in population size and concentration. Religious and ethnic identification was an ever-present source of conflict and no one envisaged the consequences that would develop from the creation of the 'colonial-settler state' of Israel.[10]

All of these new countries in the Arabian Peninsula faced the problems of becoming viable independent organisms. The Hashimite Kingdom of Jordan, for example, has had a difficult time competing in the international marketplace, let alone developing an *esprit de corps* among its own peoples.

> Jordan has the distinction of having the most artificial boundaries, the poorest endowment in natural resources and the least-developed feeling of civic loyalty of any country in the Middle East . . . . Its desert dunes were unsuited for agriculture, and no minerals were discovered . . . . Its coastal city of Aqabah, on the northeastern end of the Red Sea, was undeveloped as a port and its possession, moreover, disputed by neighbouring Saudi Arabia. All imports, therefore, had to come via the Palestinian ports of Haifa or Tel Aviv (and since 1948 via Beirut and Damascus).[11]

The modern state of Jordan was originally known as the British mandated territory of Transjordan. It was used as a military bulwark for Egypt and Palestine and as a buffer zone for the protection of the Hijaz Railway. The British had handed over the nominal reins of government to Grand Sharif Husain's son, Abdullah, in order to placate the Hashimites for unfulfilled pre-war promises and to prevent Abdullah from invading the French mandate of Syria. From a purely tactical point of view, Transjordan's resultant economic dependence in those early post-war years was advantageous to the British who had deliberately linked its Mesopotamian and Transjordan mandates across the whole of northern Arabia. The Hashimite family, who remained in control after mandate withdrawal in 1948, have since been faced with the consequences of those early decisions. The closure of the Suez Canal and hence the shipping facilities of Aqaba in 1967, as well as the influx of Palestinian refugees following conflicts with the Israeli state, created an acute economic crisis which has been repeatedly reflected in a realignment of domestic and foreign policy.

The rationale behind the European mandate settlement was that the problems arising from the economic development and political management of the Middle East would be eased by the creation of organisational apparatus under European control. It was a transitional era when most, if not all, Middle Eastern areas achieved tacit international recognition. However, new governmental systems were organised within these fixed borders that were to have ramifications far beyond this early period. No European power foresaw the continuing territorial conflicts, even war, that would result from the actual partition plan. The tremendous impact within the states of the shifts from a 'frontier mentality' to a 'border mentality', from particularistic identification with a village or tribal groups to consciousness of their national identity as defined by a state operating within fixed territorial limits, cannot be estimated.

The immediate social and political adjustment of Middle Eastern populations in the early post-war era was of a quite different character. A disparity existed between the theoretical formulations of the plan and its implementations. The inherent concepts of 'boundary' and 'nation-state' were considered neither good nor bad, although their actual enforcement created serious and, at times, irreversible effects.

For thousands of years, the cultural and material life of the nomadic pastoralists of the Arabian Peninsula had remained unchanged, despite shifts in the political and ecological balances. At the end of World War I, however, an artificial grid system of nation-states and borders, established and enforced by mandate authorities, was imposed on these communities. Theoretically, the grid was merely a device to separate uncomfortable questions of legal jurisdiction, but once machinery was created for enforcement and the framework was given life by subsequent political organisation, what was simply a structural hypothesis became a functioning entity. It was inevitable that indigenous local conditions and ultimate realities of 'nation-state' and 'border' would be mutually effective.

To understand the social and political adjustments resulting from partition, particularly those of Saudi Arabia, it is helpful to review the actual decisions made concerning boundary delineation.

As mandate authorities, France and Britain gave only secondary consideration to the needs of local populations. Their foremost concern was to secure their strategic and economic interests and this led them to focus their attention upon populous urban areas and territory advantageous for transport or communication routes. The delineation of borders and states was, for them, a political tool. As a representative of its mandates in a number of conferences where territorial settlements were being negotiated, Britain frequently forced concessions on certain countries when advantageous to its own interests. Some of these territorial settlements, such as that of Kuwait, seriously endangered the ability of the state to survive. The following statement made by British General Headquarters in Mesopotamia illustrates the problem faced in delimitating boundaries, particularly in desert territory.

> With reference to boundary you are considering along the Khabur. Being lines of convergence of interests rather than boundaries rivers are not suitable for frontiers in this country. Line through open desert preferable for a frontier and this would make administration more easy.[12]

Boundaries were designed to act as barriers separating conflicting claims to a particularly desirable area. If a boundary was delineated in a highly contested area, the difficulties of enforcing the boundary were increased. The British in the Middle East considered that the desert was not desirable and, hence, it was less contested than the areas along the Tigris and Euphrates Rivers which were urbanised and promised opportunities in commercial development. The British solution for this problem—that of drawing a 'line through open desert'—did not, however, solve Britain's problem of creating secure and uncontested boundaries, for the simple reason that the desert was not 'open'. Most of the Middle East, and especially the interior of the Arabian Peninsula, had nomadic populations whose life-style required seasonal moves to pasture and water resources as well as to settled areas to obtain otherwise unavailable supplies. The new borders proposed to cut through *dira*s, traditional grazing groups of the tribes, as well as the centuries-old commercial, social and political links that had joined the interests of the *hadar* and the badu.

The mandate powers were not unaware of the difficulties

presented by the ecological relationships between nomadic and settled communities and were anxious to minimise the problems. The British government set to work to define the limits of Mesopotamia in regions that were not settled but were occupied by badu tribes. There were two proposals, both of which presented problems. The first was to create a boundary by following the limits of cultivation: tribal country would then be a 'no man's land'. The second solution was to define a boundary in terms of tribes dependent on states rather than by dividing territory (cf. Figure 5.3)

The first solution was considered unsatisfactory because it gave no thought to economic ties between nomadic and settled areas. Furthermore, such a boundary would mean that the extensive territory belonging to the Amarat Anaza, a powerful tribal confederation, would be completely left off the Iraq mandate, the southern limits of which would be considerably extended by control of this area. The British also feared that this plan did not guard against foreign interference among nomadic tribes, who might offer strong resistance to the British mandate authorities.

The second proposal was to 'treat the tribes economically dependent on a settled state as belonging politically to that State, and to secure the recognition of this by neighbouring States, while recognising in turn their sovereignty over the tribes that look towards them'.[13] Theoretically, the tribes were then free to migrate. If one defined states by certain tribes wherever they might be encamped, then a frontier became superfluous. This proposal was considered more reasonable in that natural boundaries were inclined to fall not between settled and nomadic areas but along 'elastic' lines 'in the midst of the tribal country that divide the tribes looking towards one settled area from those looking towards another'. Control of such a boundary would, however, be difficult and expensive, if not impossible.

> It is proposed that tribes shall be under jurisdiction of the Mesopotamian State when encamped inside this line, and not under it when encamped outside it. But how is this principle to be carried out? The line is a theoretical line drawn across a steppe which can only be occupied by human beings living Bedouin fashion. Is it proposed to establish a gendarmerie cordon along this line to control the tribes when they pass across

Figure 5.3: Boundaries of Mesopotamia

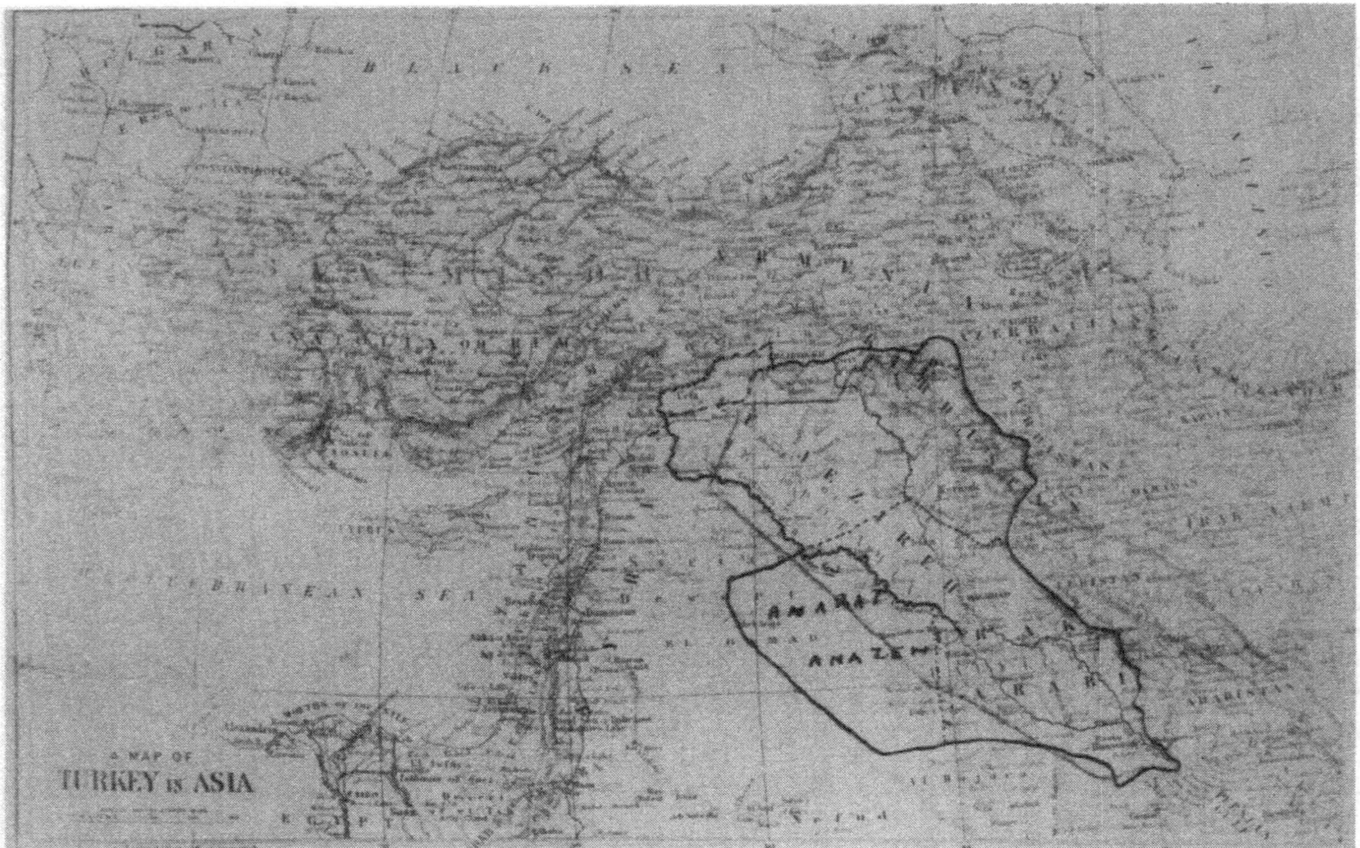

Source: Courtesy of the India Office Library and Records.

it? . . . But if it is not maintained the boundary is a dead letter, existing only on the official map, and in practice Mesopotamia is left with an open frontier.[14]

Enforcement of the laws regulating fixed borders meant considerable alteration to a tribe's livelihood, or even its death. This was typified by the so-called Road of Death in French-mandated Syria when the al-Ruwala tribal migration was forbidden. Unable to reach its other grazing ground, the tribe suffered tremendous loss in human beings and livestock. It was said that only dogs grew fat—feeding on the carcasses of animals killed by thirst and hunger.[15] Non-enforcement of the border meant continued, long-term contention between governments.

This was the dilemma confronting the mandate powers and the indigenous populations. The following chapters discuss the solutions that were applied to the delineation of borders separating Saudi Arabia from the mandate territories and the consequences of those decisions. Unlike the mandated territories, the isolated Arabian interior remained untouched by World War I and its aftermath. Arab nationalism was a virtually unknown sentiment. It was an area characterised by a great deal of regional differentiation: each region had one or more municipal centres shared by both nomadic and settled groups and a political organisation governed by a ruling family who variously based its power on religion, custom and heredity. It was not uncommon to find these so-called city-states bound in alliance against others. The larger the tribal and family groupings, the greater the tendency for them to remain associated with a particular territory, although their political allegiance was always defined by their tribal group.

During the first three decades of the twentieth century the Al Saud succeeded in establishing military and political control over the central plateau of the Arabian Peninsula and successfully took and maintained their control over the littoral areas to the east and west. At the same time they pushed north to the Euphrates and south into the Yaman as far as the coast. There has not been an uncontested inch of border on the entire circumference of what we recognise formally as the Kingdom of Saudi Arabia. Some of its boundaries and territories, such as the Buraimi Oasis, the Iraq Neutral Zone, and its boundary with Jordan continue to be contested even today.

Part II will examine the historical factors—social, economic, political, military and religious—that helped shape the course of these territorial disputes and the evolution of Arabia into a modern nation-state. Unlike other Middle Eastern border settlements, Saudi Arabia's boundaries were the result of adjustment not between two mandate powers, but between a mandate power and an autonomous independent leader, Abd al-Aziz. These disputes were particularly important as they not only illuminate the broader diplomatic issues of the time but, above all, reflect the components of political authority and socio-economic organisation present within Arabian society.

Notes

1. Dankwart A. Rustow, *Middle Eastern Political Systems* (Prentice-Hall, Englewood Cliffs, NJ, 1971), p.94.

2. India Office Records, *Political and Secret Department Separate Files 1902-1931*, L/P&S/10 (henceforward abbreviated to IO L/P&S/10): IO L/P&S/10/937, Foreign Office Memorandum on Arabian Policy, confidential, no. 7263 [E13523/9/44]. Aden had been excluded from the list because Britain did not want its status *vis-à-vis* herself to invite further discussion from other European nations. Al-Ḥijāz was also excluded because 'the boundaries of the Hedjaz have never been defined, but the Hedjaz as a State was an original member of the League of Nations, and so long as it remains so it stands on an entirely different footing from the remainder of the peninsula'.

3. IO L/P&S/10/385, memorandum from Lieutenant-Colonel Sir Percy Cox, Political Resident in the Persian Gulf, Bushire, to the Secretary for the Government of India in the Foreign Department, 2 December 1913, no. 4005-M.

4. IO L/P&S/10/385, confidential note from Captain W. H. Shakespear, Political Agent Kuwait, to Sir Arthur Hirtzel, Secretary of the Political Department, India Office, London, 26 June 1914.

5. IO L/P&S/10/769, 'Secret Operations', from the War Office to General Officer Commanding in Egypt and General Officer Commanding in Mesopotamia, 23 May 1919, Cipher 78285. See also Helmut Mejcher, *Imperial Quest for Oil: Iraq 1910-1928* (St Antony's Middle East Monographs, Oxford, 1976).

6. IO L/P&S/10/769, Minute Paper—'Points Awaiting Decision', India Office, C. C. Garbett, 20 September 1919; and 'Kurdistan', by J. E. S., Political Department, India Office, 14 December 1918, B.303. See also C. J. Edmonds, *Kurds, Turks and Arabs: Politics, Travel and Research in North-Eastern Iraq 1919-1925* (Oxford University Press, London, 1957).

7. IO L/P&S/10/769, 'Secret Operations', from the War Office to General Officer Commanding in Egypt and General Officer Commanding in Mesopotamia, 23 May 1919, Cipher 78285.

8. Rustow, *Middle Eastern Political Systems*, p.35.

9. The concept of 'supra-nationalism' was created after World War II to meet the world's new economic and political needs. It is a term that anticipated the elimination of boundaries as criteria for social, economic or political jurisdiction between nations. This is typified by international organisations such as the EEC, COMECON and the Arab League. International law and transnational institutions

such as the United Nations have also had an effect on the traditional interdictory qualities of boundaries. Even though the average Western individual of today does not theorise about such concepts as boundary and nation-state, most are so steeped in their own national identity that they could not begin to contemplate the ultimate realisation of a 'supra-nationalism' nor even a period of time when nations and nationalism did not exist. See also Elie Kedourie, *Nationalism* (Hutchinson University Library, London, 1966).

10. See Maxime Rodinson, *Israel: A Colonial-settler State?*, translated by D. Thorstad (Monad Press, NY, 1973).

11. Rustow, *Middle Eastern Political Systems*, pp.53-4.

12. IO L/P&S/10/769, telegram from General Headquarters Mesopotamia to the War Office, 1 December 1919, X.7782.

13. IO L/P&S/10/769, telegrams 10852 and 10853: 'Memorandum on the Future Frontiers of Mesopotamia', from the Chief Political Officer Iraq to the Secretary of State, 11 December 1918.

14. Ibid.

15. See Carl R. Raswan, *Black Tents of Arabia: My Life Among the Bedouins* (Hutchinson, London, 1935).

6

Expansion of Al Saud Authority 1918-1926: Territorial Conflicts and Border Delineation

Between the years 1918 and 1926 Abd al-Aziz and Great Britain attempted to settle their outstanding differences which had originated, directly or indirectly, from the juxtaposition of their territories and from Britain's delimitation of nation-states and borders in the post-World War I mandate period. Britain had begun to view Saudi authority with increasing trepidation after the Saudi thrust into Jabal Shammar in 1921 placed it in direct contact with the mandated territories of Iraq and Transjordan and alongside the Imperial Air Route. While the British sought to establish fixed territorial units with legal rights of interdictory power, Abd al-Aziz sought elastic boundaries capable of adjustment according to shifting political and ecological balances. In addition, the Saudi leader feared the establishment of an arc of Hashimite authority under European aegis across his northern frontier, since this would contain his own authority and threaten the security of Najd. Not only did the Al Saud regard these northern territories as their own family possessions; neither they nor the Ikhwan accepted the political or religious authority of the Hashimites. Ikhwan raids were instigated by the Al Saud against al-Hijaz, Iraq, Kuwait and Transjordan as they sought to regain what they considered was their lawful right as Arab and Islamic leaders.

These boundary conflicts were not questions simply of territorial jurisdiction; they related to the legitimate rights and responsibilities of governments and the people they served. The decisions of the post-war mandate period had led to new social structures and expectations within the Middle Eastern state system as it was now defined. A boundary could be effective only if the populations concerned came to recognise the rationale for its creation within the context of new patterns of political structures or if the border had to be physically enforced by police.

As an independent leader, unlike the other Arab rulers of the Peninsula who were under European mandates or protection, Abd al-Aziz was confronted by serious foreign and domestic problems, foremost of which was the need to secure the hereditary rule of his family and to extend the limits of his territory as far as possible against the mandates. Fixed borders not only curtailed the expansion of Saudi authority, which was motivated by religious and political considerations, but also prevented the seasonal migrations of the nomadic tribes. Abd al-Aziz hoped that by procrastinating in the boundary negotiations with Britain he could secure the allegiance of additional tribes by means of Wahhabi proselytising and raids and thereby obtain rights to the territory of these tribes.

This chapter deals briefly with the similarities between four of Saudi Arabia's territorial disputes in the early twentieth century—al-Khurma and Turaba, Iraq, Kuwait and Transjordan—which illustrate issues of particular importance to the Arab leaders, such as legitimate authority, rights to territory, allegiance of populations, tribal raiding and emigration. Abd al-Aziz's conquest of al-Hijaz is also discussed, not because it is typical of the inter-Arab disputes of this period, but because it shows clearly the general Saudi attitude towards the Hashimites and British as well as their deliberate policy of territorial expansion. The formal-legalistic aspect of the border negotiations is dealt with only in so far as it affected future political decisions of the Al Saud.

The Al Saud Look Towards their Eastern Frontier

The strategic position of the district of al-Qasim, lying between Jabal Shammar and Najd and juxtaposed to al-Hijaz, not only ensured that it would be a valuable entrepôt centre but also rendered it vulnerable in any conflict between its northern and southern neighbours. It was always the first district of Central Arabia to experience intermittent military incursions from al-Hijaz. In November 1915 Husain, who in the following year was to instigate the Arab Revolt and proclaim himself King of the Arabs, marched into al-Qasim, then under the control of the Al Saud, and attempted to assert his authority over the Utaiba tribe. Since the capture by the British and the Kuwaitis of Basra a year previously, Abd al-Aziz had not taken any active part in the war. His main concern was to protect his authority from the Turkish-supported Al Rashid of Jabal Shammar and the pretensions of the British-supported Hashimites in al-Hijaz. An open conflict between the Al Hashim and Al Saud eventually broke out on the frontier around the two urban centres of al-Khurma and Turaba (see Figure 3.1). This dispute has been frequently recorded by historians who regarded it as important simply because it was the first major armed conflict between these two great Arabian families and also because it was only five days' march from Mecca and a prelude to a Saudi invasion of al-Hijaz.[1] The dispute is, however, of much wider importance and provides a context for examining political motives which were relevant to the Arab leaders themselves and which have been generally misunderstood by Western observers.

Both King Husain and Abd al-Aziz claimed al-Khurma and Turaba, each for plausible reasons. The Hashimites claimed that they had previously appointed the *qadi*s and the amirs of al-Khurma, including the current amir, and in addition had paid subsidies to the town. However, when the Saudis had entered al-Hijaz in the early 1800s, they had converted the inhabitants of the region to Wahhabi beliefs and had also been responsible for appointing some of the *qadi*s. The subsidy, paid by the Hashimite Sharifs, was regarded more as a bribe paid to neighbouring areas in order to ensure the peaceful continuance of the *hajj* than as a symbol of political alliance. The whole question of territorial jurisdiction was unclear because no boundaries existed to differentiate political authorities. These fringe areas were frequently contested and all had a history of vacillating allegiances.

Briefly, the situation at the outbreak of hostilities was that, in May and again in July 1918, King Husain lost troops and arms to the Ikhwan in military actions around al-Khurma. The British asked Abd al-Aziz to desist from hostilities and the Saudi leader responded by asking them to protect rights guaranteed him under Article II of the Anglo-Saudi Treaty of 1915. These considerations were still under discussion when events accelerated. In August, Hijazi forces were destroyed by Ikhwan in a major confrontation 25 kilometres east of al-Khurma. A section of the Utaiba tribe, who were allied to Husain, defected to the Al Saud and in October this same section attacked al-Khurma itself. Meanwhile, it had become clear that the Hashimite-appointed amir, Khalid b. Luai, had adopted Wahhabi doctrines and was in close communication with the Al Saud.[2] On 21 May 1919 King Husain's son, Amir Abdullah, took Turaba, a town 30 kilometres south-west of al-Khurma. Four days later, Khalid b. Luai, now leading Ikhwan warriors, attacked, killing over five thousand of Amir Abdullah's men. Meanwhile, the pilgrimage of Abd al-Aziz's followers had been forbidden by King Husain and there was growing pressure from within Central Arabia for the Saudi leader to solve this problem; as a result the British government, in London, envisaged another Wahhabi conquest of al-Hijaz and a possible *jihad* against the mandate powers.

At this point Abd al-Aziz withdrew his troops and matters seemed to cool.[3] The British, having doubts about their continued support of Husain and worried about military security in the region, wanted to procure some agreement between the leaders and a temporary armistice was forced upon Husain in August 1920, thereby postponing hostilities in al-Hijaz for another four years.

The importance of this inter-Arab dispute is that it indicates the significance of territory and tribal allegiance to an Arab leader. This was succinctly pointed out to the British by King Husain himself when he told them that his continued recalcitrance over al-Khurma was not solely because of its strategic position. He explained that al-Khurma was situated within territory belonging to the Subai tribe and that there were large numbers of its settled and nomadic members living in the vicinity of al-Khurma. If an Arab leader were able to gain control of al-Khurma and Turaba, then he would secure the allegiance of the Subai tribe and the whole of the tribe's pasturage. Viewed in this light, the importance of al-Khurma and Turaba is easy to understand. If al-Khurma were designated as belonging to the Al Saud, the local population would recognise the boundary of Najd 16 kilometres west of al-Khurma; if it were determined in favour of the Hashimites, then the boundary would fall 193 kilometres east of al-Khurma. It was understandable that both Husain and Abd al-Aziz would regard this as a test case for similar frontier zones.[4]

The Treaty of al-Muhammara: Central Arabia's Territorial Dispute with Iraq

The territorial dispute with Iraq is illuminating because the presence of powerful nomadic tribes on the frontier between Najd and Iraq emphasised the differences between European and Central Arabian attitudes to political authority and jurisdiction. Iraq, the foreign relations of which were negotiated by the European mandate power, was interested in creating a 'defensive perimeter' around the more urbanised areas of the Tigris and Euphrates Rivers and sought the establishment of fixed boundaries through the desert as a means of control. The survival of the badu, however, necessitated a nomadic existence. Their allegiance was not to a geopolitical entity, but to their tribal responsibilities. It was a difficult, if not impossible, task to compel such people to honour a European-style boundary. The Shammar and Harb moved within their tribal *dira*s to Shinafiya (near Najaf) and Samawa; the Zafir towards Samawa, Nasiriya and Suq al-Shuyukh; the al-Ujman and Awazim towards Kuwait; and the Mutair towards Kuwait and Zubair, in order to obtain supplies from the urban centres of the north and east.

> It was not generally realized . . . especially by certain British and Arab officials in Iraq, that the trouble was almost entirely economic, aggravated . . . by the unfortunate personal hostility existing between King Faisal I and Ibn Sa'ud . . . . Badawin tribes of northern and north-eastern Najd—particularly the 'Ajmān, Harb, Mutair, Shammar, 'Awāzim and, nearer Iraq, the Dhafīr—cannot support themselves in their own country and for centuries have migrated each year . . . to obtain the necessities . . . dates, rice and . . . grazing for their camels along the rich zone lying to the south of the Euphrates from Karbala to the Persian Gulf. This applies also to the eastern 'Anizah tribes—the 'Amarāt and Dahāmshah.[5]

The migrating badu would seek permission to camp from tribes in whose territory they were entering.

> Permission was never refused, for both sides benefited . . . . The Euphrates towns and tribes—and Kuwait too—always welcomed the annual migration, while the Badu of northern

> Najd looked upon Iraq and Kuwait as their natural shopping centres at the end of summer and beginning of winter, when grazing was scarce in their homeland . . . . For the river tribes to have denied the Badu permission to pass up to the Euphrates for their *musābilah* would have been tantamount to a declaration of war . . . . But this rarely happened, and only if great heads of states—the Amīrs of Ha'il, the Al Sa'ud, the Muntafiq Sa'dūn shaikhs, etc.—were at enmity, as they sometimes were.[6]

Under normal circumstances, leaders like the Al Saud reaffirmed their control over these tribes by annual expeditions to collect tax or punish recalcitrant tribes. A unique situation developed in the 1920s when tribes in the fringe areas realised that they could take advantage of the new mandate system and the resultant hostilities between sovereigns, such as Faisal in Iraq and Abd al-Aziz in Central Arabia, to avoid this taxation. Relations between Najd, Iraq and Kuwait became critical as tribes freely raided one another and then escaped into the territory of another leader to pledge their allegiance. Rulers had to contend with a heavy loss of life and property among their allied tribes and, because of the enforced mandate frontiers, were unable to punish the offenders. The conflict intensified when, in the tenuous stability of the post-war years, the rulers sought to extend their own authority and weaken that of their neighbours by deliberately inciting tribal conflict on the frontiers and soliciting the support of previously antagonistic tribes by what the British disparagingly termed 'bribes'. As in the al-Khurma-Turaba dispute, a ruler claimed the right to a tribe's territory if that tribe had pledged its allegiance to him. Viewed in this light, Ikhwan raiding was not simply a question of lawlessness on the frontiers, but was a deliberate Saudi policy designed to extend their authority.

The particular problems of this situation may be further amplified. Ikhwan raids against the northern frontier had resulted in many tribes, particularly the Shammar, seeking refuge in Iraq, either crossing the Euphrates at Ramadi or remaining in the territory of the Amarat Anaza. The customary law of the badu prescribes that anyone supplicating for protection, even an enemy, is entitled to receive it; thus, Fahd b. Hadhdhal, chief of the Amarat Anaza, had received the Shammar even though Abd al-Aziz himself was later to question the validity of this right because the long arm of his government was now prevented from reaching its subjects. Fahd's problem was that, on the one hand, realising the economic dependence of his tribe on Baghdad, he attempted to comply with the mandatory power in Iraq, while, on the other hand, in order to secure immunity for his tribe from Ikhwan raids, he sought Abd al-Aziz's assurances of friendship. A major conflict arose when the Shammar, entitled to protection but not permitted under Arab customary law to continue hostilities while under that protection, began to use Amarat territory for counter-raids on the Wahhabis. The Saudi leader immediately claimed the allegiance of the entire Anaza tribe, maintaining that the Al Saud dynasty was of Anaza descent and that he had been donating gifts to Fahd. Fearing an intensification of hostilities, Sir Percy Cox, High Commissioner in Iraq, ordered the Shammar to cross to the left bank of the Euphrates and proposed a meeting under British auspices to reach agreement between Faisal and Abd al-Aziz on border issues and tribal affairs.

During preliminary discussions in 1920, Cox and Abd al-Aziz attempted to establish general principles according to which boundaries could be determined. Almost at once, there was disagreement: Cox advocated fixed borders while Abd al-Aziz, aware of the problems of nomadism, objected to frontiers based on territorial rather than on tribal lines. Undoubtedly he also realised that acceptance of fixed borders must ultimately limit his own authority. Cox then suggested that the tribes be allocated to one of the two states on the basis of traditionally recognised rights to pasture and wells. According to this proposal, the Amarat Anaza, Muntafiq and Zafir were to be assigned to Iraq while Abd al-Aziz was to receive the Shammar. Almost immediately this plan was upset by the actions of the tribes concerned. The Amarat Anaza was a tribal confederation with divided loyalties: the Amarat in the east preferred Iraq while the al-Ruwala in the west preferred Najd. Moreover, the Zafir eventually defected to Abd al-Aziz, seriously weakening the defences of Iraq.

The events surrounding the Zafir defection are a prime example of the inter-tribal and inter-governmental rivalries of this period. Hamud b. Suwait, Shaikh of the Zafir, had originally pledged his allegiance to the Iraqi government. However, as a punishment for the continued raids by his tribe in the frontier zone, Iraq stopped payment of a subsidy to him and also appointed Ibn Suwait's enemy, Yusuf Beg al-Sadun, head of the newly formed Camel Corps, whose duty it was to guard the Iraqi frontier with Najd. Ibn

Suwait retaliated by travelling to al-Riyad where he was received by the Saudi leader who sent him back to Iraq laden with gifts and accompanied by a Wahhabi representative sent expressly to collect tribute, presumably *zakat*, from the Zafir and all other tribes camped within the Zafir *dira*. Iraq now presented a 'soft belly' to the Ikhwan who had meanwhile camped at Hafar in the Batin, the south-western limit of Kuwait. The Camel Corps ignited the conflict by making an excursion into the Zafir *dira* and the Ikhwan responded by attacking Abu al-Ghar and Shaqra south of Nasiriya on 11 March 1922, inflicting heavy losses on the Camel Corps and on Muntafiq tribesmen camped nearby. When the British Royal Air Force was called in, there was a temporary halt of hostilities as the Ikhwan were recalled to Najd and the Camel Corps was disbanded.

Rulers like the Al Sabah in Kuwait and Abd al-Aziz in Najd recognised that the creation of boundaries presented a new complex of problems. These ruling family dynasties ensured the continuance of their authority through a system of mutual alliances established between the tribes and themselves. The tribes gave confirmation of their allegiance through taxes and military service and, in return, the paramount shaikh or amir was responsible for maintaining order and, if need be, providing military protection when any of the tribal groups were threatened. Under certain circumstances, a powerful ruler could increase the general economic prosperity of the people by forcing caravans through the territory and encouraging the presence of foreign merchants whose security would be personally guaranteed. The point of contention between Iraq, Kuwait and Najd was thus not merely boundaries as such but, rather, the complex interrelationship between boundaries and tribal life-style in the unique context of the early 1920s, as Abd al-Aziz himself stated when objecting to Cox's proposal.

> In spite of any agreement we could make the Anaizah and Dhafir would cause friction between me and Iraq for which reason it is impossible to accept them as belonging to Iraq. The Muntafik are different and not so turbulent and it is possible for them to belong to Iraq but if they settle within my borders they should pay taxes as in the past in return for protection afforded. As regards the settlement of boundaries, this is reasonable and it may be possible to arrive at an agreement.[7]

Moreover, Abd al-Aziz and the Ikhwan viewed Faisal's enthronement as a curtailment of Saudi authority and a contravention of the 'right path of Islam'. Abd al-Aziz's informal statements to the British and his captured messages indicate that he and the Ikhwan had every intention of pushing their advantage as far as was militarily possible. Indeed, the philosophy of the Ikhwan was such as to make obligatory continued raiding upon infidels and non-Wahhabis. However, in response to Britain's anger over the Ikhwan raid on Shaqra which had caused serious internal repercussions within the Iraqi government, Abd al-Aziz agreed to send an envoy to the Conference of al-Muhammara beginning on 1 May 1922. A month prior to the meeting, Cox laid down a temporary border and requested Abd al-Aziz to withdraw any of his followers who were on the Iraqi side.

The Treaty of al-Muhammara was signed on 5 May 1922. Aside from general agreements about trade and protection of pilgrims, the treaty allocated the tribes as Cox had previously decided and provided for punishment of raiding tribes. Determination of the 'ownership' of resources was to be made by a joint Iraq-Najd commission under the guidance of a British official. On this basis, a fixed frontier would be determined, although certain resources would be held in common among the tribes. Any tribe moving animals into a country to which it was not allied was liable to pay a fee. It was left to the commission to investigate the establishment of a more permanent boundary. It was significant, however, that the treaty did not preclude the possibility that tribes might change their allegiance—such disputes were thus only temporarily forestalled.

Central Arabia's Territorial Dispute with Kuwait

Relations between Central Arabia and Kuwait, like those with Iraq, were strained because of territorial and tribal problems. Kuwait's extraordinary boundaries had been delineated in the unratified Anglo-Turkish Convention of 29 July 1913 which had drawn from the focal point of Kuwait Town two semi-circles, with a twenty- and forty-mile radius respectively. In the inner or red circle the ruling Al Sabah had total autonomy, while in the outer or green circle the ruling shaikh had rather more nebulous control, but was allowed to collect tribute from the tribes.[8] The sanctity of these borders, like those with Iraq, was far from being established, as the British themselves admitted.

> The boundaries which did not give Koweit quite so much as Mubarak claimed, were straight lines drawn on the map to include certain wells which, according to the best evidence available, were used by the Koweit tribes. Such lines in fact mean very little.[9]

Trouble soon arose between the Al Saud and Al Sabah. The feud began in November 1915 when Shaikh Mubarak Al Sabah sent Kuwaiti troops under the command of his son Salim to help Abd al-Aziz overcome an insurrection by al-Ujman at al-Hufuf. Salim, although aiding the Saudi leader, gave political asylum to the unrepenting tribe in Kuwait, an act for which Abd al-Aziz never forgave Kuwait's Al Sabah.[10] Difficulties multiplied when Salim, upon his accession as ruler of Kuwait in 1917, extended his authority to the outer green circle and established a fort at Duhat Balbul where the green circle intersected the coast just north of Jabal Manifa.[11] He then went on to use the disputed land as a 'dumping ground' for tribes hostile to Abd al-Aziz, such as the al-Ujman, who were continuing in their political vacillations, and the Shammar. Abd al-Aziz then made a counterclaim to Duhat Balbul and, moreover, ordered Ibn Shuqair of the Mutair to seize and establish an Ikhwan *hijra* at Jariya Ilya,[12] which Salim also claimed. Upon receiving this news, Salim ordered Kuwaiti troops to prepare for an attack against the Ikhwan. Faisal al-Duwish of the Mutair, however, led the Ikhwan in a dawn attack against Kuwait's troops who suffered heavy losses in men and arms.[13] Salim meanwhile requested restitution of the booty taken by the Ikhwan. Abd al-Aziz replied that Salim had no right to claim anything and sent a letter to that effect for Salim's signature. Salim then requested British assistance, pointing out that Jariya Ilya was within the limits set by the Anglo-Turkish Convention; he was informed by them that the Anglo-Saudi Treaty of 1915 superseded the former document, but that they would act as an arbitrator in the dispute. Abd al-Aziz meanwhile claimed all territory right up to the walls of Kuwait Town.

Britain was faced with a dilemma: having formally claimed territory for Kuwait from the Ottomans in 1913, was she also obliged to claim for Kuwait the sanctity of territory within the green circle *vis-à-vis* the Saudis? Cox, in a telegram dated 14 December 1920, quite clearly states that, in accordance with the Anglo-Turkish Convention, 'we cannot do less but need not do more than recognise Sheikh of Koweit's rights of possession and authority within the [inner] red circle as against all comers'.[14] Because Britain had no immediate interests in Kuwait, she could arrange that some of Kuwait's territory, at least within the outer green circle, be ceded to the Al Saud in the hopes that peace might be maintained in countries of more direct concern to her, namely Iraq, Transjordan and al-Hijaz.

However, the conflict intensified when the Ikhwan attacked Jahra on 10 October 1920, killing over two hundred Kuwaitis and taking much booty from the town.[15] It is significant that in this battle Salim depended heavily on help from the townspeople, in addition to the badu, which may indicate that many of these tribes, for whatever reasons, were changing their allegiance to the Al Saud. During October, Faisal al-Duwish sent demands to Kuwait Town that the inhabitants should become Ikhwan and Britain was forced to intervene, saying that any threat to the town would be regarded as a direct attack on Britain.

Cox now realised that, before any permanent boundary could be delineated, it was essential to settle the issues concerning tribal loyalties and tribal rights to resources. H. R. P. Dickson, Political Agent at Bahrain, then proposed a creative and flexible solution for the settlement of these problems. His suggestions are, in fact, a precursor to those made by Cox at the Conference of al-Muhammara two years later concerning the problems of the Iraq-Najd border dispute.

> Bin Saud and Salim to be first asked what actual tribes they claim as belonging to him. This ought to be settled fairly easily. As we know the Ajman, Mutair, Bani Khalid, Bani Hajar etc., all belong to the former. The Rashaida, Awazim and one or two other less important elements are known to belong to Koweit. The next question to settle is the 'Mugayith' or summer camping ground of say Shaikh Salim's tribes. This will give us the names of a whole series of wells, as well as the spots where the Bedouin in summer must be on a well. If we can find out where such wells are, and if they can be proved to be the camping places of Salim's Bedouins, (this should be quite easy if say Ibn Hithlain and Hamad al Suwait were present) the rest is simple, all such

> wells to go Shaikh Salim. Similarly all wells or 'Mugayith' of Bin Saud's tribes become in Bin Saud's territory. Should a dispute arise as to the lawful owners of a particular well, a visit to the place will settle the matter as the original tribes who owned the wells will have put their 'Marks' [*wasm*s] on a rock or stone near the well.[16]

Dickson decided that grazing grounds and wells could be the only basis for a boundary since 'the tribes themselves will never abide by a decision that deprives them of an ancient right'.

> Regarding the actual dispute between Bin Saud and Shaikh Salim. From talks I have had with Shaikh Isa, Shaikh Hamad and others who know the Bedouin well, the setting of a boundary between the two rulers should not present much difficulty provided a definite line (European style) be not allowed to come into the question. Salim may possibly try to insist on this, but he should not be encouraged.[17]

The interesting aspect of this quotation from Dickson is his belief that Salim might try to insist on a fixed boundary. Salim's reason for doing so, as will be seen later, was that, because of the constant raiding by the Ikhwan, most of his tribes had 'defected' so that the 'hinterland' of Kuwait Town remained unprotected.[18] He was becoming increasingly dependent upon the British for the continued security of his rule. A fixed boundary would be a lever in bringing Abd al-Aziz to the negotiating table and forcing Britain to sanction his Arabian neighbour if he attacked Kuwaiti tribes or territory. However, on 17 February 1921 Shaikh Salim died and, on hearing the news, Abd al-Aziz immediately declared that there was no hostility between Kuwait and himself and no need to determine a boundary.

The Uqair Conference of 1922: Temporary Settlement of Central Arabia's Dispute with Iraq and Kuwait

The problem of Ikhwan raids was extending into new areas. In the west Wahhabi raiders were penetrating far up Wadi al-Sirhan, a famous strategic north-south caravan route between Central

Arabia and Transjordan. On 15 August 1922 they made an audacious strike west of the Hijaz Railway and two raids upon Bani Sakhr tribes less than 24 kilometres from Amman. Britain considered these as serious intrusions upon her interests and British armoured cars and the Royal Air Force intervened. Realising the weakness of his position, the Saudi leader agreed to resume the border negotiations begun at al-Muhammara but never ratified.

In November 1922 the Uqair Conference was convened between Najd, Iraq and Kuwait, respectively represented by Abd al-Aziz, Sabih Bey and Major J. C. More, the Political Agent for Kuwait. Sir Percy Cox acted as mediator. Negotiations soon reached an impasse with Iraq and Najd making unrealistic demands for each other's territory. Sabih Bey claimed, 'by right of God's creation', a boundary only 19 kilometres north of al-Riyad. Abd al-Aziz, claiming that he personally knew nothing about the 'creation', stated that he did know about the hereditary rights of the Al Saud and continued to argue for a tribal rather than a fixed and arbitrary boundary.

> He started off by insisting that the Dhafir [Zafir], an Iraq tribe of Badu, was his and that it was necessary for his boundary to extend right up to the Euphrates, not because he wishes to control the river, but because the Dhafir, as well as his big Badawin tribes, moved up annually to the Euphrates and would never be denied right of access, which was a question of life and death for the desert man.[19]

Cox, impatient with the lack of progress, said such a proposal was completely unfeasible in view of the most recent state of affairs. Abd al-Aziz then proposed a more flexible plan whereby he would abandon his claim to the Zafir tribe in order to secure the rights of his other tribes to water and pasture. Each tribe would lay claim to their traditional wells and pastures. *Wasms*, tribal marks, found on the wells would assist in proving these claims. Those still under dispute could be referred to the *ahl al-khibra*, 'people of wisdom', or be declared neutral.

> He advocated for instance, that the southernmost wells claimed by the 'Anizah, Dhafīr and Kuwait tribes (excluding the Mutair, 'Awāzim and 'Ajmān, which, he asserted, were under his government) should form the boundary, while any wells known

to be common property—such as existed between the 'Anizah and the Dhafīr and between the Dhafīr and the Mutair—should be declared neutral.[20]

Lengthy deliberations continued until Cox autocratically reprimanded Abd al-Aziz and said that he would himself determine the boundary: taking up a red pencil, he proceeded to do just that. A line separating Iraq from Najd started at the Arabian Gulf and continued to Jabal Unaiza near Transjordan, depriving the Saudi ruler of territory claimed by Najd. In response to tribal conflicts, Cox drew the Iraq Neutral Zone, which was actually the tribal *dira* of the Zafir. However, having lost territory in respect of Iraq, Najd was given territory claimed by Kuwait.[21] Thus on 2 December 1922 the Uqair Protocols, designed to be read with the Treaty of al-Muhammara, were signed. The first protocol delineated the boundaries between Iraq and Najd and between Kuwait and Najd.[22] Article 2 states that, if Najd tribes were closer to Iraqi wells, they would be given permission to water there instead. By virtue of Article 3, however, neither party was to fortify the wells adjoining the border or to concentrate troops in the vicinity.

Dickson, who had acted as a translator and aid during these negotiations, made a final statement about the Uqair Conference which stands alone as a scathing critique of British actions.

> This arbitrary boundary of Western type between Iraq and Najd was, in my opinion, a serious error. It resulted in Ibn Sa'ud, almost for the first time in history, restricting the annual natural movements of Najd tribes towards the north . . . . he apparently decided on a policy of slowly but surely diverting his people from their old and time-honoured communication with Iraq and Kuwait, trying instead to force them to get the necessities of life and daily requirements from 'Uqair, Qatīf and Jubail, his ports on the Persian Gulf.[23]

The results, he adds, were serious.

> natural lines of trade cannot thus be lightly interfered with or laid aside, and, as a result of this policy, we have seen nothing but trouble. Had Ibn Sa'ud left well alone, it is not improbable that we should not have had the Ikhwān rebellion of 1929-30, or

> the friction between Iraq and Najd that preceded it, or the long-drawn-out fourteen years' agony of the Kuwait blockade.[24]

Based upon his own administrative experiences, he went on to criticise Cox's decisions concerning fixed boundaries.

> a much better solution than that decided upon at 'Uqair would have been the adoption of Ibn Sa'ud's suggestion for a frontier based on tribal boundaries. When I was Political Officer of the Muntafiq, I had bitter experience of the futility of the old Turkish arbitrary boundaries between *liwas*, and found relief from inter-*liwa* tribal fighting only when I was able to persuade Sir Percy Cox to allow me to adopt tribal boundaries. He would have done well to follow the same plan at 'Uqair.[25]

Thus it was that Great Britain obtained her fixed boundaries, but the conflicts in this area were not over. Abd al-Aziz now extended Ikhwan activity west to Wadi al-Sirhan and Transjordan.

The Kuwait Conference: Central Arabia's Territorial Conflicts with Transjordan

While Ikhwan raids were continuing into Iraq and Kuwait, the British uneasily watched a third front developing in Wadi al-Sirhan, an entrepôt centre and cross-roads for north-south traffic between Central Arabia and Syria. Its major oases, Jauf and Sakaka, were the chief settlements of the area, frequented by all the *wadi* tribal groups, and were the door from Arabia into the Shamiya. At the northern end of the *wadi* were the salt villages of Qurayat al-Milh, also referred to as Kaf, and a Roman fort intended for the *wadi*'s defence in ancient times, as well as several smaller oasis settlements. Major tribal groups, such as the Ruwala Anaza of the western Shamiya and the Bani Sakhr from Transjordan, grazed throughout the major *wadi* and the four subsidiary *wadis* that entered it from the west.

British interest in Wadi al-Sirhan centred on plans for railway and pipelines which were to cross the northern end of the *wadi*. The British realised that if Wadi al-Sirhan and Kaf were under the control of the Al Saud, they would be a potential threat to Transjordan. Both Abd al-Aziz and the French were well aware that the *wadi* occupied a strategic position on the British defence corridor, cutting off Iraq from Transjordan. Abd al-Aziz was also aware that an east-west boundary in the *wadi* would be economically disastrous to the indigenous tribal groups who needed freedom of movement to graze and obtain goods from the settled area of Jauf. He lost little time in claiming the *wadi* on the grounds that the Al Rashid had controlled it and, therefore, he was heir to all their possessions by right of conquest.[26]

In the spring of 1922 the Wahhabi conquest of Wadi al-Sirhan began with the capture of Sakaka. This was closely followed by the occupation of Jauf, attacks on the oases of Khaibar and Taima, and raids on al-Ruwala tribesmen near Kaf in early summer. Amir Abdullah retaliated by occupying Qurayat al-Milh, but was unable to prevent Utaiba Ikhwan, who had recently transferred their allegiance from the Al Hashim to the Al Saud, from marching through Jauf past Kaf to Qasr al-Azraq at the extreme north-western limit of the *wadi*. On 15 August 1922 Ikhwan raided two villages of the Bani Sakhr, west of the Hijaz Railway and within 24 kilometres of Amman. Abd al-Aziz made new alliances with the tribes of western Shamiya and, in consequence, was in control of all the desert oases of Arabia up to the Fertile Crescent in the north, threatening Transjordan, Palestine and Syria.

The Uqair Conference had not attempted to settle the Transjordan or al-Hijaz disputes; nor had the signing of the protocols prevented trouble on the Iraq frontier. Ikhwan raiding to the north had continued and Wahhabi envoys had been collecting revenue from tribes who, temporarily or permanently, had transferred their allegiance to Iraq. Iraq, for her part, had continued to house Najd tribes, in particular the Shammar, and yet was unable to prevent them from conducting violent raids into Saudi territory in June 1923. In response to this, Abd al-Aziz called for their expulsion from Iraq and claimed that his authority over this tribe transcended state boundaries. Other conflicts continued, especially those concerning the restitution of booty from raids, the authority and appointment of frontier inspectors and the enlistment of troops from tribes in the territory of another government.

Hoping to stabilise the political situation, Britain began to organise the Kuwait Conference in 1923, with the intention of discussing three major problems: agreement over a Transjordan boundary, amendment of the Conference of al-Muhammara and extradition and punishment of raiders crossing established boundaries. The last problem entailed the question of which country the Shammar owed allegiance to and whether Abd al-Aziz could collect *zakat* from them when they were in Iraq territory.

The convening of this conference was not without its difficulties. At first the Saudi leader delayed, presumably (according to British records) because he wished to entice tribes to his banner.[27] The Hashimites refused to attend until the Al Saud had returned Jabal Shammar to the Al Rashid and, failing that, until the Wahhabis were at the gates of the Holy Cities. It was not long before Faisal al-Duwish obliged and arrived in al-Hijaz, destroying railway track and causing considerable consternation to the settled populace and to Britain.

The British began to fear that an Ikhwan capture of al-Madina prior to the conference would pre-empt discussion of many unsettled questions. Moreover, the Shaikh of al-Muhammara, an Arab, intruded himself upon the conference, much to the chagrin of the British who realised that Iraq and Iran had similar border problems to the ones soon to be discussed, problems they had no desire to see spread. They were also well aware that the rule of the Hashimites might be threatened in the near future, thus precluding any agreements. The British were also motivated by the necessity to stabilise Palestine, as well as their interests in Iraq and Transjordan, against an aggressive Central Arabian force. Their plan was to provide protection for the proposed pipeline and railway which were expected to run from Iraq south of Palmyra to Haifa. It was these interests that motivated Britain's concern with the allocation of Wadi al-Sirhan. She also felt that Transjordan and herself, by right of association, should have access to the Gulf of Aqaba and that the Hijaz Railway should be safely within Transjordan jurisdiction. The policy of appeasement she hoped to put forward at the conference was stated as follows.

> Thus Kaf would be given up for Aqaba by Abdulla, Khurma and Turaba would be given up by Ibn Saud for Kaf, and any claim to territory north of Mudawwara would be given up by Hussein for Khurma and Turaba.[28]

In Transjordan Abdullah rejected the British proposals on several points: Kaf was a strategic position and he saw no reason why he should surrender something he already recognised as belonging to the Hashimites, especially as he might later be accused of sacrificing territory purely for the sake of British mandatory interest. He suggested instead that Wadi al-Sirhan be restored in full to the al-Ruwala who would act as a buffer state—similar to a neutral zone—between himself and Najd. Abdullah's brother, King Faisal in Iraq, was also adamant about the position of Kaf and intransigent in his attitude towards the forthcoming conference. He was convinced that the Wahhabi attacks on the Bani Sakhr and al-Ruwala were a prelude to a major campaign on al-Hijaz itself and he would accept nothing less than the complete removal of Abd al-Aziz from al-Hijaz. If trouble arose, he would employ Iraqi tribes west of the Euphrates as a diversion to the Al Saud.

The Kuwait Conference was officially convened on 17 December 1923. Discussions centred on settlement and compensation for tribal raids and on the status of Wadi al-Sirhan. Abd al-Aziz claimed that the *wadi* was inhabited by badu and that, therefore, he had an historical right to it. Transjordan countered that there could be no peace if Central Arabia obtained Jauf or Sakaka. The people of the *wadi* had paid *zakat* to the Ottomans and, therefore, the natural boundaries of the al-Nafud should be used. They claimed Madain Salih, Taima, Jauf and Sakaka up to Jabal Unaiza where the Iraq and Najd boundaries joined. Finally it was suggested that there should be a plebiscite in Wadi al-Sirhan.[29] Abd al-Aziz agreed, with the proviso that there was also one in al-Khurma and Turaba where he was sure to win. Abdullah refused and suggested another neutral or buffer zone. The conference continued with more disagreement than accord and was adjourned twice. Abd al-Aziz, increasingly concerned by the united stance taken by Iraq, Transjordan and al-Hijaz, was prompted to ask whether they were in fact one country.[30] Meanwhile, Ikhwan raids were continuing on all fronts. Eventually, on 12 April 1924, the conference dissolved without any agreement.

The Saudi Attack on al-Hijaz Culminates with a Boundary Settlement Between Abd al-Aziz and the British

Abd al-Aziz had really very little reason for being conciliatory at the Kuwait Conference. His subsidy had been stopped on 31 March 1923, the British had not stopped Shammar raids into Najd, the

Hashimites appeared as a united block of hostile neighbours and, finally, the moral and religious significance of al-Hijaz had been debased by the corrupt rule of King Husain.[31] Not only had Husain presumed to speak as the voice of Arabs everywhere, but on 7 March 1924 he had proclaimed himself Khalifa. The knowledge that Husain's own subsidy had been stopped on 31 March 1924 could only have encouraged Abd al-Aziz in his decision to attack when Husain's tribes would be clamouring for their own subsidies. After making public appeals to the Muslim world to unite against King Husain, Saudi forces moved against southern al-Hijaz in late August 1924 while diversionary forces attacked two other Hashimite principalities—Bani Sakhr villages south of Amman in Transjordan and Zafir and Muntafiq tribesmen at Abu al-Ghar. These diversionary raids continued into January 1925, but all met with prompt resistance from British armoured cars and the Royal Air Force.

In al-Hijaz King Husain asked for British assistance but was refused. The story of his embittered, frustrated dealings with Britain and, subsequently, with the post-war peace conferences is well documented. Suffice it to say that his actions created a situation of 'diplomatic isolation' and Sir Ronald Storrs, who at that time was the Civil Governor in Jerusalem, was moved to comment that 'his pretensions bordered on the tragi-comic'.[32] He had consistently refused to sign an Anglo-Hijazi treaty and, with similar intransigence, had refused to ratify his signature to the Treaty of Versailles, with the result that his representative was refused a seat at the League of Nations. The British now regarded Husain as an albatross to their plans and claimed complete neutrality in the Hashimite-Saudi conflict which, under the circumstances, gave Abd al-Aziz an excellent advantage. On 5 September 1924 al-Taif, a summer resort used by Meccans, voluntarily surrendered to Ikhwan forces who then proceeded to slaughter all the inhabitants.[33] This created a panic and there was a massive exodus from Mecca to al-Madina. On 3 October Husain abdicated to his son Ali and two weeks later, on 16 October, Mecca fell, leaving King Ali in possession only of al-Madina, Jidda and Yanbu al-Bahr. King Husain meanwhile left for Aqaba where he used what remained of his resources in supplying men and war materials to Ali via the Red Sea.

Knowing that he would soon be answerable to all the Muslim world, Abd al-Aziz tried to curb the excesses of his Ikhwan,but was determined not to accept anything less than the complete evacuation of the Hashimites from al-Hijaz. He undertook to guarantee the safety of the 1925 pilgrimage and this, passing without incident, helped to reassure the world that Saudi intentions were, in fact, to keep the Holy Cities open to all sects of Islam.

At this juncture the interests of Abd al-Aziz and Britain coalesced through a most unusual set of diplomatic manoeuvres and military stratagems. Ever since the war Britain had tried to establish Transjordan as a viable state and secure its own tactical advantages there. The only access to the Red Sea was Aqaba and its surrounding district of Maan which both Britain and King Husain had repeatedly claimed for Transjordan and al-Hijaz respectively since the war. It is clear, however, that the British realised that al-Hijaz had a more valid claim to Aqaba and Maan, as was admitted by the Secretary of State for the Colonies in a letter to the High Commissioner for Palestine.

> as Ma'an is still nominally in the hands of the latter [King Ali] its fate may be settled in a manner contrary to the interests of Trans-Jordania . . . and position of British negotiator will be very difficult if Ibn Saud claims territory which we regard as falling within Trans-Jordan but which is actually in *de facto* Hedjaz administration.[34]

Although the British had every hope of securing the district for Transjordan, the issue was becoming increasingly difficult after Husain's arrival in Aqaba and his subsequent use of it as a military supply and training base. This left the entire area vulnerable to an Ikhwan attack.

> [The British] have always claimed and continue to claim, that Ma'an forms part of Trans-Jordan and of British Mandated Territory, but so long as it is in fact occupied by the Hedjaz and used as a training base for Hedjazi forces, it is obviously difficult for His Majesty's Government to show any good reason why Ibn Saud should not proceed to attack it should the opportunity arise.[35]

The Ikhwan, undoubtedly with the knowledge of Abd al-Aziz, did make several skirmishes around Aqaba and Maan. The British immediately made a complaint, whereupon Abd al-Aziz apologised and astutely asked where the boundary lay. The British responded that the boundary crossed the Hijaz Railway at Mudawwara. The Saudi leader withdrew his forces beyond that line, but then inquired why the British allowed the Hashimites, Abdullah and Husain, to use Aqaba to intrigue against him if it was British territory. He then expressed his desire to negotiate his boundaries with Iraq and Transjordan.[36] After years of procrastination on these two outstanding issues, Abd al-Aziz had two very sound reasons for wishing to make a permanent settlement. First, his predominant concern was no longer the boundary but the fact that his rival, Al Hashim, was supported by an even stronger potential rival—the British. By pressing the boundary issue, Abd al-Aziz forced the British to come to terms with the Hashimites. It is also possible that, by declaring his intentions to negotiate, he was assuring the British of his goodwill in order to discourage their interference with his plans in al-Hijaz. That he succeeded in this is evidenced by Britain's declaration of neutrality.

In July 1925 Britain unilaterally claimed jurisdiction over Aqaba and Maan until a final frontier delimitation could be made. The British also thanked Abd al-Aziz for withdrawing the Ikhwan from Aqaba and informed him that Husain was now exiled to Cyprus, Abdullah was in British Mandated Territory, and Ali had agreed to let Britain help him in any negotiations. In essence, the British had neutralised the Hashimites while simultaneously increasing their own chances of a united Transjordan and Iraq. It was not long before many Hijazis were defecting to Saudi positions so that, by late June, Ali was completely isolated and al-Madina cut off from any supplies. Before the final demise of al-Hijaz, however, Britain wished to negotiate the boundary issues while Abd al-Aziz was still amenable. This time Britain strongly 'invited' Iraq and Transjordan to entrust their interests to her own representation at the conference.

Sir Gilbert Clayton was chosen as Great Britain's representative and a list of instructions was sent to him which set out Britain's negotiating position: first, the Hashimite/Saudi rivalry had become an armed conflict with the former maintaining only a precarious hold while the northern district of al-Hijaz was not in either's possession and, second, Britain declared itself neutral. George Antonius, an assistant to Clayton during the forthcoming negotiations, prepared a memorandum filling in the historical and economic details of Wadi al-Sirhan. It was the customary grazing *dira* of the al-Ruwala and Bani Sakhr and, as yet, these tribes were untouched by the Wahhabi movement, in contrast to large sections of the Huwaitat and Bani Atiya in southern Transjordan who had been converted. Clayton's final instructions were that, if he was unable to come to an agreement and if the population was not settled, then he should arrange for it to be a neutral territory.

As expected, Abd al-Aziz wanted the boundary north of Jabal Unaiza so that his territory would be co-terminous with Syria. For political, economic and tribal reasons, he vehemently claimed Wadi al-Sirhan, maintaining that his family had historical ties there and that it was only his respect for Great Britain which had hitherto restrained him from occupying it.

> Wadi Sirhan was his property, and . . . he had made many concessions to Great Britain. He had Faisal on one side and 'Abdullah on the other, both new creations fencing him in on either side and both hostile towards him. When he thought of the injustices to himself he was surprised at the moderation of his demands. He would prefer to have his throat cut with a sword rather than have anyone infringe upon his rights in his own dominions.[37]

The negotiations began at Bahra in September 1925 and the results were formalised in the Hadda Agreement of 2 November, concerning Najd-Transjordan relations, and the Bahra Agreement of 1 November, concerning Najd-Iraq relations.[38] The defence corridor desired by the British War Office was left to connect Iraq with Transjordan, but Abd al-Aziz obtained all of Wadi al-Sirhan, including Kaf but excluding the four major tributary *wadis* (see Figure 6.1). Thus, the inhabitants of the *wadi*, including the al-Ruwala, fell under the control of the Al Saud. Abd al-Aziz was to refrain from fortifying Kaf and to prevent Ikhwan incursions into Transjordan while Britain undertook to restrain military activities around Qasr al-Azraq at the extreme northern end of the *wadi*.

Common to both the Bahra and Hadda Agreements were regulations regarding tribal raiding, migration and emigration. Raids were now considered acts of aggression for which tribal shaikhs were to be held accountable. Joint tribunals were to be set up between Najd and Iraq, and Najd and Transjordan, to investigate raids and ascribe guilt and compensation. The sovereign governments would have the right to disapprove of tribal migration

Figure 6.1: Najd-Transjordan Boundary Settlement 1925

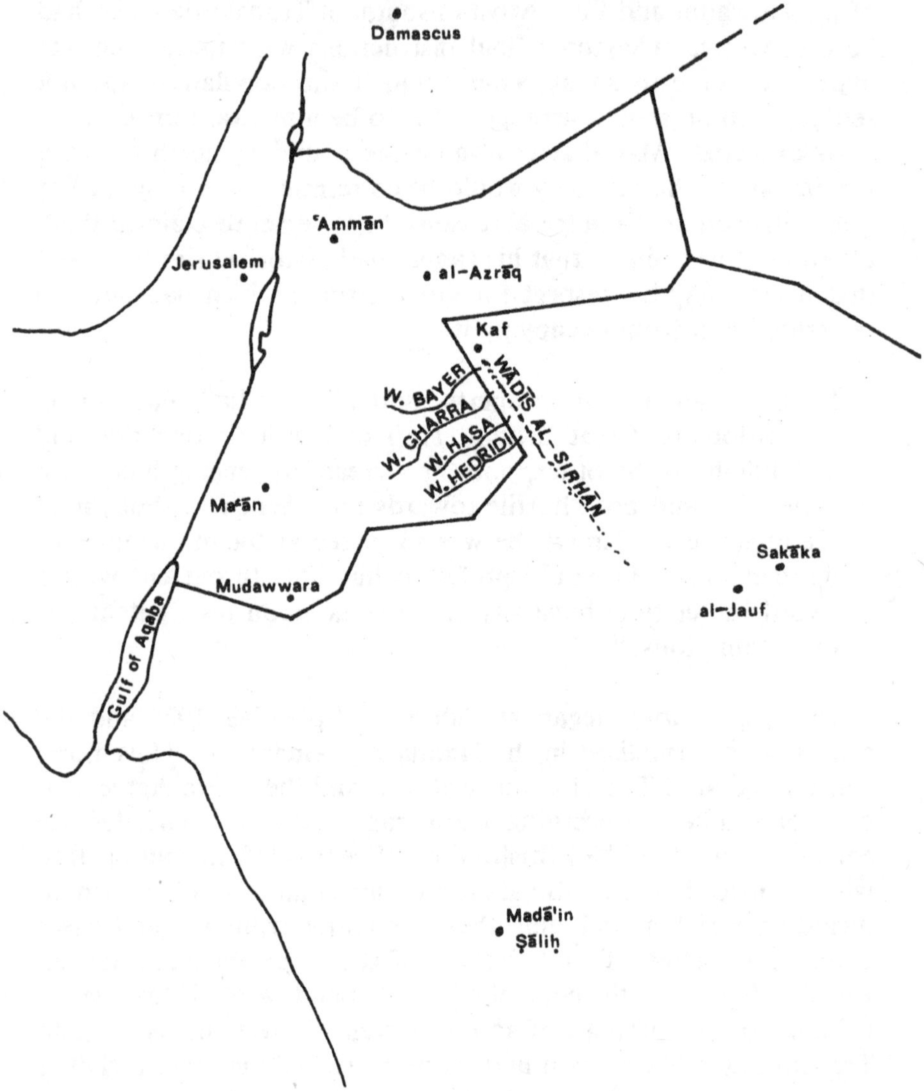

Source: IO L/P&S/10/1144. Note that the transliteration of the four tributary *wadis* is uncertain.

across national boundaries unless the migration was specifically for grazing. Governments would not have direct communication with tribal shaikhs in the territory of another government and no shaikhs would display flags or encourage tribal migrations. Military forces were forbidden to cross the frontier and tribes called up for military service were obliged to take their arms and flocks with them.

The Bahra Agreement dealt specifically with inter-tribal raiding, as the boundaries of Najd and Iraq had already been determined in the Treaty of al-Muhammara and the Uqair Protocols. This was a difficult problem and Abd al-Aziz, contrary to Arab customary law, demanded rights of extradition to which Iraq and Britain were unwilling to agree. Clayton specifically refused to extradite the Shammar from Iraq even though Abd al-Aziz insisted that they would be a constant threat to Najd unless under his direct control. Arrangements were made, however, to sanction any tribes which contravened the treaties and, as far as Britain was concerned, relations between these countries had now been regularised and legal machinery for settling claims had been arranged.

Although Clayton commented about the Saudi leader that 'the expansion of his dominion is bringing him up against problems and influences which are new and strange to him', Abd al-Aziz for his part had succeeded in these negotiations. He had obtained the whole of Wadi al-Sirhan, including Kaf, and had reached some agreement on other matters, particularly tribal raiding. He had also received, if not tacit approval, at least a benign neutrality by Britain towards his actions, especially at a point when public opinion on British military opposition might have hindered him in his attack on al-Hijaz. Al-Madina formally surrendered on 5 December 1925, Ali announced his withdrawal from al-Hijaz on 18 December, and Yanbu al-Bahr surrendered on 21 December. Abd al-Aziz entered Jidda four days later and announced that the war was over. On January 1926 he was proclaimed King of the Hijaz and Sultan of Najd and its Dependencies.

The Bahra and Hadda Agreements were followed by the Treaty of Jidda signed on 20 May 1927. This was simply a reaffirmation of continuing relations, covering general agreements about Indian pilgrimage traffic, suppression of the slave trade and, most importantly, the recognition of the independent and autonomous authority of the Al Saud.

It may generally be said that these territorial disputes and the subsequent negotiations between Central Arabia and her neighbouring countries laid a working framework for the nascent Middle East state system. In the case of Central Arabia these agreements were to help the Al Saud in their policy of social transformation and political centralisation, as will be seen in the following chapters. These new countries now had the legal machinery to prevent populations from crossing their frontiers and individual sovereigns had greater power to control and sanction recalcitrant tribes. These agreements did not, however, preclude further dispute. The Ikhwan were now becoming a powerful force in Central Arabian politics and trouble was to break out once again on the northern frontier.

Notes

1. Detailed accounts of this dispute are found in Aḥmad 'Abd al-Ghafūr Aṭṭār, *ṣaqr al-jazīra*, 7 vols (Maṭba'at al-Ḥurrīya, Beirut, 1972), pp.681-706 and 417-47; in Gary Troeller, *The Birth of Saudi Arabia: Britain and the Rise of the House of Saud* (Frank Cass, London, 1976), pp.127-58; and in various works by Philby.

2. 'Aṭṭār, *ṣaqr al-jazīra*, has given an Arab account of this period which relies heavily on correspondence between 'Abd al-'Azīz and the Hashimites. 'Aṭṭār attributes Khālid's conversion to Wahhabiism to a personal insult he had received from Amir 'Abdullāh. Khālid apparently had been struck by a shaikh of the 'Utaiba tribe from Najd and Amir 'Abdullāh, who was responsible for administering justice, had briefly imprisoned the 'Utaiba shaikh. Khālid, dissatisfied with the sanction, believed that this was the beginning of an attempt to undermine his authority in al-Khurma and Turaba.

3. The withdrawal of 'Abd al-'Azīz has often been cited as one of the major signs of his respectful obedience to the British government. There is, however, nothing to support this. It is just as likely that the Sa'udi leader found his treasury short of money as had occurred many times in the past or he may have used the dispute as a test not only for world reaction to a possible Sa'udi invasion of al-Ḥijāz but also for knowledge of his own military capabilities and the extent to which Britain would be prepared to support the Hashimites against him.

4. India Office Records, *Political and Secret Department Separate Files 1902-1931*, L/P&S/10 (henceforward abbreviated to IO L/P&S/10): IO L/P&S/10/807, particularly 'Foreign Office: Inter-Departmental Conference on Middle Eastern Affairs', 24 February 1919. See also IO L/P&S/10/389, particularly the telegram from the Political Resident in the Persian Gulf to the Foreign Secretary to the Government of India in the Foreign and Political Department, 7 September 1918, no. 7418.

5. H. R. P. Dickson, *Kuwait and Her Neighbours* (George Allen and Unwin, London, 1968), p.266. During drought years, these patterns of tribal movement could become exaggerated or entirely forsaken. Tribal *dīra*s could also change according to the varying fortunes of the tribes.

6. Ibid., p.267.

7. IO L/P&S/10/926, letter from 'Abd al-'Azīz to the British Government (date?) 1920. Ameen Rihani, *Ibn Saoud of Arabia: His People and His Land* (Constable, London, 1928), pp.59-61.

8. The fixed and arbitrary boundaries which were delimited for Kuwait can be described as follows: the end of the innermost semi-circle to the north was the juncture of the estuaries of Khaur Zubair and Khaur 'Abdullāh. The outer circle was prescribed from the south side of this juncture passing south of Ṣafwān and Jabal Sanām to the Bāṭin before turning south-west along the Bāṭin to wells at Ḥafar al-Bāṭin, then turning south-east to the wells at Sāfa, Qarā'a, Hāba and Wabra, and the village of Inta before joining the seacoast at Jabal Manīfa.

9. IO L/P&S/10/925, letter from Sir Arthur Hirtzel, Secretary of State, to Mr Churchill, 25 January 1921.

10. 'Abd al-'Azīz's desire to punish the al-'Ujmān was because of a number of incidents: their desertion from Sa'udi forces at the Battle of Jarrāb when Captain Shakespear, Political Agent Kuwait, was killed; their attempts to avoid taxation after the Sa'udi conquest of al-Aḥsā; and their assistance to the 'Arā'if, disenchanted members of the Al Sa'ūd who were challenging the authority of 'Abd al-'Azīz.

11. IO L/P&S/10/925, letter from High Commissioner of Iraq to Secretary of State, 14 December 1920.

12. Jarīya 'Ilya is, no doubt, the colloquial form of Qaryat 'Ilya.

13. When this became known, residents of Kuwait Town joined a *levée en masse* to complete a defence wall around the town in two months. Many aerial photographs still show evidence of the remains of this wall.

14. IO L/P&S/10/925, telegram from the High Commissioner of Iraq to the Secretary of State, 14 December 1920.

15. The Ikhwan reportedly lost over 13,000 men as a result of this battle (Dickson, *Kuwait and Her Neighbours*, p.255), perhaps a reflection of their belief that the death of a warrior in the cause of Allah brought many rewards in the after-life.

16. IO L/P&S/10/925, report from H. R. P. Dickson, Political Agent Bahrain, to Sir Percy Cox, High Commissioner of Iraq, 9 November 1920.

17. Ibid.

18. One of the tribes which defected was the 'Awāzim. It will be recalled that 'Abd al-'Azīz promised to free tribes from *khuwa* taxation and their so-called 'inferior status' if they gave the Al Sa'ud their allegiance.

19. Dickson, *Kuwait and Her Neighbours*, p.273.

20. Ibid.

21. Cox also delineated a Kuwait Neutral Zone not only because of tribal-related problems, but because there was the rumour of oil. The Kuwait Neutral Zone was to ensure that both governments shared the revenues (Edward Hoagland Brown, *The Saudi Arabia Kuwait Neutral Zone* (The Middle East Research and Publishing Center, Beirut, 1963)).

22. The second protocol generally concerned custom regulations and duties.

23. Dickson, *Kuwait and Her Neighbours*, pp.276-7.

24. Ibid., p.277.

25. Ibid.

26. Nūrī al-Sha'lān, paramount shaikh of the Ruwālā 'Anaza, undermined the control of the Al Rashīd in Jauf in 1909, regularly taxing the people in return for which Nūrī promised them his protection. For a brief period from 1918 to 1921, the Al Rashīd once again took control until their demise by the Al Sa'ūd when Nūrī repossessed Jauf.

27. An agreement prior to the conference stipulated that whoever a tribe had agreed to recognise as its sovereign would then be accepted by all parties.

28. IO L/P&S/10/1033, telegram from the Secretary of State for the Colonies to the Political Resident in the Persian Gulf, 8 November 1923.

29. *Oriente Moderno*, 4 (1924), pp.512-14.

30. See IO L/P&S/10/1034: Britain's personal anxiety about 'Abd al-'Azīz is evidenced by a report entitled 'A Proposal for an Air Visit to Ibn Saud at His Capital' which suggests that the establishment of an air base at Bahrain would bring him into striking distance (IO L/P&S/10/1034, J. M. Salmond, Air Marshal, Air Headquarters Iraq Command, 1 April 1924).

31. 'Abd al-'Azīz confided to Clayton that the decision to march on al-Ḥijāz was made after seeing the corrupt rule of Ḥusain interfere with the ability of Muslims to make the pilgrimage.

32. Sir Gilbert Falkingham Clayton, *An Arabian Diary* (edited by Robert O. Collins) (University of California Press, Berkeley, 1969), p.40.

33. 'Aṭṭār, *ṣaqr al-jazīra*, pp.707-14.

34. IO L/P&S/10/1144, letter from the Secretary of State for the Colonies to the High Commissioner for Palestine, 20 April 1925.

35. IO L/P&S/10/1144, letter from R. V. Vernon, Private Secretary to the Secretary of State, to N. Chamberlain, Secretary of State for Foreign Affairs, 21 May 1925.

36. IO L/P&S/10/1144, letter from Ibn Sa'ud to His Majesty's Government, 30 June 1925. See IO L/P&S/10/1144 for more information about these negotiations and also Clayton, *An Arabian Diary*.

37. Clayton, *An Arabian Diary*, pp.119-20.

38. The boundary of al-Ḥijāz and Transjordan was not discussed as 'Abd al-'Azīz did not obtain full possession of al-Ḥijāz until after the agreements were signed. Some of the articles provided for the free movement of pilgrims and merchants across the borders. In informal talks, 'Abd al-'Azīz interceded on behalf of Saiyid Aḥmad al-Sanūsī who wished to retire to Egypt or Libya.

7

The Northern Frontier 1926-1929: Britain and the Ikhwan Challenge Saudi Authority

'Nationalism' was unknown to the nomadic and settled inhabitants of Central Arabia in the early decades of the twentieth century. Traditionally, the concept of 'nation' *per se* was regarded as synonymous with the Islamic community or *umma*, which represented the most common point of identification among the people. As has been discussed, the unique doctrine of the Wahhabis led them to condemn many Muslims as 'unlawful' and, at their most extreme, to view anyone outside Najd as an inhabitant of *balad al-kuffar*, Country of the Infidels. In addition to their powerful association with the Wahhabi movement, the majority of the settled and nomadic peoples of Central Arabia identified themselves with a particular tribe or a system of tribal alliances as well as with a 'sphere of trade'. These so-called 'tribal frontiers' and 'trade frontiers' were constantly changing.

It was not until the post-World War I mandate period that Central Arabia was exposed to the phenomenon of 'nation-state', partially defined by its territorial exent within which the state had absolute and autonomous authority. Abd al-Aziz, aware that the physical limits of his own authority would be restricted by the mandates, refused to accept arbitrarily fixed boundaries. The ostensible reason for his refusal was that fixed boundaries were unsuitable for nomadic life, but there were other more personal reasons. If the allegiance of a tribe could be secured, then rights to the tribe's territory were also gained and, in this way, a ruler could continue to extend his authority as long as tribes could be induced to pledge such allegiance. The Al Saud, motivated by their Arab and Islamic heritage, wished to control all that their forefathers had had in the past and so, between 1917 and 1925, Abd al-Aziz procrastinated in all treaty negotiations while he encouraged Ikhwan raids and 'tribal conversions' on his frontiers.

> After Feisal's arrival in Iraq the treaty of El Muhammarah was forwarded to Us [Al Saud] and We refused it believing that the Iraq people had no frontiers behind Es Shutt [Shatt al-Arab], but that all the Arabs behind Es Shutt, Ez Zhafir [al-Zafir] and Eniza [Anaza] etcetera, have always been in submission to the Governor of Nejd. The people of Iraq used to pay 'El Khawa' [*khuwa*] to Nejd for crossing such frontiers both in the days of Our forefathers, of Al Er Rashid and in Our own days.[1]

By 1926, Abd al-Aziz had acquired effective control over large areas of the Arabian Peninsula, supplanting the Al Hashim in al-Hijaz and eroding their control in Transjordan and Iraq, as well as obtaining *de facto* control of Kuwait's 'hinterland'. It is evident that the only factor which prevented further Saudi expansion to the north was the military and diplomatic presence of Great Britain. Abd al-Aziz never concealed his hatred of the Hashimite rulers—Abdullah and Faisal—and felt that events would have taken a radically different course under the impetus of the Arabs themselves.

> Were We [Al Saud] not desirous not to impair the British Government's political procedure, We would have actually shewn them the standing of these two men [Abdullah and Faisal] among the Arabs. Let the British Government close their eyes a little and they will see how the face of the Arab countries will alter after a short time.[2]

This, however, was premature and by 1928 Abd al-Aziz was confronting the most serious threat to his rule that he had yet experienced. On the one hand, Britain had issued an ultimatum that Abd al-Aziz must stop the Ikhwan incursions into Iraq and Kuwait or be liable for the consequences, for 'history shows us that we shall either have a permanently settled frontier or will be driven to acquire a stable frontier ourselves'.[3] On the other hand, the Ikhwan themselves were becoming a powerful internal force. They could not understand the restraint Abd al-Aziz was now displaying towards the 'infidels' on his northern frontier and were expressing dissatisfaction among themselves with the new Saudi policy. Their strict interpretation of Islam did not allow them to compromise on any religious principle, however extreme it was, in order to obtain political guarantees or safeguards. The Al Saud, by contrast, were fully aware that their political survival was linked to the Wahhabi movement but, as in the past, they were also well aware of political practicalities.

During the years 1926 to 1929, Abd al-Aziz found himself sandwiched between two forces—Great Britain and the Ikhwan—which were hostile to each other and equally capable of challenging Saudi authority. He now accepted the finality of the boundary delimitation determined earlier, but had to make this decision acceptable to the Ikhwan. This chapter deals with the events of this period on the northern frontier, culminating in the Ikhwan rebellion against the Al Saud.

Iraq's 'Defensive Perimeter' and the Ikhwan Raid on Busaiya

The trouble that erupted on the Iraq-Najd frontier in 1927, ostensibly over the erection of an Iraqi 'police post' at Busaiya, was in reality a reflection of several deeper problems: Hashimite-Saudi rivalries, opposition between Arab Muslim forces and a foreign mandatory power, and internal dissensions within Najd which had been growing between the Ikhwan and Al Saud since 1926 or even possibly since 1924.

The Ikhwan raid on Busaiya on 5 November 1927, led by Faisal al-Duwish of the Mutair, was the first major outbreak of hostilities between Saudi and Hashimite forces since the capture of al-Hijaz in 1925. During the raid, Iraqi police and workmen were brutally massacred, their limbs sometimes being completely severed from their bodies. This gruesome detail is significant when it is remembered that the massacres committed by the Ikhwan during the conquest of al-Hijaz had ceased after the arrival of Abd al-Aziz who had punished those responsible for this atrocity. Busaiya was a departure from their normal raiding tactics and seems to have been intended as a warning not only to Iraqi authorities but also to their nominal leader, Abd al-Aziz. It is unlikely that this raid occurred with the express approval of Abd al-Aziz for it ran directly counter to the policy of appeasement which the Saudi leader had been trying to promote and to his assurances to the Muslim world that he would provide a secure and stable environment for the Holy Cities and the annual pilgrimage.

Although a contingent of 'police' had been at Busaiya since October 1925, construction on the fort had not begun until February 1927 and was still incomplete when the attack occurred. Britain and Iraq were outraged, claiming that the post was merely for police and not for military personnel. It had been built to keep out the Shammar tribesmen who had left Iraqi jurisdiction for Syria where they were carrying out raids in the direction of Kuwait in 1926. Britain argued that the post prevented raids into Najd itself.[4] This was, however, only one reason for the construction of Busaiya and other forts along the frontier. Another reason, mentioned previously, was Britain's concern for the safety of pipeline and railway routes which would, in their turn, affect the security of Haifa and Palestine, British basic trades and the dependence of the British Mediterranean fleet on oil.

> If some means cannot be devised of . . . controlling incursions of Nejd tribe of Mutair [Ikhwan] whose last raid beginning on February 20th . . ., as some twelve hundred strong, whole desert at least as far north as line from Rutbah to Damascus will become untenable and pipeline and railway must take northern route through Syrian territory.[5]

A third reason for the construction of the posts was contained in a report by the Air Headquarters of the Iraq Command.[6] It stated that 'a line of posts' was necessary for the protection of the major cities of Iraq. Failure to construct these posts would see 'the front line of defense withdrawn to the Euphrates Valley' and an Ikhwan presence could then be expected in the towns and villages of the Euphrates. Providing a 'defensive perimeter' along the Iraq-Najd desert frontier, inhabited only by badu, was less expensive than protecting the major cities like Basra and al-Najaf after hostile forces had already arrived at the gates of the city. The line of posts would preferably include Jarishan, Busaiya, Salman, Shabika, Lussuf, Muhaiwir and Rutba, although Busaiya, Salman, Shabika and Rutba were the most important (see Figure 7.1).

The fourth and final reason for the posts concerned the relationship between the government of Iraq and its tribes. Although Iraq collected a tax from the tribes of its southern desert, it was more concerned with protecting its urban centres of the north

Figure 7.1: Iraqi 'Police' Posts

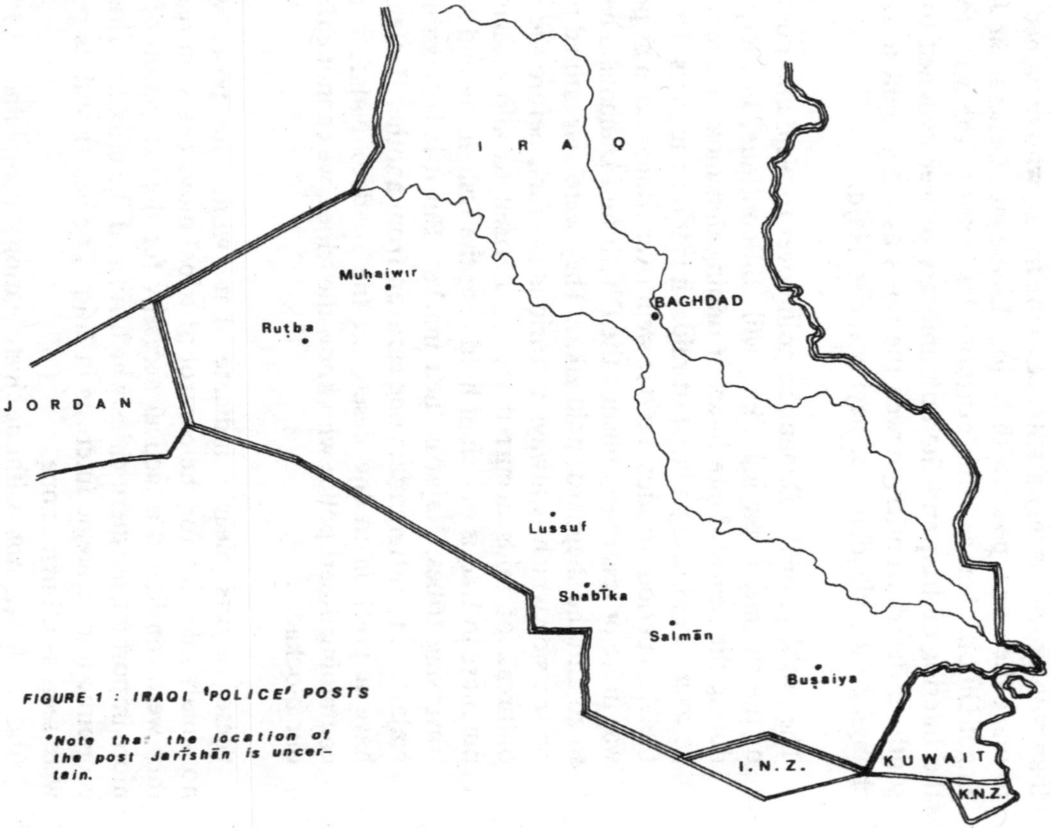

Note: The location of the post Jarishan is uncertain.

than with providing any assistance to the tribes, who remained free to make their own peace with Najd.[7] Lieutenant-General Sir John Bagot Glubb, then an Administrative Inspector to the Minister of the Interior of Iraq and the only military officer assigned to the southern desert frontier, viewed the posts as a deterrent to tribes changing their allegiance or paying tax to Najd.

> The problem of the Dahamsha going over to Nejd and possibly of the shepherds paying zikat, will still continue. In fact, it is during the peaceful interludes of raiding that most of the tribes go over . . . . during a burst of raids, it is too dangerous. During the 1924 period of raids, no one went over. But as soon as peace was more or less re-established the Dhafir and Dahamsha began to go and the shepherds paid zikat. They were determined to be on the side which is always victorious (so far), before the next outbreak of raids occurred . . . . Refusal to allow them to purchase in Iraq is our chief hold over the Dahamsha and other traversing tribes. Najaf is their market. But it is impossible in Najaf . . . to differentiate one caravan from another. Unless we have a position in the desert on the road to Najaf, a post containing desert police who know the tribes, we cannot enforce our blockade.[8]

These reports clearly indicate that, while the posts were nominally intended for the control of tribal movements, in reality they were considered a tactical necessity for the protection of the more important northern cities which formed the crux of Britain's economic and strategic interests in Iraq. The desert and its tribes were seen as a buffer zone.

Abd al-Aziz, not without justification, complained to the government of Iraq that it had contravened Article 3 of Protocol 1 of the Uqair Conference which read as follows: 'The two Governments mutually agree not to use the watering places and wells situated in the vicinity of the border for any military purpose, such as building forts on them and not to concentrate troops in their vicinity.'[9]

Britain was faced with a dilemma. What did 'in the vicinity of the border' actually mean? If Busaiya, 115 kilometres from the border, was considered a contravention of Article 3, then the proposed forts at Salman and Shabika, both 50 kilometres from the border, would certainly be objectionable. Rutba, approximately 110 kilometres from the border, would also be within the prohibited area. Moreover, when Abd al-Aziz had requested permission to build a fort at Lina, 50 kilometres from the border, he had been refused, and it was difficult to see how Iraq could be allowed to construct forts while the Saudis were forbidden similar rights.[10]

Abd al-Aziz Objects to the Iraqi Posts and *Dakhala*

Abd al-Aziz and Great Britain now opened what was to become a continuing dialogue on a number of subjects, all in some way related to the boundary issue. Two topics in particular were to remain major issues over the next few years.[11] First, the Iraqi posts were an embarrassment to the Saudi government and, if their construction continued, Abd al-Aziz would be forced to ask for legal arbitration on the dispute because of their contravention of Article 3 of the Uqair Protocols. Second, Iraq's refusal to extradite 'criminals' who crossed the border seeking refuge from Saudi authority made the position of Saudi officials difficult as they were unable to punish those guilty of raids. It also lowered the prestige of the Saudi government.

The English version of the Uqair Protocols stated that there were to be no fortifications built 'in the vicinity of the border'. This was in itself a vague phrase because it did not stipulate a precise distance from the border. The British took the view that 50 to 110 kilometres could not be construed as 'in the vicinity of the border'.[12]

Sir Percy Cox, British negotiator for the Uqair Protocols in 1922, was asked what light he could shed on the various interpretations of Article 3 and on Dickson's description of his, Cox's, dictatorial methods during the negotiations. Dealing first with Dickson's description, Cox said that his remarks were 'a little picturesque, but with this reservation his account may be accepted as relating, substantially, what passed'.[13] He went on to dismiss entirely the problems of interpreting Article 3. Sarcastically, he expressed his failure to understand that 'the phenomena of mud fortlets' could be seen 'as intolerable incitements' to those whom he facetiously described as 'the gentle bedouin'.

> the object of the agreement was to define a boundary line within which, on their side, the Iraq tribes could graze in security and

> across which Nejd tribes might not raid. I cannot admit any strained or unreasonable interpretation of the words 'in the vicinity of', or in the words used to represent them in the Arabic version [of the treaty], beyond that which any intelligent reader would assign to them. It is surely incompatible with common sense to suppose that any westerner could use or understand those words to embrace proceedings at a distance of 70 miles from the frontier . . . . The words signified to my mind, and I am sure to that of Ibn Saud at the time, 'within rifle shot of' or 'within sight of' tribes using the waterholes at a given point (the frontier being designed with reference to waterholes).[14]

It is particularly significant that Cox interpreted 'in the vicinity of' to mean 'within rifle shot of'—an interpretation which would be lost on most individuals. The Arabic version of 'in the vicinity of' reads *'alā aṭrāf al-ḥudūd* which was, perhaps, even more ambiguous than the English version in that it implied several possible meanings. Literally, it can be translated as 'right up to the extreme ends or limits of the boundaries'. According to one interpretation of this, one might imagine a line at the two opposite ends of which building would be allowed. This is not a logical interpretation, however, as boundaries do not stop in the middle of a void but continue either as boundaries with other countries or out to sea. A second explanation is based on the abstract conception of a boundary as being two lines or borders compressed into a single line fixed on the ground. To understand the phrase 'the extreme ends of the borders' one would imagine that one were going from the interior of a country straight up to the 'extreme end' of the border, that is, the extreme limit of the country. Thus, it is easy to understand the ground upon which Abd al-Aziz felt justified to contest the Protocol. The validity of the Saudi objection was explicitly recognised by the British officials, although not verbally admitted to Abd al-Aziz, in the reports between Clayton and London during the 1928 negotiations.

> Mr. Antonius [Sir Gilbert Clayton's assistant during the negotiations] now explained that as nearly exact a translation of the phrase in question as could be given, was 'on either side of' or 'at the ends or extremities of' the frontier; and that there were well established and well recognised Arabic words for 'vicinity'

or 'neighbourhood', which might have been used had the idea connoted by these terms been desired to be conveyed. Sir Gilbert Clayton indicated that the interpretation in question was to the advantage of Ibn Saud rather than of Iraq.[15]

When the British asked Abd al-Aziz upon what basis he had decided that posts 50 to 110 kilometres from the border were to be considered 'in the vicinity of', the latter replied with an even more explicit protest.

> I request . . . . His Britannic Majesty's Government to a point in the matter in question, viz., if Article 3 merely prohibited the building of *aṭrāf al-ḥudūd* there would have been cause for the British argument regarding the measurement of miles, metres, etc., but Article 3 did not prevent the building at *aṭrāf al-ḥudūd* but it prohibited the building at the waters and wells existing at *aṭrāf al-ḥudūd* . . . Busaiyah and the wells near it are all situated at *aṭrāf al-ḥudūd* and there is no argument about it.[16]

The full thrust of this statement can be understood in the light of an observation by Mr Antonius that the wells were not freely accessible to the badu if they were fortified.

> Mr. Antonius . . . is of the opinion that the real reason [for the objection of Abd al-Aziz] was that the tribes, from their experience of Turkish days, regard the presence of armed forces at watering places with the utmost apprehension, fearing that the forces will be used as a means of extortion. The consequence is that they avoid their vicinity . . . a considerable grazing area is lost to the tribes.[17]

Abd al-Aziz regarded the frontier posts as a threat to his own authority. Shaikh Hafiz Wahba, an adviser to Abd al-Aziz, told the British that there was a deliberate attempt in Najd to discredit the Saudi leader by associating him with the 'infidels'—that is, Britain.[18] The forts were rumoured to be a preliminary to the construction of a railway which would start in Baghdad and run to Hail and the Ikhwan viewed this as an attempt by the Saudi leader to dominate them. Thus, the continued construction of the forts could only hinder Abd al-Aziz in his attempts to re-establish control over the tribes, especially when the existence of the forts undermined his claims of good relations with the British and contravened the promise he had made to his Ikhwan that he would prevent such structures. Moreover, Abd al-Aziz insisted that the Hashimites were offering assistance to the Ikhwan insurgents and that on his Transjordan frontier there was now a post under construction at Mudawwara. Undoubtedly Abd al-Aziz spoke not only for his people but for himself when he wrote the following protest to the British: 'They [the inhabitants of Najd] have seen their self-respect dishonoured, their treaties broken and their neighbour waiting for his chance inside those buildings.'[19]

Although it was not confirmed, Abd al-Aziz was reported to have agreed in a December 1928 meeting with the Ikhwan that, if he could not achieve the demolition of the Iraqi posts by peaceful consultations, he would join them in attacking and destroying the posts.[20] He then raised two contentious matters with the British—the question of extradition and the use of the British Royal Air Force and armoured cars to protect the Iraq frontier. These were both emotive issues upon which the outcome of his struggle for political survival might depend.

Extradition had been a major controversy ever since the Conference of al-Muhammara. Iraq had claimed the right, by virtue of Arabian tribal custom, not to return criminals who sought refuge from Najd authorities in their territory. This custom, *dakhala*, was a point of honour among badu tribes. It is of interest that *dakhala* was one of the Arab customs which Abd al-Aziz was desirous of dispensing with entirely and the reason was understandable. As far back as the early 1900s he had complained that lack of Turkish authority in frontier areas encouraged raiding because the raiders realised that they could merely enter the territory of other amirates and shaikhdoms and claim protection. Furthermore, political refugees could use their new base for intrigue, as Abd al-Aziz himself had done when he used Kuwait as a base for his capture of al-Riyad in 1901/2. Now that the rebel Ikhwan were raiding across the border into Iraq, King Faisal claimed that his honour was at stake if he did not grant protection to those among the raiders who requested *dakhala*. Britain supported Faisal. The pressure was thus on Najd to stop the raids, although the Saudi leader maintained that he could hardly regain control of those guilty of raids if they were assured of asylum in Iraq. What, he asked, was the point of punishing Duwish and other raiders if they could then turn to Iraq and continue their activities from a safe haven?

> When the Iraq Government makes such an understanding [to extradite raiders] you will then see how we punish the Duwish and all those who took part with him in these actions of which we disapprove, it will be a punishment that, by the grace of God, will prevent them for ever from taking action on the frontier.[21]

The British justification that they were helping to honour an old Arab custom was merely an excuse, particularly as they had used Royal Air Force planes to cross the Iraq-Najd border and enter Saudi territory in order to defend their own rights.[22] Abd al-Aziz was angered and confused by the British bombing of tribes who were supposed to be guilty of raiding and he repeatedly questioned the validity of an action that killed innocent people only and had no effect on the Ikhwan at all. Furthermore, he resented what he saw as British double standards: he was not allowed to punish raiders who escaped to Iraq but Britain felt justified in crossing the border to bomb his subjects, further discrediting his leadership in the eyes of the people of Central Arabia.

> it was never explained in the past that when a raiding party goes out to another country the Government had no authority over its people and subjects. The action . . . that the British Government intend to send their aeroplanes into the interior of our country for the punishment of our subjects, this . . . is a new principle which no Government law will accept.[23]

Ikhwan Raids Destabilise Iraq-Najd-Kuwait Relations

British foreign policy makers in London began to realise that the frontier problem was less important than the general political situation which had crystallised by the end of February 1928 and which was potentially more disruptive to the stability of the region.[24] Intelligence sources were reporting that Abd al-Aziz was increasingly unpopular and 'had temporarily ceased to exist as a political factor'. His brother and nephew were suspected in a plot to assassinate one of his sons and Ibn Jiluwi, the Governor of al-Ahsa. The Ikhwan leaders—Faisal al-Duwish of the Mutair, Sultan

b. Humaid of the Utaiba and Ibn Hithlain of al-Ujman—had sworn an oath to support each other in 1926. The allegiance of the Harb was as yet unclear. Abd al-Aziz was therefore forced to be more conciliatory and the rumour spread that he had had to supply arms and ammunition to the Ikhwan for a possible *jihad* towards the north.[25] If the Saudi leader were forced to join with the Ikhwan, then his combined forces might be as many as 30,000-50,000 men.[26]

The British and Iraqis were now concerned that the ferocity of Ikhwan attacks would lead to the defection of many Iraqi tribes. Duwish had crossed the border again on 9 December, killing over 59 Iraqi shepherds in the Neutral Zone and firing at British Royal Air Force planes overhead. The Ikhwan had also driven away 7,500 animals as *ghanima*. Tribes were beginning to wear Ikhwan *iqal* and *imama* and pay dues to the tax collectors of Duwish.[27] Segments of the Anaza tribe threatened Iraq that, if Ikhwan raids could not be controlled, they would join the Ikhwan for their own protection. In addition to sustaining Ikhwan attacks, populations on the frontier suffered indirect losses because of changing environmental conditions and government restrictions on tribal movements. The following report by Glubb illustrates this dependence of the badu on their environment and, therefore, a weakness in their defence.

> If the Iraq tribes are forced to remain concentrated near the sandbelt throughout the grazing season, they suffer enormous losses in sheep. The injury inflicted by the Akhwan during the past few years in sheep looted, is probably not so great as that suffered through the tribes being concentrated in areas where grazing was insufficient . . . . On this subject it is impossible to lay down definite rules. Should rainfall be very heavy in the area north of the defended line, the tribes may not suffer at all. Rainfall in the Jazirah and in the Wadian area also affects the issue. If the former be good, many tribes spend the grazing season in the Jazirah. If bad, they all cross to the Shamiyah. If the rainfall in the Wadian be good, the Shibi, Ghazalat and Bani Salamah move there, travelling north even to the Wadi Hauran. If it be poor, they remain crowded into the Darb Zubaidah area. In some years, the best rain falls in the frontier areas.[28]

Constant raiding by the Ikhwan created conditions which

fostered the *dabka* or 'false alarm' whereby leaders attempted to suborn other tribes by instigating rumours of imminent attack which kept tribes and their flocks in a constant state of alert. Every delay or order to take up arms meant a new loss in camels and sheep as they were forced to collect in a restricted area.[29]

The Ikhwan posed a danger not only to nomadic groups, but also to urban areas where fields and animals, usually lying outside the defence walls of the cities, were vulnerable targets. A settled area could be forced into submission simply by the threat that the date palms or crops would be destroyed. Kuwait Town itself was particularly vulnerable during the pearling season from May to September when many of its residents camped along the coast, leaving the city and themselves defenceless. Dickson, Political Agent in Kuwait, described this potential danger if used against Abd al-Aziz by the Ikhwan.

> It was perfectly true that Bin Saud had possession of all the towns in Hassa, Nejd and Qassim [al-Qasim] . . . but as far as Qassim . . . this would not help him much as the inhabitants would be compelled to come to terms with the rebels who had it in their power to ruin all agriculture, gardens, etc. lying outside the town areas. As everywhere irrigation was by 'lift' from wells and as camels were the means used, these only had to be driven off by the Akhwan and all irrigation would come to a standstill. Al Duwish was perfectly aware of this fact, and once at Artawiyeh he intended to force Qassim to declare for him by means of this form of pressure.[30]

The British were now openly afraid of an Ikhwan rebellion. They had no desire to see a substitution in the leadership in Najd, particularly if that change exposed their mandates to attack and themselves to further military expenditures. The problems of defending a desert frontier 885 kilometres in length were difficult, if not impossible. The Royal Air Force was increasingly being used as a deterrent against raiding tribes, but its use was controversial because its aerial bombing could not distinguish women and children from raiders or, for that matter, friendly from hostile tribes. Kuwait, which Britain hoped would be a 'buffer state', presented similar problems of defence and initially the British decided that they could only accept responsibility for the protection of Kuwait Town itself.[31] Moreover, if Abd al-Aziz failed to gain control of the Ikhwan, it was useless to expect that a British blockade of al-Ahsa would prevent the Ikhwan from obtaining supplies: 'Smuggling is difficult to control because when the badu need something they send in the word that they need rice or whatever and every tent around Kuwait supplies one bag or so.'[32]

Britain concluded that it had to move cautiously. It had no wish to force Abd al-Aziz into making a sudden, unprepared move which would permanently antagonise the Najdis towards the Al Saud or would cause Abd al-Aziz openly to oppose the government of Britain. Moreover, it was not apparent that King Faisal of Iraq was actively instigating dissent among the refugee tribes in Iraq and offering support to the disenchanted Ikhwan. The British had no desire to become entangled in such a conflict.

Hashimite Intrigue in Najd

Abd al-Aziz had been warning Britain that the Ikhwan rebellion was a result of Hashimite instigation among his tribes and complicity with the rebels themselves. The situation could not be ameliorated and British interests in Iraq safeguarded until three matters were settled.

> *Firstly*. The Ashraf and their intrigues—both the Ashraf ruling in Iraq and Transjordania and those residing there. They are the cause of the disputes between Najd and Iraq and Najd and Transjordania. Before they came there no such difference or disputes existed. They should either leave these neighbouring countries or have their hands bound leaving them no power or authority over matters outstanding between us and Iraq and Transjordania, or over the frontiers of these two countries.
>
> *Secondly*. A 'liquidation' of former treaties should be effected so as to obviate misinterpretation and alteration, the *qaṣrs* [forts] and 'recent innovations' being removed. With this accomplished the British Government will find us anxious to ward off any occurrence against Iraq.
>
> *Thirdly*. British Officials in Iraq and Transjordania should be made the subject of an enquiry . . . and the removal effected of those . . . who have been the cause of . . . trouble.[33]

As Abd al-Aziz has so often been criticised for his territorial expansionism, it is important to examine his complaints regarding the Hashimites and their role during the Ikhwan rebellion. In a private interview with Glubb, I asked whether he had any direct knowledge of King Faisal's aid to the rebels. His reply was that, although he had no knowledge of any direct aid, Faisal's acceptance of *dakhala* by the Ikhwan rebels and the latter's subsequent use of Iraq territory for incursions into Najd constituted a major political error on the part of the British who made no move to prevent this action. Moreover, the grant of *dakhala* by King Faisal was motivated not so much by respect for the old Arab tradition as by dislike of his Saudi neighbour to the south. In this sense, Glubb regarded Faisal's action as a deliberate attempt to inflame the dissent in Najd.

King Faisal had nothing to lose by supporting the rebels and could, at the very least, feel some satisfaction that the Saudi leader who had ousted his family from al-Hijaz was now fighting for his own political survival. Faisal expressed to Hubert Young, Acting High Commissioner for Iraq, his belief that the rebels would eventually succeed in toppling Saudi authority. Moreover, Faisal told him that the British were mistaken in their support of Abd al-Aziz's 'tottering throne' because 'the continued role of King Ibn Saud over Central Arabia based as it is on constant military aggression is contrary to the interest of Iraq and Transjordan and so to the interests of His Britannic Majesty's Government'.[34] In a secret communiqué to Lord Passfield, Secretary of State for the Colonies, Young made some startling revelations about King Faisal's involvement with the Ikhwan rebels.

> In these circumstances it is impossible to expect that a man of King Faisal's character could refrain from taking more than an academic interest in the fortunes of the rebel Akhwan. There is no doubt in my mind that he has been sending agents to the rebels with messages of encouragement and in some cases with material assistance in the form of cash—though such assistance is ostensibly provided, no doubt, by the refugees from the rebel tribes now in Iraq. I have no doubt moreover that one of the reasons for the visit of the Amir Abdullah to Baghdad was the desire of the two brothers to discuss how the fall of King Ibn Sa'ud might be hastened and how it might be subsequently used to the best advantage.[35]

Young also noted that the Iraq Shammar, particularly the Shammar Abda refugees from Najd, were moving south.[36] He confirmed that they might possibly be hoping to recover their ancestral home, Hail, for the Al Rashid and that the Iraq government was taking steps to prevent potential hostilities.

> it is a fact that the Iraq Shammar are moving southward from the northern Jazirah into the Hillah and Diwaniyah Liwas. This southward move of the Shammar is however not unusual when grazing is scarce in the northern Jazirah. Similar migrations took place in 1923, 1925, and 1928 . . . . in view of possible disturbances on the Najd frontier . . . measures have been taken to keep these southward migrations of the tribe under close control. No section, for example, is permitted to cross the Euphrates into the Shamiyah.[37]

Young doubted whether the political situation would remain stable if the Ikhwan had any further successes; he believed that Duwish, King Faisal and the Shaikh of the Shammar Abda had already made a provisional agreement in case of such a success.

> if the rebels are successful and the armies of King Ibn Sa'ud are routed, as King Faisal expects, it is certain that the Shammar Abda will throw in their lot with the rebels and return to Najd to win what share they can of the spoils, nor do I consider that it will be possible to prevent them. How far a definite agreement has been reached between Shaikh Aqab Ibn Ajil of the Shammar Abda and Faisal al-Dawish, under the auspices of King Faisal, for Hail to be handed over to the Shammar in the event of a rebel victory I cannot say. But knowing that such an eventuality would precisely coincide with King Faisal's desires for the future, I should not be surprised if an agreement of this nature did exist.[38]

The evidence is strong that the meetings referred to above did occur. Duwish, like King Faisal and the displaced Shammar, had little to lose by exchanging mutual promises in the eventuality of a Saudi defeat. Dickson reported that he had heard through Shaikh Ahmad Al Sabah of Kuwait that Duwish was 'making efforts through them (the Hashimites) to get Shammar and Anaza to come in as allies by offering them Hail and Jauf respectively'.

> Remember al-Duwish is a great politician, there is no question of *Din* [religion] behind this rebellion; what Duwish is playing for is the downfall of the house of Saud and the rise of himself al-Duwish in Bin Saud's place, with success his horizon has become widened and now he hopes to become master of Nejd, and in the process does not care if the Hijaz returns to the Shereefian family or Hail to Bin Raschid.[39]

Abd al-Aziz sent the British a letter in which he listed a series of meetings he knew had taken place between the rebels and intermediaries of King Faisal in Iraq and concluded that it was obvious some agreement or aid was being offered. For example, he reported that the Iraqi Ubaid b. Faisal b. Humaid had left Baghdad on 12 June 1929 to meet the Ikhwan insurgents in Kuwait before returning to Iraq with a letter from the Ikhwan. He returned one month later with money from King Faisal and prepared to journey to Dahaina, an Ikhwan settlement of the Utaiba. On 27 June, the Iraqis Ali Abu Shuwairibat and Muhammad al-Khudari met King Faisal and then travelled to Kuwait where they met the Ikhwan leaders—Duwish, Ibn Mashhur and Ibn Hithlain. Ali Abu Shuwairibat then returned to Baghdad on 21 July with more correspondence from the rebels, while al-Khudari remained with Duwish.[40] Abd al-Aziz also listed Abdullah b. Musfir, Hamud b. Khammash, Burhan al-Jabali, Mutrik b. Hajna, Shuaifan Abu Shajara, the sons of Ali Abu Shuwairibat, Ali b. Abdullah, Rajih b. Shahin and Shukhair b. Tuwala as intermediaries of King Faisal.[41] Furthermore, he added that both Shaikh Sabah and King Faisal were sending money, food, arms and ammunition, camels and horses to Ibn Mashhur and the al-Ujman. Shaikh Sabah himself had given one thousand Riyals in mid-June to Duwish's son. The Ikhwan insurgents could be freely observed in Kuwait Town itself. In a secret report Dickson also described conversations he had had with Shaikh Ahmad which substantially confirmed the report of Hashimite collusion with the Ikhwan.

> Shaikh Ahmad told me this morning that Ali al-Shuwairabat had taken al-Duwish's signet ring to Hillal al-Mutairi, at the same time resident on his estates in the Shatt al-Arab, and that the latter had forwarded same to Baghdad with suitable covering letter by hand of Ali al-Shuwairabat . . . . Ahmad also reported this morning that a Shaikh Trad ibn Sattam al-Shaalan of Anaza

> (Syria) had arrived in Kuwait yesterday and had called on him. He has not divulged the reason of his visit yet, but it was obvious he came with a message for al-Duwish.[42]

Ahmad felt that Abd al-Aziz had little time to act against the rebels before new configurations of enemy forces were formed against him. He then related the most amazing piece of intelligence—an admission by King Faisal of communications with Duwish.

> Shaikh Ahmad replied that he had had it from Ali al-Shuwairabat when he passed through a few days ago, that King Faisal had secretly sent for all the Shammar refugee Shaikhs to Baghdad . . . including Ajil Al Yawe (Shammar Jarba) and Agab ibn Ajil (Shammar Abda), and had called them cowards for not rising against Bin Saud and making themselves masters of Hail, that the time was now ripe for action and if they did not move they deserved to be slaves for all time. That when the Shammar shaikhs excused themselves pleading their fear of al-Duwish, he the King had said, 'Have no fear, I have arranged things with al-Duwish (*'lat khafun Duwish andhi'*)'.[43]

The situation was now reaching alarming proportions. Both Abd al-Aziz and Britain were aware that, if matters continued, the Ikhwan would succeed in what was now open rebellion against the Al Saud.

The Al Saud Rule up to the Wall of Kuwait Town

The conflicts on the Iraq-Najd-Kuwait frontier culminated in 1929. In Kuwait, particularly, the tension between modern political structures and traditional structures of authority had developed to such an extreme that Kuwait Town was left without any tribes to defend itself. The events that led to this situation illustrate many of the problems between the Al Saud and the mandated territories generally and they provide a framework for understanding the succeeding events of the Ikhwan rebellion, which will be discussed in the final chapter.

The present discussion may be prefaced by a statement made by

Glubb during March 1929 regarding the question of tribal allegiance in the Iraq-Najd dispute.

> In any case, a man's nationality is settled by law or treaty, and Ibn Sa'ud's signature is attached to the Muhammerah Treaty stating that the Amarat (which includes Jazza and the Dahamshah) are Iraqis. If I like suddenly to proclaim that I am a Dutchman, my action does not make the least difference to my nationality, which is settled by law.[44]

Glubb, then a young officer in the southern desert of Iraq, fulfilled almost single-handedly the miraculous and difficult job of protecting the southern Iraqi frontier and many small defenceless tribal groups against Ikhwan raids. His statement, however, reflects a misunderstanding of political realities, although it was not an opinion he alone held. Most of the British officials in London and Baghdad and even Iraqis from the urban centres of the north shared this view. The political reality, however, was that, irrespective of the treaties and conferences of the previous ten years, tribal organisation and tribal allegiances continued to dominate politics. The badu in the frontier region were certainly aware of the existence of a boundary, but they remained totally unconcerned with an imaginary line which was not even visible on the ground. To them a man's nationality was determined by his tribe and his religious heritage and not by a law validated by the signature of Abd al-Aziz. It will be recalled that many of these tribes did not even begin to accept the suzerainty of the Al Saud until 1912 and some remained outside their control until 1925 and later.

On 3 August 1929 Shaikh Ahmad al-Jabir Al Sabah, the ruler of Kuwait, informed Colonel Dickson of three serious problems that were threatening the stability of his rule. First, there were continued raids by the Ikhwan and Abd al-Aziz's regular forces (*sariya*) into his territory and, as yet, the government of Britain had not been able to obtain restitution of property taken during these raids. Second, the economic blockade of Kuwait begun in 1921 by tribes in allegiance to the Al Saud had seen Kuwait revenues diminish by 70 per cent of their former total. Finally, and most important, Kuwait was defenceless because the Treaty of Uqair had signed away his territory and caused his tribes to change their allegiance to the Al Saud.

> we have not sufficient force or strength to defend ourselves from these constant attacks, seeing that our tribes and defenders were taken away from us, when Sir Percy Cox reduced the territories and boundaries of Kuwait, how could they remain with us seeing that they no longer had sufficient room to graze their camels and flocks, whilst the constant fear of Bin Saud's attacks hastened their going over to the other side.[45]

As discussed previously, the Shaikh of Kuwait had told the British, prior to the Uqair Conference of 1922, that there was no need to have a boundary between his territory and Najd, for the question of control over tribes, each of which had their own tribal *dira* and rights to watering places, was already recognised by the Arab parties concerned. During the rule of Shaikh Mubarak, Ahmad's grandfather, the Mutair Ilwa,[46] al-Ujman and Awazim had all declared their allegiance to Mubarak and ever since had served as the army of Kuwait. Cox, however, had arbitrarily signed away to the Al Saud much of the territory claimed by Kuwait during the Uqair Conference because, as the Political Resident in the Persian Gulf stated, 'at 'Uqair existing facts were recognized'[47]—that is, Abd al-Aziz was potentially more troublesome to Great Britain than was the Shaikh of Kuwait.

During the rule of Salim, Ahmad's uncle who ruled from 1917 to 1921, numerous tribes had already lost confidence in the leadership of the Al Sabah. When the results of the Uqair Conference were made known, many tribes 'defected' to the Al Saud who now formally controlled many of their tribal *dira*s. Those who did not immediately change their allegiance did so after continued Ikhwan raids on their tribal groups and after the economic blockade begun in 1921 by Abd al-Aziz. One of the most serious results of these events has frequently been discussed in the previous chapters: whenever a tribe declared its oath of allegiance, the ruler could then claim rights to the tribe's territory. This was precisely what happened in Kuwait and it explains why Shaikh Ahmad claimed that he was defenceless. Not only had Kuwait lost its tribes, but it had lost *de facto* control over its territory, as the Political Resident in the Persian Gulf noted: 'It is an interesting fact that Safwan, Jahara, and Subaihiya, which are situated within the present forty-mile radius boundary of Kuwait, are still considered to belong to the Mutair Alwa [Mutair Ilwa].'[48]

Because the Mutair Ilwa had since declared their allegiance to the Al Saud, these wells and the tribal *diras* were considered by all the tribal groups to constitute Saudi territory (see Figure 7.2). It was for precisely this reason that Abd al-Aziz disliked fixed boundaries.

> This has always been his claim and it was made unmistakenly clear when Bin Saud's men commanded by Abdulla bin Adwah, under the supreme command of Bin Jilawi [Ibn Jiluwi], obtained the surrender of two Najd merchants who had been guilty of bringing three camels across the border into Kuwait and had taken refuge in Kuwait town. A negro slave of Bin Jilawi promptly cut the throats of these unfortunates at the gate of Kuwait exclaiming in a loud tone: 'Thus shall my master teach you, oh people of Kuwait, that his boundary extends up to your very walls'.[49]

Shaikh Ahmad further informed the British that he had no faith in the ability of his townspeople to defend Kuwait territory against the fanatical Ikhwan and requested armoured cars to protect the frontier. He also asked the British to intervene with Abd al-Aziz and have the three tribes returned to him, particularly the al-Ujman who were known for their bravery rather than the Awazim who were not a noble tribe and were not allowed to inter-marry with the other badu tribes. It will be recalled that Abd al-Aziz had freed the Awazim from their inferior status and payment of *khuwa* to their former overlords, the al-Ujman, thus providing them with every reason for remaining under Saudi authority.

The importance of this old allegiance of the Awazim and al-Ujman and tribal organisation generally will reappear during the Ikhwan rebellion, but for the present it is enough to show that the conflict that was accelerating on the Iraq-Najd-Kuwait frontier in 1929 was partially a result of the imposition of modern political structures on traditional authority patterns. It was also the result of forces inside Saudi Arabia which had been initiated and given political-religious credence by the Al Saud—the Ikhwan. Although Abd al-Aziz had come to recognise the validity of fixed boundaries, he was no longer in control of the Ikhwan who were openly disregarding the borders and, hence, challenging the authority of the Al Saud themselves.

Figure 7.2: Overlap of Tribal Territories and State Boundaries

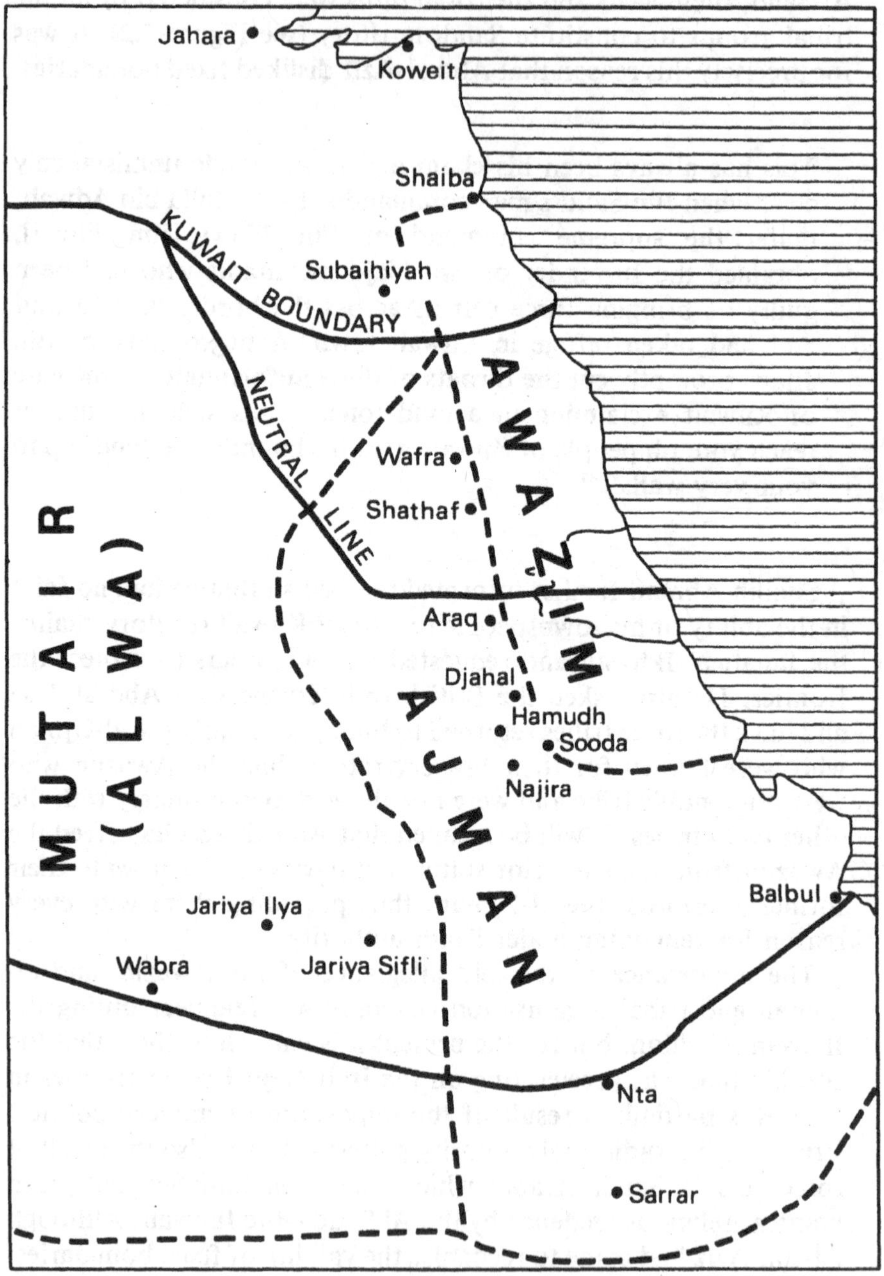

Source: From L/P&S/10/1245, drawn by Lieutenant-Colonel H. R. P. Dickson, Political Agent, Kuwait.

Notes

1. India Office Records, *Political and Secret Department Separate Files 1902-1931*, L/P&S/10 (henceforward abbreviated to IO L/P&S/10): IO L/P&S/10/1235, letter from 'Abd al-'Azīz to the British Agent, Jidda, 7 February 1928.

2. Ibid.

3. IO L/P&S/10/1234, telegram from the Political Resident in the Persian Gulf to the Secretary of State for the Colonies, 19 February 1928.

4. IO L/P&S/10/1235, letter from Lieutenant J. B. Glubb, Administrative Inspector, Dīwāniya, to the Minister of the Interior of Iraq, 23 March 1928.

5. IO L/P&S/10/1234, telegram from the High Commissioner of Iraq to the Secretary of State for the Colonies, 22 February 1928.

6. IO L/P&S/10/1236, report, Air Headquarters Iraq Command, Baghdad, 2 June 1928, ref. S10318.

7. Ibid. After the Bahra Agreement many Iraqi tribes switched their allegiance to 'Abd al-'Azīz for a variety of reasons, such as subsidies by the Al Sa'ūd and Ikhwan raids. Among the tribes to 'defect' were most of the Ẓafīr, two-thirds of the Shammar refugees, a large section of the Salqa division of 'Amarāt 'Anaza under Murdī al-Rifidī, and a section of the Dahāmisha 'Anaza under Muḥd b. Hamdān b. Mijlād. The Dahāmisha and the Salqa 'Amarāt were given Ikhwan villages and cultivation at Shaiba and Bilazīya respectively (IO L/P&S/10/1237).

8. IO L/P&S/10/1235, 'Report on the Advisability of a Post at Shabicha', from Lieutenant J. B. Glubb, Administrative Inspector, Southern Desert, Iraq, to the Adviser to the Minister of the Interior, Iraq, 23 March 1928.

9. See C. U. Aitchison, *A Collection of Treaties, Engagements and Sanads Relating to India and Neighbouring Countries* (vol. XI) (Kraus Reprint, Nendeln/Liechtenstein, 1973), pp.208-13, for the text of the 'Uqair Protocols.

10. IO L/P&S/10/1235, letter from F. H. W. Stonehewer-Bird, British Agent, Jidda, to the Secretary of State for Foreign Affairs, 10 February 1928.

11. IO L/P&S/10/1234, 'Note on Conversation of High Commissioner for Iraq with Shaikh Ḥāfiẓ Wahba on 7 January 1928 in the Presence of Captain Holt', by Sir Henry Dobbs, High Commissioner to Iraq, 8 January 1928. Aḥmad 'Abd al-Ghafūr 'Aṭṭār, *ṣaqr al-jazīra*, 7 vols (Maṭba'at al-Ḥurrīya, Beirut, 1972), pp.660-3.

12. IO L/P&S/10/1234, telegram from the Secretary of State for the Colonies to the High Commissioner to Iraq, 30 December 1927.

13. See H. R. P. Dickson's *Kuwait and Her Neighbours* (George Allen and Unwin, London, 1968) for the revealing account of how Cox, despite 'Abd al-'Azīz's protestations and humble entreaties, arbitrarily determined a boundary. Cox's task was simplified by the silence of Major J. C. More who was supposedly representing the interests of Kuwait. The role of Cox had not been one of a mediator; he had dictated the circumstances that were now laid out for the actual participants to accept without further negotiation. Even allowing for Dickson's 'picturesque language', Cox's admission is an amazing one, as dictating a settlement can hardly create a peace as effective as one that has been mutually agreed. This may also explain one reason for 'Abd al-'Azīz's lack of respect for the boundary settlement and the Shaikh of Kuwait's assistance to the Ikhwan rebels during the late 1920s.

14. IO L/P&S/10/1237, letter from Sir Percy Cox, former High Commissioner to Iraq, to J. E. Shuckburgh, Assistant Under-Secretary of State to the Colonial Office, 25 July 1928.

15. If they had wished a literal translation of 'in the vicinity of', there are several

phrases current in Arabic which might have been used, such as *fī jiwār al-ḥudūd* or *bi al-qurb min al-ḥudūd*. IO L/P&S/10/1236, memorandum from J. G. Laithwaite, Private Secretary to the Secretary of State, to Sir Arthur Hirtzel, Secretary of State for the Colonies, 22 June 1928.

16. IO L/P&S/10/1235, letter from 'Abd al-'Azīz to the British Government, dated 20 Rajab 1346 (13 January 1928).

17. IO L/P&S/10/1241, 'Report on the Raiding Situation on the Transjordan-Nejd Frontier', by Air Vice Marshal Dowding, Enclosure to Secret Dispatch of 25 January 1930.

18. IO L/P&S/10/1234, 'Note on Conversation of High Commissioner for Iraq with Shaikh Ḥāfiẓ Wahba on 7 January 1928 in the Presence of Captain Holt', by Sir Henry Dobbs, High Commissioner to Iraq, 8 January 1928.

19. IO L/P&S/10/1239, letter from 'Abd al-'Azīz to the Political Agent Bahrain, dated 12 Jamad al-Thani 1346 (7 December 1927).

20. IO L/P&S/10/1240, letter from the Political Agent Kuwait, to the Political Resident in the Persian Gulf, 14 December 1928, no. 507.

21. IO L/P&S/10/1235, letter from 'Abd al-'Azīz to the Political Agent Bahrain, dated 24 Rajab 1346 (17 January 1928).

22. IO L/P&S/10/1239, letter from 'Abd al-'Azīz to the High Commissioner of Iraq, dated 10 Jamad al-Awwal 1346 (6 November 1927), Enclosure IX to Serial no. 67, no. 3/1003. 'Aṭṭār, *ṣaqr al-jazīra*, pp.660-3.

23. IO L/P&S/10/1239, letter from 'Abd al-'Azīz to the Political Agent Bahrain, dated 28 Rajab 1346 (21 January 1928).

24. In a letter from the Secretary of State for the Colonies to the Viceroy on 24 February 1928 it was advised that the post would seem to infringe Article 3 of the 'Uqair Protocols and that Iraq should be dissuaded from continuing with its construction (IO L/P&S/10/1234).

25. IO L/P&S/10/1234, telegram from the Secretary of State for the Colonies to the High Commissioner of Transjordan, 27 February 1928, no. 10.

26. IO L/P&S/10/1234, telegram from the High Commissioner of Iraq to the Secretary of State for the Colonies, 25 February 1928, no. 110.

27. IO L/P&S/10/1239, memorandum from the High Commissioner of Iraq to the Colonial Office, 29 December 1927, no. 622.

28. IO L/P&S/10/1235, 'Memorandum on Proposed Scheme for Akhwan Defense', by Captain J. B. Glubb, Administrative Inspector, Dīwānīya, no date.

29. IO L/P&S/10/1240, 'Report on Operations in the Southern Desert of Iraq', by Captain J. B. Glubb, December 1928. See especially Sir John Bagot Glubb's *War in the Desert: An R.A.F. Frontier Campaign* (Hodder and Stoughton, London, 1960) for a detailed account of his work as an Administrative Inspector in the Southern Desert of Iraq and his extensive knowledge of tribal and boundary conflicts on the Iraq-Najd frontier.

30. IO L/P&S/10/1243, 'Intelligence Report on the Situation in Hassa and Nejd', from Lieutenant-Colonel H. R. P. Dickson, Political Agent Kuwait, to the Political Resident in the Persian Gulf, 24 September 1929, Secret no. 546.

31. IO L/P&S/10/1234, letter from the Political Resident in the Persian Gulf to the Secretary of State for the Colonies, 26 January 1928.

32. IO L/P&S/10/1243, report from Lieutenant-Colonel H. R. P. Dickson, Political Agent Kuwait, to the Political Resident in the Persian Gulf, 17 June 1929, no. 389. The al-'Ujmān and 'Awāzim were particularly well known for their skills at smuggling supplies.

33. IO L/P&S/10/1240, letter from 'Abd al-'Azīz to Sir Gilbert Clayton, dated 14 Dhu al-Qa'da 1348 (24 April 1929), no. 31.

34. IO L/P&S/10/1246, letter from Sir Hubert Young, Acting High Commissioner of Iraq, to Lord Passfield, Secretary of State for the Colonies, 21 October 1929. Secret B.

35. Ibid.

36. According to Fu'ād Ḥamza, *qalb jazīrat al-'arab* (Maktaba al-Naṣr al-Ḥadītha, al-Riyād, 1388ه(1968)), p.169, the Southern Shammar or the Shammar of Najd is composed of four divisions (*qabā'il*): 'Abda, Aslām, Sinjāra and Tūmān. The Northern Shammar or the Jarba inhabit Iraqi territory.

37. IO L/P&S/10/1246, letter from Sir Hubert Young, Acting High Commissioner of Iraq, to Lord Passfield, Secretary of State for the Colonies, 21 October 1929, Secret B.

38 Ibid. Young added that he had no evidence that the Iraq 'Anaza or the al-Ruwālā were implicated in such an agreement.

39. IO L/P&S/10/1243, Report: 'Hassa and Nejd Situation', from Lieutenant-Colonel H. R. P. Dickson, Political Agent Kuwait, to the Political Resident in the Persian Gulf, 26 September 1929, Secret no. 549.

40. IO L/P&S/10/1244, letter from 'Abd al-'Azīz to the High Commissioner of Iraq, 11 September 1929. See also 'Aṭṭār, *ṣaqr al-jazīra*, pp.981-8.

41. Some of these men, such as 'Alī Abū Shuwairibāt of the Buraih Muṭair and 'Ubaid b. Ḥumaid of the 'Utaiba, were originally Najdis who had taken refuge in Iraq and were actively encouraging discontented elements of their tribes to raid into Najd. During the Ikhwan rebellion, they also acted as intermediaries between King Faiṣal and the Ikhwan.

42. IO L/P&S/10/1243, report from Lieutenant-Colonel H. R. P. Dickson, Political Agent Kuwait, to the Political Resident in the Persian Gulf, 26 September 1929, Secret 549. In IO L/P&S/10/1241, letter from J. G. Laithwaite, Private Secretary to the Secretary of State, to J. C. Walton, Secretary of the Political Department, 18 December 1929, London confirmed that there was also Hashimite intrigue in Transjordan against 'Abd al-'Azīz: 'It appears that the position is that Eastern Transjordan is not at present effectively administered; that it is largely peopled by Bedouin tribes, who, under present arrangements, are under the control of the Amir Abdullah; that the Amir, like King Faisal in Iraq, is definitely intriguing against Ibn Saud, and not only is making no effort to control his tribes, but may—as suggested by Ibn Saud—be doing something to encourage them. For reasons of policy it is not, however, desired at present to remove the control of the Bedouin from Abdullah, though his *mala fides* is recognised.'

43. Ibid. It will be recalled that Young reported in October 1929 that the Shammar were, in fact, moving south.

44. IO L/P&S/10/1237, 'Memorandum Regarding the Seduction of Iraq Tribes by Ibn Sa'ūd', from Lieutenant J. B. Glubb to the Adviser to the Minister of the Interior, Baghdad, 19 March 1929.

45. IO L/P&S/10/1243, letter from Aḥmad al-Jābir Āl Ṣabāḥ, Ruler of Kuwait, to Colonel H. R. P. Dickson, Political Agent Kuwait, dated 27 Safar 1348 (3 August 1929).

46. According to J. G. Lorimer, *Gazetteer of the Persian Gulf, 'Omān, and Central Arabia*, 5 vols. (Gregg International, Farnborough, 1970), p.1285, the Muṭair was originally composed of two divisions: Ilwa and Braih. The Banī 'Abdillāh are sometimes classed as a third division.

47. IO L/P&S/10/1243, letter from Lieutenant-Colonel C. C. J. Barrett, Political Resident in the Persian Gulf, to the Secretary of State for the Colonies, 8 August 1929, Confidential no. 40.

48. Ibid.

49. Ibid.

8

The Ikhwan Rebellion 1929: Suppression of Internal Dissent Coincides with the Acceptance of Fixed Borders

The internal factors which influenced the evolution of political identity in Central Arabia during the early twentieth century have already been discussed in Part I, in relationship both to various interest and descent groups in the population generally and to the Al Saud in particular. Part II has briefly discussed the effects of external influences, chiefly those of the post-World War I mandate period, on the populations in the Iraq, Transjordan, Kuwait and Najd frontier zones; the foreign and domestic policy of the Al Saud; and inter-Arab relationships. The final chapter of this study is intended to relate the internal and external factors which influenced in the late 1920s the evolution of political identity in what was known by 1932 as the Kingdom of Saudi Arabia. Shaikh Ahmad Al Sabah, ruler of Kuwait, best summarised this period when explaining to the British the cause of the Ikhwan rebellion of 1929:

> when Bin Saud started his religious crusade they [the Ikhwan] were inflamed with the idea that the days of the Prophet had returned . . . . When the expansion of Bin Saud's power was checked [by the mandates] he was compelled to check his Akhwan [Ikhwan] and to renounce his 'jehad' and the 'Imam' legend was broken.[1]

It will be recalled that the delineation of boundaries and nation-states in the post-World War I period had effectively prevented further territorial expansion of the Al Saud to the north and west and, moreover, established rival Arab rulers in territories protected by the British and French. Undaunted, Abd al-Aziz procrastinated in territorial settlements between 1917 and 1925, while simultaneously encouraging Ikhwan raids against the frontier in an effort to convert tribes to Wahhabiism and, by such means, extend his authority. Britain was then forced to protect its interests. Sacrificing al-Hijaz in order to secure stable frontiers, Britain forced Abd al-Aziz to accept fixed borders through a series of treaties between himself and the mandates of Iraq and Transjordan. It also delineated the territory of Kuwait and assisted the Shaikh of Kuwait to enforce the sanctity of his borders with a loan of British armoured cars and aeroplanes. Saudi-British agreements and other subsequent actions by Abd al-Aziz led the Ikhwan to accuse the Saudi Imamate of subverting Islamic ideals. The Ikhwan eventually rebelled in 1929, threatening both Saudi rule and the mandated and protected territories of the British.

The events and chief participants of the Ikhwan rebellion have been recorded in numerous sources among which are Wahba, Dickson, Attar, Glubb, Habib and Philby. Not all of these accounts agree in specific details, but they generally present the same picture of increasing Ikhwan discontent dating from the year 1925. Because these sources are readily available, I have not attempted to provide a detailed historical chronology of this period, but rather have tried to illustrate that there occurred between 1925 and 1929 changes in the attitudes and expectations of Abd al-Aziz and the Ikhwan towards each other. These changes, influenced by internal and external factors, were especially reflected in attitudes to the inherent rights and thereby limitations of a government and its citizens; the responsibilities of a secular government the authority of which was based on a divine right to rule; and the basis of the legality of such a government. Ironically, Abd al-Aziz had to suppress the very force that had helped him expand to the territorial limits he had reached. Not only were the Ikhwan founded on Wahhabi doctrine with which the Al Saud had legitimised their own political authority, but also they were defeated with the help of the British, a non-Muslim government, and Abd al-Aziz's personal acceptance of Western-style fixed boundaries.

Antecedents of the Ikhwan Rebellion 1924-27

The beginning of Ikhwan dissatisfaction with Saudi rule may be traced to the successful completion of their campaign against al-Hijaz. After the war, Ibn Bijad anticipated his appointment as

General Commander of the Saudi forces and Faisal al-Duwish hoped for the position of Governor of al-Madina, including its surrounding territory and dependent villages.[2] The increasing Ikhwan strength, however, must have been viewed by Abd al-Aziz as a threat to his own power for he chose not to reward either of them. Ibn Bijad, leader of the Utaiba and al-Ghatghat, was regarded as a devout and sincere Wahhabi and could potentially draw many supporters. Duwish, on the other hand, already controlled the tribal *dira* of the Mutair which extended west from al-Ahsa to the district surrounding al-Madina. If he gained al-Madina itself, he would control the entire northern frontier of Arabia.

The Saudi leader did, however, try to placate general Ikhwan demands by destroying any structure which represented *shirk* or *kufr*, such as domes over mosques or shrines, and by appointing Wahhabi shaikhs to various positions in al-Hijaz. This was not easy. As the new leader of the Holy Cities of Islam, Abd al-Aziz was responsible not only to the sophisticated urban dwellers of al-Hijaz, but also to numerous Islamic groups all over the world. He tried to conciliate them by emphasising his role as a political rather than a religious leader. This infuriated the Ikhwan who felt that the Hijazis fully deserved a divine wrath and that they personally were entitled to the *ghanima* which would result from their being God's instrument of retribution. The arrival of Abd al-Aziz in al-Hijaz, however, had prevented further massacres or looting by the Ikhwan even though their religious enthusiasm was allowed to continue unabated in other ways. The use or installation of such modern innovations as telegraph, telephone, cars and aeroplanes was delayed or halted entirely because of Ikhwan opposition. Even the bicycle was viewed as the 'vehicle of the Devil'. No one, including small children, was exempt from public flogging if the Ikhwan felt Islamic practices had been transgressed. Even Ahmad al-Sanusi, a personal guest of Abd al-Aziz, was detained by the Ikhwan because he allegedly had asked for intercession at the Tomb of Khadija and it was only after some difficulty that he was exonerated.[3]

The fanaticism of the Ikhwan was no longer appropriate under Abd al-Aziz's new policy of conciliation. Having paved the way for Abd al-Aziz's grand entrance to al-Hijaz, the Ikhwan rank-and-file were duly sent back in 1925 to the *hijras* in Central Arabia and left to nurse their grievances. Their arrival was not triumphant. The wealth they anticipated from raiding in al-Hijaz and Transjordan had not materialised and they now found that a drought had decimated many of their sheep and camels. It was reported that hundreds of tents were found just outside the oases of al-Ahsa and al-Riyad and 'women and children carry the begging bowl from house to house'.[4]

Scarcely a year passed before Ibn Bijad and Faisal al-Duwish decided to convene a meeting of the Utaiba, Mutair and al-Ujman Ikhwan at al-Artawiya. At this conference in 1926 they listed a number of complaints against the Saudi leader, foremost of which was his abandonment of *jihad* against the *mushrikun*. They also charged that Abd al-Aziz was levying *maks*; he sent his sons to lands where *kufr* and *shirk* were apparent (Saud had gone to Egypt, Faisal to England); he used cars, telegraphs and telephones, all of which were witchcraft (*sihr*) and 'innovations of the Devil'; he allowed tribes from Iraq and Transjordan to graze in Muslim (Ikhwan) territory; and he did not enforce Wahhabi doctrine among the Shiites in al-Ahsa and Iraq. Finally, if Kuwait was not a country of infidels then Najdis should not be boycotting it; and if so, then Abd al-Aziz should declare a *jihad* against it.

When Abd al-Aziz heard about the Ikhwan gathering, he returned from al-Hijaz and convened a conference in January 1927 of Wahhabi *ulama* and Ikhwan leaders, all of whom were present except Ibn Bijad.[5] A *fatwa* issued at the end of the conference conceded many of the Ikhwan demands: 'non-Islamic' laws in al-Hijaz were abolished; buildings intended for the celebration of religious festivals and mosques where people worshipped in order to ask for intercession were destroyed; the Shiite were forced to attend classes in Wahhabi doctrine and forsake their own rituals; and the Egyptians were forbidden to enter al-Hijaz with the Mahmal[6] or an armed force. The *fatwa*, however, did acknowledge that the Imam had the right to declare *jihad* and that, if *maks* taxes continued to be levied by the government, it was not sufficient reason for any Muslim to rebel against the Imam and break Islamic unity. It is clear that at this time an open conflict with the Ikhwan was temporarily forestalled because the Saudi leader was still regarded as their secular and religious leader.

The 'Imam Legend' is Broken: 1927-29

The compromise reached in al-Riyad in January 1927 was not to last for long. Abd al-Aziz could not accommodate both the Ikhwan and the British. Chapters 6 and 7 have already discussed some of the events which occurred during the next two years. It will be recalled that the Ikhwan were engaged in numerous raids against Iraq and Kuwait. In October 1927 Duwish led a group of Ikhwan in an attack on Busaiya, one of the posts built on the Iraqi frontier. Britain responded by sending aeroplanes across the border to bomb the raiders in Najd, causing Abd al-Aziz to complain that the sovereignty of his rule was being violated. In April 1928 Abd al-Aziz promised the Ikhwan he would find a way to have the Iraqi posts removed through negotiations with the British in Jidda during the next month. These talks, however, were unsuccessful and, on 5 November 1928, Abd al-Aziz convened a general assembly of some eight hundred leaders in Najd — *ulama*, Ikhwan, badu and townspeople. It is reported that Duwish, Ibn Humaid and possibly others were absent. Abd al-Aziz spoke to those leaders present, stating that continuous Ikhwan raids on the frontier had resulted in the construction of posts such as Busaiya and Salman. In this speech Abd al-Aziz once again stressed his ancestral rights and his divine right to rule. He then offered to let those present choose a new leader from any of the members of his family, an offer which they refused.

> You know how great is the gift granted to me by God namely the Islam religion by which He gathered me after separation and granted us power after weakness . . . All this caused me to gather you in this place in order to remember first of all what God has granted to us and so that we may think of what to do in thanks for this blessing and secondly as something came to my mind namely that I am afraid there may be someone who has a complaint against me or against one of my representatives or Amirs in some sort of ill-treatment done to him or in deprivation of any of his rights. I wanted to know that from you so that I may have an excuse before God and do my proper duties. Thirdly, to ask for your opinions and your views regarding the welfare of your religion and your life. Might is for God alone, and you will remember that when I appeared to you you were parties and sections killing each other and robbing each other, and all those whom God caused to rule you whether Arabs or non-Arabs used to make intrigues amongst you to keep you separated to decrease your power and to make you vanish away. In the day I went out I was weak and I had nobody to help and

assist me but God alone . . . . I did not gather you for fear of any one of you as I was alone before and there was no help for me but God. I did not care for the multitude and God granted me victory. I only gathered you as I said for fear of my God lest I should be rendered self conceited or proud . . . . All are free to say what they like in this question . . . . I wish first of all to consider the question of the one who will be in charge of ruling you other than myself. Here are the members of the family before you. Choose one of them and he whom you agree upon I will recognise and help and I want you to be as sure that I do not say so to find out something or to see what you will say; because thank God, I do not think that I am indebted for my rank to anyone of you for any favour, but it is God alone who granted it . . . . Anything approved by the Sharia I will accept and anything it forbids I will abandon. Now, you the present parties say what you have to say and mention what you have heard people say in criticism of your ruler or any officials for whom he is responsible. You, Ulamas must remember that God will have you in the day of Judgment and then you will be asked the same as you are asked about to-day and about what the Moslems entrusted you with. So you have to say the truth in everything you are asked . . . . Explain the proper duties of the ruler to his people and those of the people to their ruler in accordance with religion and the world, the things in which the ruler has to be obeyed and those in which he is to be disobeyed . . . . As regards that on which there might be a difference between you, Ulamas, I will follow in its case the way of the ancestors, that is to say I will accept concerning it what is nearer to the proof of the book of God, the tradition of the Prophet or the sayings of one of the more learned Ulamas relied upon by the Sunna and Jamas. Beware you Ulamas to conceal anything of the truth thinking that this will satisfy me; he conceals a matter which he believes to be contrary to the Sharia, is cursed by God. Show the right and explain it and speak.[7]

The *ulama* answered Abd al-Aziz that they swore by God not to conceal the truth, they acknowledged God granted him the power to rule, and they had never seen him commit any deed contrary to the Sharia. The townspeople, badu and many of the Ikhwan then reaffirmed their allegiance to Abd al-Aziz although it is believed that a number of the Ikhwan — chiefly Mutair, al-Ujman and sections of the Utaiba — privately took the opportunity to agree that they alone were true Muslims and, in the event of open conflict with Abd al-Aziz, would support each other against him.

The Battle of Sibila: March 1929

Meanwhile, Ikhwan raids grew in intensity and savageness. Long stabbing raids were made into Iraq and Kuwait and the defenceless shepherd tribes in the Iraq Neutral Zone were massacred. Two events further exacerbated the conflict. First, an American missionary was killed in January by the Ikhwan as he travelled by car from Basra to Kuwait. Then in a contretemps against time-honoured custom, Ibn Humaid, an Ikhwan leader and shaikh of the Utaiba, attacked the Uqail merchants of Central Arabia.

> Ibn Humaid not only raided the Sinjara Shammar, Najd subjects and themselves Akhwan, and the Dahamshah and Ruwallah, respectively Iraq and Syrian subjects seduced by Ibn Sa'ud and having paid taxes to him, but also a large number of Agail merchants, mostly townsmen of Buraidah, one of the most Wahhabi of the Najd towns. All of the Bedouins [Qasim badu?] . . . live largely by the sale of camels to itinerant merchants, who drive their purchases across the desert for sale in Egypt or Syria. The immunity of merchants from molestation by bedouin raiders was therefore, doubtless, originally dictated by economic needs. In the old bedouin wars, both parties depended for their livelihood on the sale of camels to such merchants and their free movement amongst the tribes, even while at war, was an economic necessity to all parties. That, however . . . soon became imperceptibly a point of honour and to raid Agail merchants, under the old Arab dispensation, was an unheard of breach of the rules of war. When the fanatic revival of Wahhabism occurred, ten to fifteen years ago, this custom remained unviolated, not only because economic necessity demanded it, as before, but also because the town of Buraidah, the home of the great majority of camel dealers, was distinguished (coupled perhaps with Riyadh) as the most religious or fanatical of Najd towns. Ibn Humaid, however, not only looted the flocks of the Agail merchants at Nawadhir, but the merchants themselves were massacred, almost, it appears to a man . . . . While Ibn

> Sa'ud has long regarded with equanimity if not with approval, the disasters inflicted on the Iraq tribes by his subjects, he could scarcely, without endangering his throne, regard with indifference the massacre.[8]

Abd al-Aziz demanded that the Ikhwan make restitution of the camels they had taken. The Ikhwan refused, requesting that the issue be settled by the Sharia and Wahhabi *ulama*. They planned to undermine the authority of Abd al-Aziz by accusing him of dealing with the infidels — that is, the British. A conference was convened near Zulfa, seven hours' march from al-Artawiya. Duwish and Sultan b. Humaid all camped in the vicinity near a plain called Sibila. The Ikhwan force has been estimated at 8,000 although this figure remains conjectural.[9] Abd al-Aziz himself claimed that his force numbered 30,000.[10] Attar gives a similar figure for the Saudi troops and states that of these there were 8,000 townspeople from the Harb, Qahtan, Hutaim, Zafir, and sections favourable to Abd al-Aziz from the Mutair, Utaiba, Shammar and Anaza.[11] It is significant that Abd al-Aziz completely changed the social composition of his military force for this battle. He deliberately went to al-Qasim before the conference and appealed to the townspeople to accompany him, just as he had appealed to townspeople when he planned to attack al-Ahsa in 1913. It will be recalled that in the campaign for al-Hijaz not a single townsperson was used in the Saudi force. From the date of the Battle of Sibila, however, until the final defeat of the Ikhwan in December. Abd al-Aziz's force would always contain townspeople. Beginning in the 1700s, the Al Saud had always identified their primary economic and political interests with the populations of the urban areas and now they were again forced to rely upon them for military assistance and political support.

Abd al-Aziz then sent the Wahhabi shaikhs—Abdullah al-Unqari and Abu Habib — to mediate, but the Ikhwan refused them. Apparently, Duwish then held several meetings with Abd al-Aziz at the Saudi camp. A number of sources have related incidents of the meeting, but for our purpose it is sufficient to state that, when Duwish returned to his own camp, he reported that all of Abd al-Aziz's 'men were cooks and know nothing except sleeping on mattresses . . . . they have much that is *ḥalāl* [permitted by Islam] and there is much *ghanā'im* [pl. of *ghanima*, lawful Islamic booty]. We will defeat this *ṭāghūt* [false God] at dawn.'[12] Duwish's reference to the wealth in the Saudi camp as *ghanaim* clearly indicates that he was in rebellion against Abd al-Aziz and the Imamate.

Abd al-Aziz ordered his troops to attack the Ikhwan forces at dawn on 30 March 1929.[13] The battle which ensued became known as the Battle of Sibila and was a decisive, although not final, victory for Abd al-Aziz. Duwish was seriously wounded and sent to al-Artawiya to recover; Abd al-Aziz himself states that most of Duwish's men were captured, that some of them were beheaded and others imprisoned.[14] Before returning to al-Hijaz, Abd al-Aziz issued a public statement to explain his punitive action against the Ikhwan. It is the first time he actually condemns the behaviour and intentions of the Ikhwan.

> We have informed you over the past three years about the Ikhwan, particularly those of al-Ghaṭghaṭ and Duwīsh, the *ghulāt* [adherents of an extreme sect]. They became fanatics and their affairs were against the instruction of the Sharī'a. They were deceived and with them were the emigrants from the desert. They thought they were right because of their love for religion.
>
> Praise God, however, who removed the veil from the Muslims [showed the nature of the Ikhwan to true Muslims]. They saw this group was divided. One devoted themselves to the service of God over ignorance. The other were malicious and greedy. Religion provided a justification for them. In these days after our return [Abd al-Aziz's return from al-Hijaz?], I gathered the Najdis and their *'ulamā* and they decided what has reached you . . . it was clear that these *ghulāt* were not in the right.
>
> We gave them friendly warnings . . . to no avail. They were meeting those days and spread the word in Najd that their intention was the people and forts on the Iraqi border . . . they united and attacked . . . We summoned them to submit to arbitration of the Sharī'a. They scorned that.
>
> We sent Shaikh 'Abdullāh al-'Unqarī and Abū Ḥabīb . . . they did not accept . . . .
>
> We ordered the Muslims [Saudi forces] to proceed to them and a portion of them [Ikhwan] were killed . . . . After that, all of them asked for a pardon . . . all received it and were spared from death and punishment except Duwīsh and Ibn Ḥumaid. They faced the judgement of the Sharī'a . . . . They accepted it for two

reasons: first, people had abandoned them and others had been pardoned and, second, they had no retreat.

The truth is that we did not like killing even one Muslim, but obedience to God is necessary against those who plot harmful things. We were compelled to do that. The result was favourable . . . . The ignorant were humbled . . . . This is all that is necessary to explain.[15]

'Abd al-'Azīz
22 Shawwal 1347
(early April 1929)

In another letter written by Abd al-Aziz to Great Britain he refers to the Ikhwan conspirators as *bughat*[16] — that is, 'those who dissent in Islam but who do not renounce the authority of the Imam'. Some Islamic schools of law have specific legal sanctions concerning the treatment of *bughat*, such that they are not liable to death or their property to confiscation as long as they do not attack the head of the Islamic community or endanger its unity. Unfortunately, it is not clear what significance Abd al-Aziz attached to the usage of this term although he must certainly have been aware of its implications.

The Murder of Hithlain: May 1929

Abd al-Aziz might have re-established his control after the Battle of Sibila but for one regrettable and, by now, very famous incident — the murder of the Ujmani Shaikh, Daidan al-Hithlain. Hithlain had been personally thanked by Abd al-Aziz for having refrained from joining the other Ikhwan at Sibila. Apparently unknown to Abd al-Aziz, however, he was invited by Fahd b. Jiluwi, the son of the Governor of al-Ahsa, to Fahd's camp under an order of safe conduct. When Daidan arrived, he was refused permission to leave and, before he could be rescued by the al-Ujman, his throat was cut. No one has ever been able to explain Fahd's actions or to determine whether he acted under the orders of his father or Abd al-Aziz.[17] In any event, the al-Ujman united, even those badu who had previously been under Fahd's command, killing Fahd and almost all of the townsmen of al-Hufuf who were with him.

Daidan's murder took place on 1 May 1929. By the middle of May the Utaiba Ikhwan had cut the roads from al-Hijaz and Najd in the west, while in the east the al-Ujman had severed any connection with al-Ahsa. They indiscriminately killed non-Ikhwan, leaving many villages completely isolated and open to further aggression.[18]

'I Have Left My Desert and My Shaikhship . . . in Seeking the Gifts of God'

After the Battle of Sibila and Daidan's murder, Faisal al-Duwish recovered from his wounds and was actively gathering support for a large-scale rebellion. Abd al-Aziz meanwhile was trying to regain the allegiance of key tribal sections of the Ikhwan, particularly the Utaiba, and enlist the assistance of urban areas. The communications which passed from June to December 1929 between the Ikhwan, Abd al-Aziz, Shaikh Ahmad Al Sabah and the British constitute the most illuminating material which concerns the rebellion. Because it has remained generally unresearched and because it reflects many of the internal factors which influenced the evolution of political identity in Saudi Arabia, this material will be quoted extensively in the following sections. It particularly illustrates the enormous difficulties encountered by the Ikhwan after their *hijra* from nomadism to a settled agricultural life-style. The conflicting attitudes of individuals and groups to political authority were also reflected in a variety of tensions: Arab *versus* non-Arab; Muslim *versus* non-Muslim; Hashimite *versus* Saudi; Saudi *versus* pure Wahhabi doctrine; and tribal *versus* regional *versus* national loyalties. In addition to these political and economic tensions in the development of political identity were the external influences: British military strength and the concepts of 'boundary' and 'nation-state' introduced during the post-World War I mandate period.

These internal and external influences would cause almost two complete cycles to occur. First, the Al Saud had depended primarily upon settled people to support them politically until Abd al-Aziz began to encourage the formation of Ikhwan settlements. During the Ikhwan rebellion the Al Saud would once again depend upon the settled inhabitants of Najd to support them militarily. Second, the Ikhwan had forsaken nomadism for a new economic, political and religious life-style only to find the transition impossible. In the late 1920s, the rebel Ikhwan evacuated their *hijras*, resorting to their old tribal alliances and to their former means of livelihood.

An important and revealing letter was written on 6 June 1929 by Duwish to the Amir Saud b. Imam Abd al-Aziz in response to a letter from Saud requesting the restitution of property taken during Ikhwan raids. After greetings, Duwish thanked Saud for his father's kindness following the Battle of Sibila, but stated that he could not comply with Saud's request for two reasons.

> 1). . . we have raided only infidels and breakers of promises who build forts and encourage your subjects to rebel against you. I have informed your father [Imam Abd al-Aziz] of this and this is the reproach of the Akhwan [Ikhwan] against your father. Otherwise, all your actions when dealing with us are agreeable, may God reward you.
>
> 2)The missing property is gone and I have nothing of it left in my possession. It has occurred to me . . . that your order is only a device to entangle me and that you will either kill me or imprison me. Saud, I have left my desert, and my shaikhship, and sacrificed my wealth in seeking the gifts of God and fighting the infidels. If you wish to prevent us from fighting them, and if when one of us commits an infraction you will either imprison or kill him, this is a calamity and oppression of your subjects, who may desert you, doubt your belief and irrevocably decide that you are hindering them in their religion, and indulging that of the Christians, and the Christians their follower Faisal [King Faisal of Iraq] have not failed to do what they can [to cause dissension].[19]

Duwish's letter is significant. It is an open accusation that the Saudi Imamate was not fulfilling its responsibilities as an Islamic government. Not only had the Imamate ceased its campaign against the infidels, but it was openly consorting with a non-Muslim government. His accusation, strictly speaking, was entirely consonant with the interpretation of Wahhabi doctrine. Duwish also referred to the desert and the shaikhdom he abandoned for Islam. Now that it was a part of the past and the avenues of legitimate Islamic wealth had been closed, he and his people had fewer expectations than before they became Ikhwan.

> You have also prevented me from raiding the Bedouins. So we are neither Moslems fighting the unbelievers nor are we Arabs and Bedouins raiding . . . and living on what we get from each other. You have kept us away from both our religious and our worldly concerns. It is true that you have not failed to do what you can for me and my people but where are the rest of my tribes to go? They will perish and how can we be contented with this? In the past you used to forgive any of us who committed a sin, but now you treat us with the sword and pass over the Christians, their religion and the forts built for your immediate destruction.[20]

If Abd al-Aziz, whom Duwish called 'the politician of us Arabs', would release the Ikhwan prisoners, promise the al-Ujman a pardon, forget the past and fight the infidels, Duwish promised that they would be faithful servants of the Al Saud, allowing them to control their lives and property. The benefits would be great, but Duwish warned the Al Saud about the consequences of their present actions, reminding them of their religious duties as an Islamic Imamate.

> If we are killed, it does not matter, and if we succeed it will be for your benefit, just as our brethren the Ghut Ghut [Ibn Bijad's Ikhwan] took the Hejaz and it became yours in your name . . . . As regards the Bedouins, if they see your treatment of us, and see how the infidels receive those who go from you to them, by God, none will remain. You know that the best of them as regards religion, and the nearest to you are those whom you have killed and imprisoned . . . . We ask you not to send us away . . . deprived of your friendship and of the religion of Islam, and compelled to go to the Christians whom we dislike and who dislike us . . . do not give up your friend for your enemy.[21]

Similar sentiments were expressed by other Ikhwan in two separate meetings held with Lieutenant-Colonel Dickson. In late June, Faisal al-Shiblain (Shiblan?), a Mutairi and assistant of Duwish, explained his anti-Saudi feelings which Dickson summarised:

> 1). . . the Akhwan were out against Bin Saud because he was trying to restrict the Bedouins' freedom to an unheard of extent.
>
> 2). . . Bin Saud had filled them with religious zeal and preached that all infidels were fair game, and the 'Sheria' was the only law. But when they interpreted the former literally, Bin Saud had . . . punished them, and . . . treacherously attacked them at the Battle of Sibila.[22]

Dickson asked Shiblain why the Ikhwan had continued their raids against Iraq even when requested not to do so. Shiblain's answer is significant in that it seems to confirm the conclusion reached in Chapter 3 that the new life-style of the Ikhwan was not so financially rewarding as their former one and the Al Saud had control over tribal *dira*s, although it is not clear to what extent: 'How could we help it when our grazing grounds and wells had been taken from us and seeing that we were persistently encouraged to do so.'[23]

Two Ikhwan leaders — al-Fuqm (Mutair) and Hazam al-Hithlain — met with Dickson on 18 July in Kuwait. Dickson summarised the following points from the conversation:

> 1)They had come . . . to inform the British Government of the reasons which had led them into rebellion against Bin Saud. This was nothing more than the latter's treachery with them . . . . Bin Saud had taught them Religion and today . . . they knew how to appreciate the Truth and honest dealing. Bin Saud had ordered them to raid Iraq and Kuwait times without number and as soldiers they had carried out his orders to the letter (I here interjected that perhaps Bin Saud had not himself given the instructions, but that they had taken their instructions from someone else. This they hotly denied saying that the Akhwan leaders accepted no orders except from Bin Saud's own mouth).
>
> 2)Then came the English they said who began to complain to Bin Saud and started demanding back stolen sheep, camels, etc. To this Bin Saud gave answer that his Akhwan were out of hand and he could not very well control them. Actually he again and again had ordered them to continue their raiding and took the 'khumus', 1/5 of all the loot they got.

> 3)Eventually under pressure from the English Bin Saud had demanded that they should hand back their share of the loot to him, and he would return same to Iraq. Their reply to him had been 'Yes we will do this and loyally obey your orders but you must do likewise as our leader.' They had also wanted to know how it was that while it suited his convenience Bin Saud had quoted to them by chapter and verse of the Koran, the virtue of jehad and attacking non-Akhwan and Mushriq tribes, and how it was that he was now asking them to return to the infidel what he had preached was lawful . . . [24]

It may be concluded from the letter of Duwish and the two meetings of the Ikhwan with Dickson that the Ikhwan definitely were not in as economically advantageous position as previously. Moreover, they unanimously concurred that it was on the encouragement of Abd al-Aziz that they had adopted Wahhabi doctrine, taking it to its logical conclusion in their raids against al-Hijaz, Transjordan, Kuwait and Iraq territory. These raids had been fully supported by the Al Saud. What the Ikhwan did not understand was that Abd al-Aziz and the Al Saud had always distinguished religious ideology from political reality and acted accordingly.

Duwish Rebels Against the Saudi Imamate

Duwish recovered from his wounds, but did not join the Utaiba and al-Ujman in their new uprising until the Al Saud made it clear that they would not meet his demands. On 19 June 1929, one-and-a-half months after Daidan's murder, Duwish collected 5,000 Mutair, al-Ujman and Utaiba tribesmen and 100,000 camels and joined the rebels just south of Kuwait territory. The major tactical problem of the Ikhwan rebels was the lack of supplies and grazing. They had evacuated the *hijras*, taking all their flocks the numbers of which continued to increase because of their constant raids. They found, however, that Britain was not preventing them access to grazing in Iraq and Kuwait and, hence, they were now able to replenish supplies from the major urban centres of these countries.

The predicament of all parties was great. The British wished to assist Abd al-Aziz, but did not want to be on the losing side. Ibn Sabah resented Britain for the loss of Kuwait territory and Abd al-

Aziz for having acquired it and yet his military weakness bound him to support British policy. Abd al-Aziz had formerly denied the validity of fixed boundaries but, because of the Ikhwan rebellion, was now forced to acknowledge them and, hence, recognise the validity of the nation-states and the rulers they represented. The predicament of the Ikhwan was perhaps the saddest and most ironic of this period. An invisible boundary on the ground meant nothing to the Ikhwan who had only known loyalties to tribes and men rather than to nation-states. Now, surrounded by their women and children and flocks swollen out of proportion, the Ikhwan could not understand why they were not permitted to cross the borders of either Iraq or Kuwait to find fresh pasture.

During the month of June Abd al-Aziz was in the process of raising an army, chiefly from al-Qasim, and in soliciting Britain for its support against the Ikhwan. In order to break the powerful union of the rebels, Abd al-Aziz was also attempting to win the Utaiba to his side. In a famous speech given to 2,000 Utaiba in Duwadami on 9 July 1929, Abd al-Aziz was quoted as saying:

> You can be classified under three headings: one part . . . is very religious and faithful to its country and Government. The second part is a follower of every troublesome leader, and the third, which . . . is the smallest . . . is the most troublesome . . . . I was unable to know who was honest and who was false . . . God has always been with me and has always revealed to me those who wish to harm their religion, King, and country . . . . we [the Al Saud] are your masters and descendants of your masters and that, by the will of God and the word 'unity' [*tauhid?*] and the sword we are your Kings . . . . I sent people to warn you, but with no result. Then came the day of Sibila and according to God's wish it was the sword that was to give the final judgment. Now you people of Nejd, if you wish to help me in carrying on this Government of which you reap the benefits and of which I bear the worries and mishaps, this will be good enough for you . . . . You people of Nejd, I have promised God three things: first, to summon the people to believe in the unity of God and . . . the Sharia in giving judgment, secondly, to kill the insolent with the sword, thirdly, to reward . . . good and to punish the evil-doers . . . . I want all of you especially those who helped me in many previous or recent happenings and those who helped the backsliders but have now returned to the fold, to

> promise me first to advise any backslider or disobedient man that if he returns to the fold, he will be given safety and security. If he does not, kill him, and let the Mohammedans be well rid of him . . . . Also note that I want to annihilate these Ajman . . . If anyone . . . is absent [from the battle] without a proper excuse, kill him . . . . arrest his army and confiscate his arms and horses.[25]

Meanwhile, the rebels had extended their activity near al-Riyad. There was also evidence that the Hashimites were actively assisting the Ikhwan and that many refugees from Najd who had taken asylum in Iraq were now arriving in Kuwait to offer their assistance to the rebels.[26] In a letter dated 9 Muharram 1348 (17 June 1929), Duwish actually requested that Ibn Sabah become the Ikhwan leader. If the Shaikh would grant him the right to pasture at the wells of Subaihiya in Kuwait, the northern Ikhwan would desist from frontier raids against Kuwait or Iraq. Duwish's emphasis on boundaries is a moving reference to the dilemma confronting many populations during the process of nation-state formation as it was realised that new rules were guiding political behaviour.

> As to us, we want your protection and nothing more; we want you to tell us where we may not go, and what boundaries we must not trespass on. We will obey. Protect us and make out our frontiers for us, and we will not disobey you . . . . Our one desire is that you become the medium between us and the High Government [Britain] in exactly the same way as Ibn Saud was our 'go between' in matters that affected or befell us.[27]

Duwish sent another message to Ibn Sabah telling him that all of Abd al-Aziz's army was revolting, including the Utaiba — badu and townspeople — who had risen together. Duwish promised the Shaikh *zakat*, *khums* from all further Ikhwan raids and subsidies formerly paid by the British to Abd al-Aziz if he would become their Imam!

> Firstly we wish you to agree with us in our beliefs and tenets of Islam.
>
> Secondly we invite you to be the Imam over the great army

> [Ikhwan] which God has put into your hands: and to become the medium (*wasta*) between us and the British Government . . . .
>
> As far as fighting with Ibn Saud and the people of Najd is concerned we excuse you from taking part, and only desire from you the thing that you can assist us with (allow us to obtain supplies?).
>
> Do not . . . be stingy . . . and you will not want for wealth.[28]

On 18 July the Ikhwan reiterated their requests directly to Lieutenant-Colonel Dickson and asked if they could formally enter into a treaty agreement with Britain which would be signed by all leaders concerned. They promised that they would remain friends with Iraq and Kuwait and not attack their tribes. All they wanted was the right to purchase supplies from Kuwait as they themselves were formerly Kuwait tribes. Now, they felt, they were strong enough to be an independent nation.[29] The British predictably answered that they were in a treaty relationship with Abd al-Aziz and could not, therefore, accede to any of the demands of the Ikhwan.

During the month of August the Ikhwan attacked several sections of the Shammar, Amarat Anaza, Subai, Suhul and Awazim tribes, hoping that the injuries these tribes suffered would convince them to abandon Abd al-Aziz.[30] They also tried unsuccessfully to enter Kuwait territory and graze at Subaihiya, but Dickson ordered them to leave immediately.[31] The only major military campaign between the Ikhwan and the Al Saud occurred in this month. Duwish had sent his son, Azaiyiz, and 500 men on a raiding expedition to northern Jabal Shammar. Ibn Musaid, Amir of Hail, intercepted them by cutting off their access to wells. The two opposing armies met in temperatures over 30° Centigrade. The Ikhwan camels had not drunk for four days. Azaiyiz lost over 450 men, and his own desiccated body and those of his five companions were found months later in the desert; Ibn Musaid himself lost over 500 men. In late August, presumably after Duwish heard that his son had been killed, he sent another letter to Ibn Sabah. Although he now admitted disillusionment with the Al Saud and religion, the survival of his tribe and its flocks remained major unsolved problems. Duwish appeared almost confused when he mentioned the boundary, but once again referred to the ancient ties of his tribe to the rulers of Kuwait and alluded to the traditional right of any tribe in the desert to grazing or water.

> You talk about a boundary, and Subaihiyeh being in Kuwait. My answer is have you told the Hakuma [Britain] that Subaihiyeh is the ancestral home of the Mutair Alwa, and of us the Dooshan [ruling family of the Mutair] in particular, also that we the Mutair and Ajman are your fighting tribes and have been since the world began. If not you had better do so quickly. We certainly have been enticed away under the name of Religion by Bin Saud but we have no further use for him and as erring children, we now wish to return to our old home and be under old Rulers . . . . We require nothing but water and grazing for our camels which cannot find enough to eat or drink in North Hassa. At Hamudh there is a famine and all grazing has finished. Here round Subaihiyeh there is plenty for all. Our idea is to leave our camels and women here and issue forth into Najd once more to carry on our fight.[32]

By September Abd al-Aziz had managed to win over large sections of the Utaiba and Ibn Musaid's forces had moved east to reinforce the Awazim tribe and the townspeople who were both assisting in the defence of al-Ahsa. This, however, did not prevent the Ikhwan from attacking the Awazim on 5 October, killing over 250 men and women. Much to the displeasure of Abd al-Aziz, this forced the Awazim to seek refuge in Kuwait and gave the rebels possession of over three-quarters of al-Ahsa. It is easy to see from the events of May to October that both the Saudi leader and the Ikhwan forces had had their diplomatic and military successes, although, ultimately, they were not to be a deciding factor in the struggle. In October, Britain told Duwish that they could not assist him in any way or protect his women from Ibn Musaid's troops[33] while he challenged the Al Saud to battle in Najd. They also remained firm in their refusal to let Duwish cross the borders of Iraq or Kuwait to find pasture.

'Nation-state' and 'Border': Determinant Factors in the Saudi Success over the Ikhwan Rebellion

Ibn Sabah had earlier informed Britain that the time for rebellion was ripe and that 'Faisal al-Duwish was a *kelb-ibn kelb* [dog the son of a dog] with the brain of an astute Hathari [townsman] and . . . was the brain of the whole movement against Ibn Sa'ud without doubt'. He predicted that there would be an Utaiba uprising in the west near al-Hijaz while there was an al-Ujman/Mutair attack on al-Ahsa. Moreover, the town of Unaiza, a large commercial town in al-Qasim, would probably help a successful rebellion because the Saudi blockade against Kuwait had substantially reduced its revenues. This is essentially what, in fact, did occur[34] and there were only two reasons — British assistance to Abd al-Aziz and the inability of the Ikhwan to obtain grazing or supplies — which caused the rebellion to fail. The second reason was a direct result of Abd al-Aziz's eventual acceptance of fixed, Western-style borders which, enforced by military personnel, prevented the passage of goods and people.

In mid-August, Abd al-Aziz explained to Britain that he could not regain absolute control over the populations in his country unless he could completely crush the Ikhwan rebels. The Ikhwan were camped close to Kuwait territory and could possibly seek refuge there, with or without the approval of the authorities. Abd al-Aziz expressed the difficulty of this position. He himself could not cross the frontier for this act would be a breach of Kuwaiti or Iraqi sovereignty, but how then could he sanction the rebels? He goes on to propose two solutions, both of which acknowledge for the first time his recognition, practically as well as formally, of the absolute sovereignty of the government of Kuwait. His recognition of the territorial rights of Kuwait in 1929 shows how his attitude had considerably altered from the period in the early 1920s when he stated that no borders were necessary between himself and other Arab rulers. It is also in stark contrast to the statement of the slave of Amir Jiluwi, the Saudi Governor of al-Ahsa, who, having slit the throat of Najd merchants outside Kuwait Town, told onlookers that that would teach them that his master, that is, Saudi authority, ruled up to the walls of Kuwait Town.

> The position, as the British Government must realise, is difficult for Us; and as We have actually marched and within a few days shall have reached the spot where the rebels are stationed, and as you are aware that it is not easy in desert warfare to co-ordinate operations and as the first opportunity of attacking the enemy is the one that should be taken, We therefore suggest the following:
>
> a)We suggest that the Government of Koweit should order their subjects to collect in an appointed region with a force placed in

front of them to protect them. This locality should be far from any likely zone of battle. The Koweit Government should then inform Us of the position of that region and they (the Government of Koweit) should also place an adequate force (We do not think that the Air Force alone is sufficient) on the borders of Koweit in order to repel any rebels who attempt to take refuge there. The British Government officials should accompany the two forces . . . This frontier force is to beat the rebels back as far as possible even to within the frontiers of Nejd in order to be sure that they do not cross the frontiers again.

If it happened that any of the rebels great or small succeeded in escaping into the interior of Koweit or Iraq, he should be arrested and handed to Us. In this case, there would be no need for Our force to cross the Koweit frontier.

b)If all this is impossible We suggest that the subjects of Koweit should be ordered to collect in a certain locality of which We may be informed. Then We should be free to act against the rebels and to pursue them wherever they may be (i.e. into Koweit) and, in this case, We undertake to protect all the subjects of the neighbouring countries and to prevent them being the object of any aggression. We further undertake not to leave a single soldier in those countries immediately Our pursuit of the criminals has come to an end. In which case the rebels will be totally annihilated by the Grace and Power of God.

This is in Our opinion the only solution of the problem and the only way of exterminating the rebels.[35]

In December many of the Ikhwan had already deserted to the Saudi forces which, in late December, were approximately 110-130 kilometres south-east of the Iraq – Kuwait frontier. The Ikhwan were trapped between a border over which they could not pass without being arrested and the inexorable movement of the Al Saud towards the north.[36] It should be noted that Abd al-Aziz's army, according to British estimates, was composed of three groups, one-third to one-half of whom were townspeople. The British summarised the military and political problems as follows:

The rebellious forces are to some extent hemmed in, though the area which they occupy is considerable. They have their backs to the Iraq – Koweit frontier, and from time to time cross that

> frontier, either on raids or in search of water and supplies. In deference to request for co-operation from Ibn Saud, a zone has been cleared some 15 miles deep along the frontier of Koweit, save for a few shepherds and woodcutters. It is not clear to what extent corresponding action has been taken in Iraq. Ibn Saud has further been assured that, should the rebels cross the frontier line into Koweit or Iraq, steps will be taken to eject them, and that instructions have been given for the concerting of military measures to this end.
>
> We had always been afraid that an embarrassing situation for His Majesty's Government would be created should any of the rebels succeed in entering Iraq or Koweit accompanied by their women and children, and refuse to evacuate. We could not use force. On the other hand, we were committed by our undertakings to Ibn Saud to 'eject' refugee rebels, and to prevent them from taking refuge. Internment presented practical difficulties: in addition it was objectionable, as enabling Ibn Saud to represent that we were taking his enemies, whom he was pursuing on our behalf, out of his reach; that ultimately they would be released to be a nuisance to both Nejd and Iraq; and that he could not be expected to conduct punitive expeditions on this scale at frequent intervals. Moreover, he would be able to allege that we were seducing his tribes.[37]

The Ikhwan position was completely untenable and by 10 January 1930 the final surrender of the major Ikhwan leaders was accepted by British representatives. In due course, they were turned over to the Saudi leader. The punishment meted out by Abd al-Aziz to the Ikhwan has been discussed at length in several sources and therefore it is not necessary to do so here. Suffice it to say that the punishment was sufficient to prevent any future outbreaks of the Ikhwan rebellion. Troublesome *hijra*s were split apart and their members dispersed among other tribes, major instigators were publicly reprimanded for their disobedience to the divine laws of Islam and then imprisoned for life and their property and that of their tribes confiscated.[38]

Conclusion

Although the alliance of the Al Saud and the badu in the early twentieth century had fulfilled specific functions, especially the military expansion of the Kingdom, it was not practical for reasons already discussed. After the conclusion of the rebellion, the badu were eventually reformed to become the core of the National Guard although strict attention was paid to tribal composition in the various regions.

In conclusion, it may be said that, while the Al Saud emphasised the unity of 'church' and 'state' as well as the legitimacy of their own authority, they were eventually forced because of external influences to define their state on a territorial basis. The irony was that in a land previously characterised by shifting political and ecological balances and a segmentary social system, the concepts of 'boundary' and 'nation-state' created, at least temporarily, major alterations in political behaviour among the Arabs themselves. When Dickson told the Ikhwan leader Faisal al-Shiblain that he must not cross the boundary on pain of being bombed, Shiblain made a poignant reply which perhaps best summarises the early period of Abd al-Aziz's rule from 1901 to 1932 and the transition from tribal or other particularistic means of political identification to identification with a nation-state: '. . . where is the boundary, we don't know any boundary, we have never been told anything. If you mean Iraq or Kuwait tribes we [Ikhwan] understand, and I tell you they are safe'.[39]

Notes

1. India Office Records, *Political and Secret Department Separate Files 1902-1931*, L/P&S/10 (henceforward abbreviated to IO L/P&S/10): IO L/P&S/10/1245, letter from H. V. Biscoe, Political Resident in the Persian Gulf, to Lord Passfield, Secretary of State for the Colonies, 15 December 1929.
2. Aḥmad 'Abd al-Ghafūr 'Aṭṭār, *ṣaqr al-jazīra*, 7 vols (Maṭba'at al-Ḥurrīya, Beirut, 1972), pp.267-70.
3. Ḥāfiẓ Wahba, *Arabian Days* (Arthur Barker, London, 1964), p.131.
4. Louis P. Dame, 'Four Months in Nejd', *Moslem World*, 14 (1924), p.354.
5. Wahba, *Arabian Days*, pp.133-6; 'Aṭṭār, *ṣaqr al-jazīra*, pp.967-74.
6. This particular *maḥmal* was a decorated litter sent to Mecca by Egyptians at the time of the pilgrimage.
7. IO L/P&S/10/1240, Translation, Speech of His Majesty the King 'Abd al-'Azīz to the Ikhwan and *'Ulamā*.
8. IO L/P&S/10/1240, 'Extract, Report of the Southern Desert Administration for March 1929', by Captain John Bagot Glubb.
9. John S. Habib, 'The Ikhwan Movement of Najd: Its Rise, Development, and Decline' (PhD. thesis, University of Michigan, 1970), p.265.
10. IO L/P&S/10/1240, letter from 'Abd al-'Azīz to Sir Gilbert Clayton, High Commissioner for Iraq, dated 14 Dhu al-Qada 1347 (24 April 1929).
11. 'Aṭṭār, *ṣaqr al-jazīra*, pp.996-1000.
12. Ibid., p.998.

13. The date of this battle has also been calculated as 29 and 31 March 1929.

14. Very few sources mention Bijād during this battle or his subsequent fate. It is interesting, however, that after the conclusion of fighting, 'Abd al-'Azīz ordered al-Ghaṭghaṭ to be completely destroyed and he forbade anyone to settle within the precincts of the town itself. No such orders were issued for al-Arṭāwīya.

15. 'Aṭṭār, *ṣaqr al-jazīra*, pp.978-80.

16. Ibid., pp.980-1.

17. Although 'Abd al-'Azīz's participation in this incident is not confirmed, it is not uncommon even today to hear Arabs of the Peninsula, particularly those with a badu heritage, speak about the treachery of the Al Sa'ūd.

18. 'Aṭṭār, *ṣaqr al-jazīra*, pp.1001-5.

19. IO L/P&S/10/1243, letter from Faiṣal b. Sulṭān al-Duwīsh to Amir Sa'ūd b. Imam 'Abd al-'Azīz b. 'Abd al-Raḥmān Āl Faiṣal Āl Sa'ūd, 6 June 1929. Duwīsh went on in his letter to say that 'Anyone who goes over to them [the Hashimites] from the Nejd people is encouraged and favoured, and told to disobey Saud ['Abd al-'Azīz] and that he will be given so and so. Since last year Abu Huneik [Glubb's nickname was Father of the Little Chin because of an injury he had suffered] had been advising me and others and I have informed you accordingly. The ready proof is that you know Ibn Sabah is not worth a hen to the Christians or the Arabs. He has . . . communicated with the Ajman [al-'Ujmān] . . . and promised to grant their requests . . . his territories are free for them to enter, and . . . he will speak to the Christians on their behalf.' The implication of Duwīsh's information was that the al-'Ujmān were seeking the safety of Kuwait territory. See also Chapter 7 for information about Hashimite intrigue with the Ikhwan rebels.

20. Ibid.

21. Ibid.

22. IO L/P&S/10/1243, letter from Lieutenant-Colonel H. R. P. Dickson, Political Agent Kuwait, to the Political Resident in the Persian Gulf, 1 July 1929, no. 406.

23. Ibid.

24. IO L/P&S/10/1243, letter ('Visit of Akhwan Leaders to Kuwait on 18 July 1929') from Lieutenant-Colonel H. R. P. Dickson, Political Agent Kuwait, to the Political Resident in the Persian Gulf, 18 July 1929, no. 433. The two Ikhwan leaders also stated that 'Abd al-'Azīz had treacherously attacked the Ikhwan at Sibila and had sent Fahd b. Jilūwī to capture Ḍaidān al-Ḥithlain. Dickson was shown the actual letter from Fahd to Ḍaidān giving him safe conduct in the name of God.

25. IO L/P&S/10/1243, 'Translation, Speech of King 'Abd al-'Azīz to the 'Utaiba at Duwadamī', 9 July 1929.

26. See Ch. 7.

27. IO L/P&S/10/1243, letter from Faiṣal al-Duwīsh to Shaikh Aḥmad Āl Ṣabāḥ, Ruler of Kuwait, dated 9 Muḥarram 1348 (17 June 1929). A similar request was also stated by Faiṣal al-Shiblain to Dickson (IO L/P&S/10/1243, letter from Lieutenant-Colonel H. R. P. Dickson, Political Agent Kuwait, to the Political Resident in the Persian Gulf, 1 July 1929, no. 406).

28. IO L/P&S/10/1243, letter from Faiṣal al-Duwīsh to Shaikh Aḥmad Āl Ṣabāḥ, Ruler of Kuwait, dated 17 Muharram 1348 (25 June 1929). It is of interest to note that whenever letters passed between important Arab leaders, a verbal message (*min al-rās ilā al-rās* or 'from one head to another') was usually delivered by a trusted messenger who waited and returned with a verbal response (IO L/P&S/10/1243, letter from Lieutenant-Colonel H. R. P. Dickson, Political Agent Kuwait, to the Political Resident in the Persian Gulf, 7 July 1929, no. 412).

29. IO L/P&S/10/1243, letter from H. R. P. Dickson, Political Agent Kuwait, to the Political Resident in the Persian Gulf, 18 July 1929, no. 433.

30. It will be recalled that the 'Awāzim were one of the tribes freed by 'Abd al-'Azīz from their inferior status and payment of *khuwa* to more noble tribes. They were therefore not likely to abandon 'Abd al-'Azīz voluntarily, as Duwīsh fully realised. He told Dickson that 'We [the Ikhwan] have cleared northern Nejd of Bin Saud's forces, and we have done the British a good turn by sending back to Iraq some of her recalcitrant tribes like the Shammar and Dhafir. We must now deal with the Awazim, those fools who will not take a hint. We wish to detach them from Bin Saud, and if they will not come by kindness, we shall have to worry them by sending snipers at night and shooting up their camps. This will bring them to their senses. We do not wish to kill them. They are not worth it.' (IO L/P&S/10/1243, letter from H. R. P. Dickson, Political Agent Kuwait, to the Political Resident of the Persian Gulf, 31 August 1929, no. 505.)

31. H. R. P. Dickson, *Kuwait and Her Neighbours* (George Allen and Unwin, London, 1968), p.307, estimated that there were over 100,000 camels, 2,000 tents and 5,000 fighting men in Duwish's camp.

32. IO L/P&S/10/1243, letter from H. R. P. Dickson, Political Agent Kuwait, to the Political Resident in the Persian Gulf, 31 August 1929, no. 505.

33. Dickson, *Kuwait and Her Neighbours*, pp.316-17.

34. IO L/P&S/10/1243, letter from Lieutenant-Colonel H. R. P. Dickson, Political Agent Kuwait, to the Political Resident in the Persian Gulf, 20 June 1929, no. 394.

35. IO L/P&S/10/1246, letter from 'Abd al-'Azīz to the British Agent and Consul, 15 Jamad al-Ukhra 1348 (? January 1930).

36. See IO L/P&S/10/1247. An independent army, formed from Banī Hajir, Banī Khālid and Al Murra badu, as well as townsmen, held northern al-Aḥsā. Ibn Musā'id controlled the second group, predominantly townspeople from Jabal Shammar and Shammar Ikhwan. 'Abd al-'Azīz's group was composed of townsmen from al-Qaṣīm and districts in Central Arabia and Muṭair, Subai', Qaḥṭān, Dawāsīr and 'Utaiba badu.

37. IO L/P&S/10/1246, Minute Paper Note, J. G. Laithwaite, Private Secretary to the Secretary of State, 2 January 1930.

38. Habib, 'The Ikhwan Movement of Najd', pp.281-91; and Dickson, *Kuwait and Her Neighbours*, pp.323-8.

39. IO L/P&S/10/1243, letter from Lieutenant-Colonel H. R. P. Dickson, Political Agent Kuwait, to the Political Resident in the Persian Gulf, 1 July 1929, no. 406.

EPILOGUE

The dichotomy of Al Saud authority after 1932 was that so-called modern bureaucratic loyalties continued to be associated with traditional economic, social and religious patterns of identification. Although the Al Saud had been forced to adopt certain Western concepts to ensure the continued survival of their rule, the changes were primarily facade. Najd remained virtually isolated from non-Arab and non-Muslim influences well into the mid-twentieth century. Foreign consular offices were established in Jidda rather than al-Riyad. The Al Saud maintained a roving court or *majlis* even though it centralised political decision making. The middle class was nascent and remained so. Skilled help was imported and then kept in separate communities. Labour unions were banned. Government functions became delineated very late on. Many of the Ministries — Education, Interior, Agriculture, Health, Commerce and Industry — were not established until the 1950s. The Ministry of Justice was established only in 1970. This is, however, a story for another time.

The single major factor which differentiated Saudi authority in the first three decades of the twentieth century from earlier periods of Saudi rule was the firm establishment of control through enforcement of the Western concepts of 'boundary' and 'nation-state'. These concepts, introduced during the post-World War I mandate period, formed the basis of the Middle East state system as it is known at present. Even though revolutions sometimes were to change the actual governing power within these countries, the 'state' persisted, affecting patterns of political behaviour between Arab rulers and between a ruler and the populations of his country.

In the case of Saudi Arabia, government functions and authority were centralised in the hands of one family — the Al Saud — whose authority was further reinforced after 1932 by the international recognition of Saudi hereditary 'kingship' and previously unexploited oil wealth, the revenues of which were controlled by the Al Saud.

APPENDIX

Al Saud Leadership In Central Arabia Prior To World War I

The period between 1910 and 1914 witnessed a series of informal meetings between Abd al-Aziz and the British, Abd al-Aziz and the Ottoman Porte, and the British and the Ottomans. It was a time for bargaining. The Al Saud gradually increased their control in Najd, but sought support for their continued rule from either Britain or the Ottoman Porte. Meanwhile, Great Britain was making every effort to appease the Ottomans and assure them of her continued loyalty, although suspicion began to grow on both sides as the war approached. With the advent of World War I, the first stage of Britain's Middle Eastern diplomacy ended, as Britain and the Ottomans became adversaries. Britain then began to enter into direct treaty relations with Middle Eastern leaders, her policy being to deal with a single representative in what she considered was an autonomous political unit.

Until the war, Britain had concentrated on establishing her influence in the area under the auspices of the Ottoman Porte. This did not preclude informal, if controversial, contacts with local leaders in Ottoman territories and Britain made just such contacts with the Al Saud. In February 1910 and again in March 1911, Captain W. H. Shakespear, British Political Agent in Kuwait, met Abd al-Aziz in the Kuwait hinterland. No politics were discussed at their first meeting, but at a subsequent meeting Abd al-Aziz expressed his dislike of the Ottomans and their methods of government and his desire for British protection similar to that which had been extended to the Arabian Gulf shaikhs. His aim was clear: if his rule were contested by other Central Arabian leaders he could call upon the British for their promised support. His major rivals, the Al Rashid in northern Najd, were already supported by the Ottomans. However, British policy in the Middle East was to support 'a strong Turkey in Asia', which would act as a buffer between her own interests in India and the interests of her European rivals there. Britain was thus reluctant to make formal agreements with local leaders in territory recognised *de jure* as Ottoman, as this might adversely affect her own relationship with Turkey. This was particularly true of an area such as Najd which was of little immediate importance to Britain, either geographically or politically.

The Ottomans meanwhile were worried because they had heard rumours of an impending coalition between the disenchanted Arabian leaders on the fringes of their empire. These leaders included the Al Saud, Al Rashid, Hashimites in al-Hijaz, and tribal leaders in Asir and Mesopotamia. The Ottomans feared that Britain's Middle East presence might undermine the loyalty of their own subjects. Consequently, a series of discussions opened in 1911 between the Ottomans and the British with the primary aim of delimiting their various spheres of control in the Arabian Gulf littoral and in the southern region of the Arabian Peninsula, as well as discussing general issues regarding the Baghdad Railway and customs duties.

These discussions led to an agreement in 1913 which was eventually incorporated into a broader set of provisions known as the Anglo–Turkish Convention. It was signed in March and ratified on 5 June 1914. One result of the treaty was that the Ottomans relinquished territory of which they were no longer in *de facto* control. In Article II Ottoman authority was recognised in Central Arabia and al-Hijaz in exchange for the Ottomans' formal relinquishment of control over certain areas such as Qatar on the Arabian Gulf and Aden in Yaman. Najd was signed away by the British to the Ottomans although Abd al-Aziz was in *de facto* control of Najd and al-Ahsa. An attempt was made to placate the Saudi leader by conferring upon him the Ottoman title Mutasarrif of Najd.

Undoubtedly the British entered into this treaty with hopes of strengthening the Ottoman Empire and securing the latter's goodwill in the event of war. This did not happen: four months later Turkey allied itself to the Central Powers and Britain was placed in a most 'awkward' position. As she was already the predominant influence in the Arabian Gulf, whatever rights or advantages Britain might have gained by the Anglo – Turkish Convention were abrogated by the war. Leaders such as the Al Saud remained in *de facto* possession of territory that Britain had just agreed was to be under Ottoman jurisdiction.

Be that as it may, the British were committed to the support and encouragement of the Ottomans until the war, and any moves on the part of the local Arab leaders 'to combine either in a constitutional agitation for devolution or autonomy or in an avowedly Separatist movement' would cause serious problems. Sir Louis Mallet, British Ambassador to Istanbul, summed up the potential difficulties of the situation in a letter dated 18 March 1914 to Sir Edward Grey of the Foreign Office.

> The need for caution is apparent at the present moment, when there is evidence of a concerted movement on the part of the Arabs. If these projects should mature, and if the Arabs are eventually successful in defeating the Ottoman armies, the loss of the Caliphate would probably follow, when, shorn of a further large portion of territory and of the religious leadership, Turkish rule, as it exists to-day, would presumably disappear. Europe might then be faced with the question of a partition of the Turkish Empire, which might easily produce complications of a serious nature.[1]

The need for caution was apparent and right until the last moment Britain hoped to conciliate the Ottomans. Meanwhile she began to receive disturbing reports about the dissatisfaction of Arab leaders on the fringes of the Ottoman Empire who were 'sinking their personal differences in order to enforce nationalist aspirations as against the Central Government'. The Ottoman Porte was also aware of a possible Arab alliance. In January 1914 Colonel Erskine, Britain's Acting Consul-General in Baghdad, reported that the coalition consisted of the Grand Sharif Husain of Mecca, Al Rashid in northern Najd, Al Sadun of the Muntafiq in southern Mesopotamia, Saiyid Talib of Basra and Al Saud of Najd.[2] Erskine felt that there was little chance of cohesion because of internal frictions. A further report was received in May 1914 from Shakespear who was in the privileged position of being shown the actual correspondence between Abd al-Aziz and Saiyid Muhammad al-Idrisi, Imam Yahya of Sanaa, Ibn Shalan of the great Anaza tribe, and others of lesser importance. He reported that Ibn Rashid, who had succeeded to the leadership of northern Najd, was just a young boy with 'no real authority over his own tribesmen' and had therefore been excluded from the alliance.

> During the past year there has arisen a loose kind of confederation or alliance between the following Chiefs — Bin Saud, Imam Yahyah, Sayid Mahomed al-Idrisi, Bin Sha'alan and the Sharif of Mecca [Husain], with only Ibn Rashid the Shammar Chief left outside the coalition. The basis of the alliance is that the allied chiefs should endeavour to settle their differences by agreement or arbitration as war between them only weakens all parties as against the common enemy [Ottomans], that in the event of any aggression by the Porte upon any one of these Sheikhs all should combine for resistance and mutual help.[3]

It is interesting to note that, in an earlier meeting between Abd al-Aziz and Shakespear in 1913, and in a meeting of 1914, the former had stated that all the Arab leaders had formed a loose alliance, with the exception of Sharif Husain of Mecca who feared a Wahhabi invasion of al-Hijaz and, consequently, was allied to the Turks. The Hashimites and the Al Saud had an historic antipathy towards each other, which increased from this time on, culminating in the capture of al-Hijaz in 1925. Although there was correspondence between the Al Saud of Najd and Al Hashim of al-Hijaz, there is no evidence to show that Sharif Husain ever considered participation in this alliance. As is now known, the Sharif began negotiations with Great Britain in 1914.

The British were uncomfortably aware that these Arab 'malcontents' were inclined 'to look to His Majesty's Government for sympathy in their movement and even for eventual protection if they are successful in achieving their independence' and that the Ottomans undoubtedly suspected this. In 1914 Sir Louis reported from Istanbul that Ottoman doubts about British intentions had turned to outright distrust when they heard that a British agent had visited Kuwait and talked with Abd al-Aziz shortly before the latter's capture of al-Ahsa from Turkish troops.[4] Official records indicate that this was in fact a straightforward meeting and that Shakespear, who was the agent in question, had told Abd al-Aziz that the British could not help him in any way. However, the coincidence between the timing of this meeting and the Saudi capture of al-Ahsa was too remarkable to be believed by the Ottomans. Sir Louis stated in strong terms that Britain was effectively bound by the July 1913 agreement with the Ottomans and was thus prevented from dealing further with the Al Saud for the moment.

> . . . for the present . . . impossible to expect the Turkish Government to believe in the innocence of our motives and intentions. If we speak to them of a new situation of fact they will say that the new situation dates from before our agreement with them of July last. If we say that our only desire is to promote peace in Arabia and the integrity of the Empire, they will say, or rather, think, without saying it, that for us to treat Bin Sa'ud in a way which he and all his neighbours will construe as a sort of recognition of his *de facto* independence is a singular way of helping them to keep their Empire together. If we say that we have [no] axes to grind in the Ottoman World in Turkey, and foresee no profit to ourselves in an upheaval, they will receive our assurances with the politest incredulity.[5]

Unknown to Sir Louis, events had begun to develop their own momentum and it was beyond anyone's ability to alter them. Abd al-Aziz had heard through Saiyid Talib of the proposals in the Anglo – Turkish Convention and an offer to make him Mutasarrif of Najd. During a third meeting, from 30 March to 4 April 1913, he confronted Shakespear and asked why the British would not support him against the Turks, whom he continually stigmatised for moral laxity. Corrupt in their religious duties, it was inevitable that Ottoman rule would be irresponsible. They were

> a people who, calling themselves Musalmans, had for years neglected their faith, oppressed their subjects, embezzled religious endowments, broken every ordinance of the Koran and subverted the Khalifat . . . and would be ready to find another Khalifa tomorrow if a change should suit them.[6]

Moreover, the Ottomans had been continually harassing the Arab leaders to accept Turkish titles and to send members of their families for education in Istanbul and for service in the Ottoman army as well as demanding to see all their correspondence with foreign powers, a reflection of their desire to be sole arbiter in

Arabian affairs and to circumvent British influence. Abd al-Aziz knew it was only a question of time before the Ottomans would exploit differences in the Arab alliance and prise loose the pieces which were so essential to the united strength of the Arabs in the Peninsula. He himself could not stand alone and with astute foresight he intimated that time was now his enemy. If the British would not lend their support, then he must determine a course for the future and rely upon his own powers.

Abd al-Aziz's conversation displayed considerable knowledge about events beyond the Peninsula. He discussed the recent Ottoman defeats in Tripoli and the Balkans, the disorganisation of her army and her bankrupt treasury, and the Arab nationalist demands for reform and freedom in Beirut, Baghdad, Damascus and Basra. Shakespear noted that Abd al-Aziz 'was determined sooner or later to turn the Turks from Hasa [al-Ahsa] and Katif [al-Qatif] and if it could not be managed by diplomacy, it would be done by resort to arms'.[7] Because of the expansion of the Saudi family in the previous two centuries, the Al Saud claimed an ancestral right to these domains. There were also, however, important tactical and economic incentives for the acquisition of al-Ahsa, as Abd al-Aziz himself told Shakespear in 1913 in a candid appraisal of Najd finances which was one of the few statements ever made on the subject. Finance was a constant motivating factor in the events of the succeeding two decades.

> To withstand the Turks from both directions they [Al Saud] felt was beyond their strength and to render secure their eastern borders, thus making their full force available for the defence of their western boundaries, was one of the reasons for their desire to evict the Turks from Hasa and Katif. Another most important one was that the possession of these rich districts with their ports and especially Ojair [al-Uqair], would furnish a valuable source of revenue to what was at present an extremely poor state.[8]

Shakespear made the expected diplomatic reply to the Al Saud: he had no power other than relaying Abd al-Aziz's requests and opinions to His Majesty's Government. He warned Abd al-Aziz that there was no hope whatever of British aid if he planned offensive action and that the Turks might retaliate by entering Najd itself.

Interestingly, Shakespear's report to the British Government regarding future events was considerably less firm. With great candour he said that the Arab hatred of Ottoman policies was growing and that, if the latter continued their present stratagems, they would be doomed to failure. Not long before, Shakespear had been informed that the newly appointed Ottoman Wali to Basra had arrived only to be told bluntly that unless he fell into line with local notables he had better depart at once for Istanbul. Shakespear's assessment of Abd al-Aziz and his intentions was an accurate portrayal of future events.

> The man is a ruler of the best Arab type and his personality is one which is likely to lead Arabia should any extensive combination come into being among its tribes, an event which to me seems exceedingly probable in the near future, unless some radical change takes place in Turkish policy towards the Arabs. As soon as some such combination occurs and perhaps even before, I do not think that there is the least doubt that Bin Saud's first move will be on Hasa and Katif, and when that happens it seems to me that we shall be forced into relations with the Amir of Nejd, however much we may desire to avoid him.[9]

Shakespear also reported that, although Abd al-Aziz was disappointed at Britain's lack of encouragement, 'he showed no annoyance or resentment but merely remarked that someday we would be forced by circumstance to take up his case'. The British government did not have to wait long before Shakespear's prophecy and Abd al-Aziz's remark came true. Less than five days after Shakespear sent his first report about their meeting to the Political Resident in the Persian Gulf, he sent a second report announcing the details of a Saudi conquest of al-Ahsa region.[10]

The swiftness of Saudi movements surprised everyone, including the Kuwait Arabs who had been in frequent contact with them. Camped outside al-Hufuf, capital of al-Ahsa, on 4 May 1913, Abd al-Aziz explained to his followers that the Turks had created a state of chaos in the district by allowing indiscriminate raiding by badu tribes.[11] Furthermore, individuals deserving of punishment had taken refuge in al-Ahsa and local leaders had requested that he intervene in their affairs. He had decided to do so. It was typical of desert policy and his own diplomacy that Abd al-Aziz should seek the opinion and support of his men. All expressed their support for the undertaking and, in an often-used offensive stratagem for the conquest of fortified oasis towns, a small band scaled the walls and opened one of the city's gates so that the remaining troops could enter. The Saudi troops consisted of Najd townsmen and only a few badu — in sharp contrast to the heavy reliance placed on the badu forces in later engagements. There was little resistance from the Turkish garrisons, perhaps, as one rumour suggested, because the troops were predominantly Arabs. This rumour was not confirmed, but certainly the open support shown by the citizens of al-Hufuf for Saudi troops could not have helped Ottoman morale. On 5 May the Ottomans surrendered and requested all outlying Turkish garrisons to do the same. At Kut Castle in al-Hufuf, Abd al-Aziz's men obtained twelve guns of different calibres, two mitrailleuses, large quantities of rifles and ammunition, as well as £T.40,000. Word was sent by al-Ahsa leaders and the chief Shiite *mujtahid* for the Kaimakam of al-Qatif to surrender. All Ottoman soldiers were safely escorted to the coast whence they left, never to re-establish control again. Saudi troops also took al-Uqair, replacing the Turkish customs men with their own and lowering the customs duties from eleven per cent to four per cent.

Abd al-Aziz then proceeded to play both ends against the middle, displaying his subtle understanding of the finer points of diplomacy. He presented the British with a *fait accompli* in his capture of al-Ahsa and his new position on the Gulf. That his military manoeuvre gave him a diplomatic success cannot be doubted and he continued to solicit British aid while not yet severing his Ottoman links. The following statement is representative of the vast number of communications that passed in the next months between the lowest and the highest decision-making offices in the British government.

> Bin Saud is becoming a more and more prominent factor in the politics of the Persian Gulf littoral, and has thus brought himself within the sphere of our interests and influence. As long as Bin Saud confined himself to El Hasa [al-Ahsa] he could be ignored with impunity. Such a policy, however, cannot in our opinion safely be pursued now that there is a possibility of his interference in El Katr, with the Trucial Chiefs, and possibly in Oman where rebellion may give him an opportunity for encroachment on Muscat territory. It seems to us therefore that we must now decide whether he is to be conciliated or estranged.[12]

Abd al-Aziz unilaterally informed the Ottomans through the medium of Talib in Basra that he was a loyal Ottoman, but that they were corrupt and had failed to subsidise him so that he was 'resuming direct administration' of the Sanjaq of al-Ahsa. The use of the term *sanjaq* was a reference to an Ottoman administrative district and thus Abd al-Aziz was attempting to placate the Ottoman Porte.[13]

Britain was now confronted with a dilemma. If Abd al-Aziz's *de facto* control of al-Ahsa was recognised, as it generally was, then the only question affecting Britain's long-term strategy in the Middle East was whether his control would be temporary or permanent. As regards short-term policy, the British knew that they could not continue to hold al-Ahsa as 'politically derelict and having no administrative head with whom we can deal in matters affecting British subjects'.[14]

Therefore, on 15 and 16 December 1913 the first formal meeting was held between the British government, represented by Captain Shakespear and Major A. P. Trevor, and the Al Saud, represented by Abd al-Aziz, at al-Uqair. Wrapped cautiously in diplomatic language was the tentative beginning of a relationship which would lead to mutual recognition of their strengths. Despite the Saudi capture of al-Ahsa, however, it is important to realise that at this early date Abd al-Aziz was still regarded by the British as simply the 'amir of southern Najd'. The British were negotiating the Anglo – Turkish Convention at this very time and, while they might recognise the wisdom of establishing contact with the Saudi family, they had little reason as yet to be seriously alarmed.

By contrast, Abd al-Aziz in 1913 was maintaining a tenuous balance between an Ottoman Empire that had *de jure* control over his territory and a European government which could tangibly encourage his hopes of independence under the autonomous rule of his family. He admitted to Shakespear and Trevor that he felt a relationship with Britain was a necessary safeguard to himself and asked them what the stated 'goodwill' of their government actually meant. He further revealed that his position was crucial from several points of view. On the one hand, he had been pressed by the Turks since August 1913 to recognise their suzerainty; on the other hand, he was concerned about three major issues of diplomatic importance. First, as mentioned earlier, there was a great deal of badu raiding and general unrest resulting from Ottoman rule. The Al Rashid, who were pro-Ottoman, remained a potential threat in northern Najd. Second, by his own admission, Abd al-Aziz's finances were extremely low and he was having difficulty simply maintaining a military force, although this was not to be revealed to the British envoys until the next meeting. Third, the Araif, exiled members of another branch of the Al Saud, and other recalcitrant badu tribes had contested Abd al-Aziz's rule from the sanctuary of territories under British influence. Abd al-Aziz protested on the grounds of customary tribal law.

> Bin Saud raised the question of the policy of the British Government in Katar and Trucial Oman with special reference to their attitude in regard to enemies of his who might take sanctuary in these states and then use them as a base for intriguing against him, or as a retreat after inciting some Bedouin tribe to revolt against him. He said that of course he had not the slightest objection to fugitives from his wrath taking refuge with the neighbouring Shaikhs in accordance with the usual Arab custom, provided that they did not use their sanctuary as a base for intrigue; but if they did so he would be compelled to take steps for his own safety.[15]

During this December 1913 meeting Shakespear and Trevor were also informed about the conditions of a proposed treaty between the Ottomans and Abd al-Aziz. Of the eleven articles which it contained, five had been proposed by Abd al-Aziz and were aimed at securing 'an assured, autonomous, and probably hereditary' authority. Trevor reported that Abd al-Aziz had insisted that he was to have control of the coast and over the appointment of its local officials. The British themselves had no worries regarding these demands, especially as they were well aware that Turkish rule had been ineffective in al-Ahsa. Badu tribes raided freely and then escaped from control by crossing the political frontiers. Owing to their physical elusiveness and their shifting alliances, it was virtually impossible to establish security. There was a general dissatisfaction among the merchant/agriculturalist communities of the settled areas. The British did, however, have cause to be worried about the six articles proposed by the Turks: reinstatement of Turkish garrisons, appointment by the Ottoman Porte of judicial officers, payment of tribute to the Ottoman Porte of £T.3,000 *per annum*, no concessions to be granted by the Saudis for foreign rail and motor services, exclusion of foreign merchants and political representatives, and all communications with foreign powers to be mediated by the Turks. The last two were of particular economic and political importance to the British, to her Arab partners in the Arabian Gulf and to her Indian Muslim merchants who frequently traded with al-Ahsa from Bahrain during the pearling season. They were precisely the issues over which Britain itself had insisted on maintaining control.

The meeting was adjourned on the understanding that, if Britain intervened and recognised the *de facto* as well as *de jure* position of Abd al-Aziz in Najd, then the Saudis would suppress piracy, arms traffic and slaving, respect the conditions of the Maritime Truce and the inviolability of British authority in Qatar and Trucial Oman, admit traders, and co-operate in all other matters of joint interest. Abd al-Aziz further arranged to delay any formal agreements with the Turks for three months, by which time he hoped to have an agreement with the British.

Abd al-Aziz himself stressed that he would not under any circumstances agree to the garrisoning of Turkish troops in Najd again, as this would signal the end of his political independence. No doubt he also remembered with hatred the earlier occupation of Najd and the deportation and execution of his ancestors in the early 1800s. Shakespear for his part reported that any military operation to occupy Najd or al-Ahsa would be exceedingly difficult, if not impossible.

> I would hesitate to suggest that less than two divisions, completely equipped for a long desert war, would be able to re-establish and maintain effectively the former Turkish occupation of the Hasa province. The Turkish occupation before May 1913 was not effective in any sense . . . he could have carried out his coup of May 1913 at any time in the last five years.[16]

Three months later, on 9 March 1914, Shakespear reached al-Riyad on an unofficial visit lasting six days. Abd al-Aziz was anxious about Britain's reaction to the earlier December meeting and once again reiterated his wishes and needs to the British, but Shakespear could promise nothing. Shakespear reported to Sir Arthur Hirtzel, Secretary to the Political Department in London, the motivating forces behind Abd al-Aziz's policies, highlighting the importance of economic considerations.

> He said he had no intention of committing himself definitely to the Turks so long as he had any chance of arriving at an arrangement with the British Government or at least of obtaining our support or good offices in his negotiations with the Turks, but at the same time he could not wait indefinitely and continue to maintain a large force in the field; and, unless he could obtain some sort of assurance he would be compelled to make his own arrangements in order to obtain a temporary respite at least from having to remain continually on guard.[17]

However, Abd al-Aziz was informed on 29 April 1914 by Lieutenant-Colonel W. G. Grey, Political Agent in Kuwait, that the British could do nothing to help him. They suggested that Abd al-Aziz should negotiate directly with the Ottomans as Britain had made its own treaty with the Turks in the interim. Grey's report concluded that 'I confess that I return to Kuwait without a clear idea of what course Bin Sa'ud was likely to take, in fact I doubt whether he has himself come as yet to a definite decision'.[18]

In May Abd al-Aziz did in fact meet the Turks and Crow reported to Sir Louis what he had heard of the meeting.

> I am informed that, when the Turkish Commission met Bin Saud at Koweit, the Mutessarif of Hasa presented the latter with a letter from Enver Pasha, together with a revolver and a Koran. The letter requested Bin Saud to restore Hasa to the Ottoman Government. Bin Saud, in reply, is reported to have sent Enver Pasha his own dagger, and to have informed the Commission that El Hasa was his property, and therefore he could not hand it over to the Turks, as he was the Amir of Nejd.[19]

It was also reported, however, that the Turks had been openly soliciting the Al Rashid. Asked whether they could recapture al-Ahsa, the Al Rashid had replied in the affirmative provided that they could have Turkish troops. Because of these Ottoman manoeuvres and Britain's inability to offer support, the Al Saud were forced to enter into discussions with the Turks for their political survival.

The only way of guarding the rights of Abd al-Aziz was

undoubtedly the establishment of an assured, autonomous rule in Najd under the leadership of the Al Saud. A treaty was subsequently signed on 15 May 1914. Article 2 of the treaty provided for the rule of Abd al-Aziz to succeed to his 'sons and grandsons'. Although the treaty was signed, it was never ratified, owing to the outbreak of war. It is unlikely that, even if it had been ratified, Abd al-Aziz would have regarded it as anything more than a temporary hindrance to his ambitions. He was well aware that the Ottoman policy of *divide et impera* would at some stage be directed against him. In the six months preceding February 1914, a large arms consignment had been shipped to Hail, the capital of the Al Rashid, from Damascus. Arab leaders in al-Hijaz had confirmed reports that some 30,000 Mauser and Mannlicher rifles with bayonets, hundreds of boxes of ammunition and three breech-loading mountain guns each with 500 shrapnel shells had been shipped. Three Europeans, supposedly artillerymen, had been sent overland by car. It is easy to understand Al Saud distrust of the Turks, and the Turks, for their part, could hardly trust the gradually increasing power of the Al Saud and their leadership of an Arab alliance.

> the Arabs have now found a leader [Abd al-Aziz] who stands head and shoulders above any other chief and in whose star all have implicit faith. The other sheikhs of the Arab alliance refer all kinds of matters to Bin Sa'ud for his advice, more especially those affecting their relations with the Porte.[20]

Between 1910 and 1914 every power — Ottoman, British, Arab — was jockeying for a stronger position. Each had something to bargain with. The British wanted a 'strong Turkey in Asia', but that did not preclude their informal and serious discussions prior to World War I with Arab leaders in territory the Ottomans recognised as theirs. While the Ottomans were attempting to have the Al Saud recognise their authority, they were simultaneously shipping arms and advisers to a Saudi rival. Great Britain and the Ottomans concluded an agreement to delineate their spheres of influence, but local leaders in *de facto* control of their territory were not consulted and Arab dissatisfaction in the Arabian Peninsula increased, leading to the formation of an alliance by Arab leaders. Individual leaders like Abd al-Aziz could hate the Turks for their oppression of his family and the abuse of his people, but he could not yet make an outright break with them without risking the personal loss of his rule. The British represented not so much a substitute for Turkish rule as a means to an end: they were a political tool that could ensure Saudi political survival until the time came when Al Saud strength could stand independently.

Notes

1. India Office Records, *Political and Secret Department Separate Files 1902-1031*, L/P&S/10 (henceforward abbreviated to IO L/P&S/10): IO L/P&S/10/385, telegram from Sir Louis Mallet, British Ambassador, Istanbul, to Sir Edward Grey, Secretary of the Foreign Office, 18 March 1914 [13871], no. 193.
2. Ibid.
3. IO L/P&S/10/385, letter from Captain W. H. I. Shakespear, Political Agent Kuwait, to Sir Arthur Hirtzel, Secretary of the Political Department of the India Office, 26 June 1914.
4. IO L/P&S/10/385, telegram from Sir Louis Mallet, British Ambassador, Istanbul, to Sir Edward Grey, Secretary of the Foreign Office, 12 May 1914 [22042], no. 335.
5. Ibid.
6. IO L/P&S/10/384, letter from Captain W. H. I. Shakespear, Political Agent Kuwait, to the Political Resident in the Persian Gulf, 15 May 1913, no. C-10.
7. Ibid.
8. Ibid.
9. Ibid.
10. IO L/P&S/10/384, letter from Captain W. H. I. Shakespear, Political Agent Kuwait, to the Political Resident in the Persian Gulf, 20 May 1913, no. C-12.
11. Aḥmad ʻAbd al-Ghafūr ʻAṭṭār, *ṣaqr al-jazīra*, 7 vols (Maṭbaʻat al-Ḥurrīya, Beirut, 1972), pp.393-409.
12. IO L/P&S/10/384, telegram from the Viceroy to the Secretary of State, 10 August 1913, Foreign Secret.
13. IO L/P&S/10/212, 'Turkish Arabian Summaries', compiled by J. G. Lorimer, Political Resident in the Persian Gulf.
14. IO L/P&S/10/385, letter from J. G. Lorimer, Political Resident in the Persian Gulf, to the Secretary to the Government of India in the Foreign Department, Delhi, 4 January 1914, no. 24.
15. IO L/P&S/10/385, letter from Major A. P. Trevor, Political Agent Bahrain, to the Political Resident in the Persian Gulf, 20 December 1913, no. T-805.
16. IO L/P&S/10/385, letter from Captain W. H. I. Shakespear, Political Agent Kuwait, to Sir Arthur Hirtzel, Secretary of the Political Department of the India Office, 26 June 1914.
17. Ibid.
18. IO L/P&S/10/385, telegram from F. E. Crow, British Consul in Basra, to Sir Louis Mallet, British Ambassador in Istanbul, 16 May 1914 [27968], no. 32.
19. IO L/P&S/10/385, letter from Lieutenant-Colonel W. G. Grey, Political Agent Kuwait, to the Political Resident in the Persian Gulf, 29 April 1914, C-16 (confidential).
20. IO L/P&S/10/385, letter from Captain W. H. I. Shakespear, Political Agent Kuwait, to Sir Arthur Hirtzel, Secretary of the Political Department of the India Office, 26 June 1914.

BIBLIOGRAPHY

A. Government Documentation

India Office Records: *Political and Secret Department Separate Files 1902-1931*, L/P&S/10

Great Britain: *United Kingdom Memorial* or *Arbitration Concerning Buraimi and the Common Frontier Between Abu Dhabi and Sa'udi Arabia: Memorial Submitted by the Government of Great Britain and Northern Ireland*, 3 vols (1955)

Saudi Arabia: *'arḍ ḥukūmat al-mamlaka al-'arabīya al-sa'ūdīya: al-taḥkīm ma'a masqaṭ wa abū ẓabī*, or *The Sa'udi Memorial*, 3 vols (1374ه (1955))

B. Unpublished Reference Material

Butler, S. S., 'A Journey into Unknown Arabia, in 1908, living as, and with, the Bedouin' (travel diary)

Dragnich, George Stephen, 'The Bedouin Warrior Ethic and the Transformation of Traditional Nomadic Warriors into Modern Soldiers within the Arab Legion, 1931-48' (MA thesis, Georgetown University, 1975)

Habib, John S., 'The Ikhwan Movement of Najd: Its Rise, Development, and Decline' (PhD thesis, University of Michigan, 1970)

Kelly, J. B., 'The Qatar Frontier, Khaur al-'Udaid and the North-Western Frontier of Abu Dhabi' (confidential research paper, 1977)

Philby, H. St John B., *Private Papers Collection* (diaries, engagement books, memoranda, letters) (St Antony's College, Middle East Centre, Oxford)

Rentz, George S., 'Muḥammad ibn 'Abd al-Wahhāb (1703/04-1792) and the Beginnings of the Unitarian Empire in Arabia' (PhD thesis, University of California at Berkeley, 1948)

Shakespear, W. H., *Private Papers Collection* ('Journal of a Trip via Central Arabia to Egypt', memoranda, letters, photographs) in the possession of Major-General J. D. Lunt, Oxford

Silverfarb, Daniel, 'British Relations with Ibn Saud of Najd 1914-1919' (PhD thesis, University of Wisconsin, 1972)

C. Published Reference Material

'Abd al-Wahhāb, see Wahhāb, Muḥammad b. 'Abd al-

Abu Hakima, Ahmad Mustafa, *History of Eastern Arabia 1750-1800: The Rise and Development of Bahrain and Kuwait* (Khayats, Beirut, 1965)

Aḥmed, Manzooruddīn, 'Key Political Concepts in the Qur'ān', *Islamic Studies*, 10 (1971), pp.77-102

Ahmed, Ziauddin, 'Aḥmad B. Ḥanbal and the Problems of 'Īmān', *Islamic Studies*, 12 (1973), pp.261-70

—— 'Some Aspects of the Political Theology of Aḥmad B. Ḥanbal', *Islamic Studies*, 12 (1973), pp.53-66

Aitchison, C. U., *A Collection of Treaties, Engagements and Sanads Relating to India and Neighbouring Countries*, vol. XI (Kraus Reprint, Nendeln/Liechtenstein, 1973)

Albaharna, Husain M., *The Legal Status of the Arabian Gulf States: A Study of Their Treaty Relations and Their International Problems* (Manchester University Press, Manchester, 1968)

Ali, Moulavi Cherágh, *A Critical Exposition of the Popular 'Jihád', Showing That All the Wars of Mohammad Were Defensive; and That Aggressive War, or Compulsory Conversion, Is Not Allowed in the Koran* (Thacker and Spink, Calcutta, 1885)

Alireza, Marianne, *At the Drop of a Veil* (Houghton Mifflin, Boston, 1971)

Allan, Mea, *Palgrave of Arabia: The Life of William Gifford*

Palgrave 1826-1888 (Macmillan, London, 1972)
'Alun Yale', 'The Future of the Caliphate', *Moslem World*, 14 (1924), pp.342-53
Amīn, Bakrī Shaikh, *al-ḥarakat al-adabīya fī al-mamlaka al-'arabīya al-su'ūdīya* (Dār Ṣādir, Beirut, 1972)
Anderson, M. S., *The Eastern Question 1774-1923: A Study in International Relations* (Macmillan, London, 1974)
Anonymous, 'The Boundaries of the Nejd: A Note on Special Conditions', *Geographical Review*, 17 (1927), pp.128-34
Antonius, George, *The Arab Awakening: The Story of the Arab National Movement* (Librairie du Liban, Beirut, 1969)
Arnold, Sir Thomas W., *The Caliphate* (Clarendon Press, Oxford, 1924)
Asad, Muhammad, *The Principles of State and Government in Islam* (University of California Press, Berkeley, 1961)
'Aṭṭār, Aḥmad 'Abd al-Ghafūr, *ṣaqr al-jazīra*, 7 vols (Maṭba'at al-Ḥurrīya, Beirut, 1972)
Bacon, Elizabeth, 'Types of Pastoral Nomadism in Central and Southwest Asia', *Southwestern Journal of Anthropology*, 10 (1954), pp.44-68
Beaumont, Peter, 'Water and Development in Saudi Arabia', *Geographical Journal*, 143 (1977), pp.42-60
Belhaven, Lord, *The Uneven Road* (John Murray, London, 1955)
Blondel, Jean, *Thinking Politically* (Penguin, Harmondsworth, 1978)
Blunt, Lady Anne, *A Pilgrimage to Najd*, 2 vols (John Murray, London, 1881)
—— *Bedouin Tribes of the Euphrates*, 2 vols (John Murray, London, 1879)
Brown, Edward Hoagland, *The Saudi Arabia Kuwait Neutral Zone* (The Middle East Research and Publishing Center, Beirut, 1963)
Brydges, Harford Jones, *An Account of the Transactions of His Majesty's Mission to the Court of Persia in the Years 1807-11, to which is Appended a Brief History of the Wahauby*, 2 vols (James Bohn, London, 1834)
Bullard, Sir Reader, *The Camels Must Go: An Autobiography* (Faber and Faber, London, 1961)
Burckhardt, John Lewis, *Notes on the Bedouins and Wahábys*, 2 vols (no publisher listed, London, 1831)
—— *Travels in Arabia* (no publisher listed, London, 1829)

Burton, Sir Richard F., *Pilgrimage to Al Medinah and Meccah*, 2 vols (George Bell and Sons, London, 1907)

Busch, Briton Cooper, *Britain and the Persian Gulf, 1894-1914* (University of California Press, Berkeley, 1967)

Caskel, Werner, 'The Bedouinization of Arabia', in C. E. Von Grunebaum (ed.), *Studies in Islamic Cultural History* (The American Anthropological Association Memoirs no. 76, Menasha, Wisconsin, 1954)

Cheesman, R. E., *In Unknown Arabia* (Macmillan, London, 1926)

Clayton, Sir Gilbert Falkingham, *An Arabian Diary* (edited by Robert O. Collins) (University of California Press, Berkeley, 1969)

Cohen, Saul B. and Lewis D. Rosenthal, 'A Geographical Model for Political Systems Analysis', *Geographical Review*, 61 (1971), pp.5-31

Cole, Donald, *Nomads of the Nomads: The Āl Murrah Bedouin of the Empty Quarter* (AHM Publishing Corporation, Arlington Heights, Illinois, 1975)

Cragg, Kenneth, *The Event of the Qur'ān: Islam in its Scripture* (George Allen and Unwin, London, 1971)

Dakhīl, Sulaimān al-, '*aqsām imārat al-su'ūd*', *Lughat al-'Arab*, 3 (1914), pp.350-9

—— '*al-arṭawīya au balad jadīda fī diyār najd*', *Lughat al-'Arab*, 2 (1913), pp.481-8

Dame, Louis P., 'Four Months in Nejd', *Moslem World*, 14 (1924), pp.353-62

Dawn, C. Ernest, *From Ottomanism to Arabism: Essays on the Origins of Arab Nationalism* (University of Illinois Press, Urbana, 1973)

De Gaury, Gerald, *Arabia Phoenix* (George G. Harrap, London, 1946)

Dickson, H. R. P., *The Arab of the Desert: A Glimpse into Badawin Life in Kuwait and Sa'udi Arabia* (George Allen and Unwin, London, 1972)

—— *Kuwait and Her Neighbours* (George Allen and Unwin, London, 1968)

Donner, Fred McGraw, 'Mecca's Food Supplies and Muhammad's Boycott', *Journal of the Economic and Social History of the Orient*, 20 (1977), pp.249-66

Doughty, Charles M., *Travels in Arabia Deserta* (Jonathan Cape and The Medici Society, London, 1926)

Edmonds, C. J., *Kurds, Turks and Arabs: Politics, Travel and Research in North-Eastern Iraq 1919-1925* (Oxford University Press, London, 1957)

Elphinston, W. G., 'The Future of the Bedouin of Northern Arabia', *International Affairs*, 21 (1945), pp.370-5

Evans-Pritchard, E. E., *The Sanusi of Cyrenaica* (Clarendon Press, Oxford, 1973)

Fisher, W. B., *The Middle East: A Physical, Social and Regional Geography* (Methuen, London, 1971)

Forand, Paul G., 'Notes on *'ušr* and *maks*', *Arabica*, 13 (1966), pp.137-41

Gibb, H. A. R., 'Al-Māwardī's Theory of the Khilāfah', *Islamic Culture*, 11 (1937), pp.291-302

—— *Modern Trends in Islam* (University of Chicago Press, Chicago, 1947)

—— *Mohammedanism: An Historical Survey* (Oxford University Press, Oxford, 1969)

Glubb, Sir John Bagot, *Arabian Adventures: Ten Years of Joyful Service* (Cassell, London, 1978)

—— *War in the Desert: An R.A.F. Frontier Campaign* (Hodder and Stoughton, London, 1960)

Graves, Philip P., *The Life of Sir Percy Cox* (Hutchinson, London, 1941)

—— *Memoirs of King Abdullah of Transjordan* (edited by Graves) (Jonathan Cape, London, 1951)

Guarmani, Carlo, *Northern Najd: A Journey from Jerusalem to Anaiza in Qasim* (edited by Douglas Carruthers) (N. Israel, Amsterdam, 1971)

Gubser, Peter, *Politics and Change in Al-Karak, Jordan: A Study of a Small Arab Town and its District* (Oxford University Press, London, 1973)

Haidar, Princess Musbah, *Arabesque* (Hutchinson, London, 1948)

Haim, Sylvia G. (ed.), *Arab Nationalism: An Anthology* (University of California Press, Berkeley, 1976)

Ḥamza, Fu'ād, *qalb jazīrat al-'arab* (Maktaba al-Naṣr al-Ḥadītha, al-Riyāḍ, 1388 (1968))

Harrison, Paul W., 'Al Riadh, The Capital of Nejd', *Moslem World*, 8 (1918), pp.412-19

—— *The Arab at Home* (Thomas Y. Crowell, New York, 1924)

—— 'Economic and Social Conditions in East Arabia', *Moslem World*, 14 (1924), pp.163-71

Hasan, Mohammed Salman, 'The Role of Foreign Trade in the Economic Development of Iraq, 1864-1964: A Study in the Growth of a Dependent Economy', in A. M. Cook (ed.), *Studies in the Economic History of the Middle East* (Oxford University Press, London, 1970)

Hogarth, David George, *Arabia* (Clarendon Press, Oxford, 1922)

—— *Hejaz Before World War I* (Oleander Press/Falcon Press, Cambridge, 1978)

—— *The Penetration of Arabia* (Alston Rivers, London, 1905)

Holt, P. M., *Egypt and the Fertile Crescent 1516-1922: A Political History* (Cornell University Press, Ithaca, 1966)

Hopwood, Derek (ed.)., *The Arabian Peninsula: Society and Politics* (George Allen and Unwin, London, 1972)

Howarth, David, *The Desert King: Ibn Saud and His Arabia* (McGraw-Hill, New York, 1964)

Ibn Bishr, 'Uthmān b. 'Abdullāh, al-Najdī al-Ḥanbalī, *'unwān al-majd fī ta'rīkh najd* (Ṣādir, Beirut, 1387 (1967))

Ibn Khaldūn, *The Muqaddimah: An Introduction to History* (Routledge and Kegan Paul, London, 1967)

Ibn Taimīya, *al-siyāsat al-shar'īya* (Dār al-Kutub al-'Arabīya, Beirut, 1966)

—— *Ibn Taimiyya on Public and Private Law in Islam or Public Policy in Islamic Jurisprudence* (Khayats, Beirut, 1966)

Iqbal, Sheikh Muhammad, *Emergence of Saudi Arabia: A Political Study of King Abd al-Aziz ibn Saud 1901-1953* (Saudiyah, Shrinagar, Kashmir, 1977)

Jabbur, Jibra'il, 'Abū al-Duhūr, the Ruwalah '*Uṭfah*', in James Kritzeck and R. Bayly Winder (eds), *The World of Islam* (Macmillan, London, 1959)

Johnson, Douglas L., *The Nature of Nomadism: A Comparative Study of Pastoral Migrations in Southwestern Asia and Northern Africa* (Department of Geography Research Paper no. 118, University of Chicago, Chicago, 1969)

Jones, Stephen B., 'A Unified Field Theory of Political Geography', in Roger E. Kasperson and Julian V. Minghi (eds), *The Structure of Political Geography* (University of London Press, London, 1969)

Jurji, E. J., 'The Islamic Theory of War', *Muslim World*, 30 (1940), pp.332-42

Juynboll, G. H. A., 'The Date of the Great *Fitna*', *Arabica*, 20 (1973), pp.142-59

Karpat, Kemal H., *Political and Social Thought in the Contemporary Middle East* (Frederick A. Praeger, London, 1968)

Kedourie, Elie, *Nationalism* (Hutchinson University Library, London, 1966)

—— 'The Surrender of Medina, January 1919', *Middle East Studies*, 13 (1977), pp.124-43

Kelly, J. B., *Britain and the Persian Gulf 1795-1880* (Clarendon Press, Oxford, 1968)

—— *Eastern Arabian Frontiers* (Faber and Faber, London, 1964)

Kennett, Austin, *Bedouin Justice: Law and Customs Among the Egyptian Bedouin* (Frank Cass, London, 1968)

Khadduri, Majid, *War and Peace in the Law of Islam* (Johns Hopkins Press, Baltimore, 1955)

Kirkbride, Sir Alec, *An Awakening: The Arab Campaign 1917-18* (University Press of Arabia, Tavistock, England, 1971)

Kristof, Ladis K. D., 'The Nature of Frontiers and Boundaries', in Roger E. Kasperson and Julian V. Minghi (eds), *The Structure of Political Geography* (University of London Press, London, 1969)

Kurd 'Alī, Muḥammad, *al-qadīm wa al-ḥadīth* (Al-Maṭba'at al-Raḥmānīya, Cairo, 1343ﻫ (1925))

Lambton, Ann K. S., 'The Theory of Kingship in the *Naṣīhat Ul-Mulūk* of Ghazālī', *The Islamic Quarterly*, 1 (1954), pp.47-55

Laoust, Henri, *Essai sur les doctrines sociales et politiques de Taḳī-d-Dīn Aḥmad b. Taimīyah, canoniste ḥanbalite* (Imprimerie de l'Institut Francais d'Archéologie Orientale, Cairo, 1939)

Lapidus, Ira M., 'The Separation of State and Religion in the Development of Early Islamic Society', *International Journal of Middle Eastern Studies*, 6 (1975), pp.365-85

Lawrence, T. E., *Seven Pillars of Wisdom: A Triumph* (Penguin, Harmondsworth, 1973)

Leachman, G. E., 'A Journey in North-Eastern Arabia', *Geographical Journal*, 37 (1911), pp.265-74

Lewis, Bernard, *The Arabs in History* (Hutchinson University Library, London, 1950)

Lockhart, Laurence, 'Outline of the History of Kuwait', *Royal Central Asian Journal*, 34 (1947), pp.262-74

Løkkegaard, Frede, *Islamic Taxation in the Classic Period with Special Reference to Circumstances in Iraq* (Branner and Korch,

Copenhagen, 1950)

Longrigg, Stephen Hemsley, *Four Centuries of Modern Iraq* (Gregg International, Farnborough, 1968)

Lorimer, J. G., *Gazetteer of the Persian Gulf, 'Omān, and Central Arabia*, 5 vols (Gregg International, Farnborough, 1970)

Lunt, James, 'Abu Henaik', *Blackwood's Magazine*, 279 (1956), pp.419-29

—— *The Barren Rocks of Aden* (Harcourt, Brace and World, New York, 1967)

—— 'Watch and Ward', *Blackwood's Magazine*, 279 (1956), pp.253-61

Macdonald, D. B., 'The Caliphate', *Moslem World*, 7 (1917), pp.349-57

Mackenzie, W. J. M., *Political Identity* (Penguin, Harmondsworth, 1978)

Mackie, J. B., 'Hasa: An Arabian Oasis', *Geographical Journal*, 63 (1924), pp.189-207

Madanī, Muḥammad Mughairabī Fatīḥ, al-, *firqat al-ikhwān al-islāmīya bi najd au wahhābīya al-yaum* (no publisher listed, 1342 ▲ (1923))

Makdisi, George, 'Ibn Taimīya: A Ṣūfi of the Qādiriya Order', *American Journal of Arabic Studies*, 1 (1973), pp.118-29

—— 'The Tanbīh of Ibn Taimīya on Dialectic: The Pseudo-'Aqīlian Kitāb Al-Farq', in Sami A. Hanna (ed.), *Medieval Middle Eastern Studies* (E. J. Brill, Leiden, 1972)

Margoliouth, D. S., 'The Latest Developments of the Caliphate Question', *Moslem World*, 14 (1924), pp.334-41

Mauss, Marcel, *The Gift: Forms and Functions of Exchange in Archaic Societies* (W. W. Norton, New York, 1967)

Maxwell, Gavin, *People of the Reeds* (Pyramid Books, New York, 1966)

Mejcher, Helmut, *Imperial Quest for Oil: Iraq 1910-1928* (St Antony's Middle East Monographs, Oxford, 1976)

Melamid, Alexander, 'Boundaries and Petroleum Developments in Southern Arabia', *Geographical Review*, 47 (1957), pp.589-91

—— 'The Economic Geography of Neutral Territories', *Geographical Review*, 45 (1955), pp.359-74

—— 'Oil and the Evolution of Boundaries in Eastern Arabia', *Geographical Review*, 44 (1954), pp.295-6

—— 'Political Boundaries and Nomadic Grazing', *Geographical Review*, 55 (1965), pp.287-90

Memon, Muhammad Umar, *Ibn Taimīya's Struggle against Popular Religion: With an Annotated Translation of his Kitāb iqtiḍā' as-sirāt al-mustaqīm mukhālafat aṣḥāb al-jahīm* (Mouton, Mouton, 1976)

Monroe, Elizabeth, *Philby of Arabia* (Faber and Faber, London, 1973)

Montagne, Robert, 'Notes sur la vie sociale et politique de l'Arabie du Nord', *Revue des Études Islamiques*, 6 (1932), pp.61-79

Moorehead, Alan, *The White Nile* (Harper and Brothers, New York, 1960)

Morgenstern, Julian, *The Ark, the Ephod, and the 'Tent of Meeting'* (Hebrew Union College Press, Cincinnati, 1945)

Musil, Alois, *Arabia Deserta* (American Geographical Society/Oriental Explorations and Studies no. 2, New York, 1927)

—— *The Manners and Customs of the Rwala Bedouins* (American Geographical Society/Oriental Explorations and Studies no. 6, New York, 1928)

—— *A Musil Map of Northern Arabia* (American Geographical Society/Oriental Explorations and Studies nos. 2-5, New York, 1926)

—— *Northern Najd* (American Geographical Society/Oriental Explorations and Studies no. 5, New York, 1928)

Naqvi, Ali Raza, 'Laws of War in Islam', *Islamic Studies*, 13 (1974), pp.25-43

Nasir, Sari J., *The Arabs and the English* (Longman Group, London, 1976)

Nelson, Cynthia (ed.), *The Desert and the Sown: Nomads in the Wider Society* (University of California Institute of International Studies, Berkeley, 1973)

Niebuhr, C., *Travels Through Arabia, and other Countries in the East*, 2 vols (no publisher listed, 1792)

Palgrave, William Gifford, *Narrative of a Year's Journey Through Central and Eastern Arabia*, 2 vols (Gregg International, Farnborough, 1969)

Patai, Raphael, 'Nomadism: Middle Eastern and Central Asian', *Southwestern Journal of Anthropology*, 7 (1951), pp.401-14

Patton, Walter M., *Aḥmed Ibn Ḥanbal and the Miḥna, a biography of the Imām including an account of the Mohammedan inquisition called the Miḥna 218-234 A.H.* (E. J. Brill, Leiden, 1897)

Peake, Frederick G., *History and Tribes of Jordan* (University of Miami, Coral Gables, 1958)

Pelly, Lewis, *Report on A Journey to Riyadh in Central Arabia (1865)* (Oleander Press, Cambridge, 1977)

Philby, H. St John B., *Arabia of the Wahhabis* (Frank Cass, London, 1977)

—— *Arabian Days* (Robert Hale, London, 1948)

—— *Arabian Highlands* (Cornell University Press, Ithaca, 1952)

—— *Arabian Jubilee* (John Day, New York, 1953)

—— *The Empty Quarter* (Constable, London, 1933)

—— *Forty Years in the Wilderness* (Robert Hale, London, 1957)

—— *The Heart of Arabia*, 2 vols (Constable, London, 1922)

—— 'Jauf and the North Arabian Desert', *Geographical Journal*, 62 (1923), pp.241-59

—— *A Pilgrim in Arabia* (Robert Hale, London, 1946)

—— *The Land of Midian* (Ernest Benn, London, 1957)

—— *Report on Najd Mission 1917-1918* (India Office File L/P&S/10/2182, 1913, no. 122, Pts. 9 and 10) (Government Press, Baghdad, 1918)

—— *Sa'udi Arabia* (Ernest Benn, London, 1955)

Rahman, Fazlur, *Islam* (Weidenfeld and Nicolson, London, 1966)

Rashid, Ibrahim al-, *Documents on the History of Saudi Arabia*, 3 vols (Documentary Publications, Salisbury, North Carolina, 1976)

Raswan, Carl R., *Black Tents of Arabia: My Life Among the Bedouins* (Hutchinson, London, 1935)

—— 'Tribal Areas and Migration Lines of the North Arabian Bedouins', *Geographical Review*, 20 (1930), pp.494-502

Raunkiaer, Barclay, *Through Wahhabiland on Camelback* (Routledge and Kegan Paul, London, 1969)

Rentz, George, 'Literature on the Kingdom of Saudi Arabia', *The Middle East Journal*, 4 (1950), pp.244-9

—— 'Notes on Dickson's *The Arab of the Desert*', *The Muslim World*, 41 (1951), pp.49-64

Rihani, Ameen, *Ibn Sa'oud of Arabia: His People and His Land* (Constable, London, 1928)

Ritter, Wigand, 'Central Saudi Arabia', *Wiener Geographische Schriften 43/44/45 Beiträge zur Wirtschaftsgeographie*, 1 (1975), pp.205-28

—— 'A Note on the Sedentarization of Nomads in Eastern Saudi-Arabia', *Studien zur allgemeinen und regionalen Geographie*

(Frankfurter Wirtschafts- und Sozialgeographische Schriften, 1977), pp.407-34

Rosenfeld, Henry, 'The Social Composition of the Military in the Process of State Formation in the Arabian Desert—Part I', *Journal of the Royal Anthropological Institute*, 95 (1965), pp.75-86

—— 'The Military Force used to Achieve and Maintain Power and the Meaning of its Social Composition: Slaves, Mercenaries and Townsmen—Part II', *Journal of the Royal Anthropological Institute*, 95 (1965), pp.174-94

Rustow, Dankwart A., *Middle Eastern Political Systems* (Prentice-Hall, Englewood Cliffs, New Jersey, 1971)

—— 'The Politics of the Near East', in Gabriel A. Almond and James S. Coleman (eds), *The Politics of Developing Areas* (Princeton University Press, Princeton, 1960)

Sadleir, George Foster, *Diary of a Journey Across Arabia (1819)* (Oleander Press, Cambridge, 1977)

Sanger, Richard H., *The Arabian Peninsula* (Cornell University Press, Ithaca, 1954)

Schacht, Joseph, *An Introduction to Islamic Law* (Clarendon Press, Oxford, 1964)

—— *Origins of Muhammadan Jurisprudence* (Clarendon Press, Oxford, 1950)

Seale, Morris S., *The Desert Bible: Nomadic Tribal Culture and Old Testament Interpretation* (Weidenfeld and Nicolson, London, 1974)

Shamekh, Ahmed A., *Spatial Patterns of Bedouin Settlement in al-Qasim Region Saudi Arabia* (University of Kentucky Press, Lexington, 1975)

Shoufany, Elias, *Al-Riddah and the Muslim Conquest of Arabia* (University of Toronto Press, Toronto, 1972)

Sinderson Pasha, Sir Harry C., *Ten Thousand and One Nights: Memories of Iraq's Sherifian Dynasty* (Hodder and Stoughton, London, 1973)

Smalley, W. F., 'The Wahhabis and Ibn Sa'ud', *Moslem World*, 22 (1932), pp.227-46

Smith, W. Robertson, *Kinship and Marriage in Early Arabia* (Adam and Charles Black, London, 1903)

—— *The Religion of the Semites* (Adam and Charles Black, London, 1894)

Spooner, Brian, 'Towards a Generative Model of Nomadism',

Anthropological Quarterly, 44 (1971), pp.198-210

Stitt, George, *A Prince of Arabia: The Emir Shereef Ali Haidar* (George Allen and Unwin, London, 1948)

Storrs, Sir Ronald, *Orientations* (Ivor Nicholson and Watson, London, 1937)

Sweet, Louise E., 'Camel Raiding of North Arabian Bedouin: A Mechanism of Ecological Adaptation', *American Anthropologist*, 67 (1965), pp.1132-50

Thesiger, Wilfred, *Arabian Sands* (Longmans, London, 1959)

—— *The Marsh Arabs* (Penguin, Harmondsworth, 1976)

Thomas, Bertram, *Alarms and Excursions in Arabia* (George Allen and Unwin, London, 1931)

Tibawi, A. L., *A Modern History of Syria including Lebanon and Palestine* (Macmillan, London, 1969)

Toynbee, Arnold J., *Survey of International Affairs 1925: The Islamic World since the Peace Settlement*, vol. I (Humphrey Milford, London, 1927)

Troeller, Gary, *The Birth of Saudi Arabia: Britain and the Rise of the House of Sa'ud* (Frank Cass, London, 1976)

Van der Meulen, Daniël, *The Wells of Ibn Sa'ud* (John Murray, London, 1957)

Vidal, F. S., *The Oasis of Al-Hasa* (Arabian American Oil Company, New York, 1955)

Wagtendonk, K., *Fasting in the Koran* (E. J. Brill, Leiden, 1968)

Wahba, Ḥāfiz, *Arabian Days* (Arthur Barker, London, 1964)

—— *Jazīrat al-'arab fī al-qarn al-'ishrīn (Maṭba'at Lajnat al-Ta'līf wa al-Tarjama wa al-Nashr*, no place of publication listed, 1354▲ (1935))

Wahhāb, Muḥammad b. 'Abd al-, and other Wahhabi *'ulamā, majmū'at al-rasā'il wa al-masā'il*, 3 vols (edited by Rashīd Riḍā) (Al-Manar, Cairo, 1344▲-1349▲ (1925-1930))

—— *majmū'at al-tauḥīd al-najdīya* (edited by Rashīd Riḍā) (Al-Manār, Cairo, 1346▲(1927))

Wallin, George Augustus, 'Narrative of a Journey from Cairo to Medina, and Mecca, by Suez, Arabá, Tawilá, al-Jauf, Jubbé, Háil, and Nejd, in 1845', *Journal of the Royal Geographical Society*, 24 (1854), pp.115-207

Wenner, Manfred W., 'Saudi Arabia: Survival of Traditional Elites', in Frank Tachau (ed.), *Political Elites and Political Development in the Middle East* (Schenkman, Cambridge, Massachusetts, 1975)

Wensinck, A. J., 'Wine in Islam', *Moslem World*, 18 (1928), pp.365-73

Wilkinson, J. C., 'The Ibāḍī *imāma*', *Bulletin of the School of Oriental and African Studies*, 39 (1976), pp.535-51

—— 'Islamic Water Law with Special Reference to Oasis Settlement', *Journal of Arid Environments*, 1 (1978) pp.87-96

—— 'Problems of Oasis Development' (School of Geography Research Paper no. 20, Oxford University, 1978)

—— *Water and Tribal Settlement in South-East Arabia: A Study of the Aflāj of Oman* (Clarendon Press, Oxford, 1977)

Winder, Bayly R., *'al-'awāmil allatī sā'adat 'alā tauṭīd al-mulk al-su'ūdī'*, *Al-Abḥāth*, 1 (1948), pp.3-14

—— *Saudi Arabia in the Nineteenth Century* (Macmillan, London, 1965)

Winstone, H. V. F., *Captain Shakespear: A Portrait* (Jonathan Cape, London, 1976)

Zeine, Zeine N., *The Struggle for Arab Independence: Western Diplomacy and the Rise and Fall of Faisal's Kingdom in Syria* (Khayats, Beirut, 1960)

Ziriklī, Khair al-Dīn, *shibh al-jazīra fī 'ahd al-malik 'abd al-'azīz*, 3 vols (Maṭābi' Dār al-Qalam, Beirut, 1390▲ (1970))

INDEX